SWEET MARIA'S

BIG BAKING
BIBLE

ALSO BY MARIA BRUSCINO SANCHEZ

The New Lasagna Cookbook:
A Crowd-Pleasing Collection of Recipes from Around
the World for the Perfect One-Dish Meal

SWEET MARIA'S

BIG BAKING BIBLE

300 Classic Cookies, Cakes, and Desserts from

an Italian-American Bakery

MARIA BRUSCINO SANCHEZ

ST. MARTIN'S PRESS ✿ NEW YORK

Sweet Maria's

ITALIAN COOKIE TRAY

Sweet Maria's

ITALIAN COOKIE TRAY

MARIA BRUSCINO SANCHEZ

FOR MOM AND DAD

CONTENTS

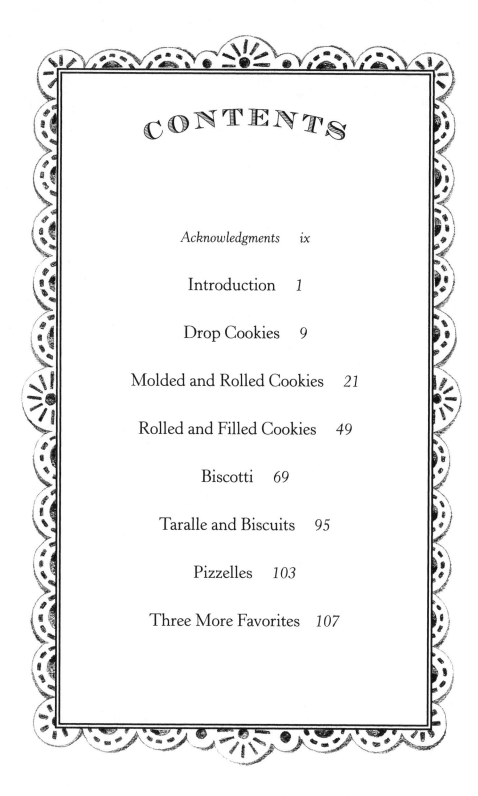

ACKNOWLEDGMENTS

Many thanks to my agent, Carla Glasser, whose expertise
and support made this book a reality.

And to my editor, Marian Lizzi, for effortlessly guiding me through this project,
and for her enthusiasm every step of the way.

To my husband, Edgar, for his constant support and patience.

To my Dad, for the great stories.

To all who shared their recipes and techniques:
Mom, Philomena Parrillo, Gemma Luciano, Josephine Reynolds,
Mary Tropasso, Winnie Cerasulo, Jane Briotti, Lena Chillemi,
Ann Chillemi, Terry Sanchez, Sabina Figluizzi,
Antoinette Vaccarelli, and Louise Donnarumma.

For Grandma Bruscino and Aunt Giulia's inspiration.

And to all the Sweet Maria's staff:
Clotilda DelGobbo, Sarah Figluizzi, Louise Mastronunzio,
and Susan Tropasso, for their cookie sampling and honest opinions.

INTRODUCTION

Because I grew up second-generation Italian, my family life has been filled with lots of rituals and traditions, many of which revolve around large gatherings and great food. When I was a child, some of these customs seemed silly and I soon found that many of my friends, away from my neighborhood, did not observe similar traditions. As I've grown older, I've come to appreciate these traditions and have strived to understand their meanings. I've also tried to preserve some of these customs and recipes for future generations.

As in most American-Italian households, our customs and foods often correspond to specific Catholic holidays. *Panettone* (sweet raisin bread) and *strufoli* (honey clusters) for Christmas, and sweet rice pies and *pizza piena* (meat pie) to celebrate Easter and the arrival of spring. Although many of these customs seemed antiquated even to my Mom, we both respected and learned the traditional ways of my grandparents. Even now that they're gone, we still preserve many of their ways, both from respect and a desire to stay connected with the past.

Each region of Italy has its own unique history, foods, customs, and dialects. Even each small town, or *paese*, may have its own specialties. Most of these cookie recipes are originally from the Neopolitan (towns surrounding Naples) region of Italy. A few of the recipes, where noted, are from the Sicilian side of my husband's family. Some are simple, such as traditional plain biscuits, while others are fancy, like the jelly- and nut-filled cookies. Some of the recipes were adjusted when my grandparents first came to the United States. Because ingredient quality and availability differ from country to country, these recipes have truly become American-Italian.

Many of them existed only as "a handful of sugar" or "enough flour to make a soft dough." I've translated these directions to more universal and practical measures. I've also included a few original recipes that I've developed, inspired by the Italian tradition of rich flavorings and spices.

Italian cookie trays aren't just platters of cookies in a single layer. They are usually large mounds of a large variety of cookies. Cookie trays were always on our tables during baptisms, birthdays, weddings, and even funeral gatherings. Everyone has their favorite cookie, and every baker has her specialty. In fact, many trays were made by each woman baking a batch of her specialty, and then collecting all the varieties together.

These are the cookies that I grew up with. They became a part of my life and its celebrations. Now, they've become part of my business. Sweet Maria's is a custom cake and cookie bakery. Our product line is similar to my upbringing—American, with an Italian accent. This collection of recipes is by no means definitive, but rather a slice of life. I hope they provide you with a little flavor and spice, and encourage you to preserve the oral recipes and traditions that exist in your own family, whatever the origin.

INGREDIENTS

FLOUR: All of the recipes in this collection use either all-purpose or unbleached flour. These types of flour are readily available and the most consistent for flavor and texture. I've found that the most consistent way to measure flour is to spoon it into the measuring cup.

SUGAR: Extra-fine granulated sugar, unless otherwise specified, is used in most of these recipes. The finer the grain, the easier the sugar will blend with the butter and other ingredients in the dough.

CONFECTIONERS' SUGAR: Confectioners' sugar, or powdered sugar, is sugar that has been ground to a fine powder with a little cornstarch added to prevent clumping. "10-x" sugar is the most commonly used and most readily available type of confectioners' sugar.

BROWN SUGAR: Brown sugar is granulated sugar that has been processed with molasses for a rich flavor. When a recipe uses brown sugar, you can use either light or dark, loosely packed.

EGGS: Whole, grade A, large eggs work the best in these recipes. If you need to separate eggs, it's easier to do it when the eggs are cold.

BUTTER: Unsalted butter is recommended for the best flavor and texture. It is more perishable than salted butter, yet has a freshness and sweetness that are unmatched. If you are using salted butter, you may want to reduce the amount of salt called for in the recipe. If butter is a dietary concern, you can certainly substitute margarine.

SHORTENING: Some of these recipes call for shortening instead of butter. All-purpose vegetable shortening is recommended for a flaky texture.

OIL: Vegetable oil, unless otherwise noted, is preferable for these cookie recipes. Olive oil is not only expensive, but often too flavorful and heavy for cookie baking or frying.

CHOCOLATE: Always use the finest quality chocolate for baking or dipping. Most of these recipes use semisweet chips or baking bars that are readily available in most supermarkets.

COCOA: Because of the processing technique used to make Dutch process cocoa, it provides the fullest flavor for baking.

PINE NUTS: There are several types of pignoli, or pine nuts. The Spanish variety are the smoothest and the purest white in color. These have a good, consistent flavor and are a bit more expensive than other types. The Chinese pine nut is more yellow in color and irregular in shape. It is still a good option for flavor and is less expensive. Most varieties of pine nuts can be found in gourmet sections of supermarkets or your local gourmet retailer.

OTHER NUTS: Almonds, pecans, hazelnuts, and walnuts are used in many of these recipes. If you have a large amount left over, place the nuts in a plastic bag and freeze for later use.

If you need to coarsely chop the nuts, it's best to use a cutting board and a sharp straight knife. For nuts that are finely ground, I recommend a food processor.

BAKING SODA AND BAKING POWDER: It is necessary that both of these leavening agents be fresh. When not in use they should be stored, separately, in airtight containers so that they do not absorb moisture and odors.

EXTRACTS: Pure extracts are the essence of the flavor in an alcohol-based liquid. They are the richest tasting and are highly recommended. Imitation flavors are cheaper, but you can really taste the difference.

SPICES: Most of the spices used in these recipes are ground. For the best flavor, be sure your supply is fresh.

LEMON OR ORANGE RIND: Citrus rinds provide a rich flavoring. When grating rind, be sure to avoid the pith, the white, fleshy, bitter part of the fruit under the rind.

GLACÉ CHERRIES: This is the type of cherry commonly used in fruitcakes. They are sugared and are available in red or green.

LIQUEURS: A few of these recipes call for various types of flavored alcoholic liqueurs, which add flavor in the same way that extracts do. These can be any brand name. The most commonly used flavors are coffee, amaretto (almond), or hazelnut.

EQUIPMENT

Most of the equipment used to make these cookies are everyday kitchen utensils such as mixing bowls, measuring cups and spoons, electric mixers, wire whisks, rubber and metal spatulas, and saucepans.

COOKIE SHEETS: Sturdy, firm, clean sheets are definitely necessary for successful cookie baking.

ROLLING PINS: I find the heavy marble type the easiest to use. The heaviness helps to flatten your dough evenly, and the rolling mechanism rolls easily, with less pressure on your arms than the old-fashioned wooden pins.

PARCHMENT PAPER: Using parchment paper is a great way to line cookie sheets. Not only does it provide a nonstick surface, it helps to make the cleaning of cookie sheets a little easier. You can purchase parchment paper from most kitchen stores and supermarkets.

ELECTRIC MIXER: A stand-up model electric mixer is a great tool. While your dough is mixing, you can turn to another task, like preparing cookie sheets.

MIXING BOWLS: Large stainless steel bowls, with approximately a 15-inch diameter, are ideal for the "making a well" technique and hand mixing. These bowls allow you to combine dry ingredients, then wet ingredients, and still give you enough side room to mix the dough before turning it out on a floured surface for kneading.

WIRE RACKS: Wire cooling racks are the best way to let cookies cool when removed from a cookie sheet. The air circulates underneath to cool the entire cookie. After frosting cookies, place them on wire cooling racks to allow excess icing to drip. For easier cleanup, place a piece of parchment or waxed paper underneath the rack to catch the excess frosting.

CONTAINERS: Airtight containers are essential for storing baked cookies. These can be cookie tins or Tupperware-type sealable containers. If the cookies aren't too fragile, you can also use plastic bags.

GENERAL INFORMATION AND TECHNIQUES

Making a Well

This is a technique I use often. The concept is to combine all the dry ingredients in a large bowl and mix with a wooden spoon. After the ingredients are blended, make a mound of the mixture, then make a hole on top of the mound. This is your "well" to catch the wet ingredients.

In a separate bowl, the wet ingredients are blended together as directed. Pour the wet ingredients into your "well" and blend thoroughly with a wooden spoon or rubber spatula.

Turning Dough Out onto a Lightly Floured Surface

While you are using an electric mixer on low speed, the dough will sometimes get too heavy to mix. When this happens, simply empty the contents of the mixer onto a counter or table dusted with flour. Knead together the ingredients to form your dough.

Chopping Nuts

You can purchase nuts in a variety of sizes, or you can chop them to suit an individual recipe. Freshly chopping nuts helps to bring out their natural oils and flavors. Here are a few guidelines to the size references in this book.

WALNUT HALVES: These are the actual walnut halves, unchopped, usually used for decorative purposes.

COARSELY CHOPPED: The nut is cut into smaller pieces than the nut halves, but not as small as finely chopped nuts. It's best to use a cutting board and a sharp, straight-edged knife using a chopping motion.

FINELY CHOPPED: Finely chopped nuts can be made with a nut chopper or food processor. If using a food processor, a few quick pulses will do the trick.

FINELY GROUND: Finely ground nuts are pulverized in a food processor or blender. They resemble the texture of flour.

Cooling on Parchment

For some cookies it is easier to cool them right on the parchment paper instead of trying to remove them with a metal spatula while they are hot. Certain varieties of cookies, such as Pine Nut Cookies, Coconut Macaroons, and Ladyfingers, are soft and sticky and need to be fully cooled before removing them from the parchment paper. To cool on parchment, simply slip the parchment paper off of the cookie sheet and onto a wire cooling rack.

Egg Wash

This refers to brushing cookies with a beaten egg, which adds a professional, shiny finish. Use a pastry brush to spread a beaten egg on the tops of biscotti loaves before baking.

Dusting or Rolling with Confectioners' Sugar

Many of these cookies are finished with a coating of confectioners' sugar. There are a few ways to do this. To dust cookies, put a small amount of confectioners' sugar into a small, dry strainer. Shake the strainer over the cookies that you wish to dust. Refill the strainer as needed.

To coat cookies, place a small amount of confectioners' sugar in a medium size mixing bowl. Put about 10 to 12 cookies at a time in the bowl with the sugar. Using your fingers or two spoons, carefully toss the cookies around in the sugar, being careful not to break them. Repeat until all cookies are coated.

Or place a small amount of confectioners' sugar in a medium-size plastic bag. Add 10 to 12 cookies at a time and close the bag tightly with a twist tie. Shake the bag to coat the cookies. Repeat as necessary. This method is the most fun, but only works if your cookies are completely cool and not too fragile.

Dipping and Decorating with Chocolate

TO MELT CHOCOLATE: I've always found using a double boiler the most consistent way to melt chocolate. Over slightly simmering water, stir the chocolate constantly so it melts slowly and evenly.

TO DRIZZLE: Dip a fork into melted chocolate and shake quickly back and forth over cookies to produce a drizzled effect.

TO DIP: Dip one end of cookie diagonally into chocolate. Pull out, shake off excess, and place on a parchment-lined tray. While chocolate is still moist, sprinkle with chopped nuts or sprinkles. Let dry.

Grating Lemon and Orange Rind

The zest of an orange or lemon is a great addition for natural flavor. I find it easiest to use a zester. You could also use a regular four-sided hand grater. Grate the skin, being careful not to include the bitter, fleshy pith underneath. Use a dry pastry brush to help remove rind that may stick to the grater.

Filling a Pastry Bag

Using a pastry bag is a great way to make professional-looking cookies and decorations. For beginners, here's an easy technique. Place the empty bag, tip side down, in a tall drinking glass. Fold the top edges of the bag down over the outside of the glass. This will give you a steady open bag. Spoon dough into the open end, being careful not to overfill it. Gather up the edges and remove from the glass. To use, simply squeeze and add pressure to the center of the bag, releasing the dough from the bottom tip. Practice will help you to regulate the size of the cookies as you squeeze. When piping cookies onto parchment, gently press the tip onto the surface of the paper to release dough.

Figuring Cookie Quantities

You can usually figure on 4 to 5 cookies per person. Of course, some people will eat more, and some people will eat less. If you are serving another dessert as well as the cookies, you can probably cut the amount to 2 to 3 cookies per person.

Storage

The best way to store baked cookies for short periods is to put them in airtight containers and leave at room temperature. Cookie tins or Tupperware-type sealable bins are ideal. Because so many of these cookies are flavorful, it is best to keep each flavor in its own container until you're ready to make your tray. If you need to store baked cookies for longer periods of time, freezing is your best option. Freezing stops the staling process immediately. Refrigeration, on the other hand, only speeds up the staling process, robbing the cookies of their moisture and flavor.

Freezing Dough

Some of the cookie doughs in this book can be frozen, thawed, and then baked. The ones that can be frozen and used later include many of the butter-based doughs that are used for molded, rolled, and filled cookies. Many of the doughs for drop cookies, biscotti, and any type of fried cookies do not freeze successfully.

To freeze dough, double wrap in plastic bags and be sure to label and date them. Most dough can be frozen up to 3 months. To defrost, set the dough aside at room temperature for 40 to 45 minutes, or until desired texture returns.

Freezing Baked Cookies

By freezing cookies that are already baked, you can always have cookies ready to serve, or stock up for an upcoming party. A great way to freeze biscotti is to freeze the loaves before slicing. Carefully wrap in foil, then plastic freezer bags. When thawed, cut into slices and re-toast to bring out additional flavor.

Any cookie that requires frosting or dusting with sugar is best frozen unfrosted. Freeze drop cookies in plastic freezer bags, thaw, then frost with appropriate frosting. To defrost cookies, remove from freezer and let stand at room temperature for 10 to 15 minutes.

A few cookies in this book are fried instead of baked. They do not freeze well because they get quite soggy and flavorless during the thawing process. It is best to fry these confections and enjoy them when they're at their freshest.

"Traying," or making a tray of cookies, requires little practice and these tips.

To build the perfect mound of cookies, start with a flat plate, platter, or basket. You may want to add a lace doily to the plate or line a basket with a colorful linen napkin. You should layer the bottom of the plate with some durable type of cookie like a biscotti. Be sure to lay the cookies flat on the bottom of the plate. Continue with layer after layer of various types of cookies, making sure the lighter, softer types are on the upper levels. As you add more layers, gradually decrease the number of cookies on each layer to build a mountain effect. Be sure to pay attention to color, alternating rows of chocolate, vanilla, and jelly cookies. Traditionally, many people choose to add candy-coated almonds or other candies to their cookie trays. This is a personal choice, but I like my cookies to be the center of attention.

Fried cookies are best on their own platter and not combined with other varieties, because they tend to be softer and more fragile.

Suggestions for Containers

Use your favorite plates or cake platters for your cookie tray. Or if the cookie tray is a gift, buy a plate that becomes part of the gift. Baskets are another alternative, or a terra-cotta planter lined with a napkin. Festive cookie tins, trays, and gift boxes are great for holiday gift giving. For a professional finished look, use a clear or colored cellophane or plastic wrap. Add fancy fabric ribbons to accent your tray.

DROP COOKIES

These cookies are formed by dropping the cookie dough off an everyday teaspoon onto the cookie sheet, using your index finger to push the dough off the teaspoon. If the dough is sticky, lightly dust your fingers with flour.

These are the easiest type of cookies to bake. There's no rolling, cutting, or filling. They are practically foolproof, and a great place to start your adventure into Italian cookie baking.

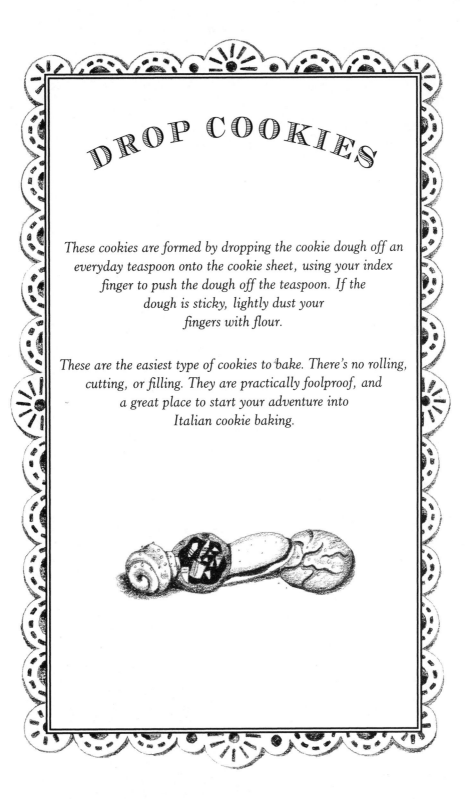

LEMON DROP COOKIES

ANGINETTI

When most people think of "Italian cookies," they're usually referring to these light, frosted treats. Our family has always frosted them pure white, but feel free to add a few drops of food coloring to the frosting or sprinkle the moist frosting with colored sprinkles.

3 EGGS

½ CUP MILK

2 TEASPOONS LEMON EXTRACT

½ CUP SUGAR

½ CUP VEGETABLE OIL

3 CUPS FLOUR

8 TEASPOONS BAKING POWDER

1. Preheat oven to 350°F.

2. In an electric mixer on medium speed, beat eggs, milk, lemon extract, sugar, and oil until well blended.

3. On low speed, add flour and baking powder. Mix until just blended. The dough should be soft and sticky.

4. Lightly dust the dough and your fingers with a little additional flour.

5. Drop the dough from a teaspoon onto a lightly greased cookie sheet, spacing the cookies 2 inches apart.

6. Bake immediately for 8 to 10 minutes, or until slightly browned.

7. Remove cookie sheet from oven. Using a metal spatula, remove cookies from sheet onto wire racks.

8. Cool on wire racks.

9. Frost with Lemon Confectioners' Frosting (see the following recipe). If it is necessary to freeze cookies, use heavy-duty plastic freezer bags and freeze the cookies unfrosted.

YIELDS 50 COOKIES

CONFECTIONERS' FROSTING

This is a basic glaze that can be used for several different cookies. It is a very versatile icing. You can substitute anise or another extract to create different flavors.

6 CUPS CONFECTIONERS' SUGAR   ½ CUP WATER

2 TEASPOONS VANILLA EXTRACT

1. In an electric mixer on medium speed, beat all ingredients until smooth.

2. Using a metal spatula, frost the tops of the cookies. The frosting will drip down the sides and coat the cookies.

3. Dry the frosted cookies on wire cooling racks. Store in an airtight container.

YIELDS ENOUGH FOR 50 COOKIES

LEMON CONFECTIONERS' FROSTING

6 CUPS CONFECTIONERS' SUGAR   ½ CUP WATER

2 TEASPOONS LEMON EXTRACT

Follow instructions in steps 1 to 3 above.

ORANGE CONFECTIONERS' FROSTING

6 CUPS CONFECTIONERS' SUGAR   ½ CUP ORANGE JUICE

2 TEASPOONS ORANGE EXTRACT

Follow instructions in steps 1 to 3 above.

CHOCOLATE CLOVE DROPS

This cookie is a Christmas favorite of many families I know. It has an uncommon flavor combination of cocoa and cloves. We always leave a few of these cookies and a fresh cup of cappuccino for Santa.

2½ CUPS FLOUR	½ TEASPOON CINNAMON
3 TEASPOONS BAKING POWDER	2 EGGS
½ TEASPOON BAKING SODA	¾ CUP SUGAR
¼ CUP COCOA	½ CUP MILK
1 TEASPOON GROUND CLOVES	½ CUP VEGETABLE SHORTENING, MELTED, THEN COOLED
½ TEASPOON NUTMEG	

1. Preheat oven to 350°F.

2. In a large stainless-steel bowl, with a wooden spoon, mix together 2 cups of the flour, the baking powder, baking soda, cocoa, cloves, nutmeg, and cinnamon.

3. Make a well in the center of the dry ingredients. Set aside.

4. In an electric mixer or with a wire whisk, beat eggs and sugar. Add milk and melted shortening. Mix well.

5. Pour egg mixture into the well and begin to mix with a wooden spoon.

6. With a wooden spoon, mix in the remaining ½ cup flour. This will give you a slightly sticky dough. Drop from a teaspoon onto a parchment-lined cookie sheet, spacing cookies 2 inches apart.

7. Bake for 8 to 10 minutes, or until lightly browned. Remove cookie sheet from the oven.

8. Using a metal spatula, remove cookies from the baking sheet onto wire cooling racks. Cool, then frost with Chocolate Clove Frosting (see following recipe). Let frosting dry for a few hours before serving. Store frosted cookies in an airtight container. Freeze unfrosted cookies in plastic freezer bags.

YIELDS 50 COOKIES

CHOCOLATE CLOVE FROSTING

Use this tasty icing to accent the chocolate clove drops.

½ CUP MILK

1 TEASPOON GROUND CLOVES

½ TEASPOON NUTMEG

3 CUPS CONFECTIONERS' SUGAR

½ TEASPOON CINNAMON

½ CUP COCOA

1. With an electric mixer, mix all ingredients until smooth.

2. Using a metal spatula or butter knife, frost the tops of the cookies. If the frosting is too stiff to spread, add a few drops of water to it and dip your butter knife or spatula in water before spreading.

YIELDS ENOUGH FOR 50 COOKIES

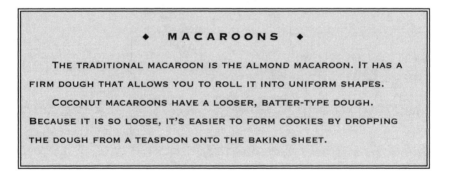

◆ **MACAROONS** ◆

THE TRADITIONAL MACAROON IS THE ALMOND MACAROON. IT HAS A FIRM DOUGH THAT ALLOWS YOU TO ROLL IT INTO UNIFORM SHAPES. COCONUT MACAROONS HAVE A LOOSER, BATTER-TYPE DOUGH. BECAUSE IT IS SO LOOSE, IT'S EASIER TO FORM COOKIES BY DROPPING THE DOUGH FROM A TEASPOON ONTO THE BAKING SHEET.

CHRISTMAS FRUIT DROPS

These are dense little fruit-filled drops, like tiny fruitcakes. Be sure to use a combination of red and green cherries for the Christmas holidays.

In Italian homes, Christmas Eve is always the bigger celebration than Christmas Day. We enjoy a large dinner of pasta and fish followed by special holiday sweets. We even open all our gifts on Christmas Eve!

2 CUPS GLACÉ CHERRIES, CHOPPED	½ CUP SUGAR
1 CUP WALNUTS, CHOPPED	1 TEASPOON VANILLA EXTRACT
1¾ CUPS FLOUR	3 EGGS
¼ POUND BUTTER, SOFTENED	PINCH OF SALT

1. Preheat oven to 375°F.

2. In a medium mixing bowl, mix cherries and nuts with 2 tablespoons of the flour. Use a wooden spoon and mix until fruit and nuts are coated. Set aside.

3. With an electric mixer, cream butter, sugar, and vanilla until light. Add eggs and mix until blended.

4. On low speed, gradually add the remaining flour and salt to make a soft dough. Stir in floured nuts and cherries.

5. Drop cookie dough from a rounded teaspoon onto a parchment-lined cookie sheet, spacing cookies about 2 inches apart.

6. Bake for 12 to 15 minutes, or until lightly browned. Remove cookie sheet from the oven.

7. Using a metal spatula, remove cookies from the cookie sheet and place on wire cooling racks.

8. Cool. Serve plain, dust with confectioners' sugar, or frost with Lemon Confectioners' Frosting (see recipe page 12).

YIELDS 55 COOKIES

FLORENTINES

These crispy, almost candylike cookies are the highlight of any tray.
They have a zesty, fresh orange flavor that complements the rich chocolate coating.
Festively wrapped in a candy box or cellophane bag tied with a
fabric ribbon, they make great holiday gifts.

4 TABLESPOONS UNSALTED BUTTER	⅓ CUP FLOUR
3 TABLESPOONS HEAVY CREAM	JUICE OF 1 ORANGE
3 TABLESPOONS HONEY	ZEST OF 1 ORANGE
¾ CUP CONFECTIONERS' SUGAR	1½ CUPS ALMONDS, FINELY GROUND

CHOCOLATE SPREAD

6 OUNCES SEMISWEET CHOCOLATE (6 SQUARES)	¼ CUP ADDITIONAL ALMONDS, SLICED, FOR GARNISH
2 TEASPOONS CORN SYRUP	

1. Preheat oven to 350°F.

2. In a medium saucepan, melt butter over medium heat. Add heavy cream, honey, confectioners' sugar, flour, and orange juice. Mix with a wire whisk to break up any lumps you may have from the flour or sugar. Bring to a boil, stirring constantly with a wooden spoon. Boil until thickened, about 1 minute.

3. Remove the pan from the heat and stir in orange zest and almonds. Allow batter to cool enough to the touch, about 5 minutes

4. Drop ¾ teaspoon of batter onto a parchment-lined cookie sheet, spacing the cookies 2 inches apart to allow for spreading.

5. Bake for 15 to 20 minutes, or until the entire cookie is lightly browned. Remove cookie sheet from the oven.

6. Cool cookies on parchment paper. When cool, remove from parchment paper with a metal spatula.

7. Melt chocolate slowly in a double boiler over simmering water. Stir constantly with a wooden spoon. Remove from heat.

8. Stir in corn syrup. Using a butter knife or a metal spatula, put a dab of chocolate on the underside of each cookie. Spread to coat the cookie and sprinkle with sliced almonds while chocolate is still moist. If the chocolate gets too thick for spreading, return it over the simmering water to thin the chocolate back to spreading consistency.

9. Let cookies dry, chocolate side up, for approximately 1 hour. Store in an airtight container.

YIELDS 40 COOKIES

COCONUT MACAROONS

These classic cookies are traditionally a part of bridal shower cookie trays. Not only are the cookies enjoyed at the shower, but many women bring plastic bags or fill their napkins with cookies to take home for the men to enjoy. The light and spongy texture comes from really whipping the egg whites.

3 EGG WHITES

1 TEASPOON VANILLA EXTRACT

¾ CUP CONFECTIONERS' SUGAR

1¼ CUPS SWEETENED FLAKED COCONUT

½ CUP FLOUR

1. Preheat oven to 350°F.

2. In an electric mixer, with the whisk attachment, beat egg whites and vanilla until stiff peaks form.

3. Gradually add confectioners' sugar. Mix well.

4. Using a rubber spatula, fold in the coconut and flour until blended.

5. Drop from a teaspoon onto a parchment-lined cookie sheet, spacing cookies 2 inches apart.

6. Bake for 10 to 12 minutes, or until lightly browned. Remove cookie sheet from the oven.

7. Cool cookies on parchment paper. When fully cool, carefully remove cookies using a metal spatula. Store in an airtight container to retain softness.

YIELDS 30 COOKIES

ORANGE ALMOND DROPS

These cookies have a popular Italian flavor combination—orange and almond. As a child, I never liked orange rind. My mom always said that my taste would change, and she was right. Now these orange almond drops are one of my favorites.

After cooling the cookies, you can either dust them with confectioners' sugar or frost them with an orange variation of confectioners' icing.

¼ POUND BUTTER, SOFTENED	2½ CUPS FLOUR
1 CUP SUGAR	½ TEASPOON SALT
2 EGGS	½ TEASPOON BAKING SODA
GRATED RIND OF 1 ORANGE	¾ CUP CHOPPED ALMONDS
½ CUP ORANGE JUICE (FROM ORANGE AFTER GRATING)	

1. Preheat oven to 375°F.

2. Using an electric mixer, cream the butter and sugar until light. Add eggs, orange rind, and orange juice. Mix until blended.

3. Gradually add flour, salt, and baking soda on low speed and mix just until blended. The dough should be soft. Stir in chopped almonds.

4. Drop from a teaspoon onto a parchment-lined cookie sheet, spacing cookies 2 inches apart.

5. Bake for 10 to 12 minutes, or until lightly browned. Remove cookie sheet from the oven.

6. Remove cookies from the cookie sheet using a metal spatula. Cool on wire cooling racks.

7. Dust with confectioners' sugar just before using. Or frost with Orange Confectioners' Frosting (see recipe on page 12). Let frosted cookies dry on wire cooling racks.

YIELDS 50 COOKIES

ALMOND WINE COOKIES

These cookies have a delicate sweetness and a rich toasted almond flavor.
They are a great springtime dessert, perfect wrapped
in a special Easter basket.

¼ POUND BUTTER, SOFTENED	1 CUP FLOUR
½ CUP SUGAR	¼ CUP DRY WHITE WINE
2 EGG YOLKS	½ CUP CHOPPED ALMONDS
½ TEASPOON ANISE EXTRACT	½ CUP SLIVERED ALMONDS

1. Preheat oven to 375°F.

2. In an electric mixer, cream the butter and sugar until light. Add the egg yolks and anise extract. Mix until blended.

3. On low speed, add flour and wine alternately and mix until blended. Mix in chopped almonds to form a soft dough.

4. Using a teaspoon, drop dough into slivered almonds and roll around to coat.

5. Place on a parchment-lined cookie sheet, spacing cookies 2 inches apart. Press the tops of the cookies to flatten.

6. Bake for 12 to 15 minutes, or until lightly browned.

7. Remove cookie sheet from the oven. Using a metal spatula, remove the cookies from the cookie sheet onto a wire cooling rack. Cool.

8. Store cookies in an airtight container.

YIELDS 35 COOKIES

MOLDED AND ROLLED COOKIES

These are cookies that are shaped or rolled into balls,
or cut from cookie cutters.

TO ROLL INTO BALLS: Break off a teaspoon-size piece of dough. Roll between your palms into a small, tight ball. If the dough is sticky, lightly flour your hands.

BAGGED: To press dough from a pastry bag, the dough must be soft. Press from a bag onto a parchment-lined cookie sheet in desired shape.

ROLLED AND CUT: Roll dough with a rolling pin on a lightly floured surface. If necessary, dust rolling pin with flour to avoid sticking. Just be sure not to overflour or the dough will become tough. Lightly dust cookie cutters with flour to avoid sticking.

BUTTER COOKIES

These are rich and buttery treats. Dress them up by adding a cherry or nut before baking. Or after baking, dip them in melted chocolate and sprinkle with chopped nuts.

½ POUND BUTTER, SOFTENED	2½ CUPS FLOUR
¾ CUP SUGAR	½ TEASPOON BAKING POWDER
1 EGG	PINCH OF SALT
1 TEASPOON VANILLA EXTRACT	GLACÉ CHERRY HALVES, OPTIONAL

1. Preheat oven to 350°F.

2. In an electric mixer, cream the butter and sugar until really fluffy, 3 to 4 minutes. Add eggs and vanilla. Mix until well blended.

3. With mixer on low speed, add flour, baking powder, and salt. Mix just until blended. Overmixing the dough will make it tough to squeeze through a pastry bag.

4. Fill a pastry bag fitted with a large open star tip with the cookie dough. Pipe cookies onto a parchment-lined cookie sheet, spacing them 2 inches apart. If desired, place a cherry half in the center of each cookie before baking.

5. Bake for 10 to 15 minutes, or until edges begin to brown.

6. Using a metal spatula, lift cookies off cookie sheet and onto wire cooling racks. Cool. Store in an airtight container.

YIELDS 40 COOKIES

NOTE: *For an alternative way to form butter cookies, see page 37.*

CHOCOLATE BUTTER COOKIES

This is a rich variation of the classic butter cookie. Try combining half of this chocolate dough with half of the plain butter cookie dough for a two-toned treat.

½ POUND BUTTER, SOFTENED	2 CUPS FLOUR
½ CUP SUGAR	½ TEASPOON BAKING POWDER
1 EGG	PINCH OF SALT
1 TEASPOON VANILLA EXTRACT	WALNUT HALVES, OPTIONAL
½ CUP COCOA	

1. Preheat oven to 350°F.

2. Using an electric mixer, cream butter and sugar until very fluffy, 3 to 4 minutes. Add egg, vanilla, and cocoa. Mix until well blended.

3. On low speed, gradually add the flour, baking powder, and salt. Mix just until blended. Overbeating will make the dough tough to squeeze through the pastry bag.

4. Fill a pastry bag fitted with a large open star tip with the cookie dough. Pipe cookies onto a parchment-lined cookie sheet, spacing them 2 inches apart. You may want to place a walnut half in the center of the cookie, for decoration. If desired, simply moisten the walnut with water and press into dough.

5. Bake for 10 to 15 minutes, or until edges begin to brown.

6. Using a metal spatula, lift cookies off sheet and onto wire cooling racks. Cool. Store in an airtight container.

YIELDS 40 COOKIES

NOTE: *For an alternative way to form butter cookies, see page 37.*

PINE NUT COOKIES
PIGNOLI AMARETTI

People are just crazy about these classic almond macaroons that are generously rolled in pine nuts and baked until golden. We can't seem to make them fast enough! While rolling this dough, it helps to dip your hands in a bowl of water. This will keep the dough from sticking to your hands as you roll the dough and will help the nuts adhere to the dough.

1½ POUNDS ALMOND PASTE
(BROKEN INTO PEBBLE-SIZE PIECES)

1½ CUPS SUGAR

1 CUP CONFECTIONERS' SUGAR

4 EGG WHITES

2 CUPS PINE NUTS

1. Preheat oven to 350°F.

2. In an electric mixer, combine almond paste, sugar, confectioners' sugar, and egg whites on low speed until blended. Mix for 2 minutes on medium speed. This will make a sticky dough.

3. Roll dough into 1-inch balls. Roll balls in a bowl of pine nuts. Place the cookies on a parchment-lined cookie sheet, spacing them 2 inches apart. Using your fingers, slightly flatten the tops of the cookies.

4. Bake for 15 to 20 minutes, or until golden brown. Remove the cookie sheet from the oven. Let cookies cool on parchment for easiest removal. When cookies are completely cool, use a metal spatula to loosen them from the parchment paper. Store in an airtight container.

YIELDS 50 COOKIES

CHOCOLATE ALMOND MACAROONS
AMARETTI DI CIOCCOLATA

*These are a chocolate lover's version of the almond macaroon. To check
for doneness, bake them alongside the pine nut cookies. When the latter are golden
brown, the chocolate macaroons will be ready. Because this dough is a variation
of the pine nut cookie, it is best to use the technique described in the
previous recipe, dipping your hands in water while rolling.*

1½ POUNDS ALMOND PASTE
(BROKEN INTO PEBBLE-SIZE PIECES)

1½ CUPS SUGAR

1 CUP CONFECTIONERS' SUGAR

½ CUP COCOA

4 EGG WHITES

2 CUPS ALMONDS, SLICED

1. Preheat oven to 350°F.

2. In an electric mixer, combine almond paste, sugar, confectioners' sugar, cocoa,
   and egg whites on low speed until blended. Mix for 2 minutes on medium
   speed. This will make a sticky dough.

3. Roll dough into 1-inch balls. Roll balls in a bowl filled with almonds. Place
   cookies on a parchment-lined cookie sheet, spacing them 2 inches apart. Using
   your fingers, slightly flatten the tops of the cookies.

4. Bake for 15 to 20 minutes. Remove cookie sheet from the oven. Cool on parchment for easiest removal. When cookies are completely cool, use a metal spatula
   to loosen them from the parchment paper. Store in an airtight container.

YIELDS 60 COOKIES

SESAME COOKIES
BISCOTTI DI REGINA OR QUEEN'S BISCUITS

*These are very popular Sicilian cookies that have just a hint of sweetness.
Many women I know argue about whose variation is the best, but this version
has been made famous by my Aunt Ann. Everywhere she goes,
so do her sesame cookies!*

¼ POUND BUTTER, SOFTENED

½ CUP SUGAR

1 EGG

⅓ CUP MILK

1 TEASPOON VANILLA EXTRACT

2¼ CUPS FLOUR

1 TABLESPOON BAKING POWDER

ADDITIONAL MILK

1 CUP SESAME SEEDS

1. Preheat oven to 375°F.

2. In an electric mixer, cream butter and sugar until light. Add egg, milk, and
   vanilla. Mix until well blended. On low speed, gradually add the flour and baking powder. Turn out dough onto a lightly floured surface and knead until
   blended. This will be a soft dough.

3. Roll dough into 1-inch balls. Roll balls in a bowl filled with additional milk
   (about ½ cup) then in a bowl filled with the sesame seeds. This will help the
   seeds adhere. Place the cookies on parchment-lined cookie sheets, spacing them
   2 inches apart. Gently press the tops of cookies to flatten.

4. Bake for 12 to 15 minutes, or until lightly browned. Remove cookie sheet from
   the oven. Use a metal spatula to transfer cookies from the cookie sheet onto a
   wire cooling rack. Cool. Store in an airtight container.

YIELDS 40 COOKIES

THUMB COOKIES

These jelly-filled cookies are an international favorite. They get their name from using your thumb to make a hole in the center that holds the jelly. This recipe can easily be doubled to make a larger batch. For a tasty variation, try rolling the cookies in shredded coconut in place of the chopped nuts.

½ POUND BUTTER, SOFTENED

½ CUP SUGAR

2 EGGS, SEPARATED

2 TEASPOONS VANILLA EXTRACT

½ TEASPOON SALT

2 CUPS FLOUR

2 CUPS CHOPPED WALNUTS, OR HAZELNUTS

¾ CUP JELLY, ANY FLAVOR

1. Preheat oven to 350°F.

2. In an electric mixer, cream the butter and sugar until light. Add the egg yolks and vanilla. Mix until well blended.

3. On low speed, gradually add salt and flour. Mix just until blended to form a soft dough.

4. Shape the dough into 1-inch balls.

5. In a small bowl, beat egg whites with a fork until fluffy. Place chopped nuts in another small bowl.

6. Dip balls into egg whites and then roll in nuts. Coat thoroughly. Place balls on a parchment-lined cookie sheet, spacing them 2 inches apart.

7. Using your fingers, press the tops of the balls to flatten. With your index finger, make a hole in the center of each cookie.

8. Spoon ½ teaspoon of jelly into the hole. Repeat until all cookies are coated and filled.

9. Bake for 15 to 20 minutes, or until lightly browned. Remove cookie sheet from the oven.

10. Using a metal spatula, remove cookies from the cookie sheet and place on a wire cooling rack. Cool. Store in an airtight container.

YIELDS 35 COOKIES

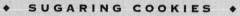

◆ SUGARING COOKIES ◆

MANY COOKIES IN THIS BOOK NEED TO BE ROLLED IN CONFECTION-ERS' SUGAR FOR THEIR FINISHING TOUCH. IF YOU CHOOSE TO ROLL THE COOKIES BY HAND, BE SURE TO WASH YOUR HANDS WHEN YOU'RE DONE. YOU'LL END UP WITH POWDERED FINGERPRINTS ON EVERYTHING ELSE YOU TOUCH!

HALF-MOONS

MEZZA LUNA

This is my own variation of my father's favorite cookie. It's a basic butter cookie shaped with a half-moon cookie cutter and brushed with a beaten egg. For years we bought them at Ortone's, a popular local bakery operated by family friends. They had a great business during World War 11, shipping these cookies overseas to homesick troops. I've developed my own version, and Dad likes them just fine.

½ POUND BUTTER, SOFTENED

½ CUP SUGAR

½ CUP CONFECTIONERS' SUGAR

1 TEASPOON VANILLA EXTRACT

2 TABLESPOONS ORANGE JUICE

1 TEASPOON ALMOND EXTRACT

2 EGGS

2½ CUPS FLOUR

1. In an electric mixer, cream the butter, sugar, and confectioners' sugar. Add vanilla, orange juice, almond extract, and 1 egg. Mix until well blended.

2. On low speed, gradually add the flour and mix until just blended.

3. Wrap the dough in plastic wrap and refrigerate 1 to 2 hours or overnight.

4. Preheat oven to 350°F.

5. Roll out dough on a lightly floured surface to a ¼-inch thickness. Cut shapes using a 3-inch half-moon cookie cutter. Place cookies 2 inches apart on a parchment-lined cookie sheet.

6. In a small bowl, beat remaining egg until blended. Using a pastry brush, brush the top of the crescents with the beaten egg.

7. Bake for 12 to 15 minutes, or until golden brown. Using a metal spatula, carefully lift cookies off the cookie sheet and onto a wire cooling rack. Cool. Store in an airtight container.

YIELDS 30 COOKIES

FORK COOKIES

These cookies get their name from the design on top. My mom loves them because they are crispy and have a subtle anise flavor. We always have a lively debate over which is better, chewy or crunchy cookies (she prefers crunchy!).

¼ POUND BUTTER, SOFTENED

¾ CUP SUGAR

½ CUP CONFECTIONERS' SUGAR

2 EGGS

2 TEASPOONS ANISEED

2½ CUPS FLOUR

1 TEASPOON BAKING SODA

½ TEASPOON CREAM OF TARTAR

¼ TEASPOON SALT

1. Preheat oven to 350°F.

2. In an electric mixer, cream the butter, sugar, and confectioners' sugar. Add eggs and aniseed. Mix until well blended.

3. On low speed, gradually add the flour, baking soda, cream of tartar, and salt. Knead to make a soft dough. Shape dough into ½-inch balls. Place cookies 2 inches apart on parchment-lined cookie sheets.

4. Using a fork, press tines into the tops of the cookies in a crisscross design. Dust the fork with flour to avoid sticking.

5. Bake for 10 to 12 minutes, or until golden brown. Remove cookie sheet from the oven.

6. Remove cookies from the cookie sheet using metal spatula. Placing on wire cooling racks. Cool. Store in an airtight container.

YIELDS 50 COOKIES

ALMOND CRESCENTS

*These horseshoe-shaped cookies are best when rolled in confectioners' sugar.
Because they are a bit fragile, be sure to place them on the top of
your cookie tray to prevent breaking.*

½ POUND BUTTER, SOFTENED

½ CUP SUGAR

2 EGGS

1 TEASPOON ALMOND EXTRACT

2 CUPS FLOUR

¼ TEASPOON SALT

1 CUP ALMONDS, SLICED

CONFECTIONERS' SUGAR FOR
COATING

1. Using an electric mixer, cream the butter and sugar. Add eggs and almond extract. Mix until well blended.

2. On low speed, gradually mix in flour, salt, and almonds. Mix just until blended. Wrap dough in plastic wrap and refrigerate for 1 to 2 hours.

3. Preheat oven at 350°F.

4. Roll the dough into long pencil-like strips about ½ inch in diameter. Cut these strips into 3-inch-long pieces and bend into horseshoe shapes. Place on a parchment-lined cookie sheet, spacing them 2 inches apart.

5. Bake for 15 to 20 minutes, or until lightly browned. Remove carefully from the cookie sheet with a metal spatula. While hot, gently roll crescents in confectioners' sugar.

6. Cool on wire racks. Store cookies in an airtight container.

YIELDS 70 COOKIES

BUTTER NUTS

NOCI DI BURRO

These buttery cookies are rolled in confectioners' sugar. Rich and fancy cookies, like these cookie balls, are usually made for special occasions and holidays. My brother and I used to steal these from the cookie tray and fill our pockets for our own personal supply.

½ POUND BUTTER, SOFTENED

⅓ CUP CONFECTIONERS' SUGAR

1 TEASPOON VANILLA EXTRACT

2 CUPS FLOUR

1 CUP HAZELNUTS, CHOPPED

CONFECTIONERS' SUGAR FOR COATING

1. Preheat oven to 350°F.

2. Using an electric mixer, cream butter, confectioners' sugar, and vanilla until well blended.

3. Add the flour and hazelnuts on low speed.

4. Roll dough into ½-inch balls and place on parchment-lined cookie sheets, spacing them about 2 inches apart. Bake for 15 to 20 minutes, or until lightly browned. Remove the cookie sheet from the oven. While cookies are hot, roll in confectioners' sugar to coat. Store in an airtight container.

YIELDS 50 COOKIES

KNOTS

These are one of my Aunt Lena's specialties. They are traditional, plain biscuits that are rolled in various shapes and twists. Every family rolls and shapes them differently. They can be braided or made into rings and frosted with confectioners' icing. When we were kids, we used to eat all of the frosting off the cookies first, and then bite into the cookie.

3 EGGS

½ CUP VEGETABLE OIL

½ CUP SUGAR

1 TEASPOON VANILLA EXTRACT

2¾ CUPS FLOUR

3 TEASPOONS BAKING POWDER

PINCH OF SALT

1. Preheat oven to 350°F.

2. In an electric mixer, mix eggs, oil, sugar, and vanilla on medium speed.

3. On low speed, gradually add flour, baking powder, and salt. Turn out dough onto a lightly floured surface. Knead to make a soft and elastic dough. Cover the dough with plastic wrap and let rest at room temperature for 15 to 20 minutes.

4. Break off small pieces of the dough and roll into ¼-inch-thick logs about 4 inches long. Twist dough pieces to make knots and braids. Place on a parchment-lined cookie sheet.

5. Bake for 15 to 20 minutes, or until lightly browned. Remove the cookie sheet from the oven.

6. Remove cookies from the cookie sheet using a metal spatula. Cool on wire racks.

7. When cool, frost with Confectioners' Frosting (see recipe page 12).

YIELDS 36 COOKIES

MOCHA WALNUT BUTTER COOKIES

This recipe is a family favorite that uses a combination of coffee and chocolate. My mom first learned how to make these cookies from my grandmother, when my brother and I were toddlers. She diligently rolled the dough into balls and placed them on the cookie sheet, ready for baking. When she wasn't looking, my brother and I smashed all the balls flat. Of course, we then learned a lesson—how to re-roll cookies.

½ POUND BUTTER, SOFTENED

½ CUP SUGAR

2 TEASPOONS VANILLA EXTRACT

2 TEASPOONS FINELY GROUND
ESPRESSO BEANS

1¾ CUPS FLOUR

¼ CUP COCOA

½ CUP WALNUTS, CHOPPED

CONFECTIONERS' SUGAR FOR
COATING

1. Preheat oven to 350°F.

2. Using an electric mixer, cream the butter and sugar. Add vanilla and espresso. Mix until well blended. On low speed, mix in flour, cocoa, and walnuts. Mix until just blended.

3. Roll dough into 1-inch balls and place on parchment-lined cookie sheets, spacing cookies 2 inches apart.

4. Bake for 15 to 20 minutes, or until firm. Carefully touch the top of the cookie with your fingers to check firmness. Remove cookie sheet from the oven.

5. Using a metal spatula, remove cookies from the cookie sheet onto a wire cooling rack. Cool. Roll cookies in confectioners' sugar. Store in an airtight container. To freeze, place uncoated cookies in a plastic freezer bag.

YIELDS 50 COOKIES

CINNAMON NUTMEG COOKIES

This recipe was given to me by Sabina Figluizzi, another cousin originally from New York. The cream cheese in the dough adds a rich, distinctive flavor. The sprinkle of cinnamon and nutmeg is just the right amount of sweetness and spice.

If you don't want to use a pastry bag to form these cookies, simply roll the dough into 1-inch balls, roll in spice mixture, and place on a parchment-lined cookie sheet. Press the tops of the balls slightly to flatten.

½ POUND BUTTER, SOFTENED

1 CUP SUGAR

3 OUNCES CREAM CHEESE, SOFTENED

1 EGG YOLK

2½ CUPS FLOUR

TOPPING:

¼ CUP SUGAR

1 TEASPOON CINNAMON

1 TEASPOON NUTMEG

1. Preheat oven to 375°F.

2. In an electric mixer, cream the butter, sugar, and cream cheese. Add the egg yolk and mix until well blended. On low speed, gradually add flour until just blended.

3. Spoon the dough into a pastry bag fitted with a large open star tip. Pipe 1½-inch rounds onto a parchment-lined cookie sheet, spacing them 2 inches apart.

4. In a small bowl, combine sugar, cinnamon, and nutmeg. Using your fingers or a small spoon, sprinkle the spice mixture over the tops of the cookies.

5. Bake for 10 to 12 minutes, or until lightly browned. Remove the cookie sheet from the oven.

6. Using a metal spatula, gently remove cookies from the cookie sheet onto a wire cooling rack.

7. Cool. Store cookies in an airtight container.

YIELDS 45 COOKIES

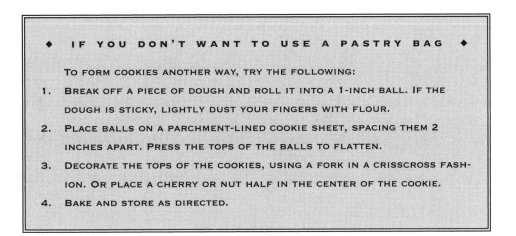

◆ IF YOU DON'T WANT TO USE A PASTRY BAG ◆

TO FORM COOKIES ANOTHER WAY, TRY THE FOLLOWING:

1. BREAK OFF A PIECE OF DOUGH AND ROLL IT INTO A 1-INCH BALL. IF THE DOUGH IS STICKY, LIGHTLY DUST YOUR FINGERS WITH FLOUR.

2. PLACE BALLS ON A PARCHMENT-LINED COOKIE SHEET, SPACING THEM 2 INCHES APART. PRESS THE TOPS OF THE BALLS TO FLATTEN.

3. DECORATE THE TOPS OF THE COOKIES, USING A FORK IN A CRISSCROSS FASHION. OR PLACE A CHERRY OR NUT HALF IN THE CENTER OF THE COOKIE.

4. BAKE AND STORE AS DIRECTED.

CHOCOLATE PUFFS

*These are light, chewy chocolate cookies that have always been a personal favorite.
The recipe was given to me by a "cousin." (Sometimes it seems that
I have so many neighbors and relatives, by the time I explain their exact
relationships, it's just easier to call everyone a cousin!)*

¼ POUND BUTTER, SOFTENED	2 CUPS FLOUR
1½ CUPS SUGAR	2 TEASPOONS BAKING POWDER
1 TEASPOON VANILLA EXTRACT	PINCH OF SALT
6 OUNCES SEMISWEET CHOCOLATE, MELTED	CONFECTIONERS' SUGAR
4 EGGS	

1. Using an electric mixer, cream butter and sugar. Add vanilla and melted chocolate. Mix until well blended. Add eggs. Mix well. On low speed, add flour, baking powder, and salt. This dough will be similar to a thick cake batter.

2. Cover the mixing bowl with plastic wrap and refrigerate the dough for 2 to 3 hours or overnight. The dough is ready when you can roll it into balls.

3. Preheat oven to 350°F.

4. Roll dough into ½-inch balls. Roll the balls in confectioners' sugar to coat. Place the sugared balls on a parchment-lined cookie sheet. Space the cookies 2 inches apart. They will spread.

5. Bake for 10 to 12 minutes. Cookies will spread and flatten. If you overcook these cookies they will lose their softness. Remove cookie sheet from the oven.

6. Cool cookies on parchment paper. When they are completely cool, use a metal spatula to loosen the cookies from the parchment paper. Store cooled cookies in an airtight container to retain softness.

YIELDS 50 COOKIES

CINNAMON "S" COOKIES

*These are among my favorite breakfast cookies. Their rich cinnamon flavor
is the perfect companion to a hot cup of coffee.*

¼ POUND BUTTER, SOFTENED

½ CUP BROWN SUGAR

1 EGG

1½ CUPS FLOUR

½ TEASPOON BAKING POWDER

2 TEASPOONS CINNAMON

2 TABLESPOONS BROWN SUGAR

1. Preheat oven to 375°F.

2. In an electric mixer, cream the butter and ½ cup brown sugar until light. Add the egg. Mix until blended.

3. On low speed, gradually add the flour and baking powder. Mix until just blended to form a soft dough.

4. On a lightly floured surface, roll the dough into pencil-width ropes about 5 inches long.

5. Combine cinnamon and brown sugar in a small bowl.

6. Roll dough strips in the sugar mixture. Form into an "S" shape and place on a parchment-lined cookie sheet, spacing cookies 2 inches apart.

7. Bake for 12 to 15 minutes, or until the edges begin to brown.

8. Remove cookie sheet from the oven. Using a metal spatula, remove the cookies from the cookie sheet onto a wire cooling rack. Cool. Store in an airtight container.

YIELDS 22 COOKIES

LADYFINGERS

These sponge cookies are the basis for the classic Italian dessert tiramisù.
They're also a family favorite topped with strawberries soaked in vermouth.
For the lightest ladyfingers, whip the egg whites until very stiff.

4 EGGS, SEPARATED, AT ROOM
TEMPERATURE

PINCH OF SALT

¼ TEASPOON CREAM OF TARTAR

¾ CUP SUGAR

1 TEASPOON VANILLA EXTRACT

¾ CUP FLOUR

1. Preheat oven to 375°F.

2. Using an electric mixer, with the whisk attachment, whip the egg whites, salt, and cream of tartar on high speed until soft peaks form. Gradually add ¼ cup sugar and beat until stiff.

3. In a separate bowl, beat egg yolks, vanilla, and remaining ½ cup sugar until thick. Stir in flour with a rubber spatula.

4. Gently fold egg whites into flour mixture.

5. Fill a pastry bag fitted with a plain open tip with cookie batter. Pipe batter onto a parchment-lined cookie sheet, making 3-inch ladyfingers. Space cookies 1 inch apart.

6. Bake immediately for 10 to 12 minutes, or until lightly browned. Remove cookie sheet from oven. Cool cookies on parchment paper.

7. When cool, use a metal spatula to carefully remove cookies from parchment. Store cooled cookies in an airtight container to retain softness.

YIELDS 65 COOKIES

SWEET FINGERS

DITI DI DOLCI

These cookies have a full almond flavor and a bit of chocolate—one of my favorite combinations. Try them for dessert alongside a simple gelato or spumone.

½ POUND BUTTER, SOFTENED

½ CUP SUGAR

2 EGGS

1 TEASPOON ALMOND EXTRACT

2 CUPS FLOUR

½ TEASPOON BAKING POWDER

½ CUP CHOPPED SEMISWEET CHOCOLATE

½ CUP CHOPPED ALMONDS

ADDITIONAL GRANULATED SUGAR

1. In an electric mixer, cream butter and sugar until light. Add 1 of the eggs and almond extract. Mix until blended.

2. On low speed, gradually add flour and baking powder. Mix until just blended.

3. With a wooden spoon, stir in chocolate and almonds. Wrap dough in plastic wrap and refrigerate for 1 to 2 hours.

4. Preheat oven to 350°F.

5. Turn out dough onto a lightly floured surface. Roll dough into strips about ½ inch wide. Cut the strips to measure 3 inches in length. Place on a parchment-lined cookie sheet, spacing cookies 2 inches apart.

6. In a small bowl, beat the remaining egg with a fork. Using a pastry brush, brush the tops of the cookies with the egg and sprinkle with additional sugar.

7. Bake for 15 to 20 minutes, or until golden brown.

8. Remove cookie sheet from the oven. Using a metal spatula, remove the cookies from the cookie sheet and place on a wire cooling rack. Cool. Store in an airtight container.

YIELDS 50 COOKIES

CHOCOLATE LADYFINGERS

A delicious variation. Try using a combination of vanilla and chocolate ladyfingers for a striking and tasty tiramisù.

4 EGGS, SEPARATED

PINCH OF SALT

¼ TEASPOON CREAM OF TARTAR

¾ CUP SUGAR

1 TEASPOON VANILLA EXTRACT

⅔ CUP FLOUR

3 TABLESPOONS COCOA

1. Preheat oven to 375°F.

2. Using an electric mixer with the whisk attachment, whip the egg whites, salt, and cream of tartar on high speed until soft peaks form. Gradually add ¼ cup sugar and beat until stiff.

3. In a separate bowl, beat egg yolks, vanilla, and remaining ½ cup sugar until thick. Stir in flour and cocoa, using a rubber spatula.

4. Gently fold egg whites into flour mixture.

5. Fill a pastry bag fitted with a plain open tip with cookie batter. Pipe batter onto a parchment-lined cookie sheet, making 3-inch ladyfingers. Space cookies 1 inch apart on cookie sheet.

6. Bake immediately for 10 to 12 minutes, or until lightly browned. Remove cookie sheet from the oven. Cool cookies on parchment paper.

7. When cool, use a metal spatula to carefully remove ladyfingers from the parchment. Store cooled cookies in an airtight container to retain softness.

YIELDS 75 COOKIES

DATE NUT BARS

These are cakelike squares that are easy to prepare. Shaking the bars in a plastic bag with confectioners' sugar to coat them was always one of my holiday jobs.

12 TABLESPOONS BUTTER, SOFTENED	PINCH OF SALT
1¼ CUPS SUGAR	1¼ CUPS FLOUR
2 TEASPOONS VANILLA EXTRACT	2 CUPS CHOPPED DATES
4 EGGS	2 CUPS CHOPPED WALNUTS

1. Preheat oven to 350°F.

2. Spray a 12 x 16-inch cookie sheet or jelly roll pan with a nonstick spray coating. Be sure to use a cookie sheet that has sides. Set aside.

3. Using an electric mixer, cream the butter and sugar. Add vanilla and eggs. Mix until well blended. On low speed, add salt, flour, dates, and walnuts. Mix until just blended.

4. Spread dough in prepared cookie sheet. Using a spatula, be sure to spread the dough evenly.

5. Bake for 25 to 30 minutes, or until the entire top is lightly browned. Remove pan from the oven.

6. Cool in the sheet pan on a wire cooling rack. When cool, slice into 1-inch squares. Coat the squares with confectioners' sugar.

YIELDS 95 SQUARES

CHOCOLATE SANDWICHES

*What could be better than two tasty cookies sandwiching a rich chocolate filling?
This is one of my brother's favorites. We have a lot in common,
especially our love of chocolate.*

½ POUND BUTTER, SOFTENED	1 TEASPOON VANILLA EXTRACT
¾ CUP SUGAR	PINCH OF SALT
1 EGG	1½ CUPS FLOUR

CHOCOLATE FILLING

8 OUNCES SEMISWEET CHOCOLATE (8 BAKING SQUARES)	3 TEASPOONS COFFEE LIQUEUR
3 TEASPOONS LIGHT CORN SYRUP	

1. Preheat oven to 350°F.

2. Using an electric mixer, cream the butter and sugar. Add the egg and vanilla. Mix until well blended.

3. On low speed, gradually add the salt and flour. Mix until just blended.

4. Using a pastry bag fitting with a plain tip, pipe 2-inch-long strips onto a parchment-lined cookie sheet, spacing cookies 2 inches apart. Try to pipe the cookies so they are all the same length. This will make it easier to pair them.

5. Bake for 8 to 10 minutes, or until the edges begin to brown. Remove the cookie sheet from the oven. Remove cookies from the cookie sheet using a metal spatula. Cool on a wire rack.

6. Slowly melt chocolate in a double boiler over barely simmering water. Stir constantly with a wooden spoon. When melted, add corn syrup and coffee liqueur. Remove from heat.

7. Using a butter knife, spread a dab of chocolate on the bottom of a cookie. Cover the chocolate with another cookie, forming a sandwich. The rounded sides should be on the outside. Repeat the chocolate filling with the remaining cookies. If the chocolate gets too thick, return it to over the simmering water to thin it to spreading consistency.

YIELDS 40 COOKIES

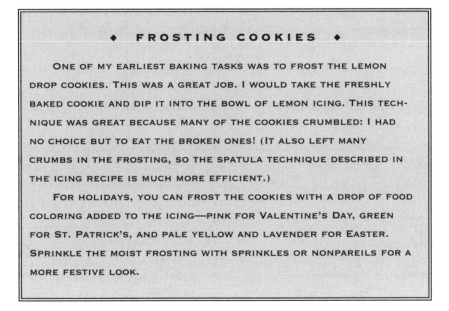

◆ FROSTING COOKIES ◆

One of my earliest baking tasks was to frost the lemon drop cookies. This was a great job. I would take the freshly baked cookie and dip it into the bowl of lemon icing. This technique was great because many of the cookies crumbled: I had no choice but to eat the broken ones! (It also left many crumbs in the frosting, so the spatula technique described in the icing recipe is much more efficient.)

For holidays, you can frost the cookies with a drop of food coloring added to the icing—pink for Valentine's Day, green for St. Patrick's, and pale yellow and lavender for Easter. Sprinkle the moist frosting with sprinkles or nonpareils for a more festive look.

PEACHES

PÈSCE

*This recipe came to our family through my Aunt Babe's neighbor, Antoinette.
When these cookies are filled and sugared, they look like real peaches.
They are whimsical cookies and a great conversation piece at parties,
especially when stacked in a basket. This is an especially great project for kids.*

COOKIE

4 EGGS

1 CUP VEGETABLE OIL

1 CUP SUGAR

4 CUPS FLOUR

4 TEASPOONS BAKING POWDER

FILLING

2 CUPS PEACH PRESERVES

2 OUNCES AMARETTO LIQUEUR

1 TABLESPOON WATER

COATING

4 PACKAGES PEACH JELL-O

¾ CUP GRANULATED SUGAR

1. Preheat oven to 350°F.

2. Mix eggs, oil, and sugar with an electric mixer. On low speed, add flour and baking powder and blend well to make a somewhat sticky dough. Let the dough rest at room temperature for 5 to 10 minutes.

3. Roll the dough into balls the size of a rounded teaspoon. Try to roll the balls uniformly because you will be matching them.

4. Bake on a lightly greased cookie sheet for 15 to 20 minutes, or until lightly browned. Remove cookie sheet from the oven.

5. Use a metal spatula to remove cookies from the cookie sheet onto a wire cooling rack. Cool.

6. Mix together the filling ingredients with a wooden spoon.

7. When cookies are cool, use a paring knife to scoop out the undersides. Break insides into fine crumbs and add the crumbs to the filling mixture. Match pairs of cookies that fit well together.

8. Fill matching pairs of cookies with filling, letting it squirt out the seam. Press flat ends together to form a sphere. Using your fingers, rub extra filling in a thin layer around each peach.

9. While still moist, roll in powdered Jell-o. Then roll in plain granulated sugar as a finish coat. Store in a cool place. Add a green leaf, if desired.

YIELDS 25 PEACHES

COLORED SUGARS

Instead of using peach Jell-o, you can create your own colored sugars to roll the cookies in.

3 CUPS GRANULATED SUGAR   LIQUID FOOD COLORING: RED, YELLOW, AND ORANGE

1. Place ¾ cup granulated sugar in each of 4 small bowls. Add several drops of red liquid food coloring to one bowl and mix well with your fingers until sugar is well blended. Repeat with the yellow and orange food coloring in two other bowls. Leave 1 bowl plain. Add as much food coloring to achieve your desired color. Use immediately. Roll the cookies lightly in each color for a natural look. Roll the peaches in ¾ cup plain sugar as a finish coat.

ROLLED AND FILLED COOKIES

These cookies are generally more labor-intensive and time-consuming than most of our recipes. Cookie dough that needs to be rolled out like a pie crust usually needs to be chilled to make it firmer for rolling. After chilling, roll out the dough with a lightly floured rolling pin on a lightly floured surface.

Use as little flour as possible; too much will toughen the dough. You should roll out and use all of the freshest dough first, saving all scraps for re-rolling at the end. Otherwise, the scraps will toughen the remaining dough. If you are splitting the dough to use one half at a time, keep the unused portion refrigerated until you are ready to roll it.

Although many of the cookies are time-consuming, you can usually split the process into two days. You can mix the dough, refrigerate it overnight, and then finish the cookies the next day.

If using cookie cutters, dust them with a little flour to reduce sticking. I remember my grandmother using the top lip of a juice glass to cut circles from cookie dough. It's not a bad idea if you don't want to invest in a lot of different-size cookie cutters.

CHOCOLATE SESAME BARS

This is one of several bar cookie recipes included in this collection. They are easy to prepare and have a rich almond flavor, chocolate filling, and a crunchy crumb topping.

FILLING

6 OUNCES SEMISWEET CHOCOLATE (SQUARES OR CHIPS)

3 OUNCES CREAM CHEESE

⅓ CUP HEAVY CREAM

½ CUP CHOPPED WALNUTS

2 TABLESPOONS SESAME SEEDS

½ TEASPOON ALMOND EXTRACT

CRUST

1½ CUPS FLOUR

½ TEASPOON BAKING POWDER

PINCH OF SALT

¼ POUND BUTTER, SOFTENED

¾ CUP SUGAR

1 EGG

1. Preheat oven to 375°F.

2. Coat an 8-inch square cake pan with a nonstick spray.

3. For the filling, melt chocolate, cream cheese, and heavy cream in a small saucepan over low heat. Stir constantly with a wooden spoon until melted.

4. Remove from heat and stir in walnuts, sesame seeds, and almond extract. Set aside.

5. In an electric mixer, combine all crust ingredients. Mix on low speed just until ingredients become blended fine crumbs.

6. Press half the crumb mixture into the prepared pan. Spread the filling mixture over the crust, spreading to the edges with a spatula.

7. Sprinkle remaining crumb mixture over chocolate filling and press down gently.

8. Bake for 20 to 25 minutes, or until the top is golden brown.

9. Remove pan from the oven. Cool pan on a wire cooling rack. When cool, cut into 1-inch squares. Store cooled bars in an airtight container.

YIELDS 36 BARS

RICH JELLY-FILLED COOKIES

These fancy jelly-filled treats are a specialty of my Aunt Babe.
You can use any flavor jelly, but raspberry has always been my favorite.
This recipe does yield a large number of cookies, but our philosophy
has always been that if you're going to make a mess, you might as well
make a lot of cookies. You can freeze some of them after they're baked,
or freeze half the dough for use at another time.

CRUST

¼ POUND BUTTER, SOFTENED	½ CUP SOUR CREAM
1 CUP SUGAR	2¾ CUPS FLOUR
½ TEASPOON VANILLA EXTRACT	1 TEASPOON BAKING POWDER
1 EGG	½ TEASPOON BAKING SODA

FILLING

1 CUP RASPBERRY OR ANY FLAVOR JELLY

1. In an electric mixer, cream the butter, sugar, and vanilla until light. Add the egg and sour cream and mix until blended. On low speed, mix in flour, baking powder, and baking soda. Turn out the dough onto a lightly floured surface and knead to make a soft dough. Wrap the dough in plastic wrap and refrigerate for 1 to 2 hours or overnight.

2. Preheat oven to 350°F.

3. Divide the dough into two equal pieces. Using a rolling pin, roll out a piece of the dough until very thin, like a pie crust, on a lightly floured surface. Using a 2-inch cookie cutter, cut circles from the dough. Spoon ½ teaspoon of jelly into the center of each circle. Pinch in two opposite sides of the circle. Place on a parchment-lined cookie sheet 2 inches apart.

4. Bake for 10 to 15 minutes, or until the edges begin to brown. Remove the cookie sheet from the oven.

5. Using a metal spatula, gently remove the cookies from the cookie sheet onto a wire cooling rack. Cool. Store cooled cookies in an airtight container.

YIELDS ABOUT 75 COOKIES

AUNT GIULIA'S JELLY AND NUT-FILLED COOKIES

Aunt Giulia, my grandmother's sister, was definitely the best baker in the family. She treated us to everything from Easter pies and Christmas strufoli to birthday sponge cakes. She seemed to produce them all with such ease and enjoyment, and she always had time for us to stop in and sample her goodies. These jelly and nut cookies were definitely her specialty, and they remind me of her the most. The dough is rolled, jelly-roll fashion, into a long loaf similar to a filled biscotti, cooled, and then sliced.

CRUST

4 TABLESPOONS BUTTER, SOFTENED	¼ CUP MILK
½ CUP SUGAR	2 CUPS FLOUR
2 EGGS	2 TEASPOON BAKING POWDER

FILLING

½ CUP CHOPPED WALNUTS	½ TEASPOON CINNAMON
3 TABLESPOONS SUGAR	1 CUP RASPBERRY JELLY

1. Using an electric mixer, cream the butter and sugar. Add eggs and milk. Mix until well blended.

2. Add the flour and baking powder on low speed. Turn out the dough onto a lightly floured surface and knead until the dough is well blended. Wrap dough in plastic wrap and refrigerate for several hours or overnight.

3. Preheat oven to 350°F.

4. In a small bowl, combine walnuts, sugar, and cinnamon.

5. Divide dough in half. With a rolling pin, roll out a piece of dough on a lightly floured surface, until about ⅛-inch thick. The dough should be rolled in an

oblong shape, not round. Spread ½ cup of jelly over the dough, using a metal spatula or butter knife. Sprinkle half of the nut mixture over the jelly.

6. Starting at the bottom long end, roll up loosely, like a jelly roll. Carefully move the roll onto a parchment-lined cookie sheet, placing seam side down.

7. Repeat rolling and filling with the other half of dough. Place each loaf about 3 inches apart on cookie sheet.

8. Bake for 25 to 30 minutes, or until light brown. Remove the cookie sheet from the oven. Cool on cookie sheets. These cookies will be easier to slice, with less breakage, if they are stored at room temperature, wrapped in foil, overnight. After cooling, slice each loaf diagonally into ½-inch slices.

YIELDS ABOUT 25 COOKIES

CECI-FILLED CALZONES
CALZONE DI SAN GIUSEPPE

This fried cookie is traditionally baked to celebrate St. Joseph's Day, March 19. As is customary on a saint's feast day, you must seek out every person named Joseph or Josephine on this day and pull their ear for good luck.

When my grandmother first told me about this chick-pea and chocolate combination, I must admit I was quite skeptical about its taste. But upon trying it, I agreed it was flavorful with an interesting texture. My mother and I always say this recipe was probably invented by an Italian woman who had a little bit of ceci and a little bit of chocolate left over and hated to throw them away.

CRUST

3 EGGS	¼ CUP WHITE WINE
1 TABLESPOON SUGAR	1 TEASPOON CINNAMON
¼ CUP VEGETABLE OIL	2¼ TO 2½ CUPS FLOUR

FILLING

10 OUNCES CANNED CHICK-PEAS	¼ CUP HONEY
3 OUNCES SEMISWEET CHOCOLATE CHIPS	½ TEASPOON CINNAMON
½ CUP FINELY CHOPPED WALNUTS	1 TABLESPOON CONFECTIONERS' SUGAR
VEGETABLE OIL FOR FRYING	

1. In a small bowl, beat eggs, sugar, oil, wine, and cinnamon with a fork. Add 2 cups of flour and knead until dough is smooth and elastic. Knead in additional flour if dough is too sticky. Wrap dough in plastic wrap and refrigerate while you make the filling.

2. Drain chick-peas. Pour into a small saucepan and cover with water. Over medium heat, boil, uncovered, until tender, 10 to 12 minutes. Drain. Remove and discard any skins that have been loosened during boiling. Mash the chick-peas until smooth using a fork or potato masher.

3. While hot, mix in all other filling ingredients. Blend well until chocolate is melted. Set aside.

4. Roll out crust to a ⅛-inch thickness. With a 4-inch round cookie cutter, cut dough into circles. Before filling the circles, slightly stretch each circle similar to stretching a pizza crust.

5. Place ¾ teaspoon of filling into the center of each circle. Fold the dough over to form a mini-turnover. Seal seams of dough with a fork. Fill all circles, then let them set for 10 to 15 minutes.

6. Preheat a medium saucepan filled with 3 inches of vegetable oil.

7. Deep-fry calzones in preheated vegetable oil for 1 to 2 minutes, until just browned on both sides. Remove from oil with a slotted spoon. Drain on paper towels. Dust with confectioners' sugar and serve warm or cooled.

YIELDS ABOUT 30 COOKIES

◆ **CHICK-PEAS** ◆

CHICK-PEAS ARE COMMONLY USED IN SALADS OR WITH PASTA BUT MAKE A UNIQUE FILLING FOR OUR "CALZONES." THEY ARE ALSO KNOWN AS CECI OR GARBANZO BEANS AND ARE READILY AVAILABLE CANNED IN MOST SUPERMARKETS.

BUTTER HORNS

*These cookies, which have a great flaky dough and are filled
with cinnamon and sugar, have always been a part of fancy wedding cookie trays.
Years ago, it was a tradition for the bride and groom to visit all
of the guest tables with a large platter of cookies. This gave everyone an opportunity
to visit, taste the cookies, and in a very subtle way, allowed the bride and groom
to collect the gift envelopes.*

CRUST

½ POUND BUTTER, SOFTENED	¾ CUP SOUR CREAM
1 EGG YOLK	2 CUPS FLOUR

FILLING

1 CUP SUGAR	1 CUP CHOPPED WALNUTS
1 TEASPOON CINNAMON	

1. In an electric mixer, cream the butter. Add egg yolk and sour cream. Blend well.
   On low speed, gradually add the flour. Turn out dough onto a lightly floured
   surface and knead until well blended. Wrap dough in plastic wrap and refrigerate for 1 to 2 hours or overnight.

2. Preheat oven to 375°F.

3. In a small bowl, mix sugar, cinnamon, and nuts. Set aside.

4. Divide the dough into three equal pieces. Using a lightly floured rolling pin,
   roll out each piece until very thin, like a pie crust, on a lightly floured surface.
   Spread a third of the sugar mixture over the circle of dough.

5. Using a pastry cutter, cut the circle into 16 wedges.

6. Roll each wedge, starting at the wide end, toward the center of the circle. Pinch
   at the middle to adhere loose end of the dough. Slightly curve the cookie into a

half-moon shape and place on a parchment-lined cookie sheet. Be sure to tuck the loose end of the dough underneath the cookie so it doesn't open while baking.

7. Bake for 15 to 20 minutes, or until lightly browned. Remove the cookie sheet from the oven.

8. Remove the cookies from cookie sheet with a metal spatula onto a wire cooling rack. Cool. Store cooled cookies in an airtight container.

YIELDS ABOUT 48 COOKIES

FILLED CRESCENTS

CALZONE

These are baked crescents with a light and flaky crust. The date nut and fig fillings are family favorites. These types of cookies and other rich foods were used to celebrate Shrove Tuesday, or Mardi Gras.

CRUST

½ POUND BUTTER, SOFTENED   2 CUPS FLOUR

1 CUP COTTAGE CHEESE   PINCH OF SALT

DATE NUT FILLING

1 CUP CHOPPED WALNUTS   ½ CUP CHOPPED DATES

1 CUP BROWN SUGAR   ½ CUP HEAVY CREAM

½ CUP RAISINS

1. In a medium mixing bowl, blend butter and cottage cheese with a rubber spatula. Gradually mix in flour and salt. Turn out dough onto a lightly floured surface and knead until well blended. This will be a soft dough. Wrap dough in plastic wrap and refrigerate for 1 to 2 hours or overnight.

2. When dough has been chilled, remove from the refrigerator.

3. Preheat oven to 350°F.

4. Combine all filling ingredients in a medium saucepan. Cook, stirring constantly over medium heat, until thickened, 6 to 8 minutes. Cool. Set aside.

5. Roll out crust dough on a lightly floured surface until about ⅛ inch thick. Using a 3-inch cookie cutter, cut dough into rounds. Re-roll and re-cut dough as necessary.

6. Spoon 1 teaspoon of filling into the center of each circle. Brush the edge of the dough with water. Fold dough over to form a turnover. Seal edges with a fork. Place 2 inches apart on a parchment-lined cookie sheet.

7. Bake 10 to 15 minutes, or until lightly browned. Remove the cookie sheet from the oven. Using a metal spatula, remove the hot crescents from the cookie sheet and place on a wire cooling rack. Cool.

8. Dust with confectioners' sugar.

YIELDS ABOUT 48 CRESCENTS

VARIATION: FIG FILLING

12 OUNCES DRIED FIGS	½ CUP APRICOT PRESERVES
½ CUP SUGAR	¼ TEASPOON GROUND CLOVES
1 TEASPOON CINNAMON	2 TABLESPOONS RUM

1. Place figs in a medium saucepan and cover with water. Boil, uncovered, over medium heat for 10 minutes. Drain.

2. Place cooked figs in a food processor. Pulse 1 to 2 minutes, or until puréed.

3. In a small mixing bowl, combine puréed figs, sugar, cinnamon, preserves, cloves, and rum. Mix with a rubber spatula until blended.

FILLED TWISTS

These are fancy Christmas cookies that look like twisted ribbons.
They are fragile, so be sure to place them on the top of your cookie tray
or on their own separate platter.

CRUST

¼ POUND BUTTER, SOFTENED	1 EGG YOLK
3 OUNCES CREAM CHEESE, SOFTENED	1 CUP FLOUR

FILLING

2 TABLESPOONS SUGAR	¼ CUP APRICOT PRESERVES
1 TEASPOON CINNAMON	(OR ANY OTHER FLAVOR)
¼ CUP FINELY CHOPPED WALNUTS	

1. In an electric mixer, cream butter and cream cheese. Add egg yolk. Mix until well blended. On low speed, add flour until just mixed. Turn out dough onto a lightly floured surface. Knead until blended. Wrap dough in plastic wrap and refrigerate for 1 to 2 hours or overnight.

2. Preheat oven to 375°F.

3. In a small bowl, mix together sugar, cinnamon, and nuts. Set aside.

4. Divide chilled dough in half. Using a lightly floured rolling pin, roll a piece of the dough into a rectangle approximately 20 by 5 inches. Roll the dough as thin as possible.

5. Spread a thin layer of preserves on the dough. Sprinkle half the sugar mixture on top.

6. Take the top piece of the dough and fold it over to meet the bottom evenly. Press down lightly.

7. Using a pastry cutter, cut the filled dough into strips about ½ inch wide by 3 inches long. Take the strip of filled dough and gently twist. Place twists on parchment-lined cooked sheets, spacing them about 2 inches apart.

8. Bake for 12 to 15 minutes, or until lightly browned. Remove cookie sheet from the oven. Cool cookies on parchment paper. When cool, use a metal spatula to remove cookies from the parchment. Store in an airtight container.

YIELDS 36 COOKIES

◆ OLD RECIPE BOXES ◆

MANY OF MY OLDER AUNTS HAD RECIPE BOXES IN WHICH GREASE-STAINED INDEX CARDS HELD THE SECRETS TO THEIR CREATIONS. UNFORTUNATELY, THEIR NOTES AND DIRECTIONS ARE VERY INCOMPLETE. THE BEST WAY TO RE-CREATE THEIR DELICACIES IS TO ACTUALLY WATCH THEM PREPARE THE ACTUAL DISH.

CINNAMON NUT BARS

The buttery crust and rich nut topping make these squares a special candylike dessert. You can cut them into triangles or diamonds for fancier additions to your cookie tray.

CRUST

½ POUND BUTTER, SOFTENED	1 EGG
½ CUP BROWN SUGAR	2 CUPS FLOUR
½ TEASPOON VANILLA EXTRACT	

TOPPING

2½ CUPS CHOPPED WALNUTS	½ CUP HONEY
2 TEASPOONS CINNAMON	¼ CUP BROWN SUGAR
½ TEASPOON NUTMEG	¼ CUP MILK
¼ POUND BUTTER, SOFTENED	

1. Preheat oven to 350°F.

2. For the crust, cream butter and sugar in an electric mixer until light. Add vanilla and egg. Mix until well blended.

3. On low speed, gradually add the flour to make a soft dough.

4. Press the dough into a greased 10 x 10-inch baking pan. Cover the bottom of the pan and let the crust go slightly up the sides as well.

5. Bake the crust for 10 to 15 minutes, or until lightly browned. Remove the pan from the oven. Place on a wire cooling rack.

6. For the topping, combine walnuts, cinnamon, and nutmeg in a medium bowl. Mix until blended. Set aside.

7. In a medium saucepan over medium heat, melt butter. Add the honey and brown sugar. Using a wooden spoon, stir until boiling. Let boil for 2 to 3 minutes, stirring constantly.

8. Remove saucepan from the heat. Pour hot mixture into nuts and spices. Add milk. Mix with a wooden spoon and spread evenly over crust.

9. Bake for 15 to 20 minutes, or until bubbling. Remove pan from the oven. Place pan on a wire cooling rack.

10. Cool cookies in the pan. Cut into squares. Store in an airtight container.

YIELDS 45 SQUARES

◆ GELATO AND SPUMONE ◆

MANY OF THESE COOKIES ARE A GREAT COMPANION TO A DISH OF ICE CREAM OR GELATO OR SPUMONE. GELATO CAN BE ANY FLAVOR, SPUMONE IS TRADITIONALLY PART VANILLA, PART CHERRY, AND PART PISTACHIO, REPLICATING THE RED, WHITE, AND GREEN OF THE ITALIAN FLAG. FRUIT-FLAVORED SORBETS OR ITALIAN ICES ARE ALSO POPULAR DESSERTS THAT GO WELL WITH COOKIES.

SWEET RAVIOLI

RAVIOLI DOLCI

The cookies have a sweet crust and a ricotta filling. They are like a smaller version of the sweet ricotta pies we traditionally bake for Easter.

CRUST

¼ POUND BUTTER, SOFTENED

½ CUP SUGAR

1 EGG

2 TABLESPOONS SOUR CREAM

2 CUPS FLOUR

1½ TEASPOONS BAKING POWDER

PINCH OF SALT

FILLING

1 CUP RICOTTA

¼ CUP SUGAR

1 EGG YOLK

½ TEASPOON LEMON EXTRACT

TOPPING

1 EGG WHITE, LIGHTLY BEATEN

2 TABLESPOONS SUGAR

1 TEASPOON CINNAMON

1. In an electric mixer, cream the butter and sugar. Add the egg and sour cream. Mix until well blended. On low speed, add flour, baking powder, and salt. Turn out dough onto a lightly floured surface and knead until well blended. Wrap the dough in plastic wrap and refrigerate for 1 to 2 hours or overnight.

2. Preheat oven to 350°F.

3. In a small bowl, mix ricotta, sugar, egg yolk, and lemon extract using a wooden spoon. Set aside.

4. Remove chilled dough from the refrigerator. Using a lightly floured rolling pin, roll out the dough on a lightly floured surface. Roll the dough thin like a pie crust, about ⅛ inch thick. Cut circles from the dough using a 2½-inch round cookie cutter. Continue rolling until all the dough has been cut into circles. Try to have an even number of circles.

5. Place ¾ teaspoon of filling into the center of half the circles. With a pastry brush, brush some egg white around the edge of the filled circle. This will help to seal it.

6. Place another circle of dough on top of a circle that has a dab of filling. Press the edges firmly to seal. You can use a flour-dusted fork to create a design along the sealed edge. Use a metal spatula to carefully place the ravioli on a parchment-lined cookie sheet. Repeat filling and sealing all the rounds.

7. In a small bowl, combine sugar and cinnamon. Brush the tops of the ravioli with egg white and sprinkle the tops with the cinnamon and sugar mixture.

8. Bake 12 to 15 minutes, or until golden brown. Remove cookie sheet from the oven.

9. Use a metal spatula to remove ravioli from the cookie sheet onto a wire cooling rack. Cool. Store in an airtight container in the refrigerator.

YIELDS ABOUT 25 COOKIES

BISCOTTI

Biscotti are Italian cookies that are twice baked. In most older traditional biscotti recipes, there was no type of shortening added to the dough. This produced a hard biscuit that could only be enjoyed by dunking into coffee or wine. This gave many people the impression that biscotti were stale, hard biscuits. Luckily, biscotti has shed the image of jawbreakers. Many of the biscotti recipes in this book call for some type of fat to produce a slightly softer, more cookielike texture. These biscotti are still crunchy, but have richer flavor.

The following technique is a universal method for making biscotti. The cookie dough is formed into a long, thin loaf and baked. The loaves can be cooled on wire racks, or if you have enough cookie sheets, they can simply cool on the sheets. It is a good idea to let the loaves cool thoroughly before slicing them into strips. This will make the biscotti less crumbly. You can cool the loaves overnight. Be sure they are cool, then wrap each loaf in a plastic bag and store at room temperature overnight.

The loaves are sliced diagonally into $\frac{1}{2}$-inch strips. Use a sharp straight knife in a chopping motion. (If the loaves are warm, use a large serrated knife with a sawing motion.) The strips are then placed back on the cookie sheet, in a single layer, and toasted in the oven again. This creates a crunchy, toasted cookie.

ANISE TOASTS

These flavorful biscuits are one of the first I learned to bake. Using anise extract or oil produces a greater flavor than using the actual Anisette or Sambuca liqueurs. Whenever we bake them, the whole neighborhood can smell them!

6 EGGS

1 CUP SUGAR

1 CUP VEGETABLE OIL

1½ TABLESPOONS ANISE OIL
OR EXTRACT

6 TEASPOONS BAKING POWDER

4½ CUPS FLOUR

1. Preheat oven to 350°F.

2. In an electric mixer, or with a wire whisk, beat eggs, sugar, oil, and anise until well blended.

3. On low speed, gradually mix in baking powder and 3 cups of flour. Turn out dough onto a lightly floured surface and knead in the additional 1½ cups flour to make a soft dough. The dough should be soft but not sticky. Dust with flour if dough is too sticky to handle.

4. Divide the dough into four equal pieces and roll each piece to form a 12-inch-long loaf.

5. Place on a parchment-lined cookie sheet, spacing loaves 3 inches apart.

6. Bake 20 to 25 minutes, or until golden brown. Remove cookie sheet from the oven.

7. Using two metal spatulas, carefully lift the loaves off the cookie sheet and onto a wire cooling rack. Cool.

8. Place cooled loaves on a cutting board. Using a large sharp knife, slice loaves diagonally into ½-inch-wide strips and place in a single layer on the cookie sheet.

9. Return to the oven for 12 to 15 minutes, or until lightly browned. Remove cookie sheet from the oven. Cool toasted biscotti on a wire cooling rack. Store in an airtight container.

YIELDS 48 COOKIES

APRICOT PECAN BISCOTTI

I developed this recipe to combine two of my favorite things, apricots and pecans. These are a great summer treat with a tall glass of iced tea.

1½ CUPS DRIED APRICOTS, CHOPPED

1½ CUPS PECANS, COARSELY CHOPPED

2¾ CUPS FLOUR

¼ POUND BUTTER, SOFTENED

1 CUP BROWN SUGAR

3 EGGS

1 TEASPOON VANILLA EXTRACT

3 TEASPOONS BAKING POWDER

PINCH OF SALT

1. Preheat oven to 350°F.

2. In a small bowl, mix apricots and pecans with 2 tablespoons of the flour. Stir with a wooden spoon to coat the fruit and nuts. Set aside.

3. In an electric mixer, cream the butter and brown sugar. Add eggs and vanilla. Mix until well blended.

4. On low speed, gradually add the remaining flour, baking powder, and salt. Mix until just blended. Stir in apricots and pecans. Turn out dough onto a lightly floured surface. Divide dough into three pieces. Roll each piece into a loaf about 12 inches long. Place loaves 3 inches apart on a parchment-lined cookie sheet.

5. Bake 20 to 25 minutes, or until golden brown. Remove cookie sheet from oven.

6. Using two metal spatulas, carefully remove the loaves from the cookie sheet onto a wire cooling rack. Cool.

7. Place cooled loaves on a cutting board. Using a sharp knife, slice diagonally into ½-inch-wide strips. Place in a single layer on the cookie sheet and return to the oven for about 10 to 15 minutes, or until lightly browned. Remove cookie sheet from oven. Cool toasted biscotti on wire cooling racks. Store in an airtight container.

YIELDS 40 COOKIES

CHOCOLATE BISCOTTI

BISCOTTI DI CIOCCOLATA

This is a great biscotti for chocoholics. The recipe is inspired by my Aunt Dolly, who loves chocolate cookies so much, everyone calls her Auntie Cookie.

Be sure to use imported Dutch cocoa for the fullest flavor.
Try serving these biscotti with an iced cappuccino.

¼ POUND BUTTER, SOFTENED	2 CUPS FLOUR
¾ CUP SUGAR	½ CUP COCOA
2 TABLESPOONS COFFEE LIQUEUR	1½ TEASPOONS BAKING POWDER
2 EGGS	

1. Preheat oven to 375°F.

2. With an electric mixer, beat butter, sugar, and coffee liqueur until light in color and fluffy in texture. Add the eggs and blend well.

3. On low speed, gradually add flour, cocoa, and baking powder.

4. Divide the dough in half. Shape into two loaves about 10 inches long. Place on a parchment-lined cookie sheet, spacing them 3 inches apart.

5. Bake for 20 to 25 minutes, until tops of loaves are firm. Remove cookie sheet from the oven.

6. Using two metal spatulas, carefully remove loaves from hot cookie sheet onto wire racks. Cool. Place cooled loaves on a cutting board. Using a sharp knife, slice the loaves diagonally into ½-inch-wide slices.

7. Place the slices on the cookie sheet in a single layer. Return to the oven for 12 to 15 minutes, or until lightly browned. Remove cookie sheet from the oven. Cool toasted biscotti on a wire cooling rack. Store cooled cookies in an airtight container.

YIELDS 24 BISCOTTI

CINNAMON DATE NUT BISCOTTI

*This is one of my personal favorites, made famous by my Grandma Bruscino.
She was such a devoted wife and mother, she counted out 100 pieces
of linguine each day for my father's lunch!*

*The beaten egg brushed on top of these biscotti adds a professional finished look.
They have a great flavor baked only once,
without the traditional toasting.*

4 CUPS FLOUR	5 EGGS
1 TEASPOON CINNAMON	1 CUP VEGETABLE OIL
1 TEASPOON BAKING SODA	1 CUP SUGAR
1 CUP WALNUTS, COARSELY CHOPPED	1 CUP BROWN SUGAR
1 CUP DATES, CHOPPED	

1. Preheat oven to 350°F.

2. In a large bowl, using a wooden spoon, combine flour, cinnamon, baking soda, walnuts, and dates. Form a well in the center of the dry ingredients. Set aside.

3. In another bowl, with a wire whisk, beat 4 of the eggs with the oil, sugar, and brown sugar. Pour egg mixture into the well of dry ingredients. Mix with a wooden spoon. Turn out dough onto a lightly floured surface and knead until dough is blended. If dough is sticky, dust with additional flour.

4. Divide dough into four equal pieces. Form each piece into a loaf approximately 12 inches long. Place loaves 3 inches apart on parchment-lined cookie sheets.

5. In a small bowl, beat remaining egg with a fork. Using a pastry brush, brush the tops of the loaves with beaten egg.

6. Bake for 20 to 25 minutes, or until golden brown.

7. Remove cookie sheet from the oven.

8. Using two metal spatulas, carefully remove loaves from hot cookie sheet onto wire racks. Cool.

9. Place cooled loaves on a cutting board. Using a large sharp knife, slice diagonally into ½-inch-wide slices. Serve without toasting. Store cooled cookies in an airtight container.

YIELDS 50 COOKIES

◆ SUNDAY DINNERS ◆

SUNDAY DINNERS ARE USUALLY A BIG PRODUCTION IN MOST AMERICAN-ITALIAN HOUSEHOLDS. THE BIG MEAL IS ALWAYS THE AFTERNOON MEAL, STARTING GENERALLY AT NOON OR 1 O'CLOCK. WHEN I WAS A CHILD, THE MEAL SEEMED TO LAST ALL AFTERNOON, SOUP TO NUTS. NOW WITH EVERYONE'S BUSIER LIFESTYLE, THE SUNDAY AFTERNOON MEAL HAS BEEN A BIT STREAMLINED. IT'S STILL AN IMPORTANT TRADITION AND ALWAYS A GREAT TIME TO CATCH UP WITH FAMILY.

COCONUT BISCOTTI

*This nice, basic biscotti is ideal plain or drizzled with chocolate.
These biscotti always remind me of the warm weather—probably because I love to
serve them with ice cream. As a child I spent many summer afternoons
at my Uncle Nick's cottage munching on biscotti like these.*

¼ POUND BUTTER, SOFTENED

1 CUP SUGAR

2 EGGS

2 TEASPOONS VANILLA EXTRACT

2 CUPS SWEETENED FLAKED
COCONUT

2 CUPS FLOUR

1½ TEASPOONS BAKING POWDER

¼ TEASPOON SALT

1. Preheat oven to 350°F.

2. In an electric mixer, beat the butter and sugar until light. Add the eggs and vanilla. Mix well.

3. On low speed, add coconut. Gradually add the flour, baking powder, and salt. Divide the dough into three equal pieces. If the dough is sticky, dust with additional flour. Form the pieces of dough into loaves about 12 inches long. Place loaves on a parchment-lined cookie sheet, spacing them 3 inches apart.

4. Bake until golden brown, 20 to 25 minutes.

5. Remove cookie sheet from oven.

6. Carefully remove loaves, using two metal spatulas, onto wire cooling racks. Cool.

7. Place cooled loaves on a cutting board. Using a large, sharp knife, slice diagonally into ½-inch-wide slices.

8. Return slices to the cookie sheet, in a single layer, and toast for 12 to 15 minutes, or until lightly browned. Remove cookie sheet from oven. Cool toasted biscotti on wire cooling racks. Store in airtight containers.

YIELDS 45 COOKIES

ALMOND BISCOTTI
BISCOTTI DI PRATO

*These cookies are one of the original, classic biscotti of Italy. This recipe does not
use any fat, so the biscotti produced are a lot crunchier than the other biscotti
in this chapter. They are at their best when dunked in a fresh cup of cappuccino.
Because they harden quickly, be sure to slice them while they are warm.*

2 CUPS FLOUR	½ CUP SLICED ALMONDS
½ CUP SUGAR	3 EGGS
1½ TEASPOONS BAKING POWDER	¼ CUP MILK
¼ TEASPOON SALT	

1. Preheat oven to 375°F.

2. In a large bowl, combine flour, sugar, baking powder, salt, and almonds. Make a well in the center. Set aside.

3. In a separate bowl, mix 2 of the eggs and milk with a wire whisk. Add the egg mixture to the well. Stir with a wooden spoon. Turn out dough onto a lightly floured surface. Knead until dough is blended. It will be a little sticky.

4. Divide dough in half. Roll into two loaves, about 12 inches long. Place the loaves on parchment-lined cookie sheets, spacing them 3 inches apart.

5. In a small bowl, beat remaining egg. Brush the tops of the loaves with the egg, using a pastry brush.

6. Bake for 20 to 25 minutes, or until golden brown.

7. Remove cookie sheet from the oven.

8. Carefully remove hot loaves from the cookie sheet and place on a cutting board. While still warm, slice the loaves diagonally into ½-inch-wide slices.

9. Place slices in a single layer on the cookie sheet. Return to the oven for 15 to 20 minutes, or until lightly browned. Remove cookie sheet from the oven. Cool toasted biscotti on a wire cooling rack. Store in an airtight container.

YIELDS 24 COOKIES

MARBLE BISCOTTI

For those who can't decide on chocolate or vanilla, choose both!
Making this dough is like making two different doughs at once. It can be a messy
process, but great fun. Just don't be afraid to get your hands dirty.

7 EGGS

1½ CUPS SUGAR

1 TEASPOON VANILLA EXTRACT

¼ CUP MILK

¼ POUND BUTTER, MELTED, THEN
COOLED

3 TEASPOONS BAKING POWDER

4½ CUPS FLOUR

¾ CUP COCOA

1. Preheat oven to 350°F.

2. In an electric mixer, mix 5 of the eggs, sugar, and vanilla until well blended.
   Add milk and melted butter. Mix well.

3. Divide this egg mixture in half, placing each half in a medium mixing bowl.
   This will be about 1½ cups of the egg mixture per bowl.

4. To make the vanilla portion of our marble biscotti, add 1½ teaspoons baking
   powder and 2¼ cups of flour to one of the egg mixtures. Mix until blended.
   Turn out dough onto a lightly floured surface and knead to make a soft dough.
   Cover the dough with plastic wrap and set aside.

5. To make the chocolate portion of our marble biscotti, add 1½ teaspoons of
   baking powder, ¾ cup cocoa, and 2¼ cups flour to the remaining egg mixture.
   Mix with a wooden spoon. Turn out dough onto a lightly floured surface and
   knead until well blended. This will give you a soft dough similar to the vanilla
   portion.

6. Divide the chocolate dough into four equal pieces. Divide the vanilla dough
   into four equal pieces. Roll each piece into a cylinder about 12 inches long.
   Take one vanilla and one chocolate cylinder and twist around each other.
   Knead this piece for just a minute to give it a two-tone look. Form a loaf with
   this marbled dough about 12 inches long.

7. Repeat the marbling process with the remaining dough for a total of four loaves.

8. Place the loaves on a parchment-lined cookie sheet, spacing them about 3 inches apart.

9. In a small bowl, beat the remaining egg. Brush the tops of the loaves with the egg, using a pastry brush.

10. Bake for 20 to 25 minutes, or until lightly browned.

11. Remove cookie sheet from the oven.

12. Remove loaves, using two metal spatulas, onto a wire rack for cooling. When cool, place the loaves on a cutting board. Cut each loaf into ½-inch-wide diagonal slices.

13. Place slices on cookie sheet and return to the oven for 12 to 15 minutes, or until lightly browned. Store cookies in an airtight container.

YIELDS 48 COOKIES

MOLASSES SLICES

"DA-DUNES"

These are a traditional Neopolitan Christmas cookie, introduced to our family years ago by our friend Mary Tropasso. These tasty cookies are formed into loaves like traditional biscotti, yet they don't require additional toasting to bring out their flavor. The original recipe called for "sugar, enough to taste" and a "whole bottle of molasses." After a few rounds of experimentation, I've found the following works best. Try to find the darkest molasses for the fullest flavor. The nickname "da-dunes" is still a mystery.

5 CUPS FLOUR	1 CUP DARK MOLASSES
3 TEASPOONS BAKING POWDER	⅔ CUP SUGAR
½ TEASPOON NUTMEG	1 TEASPOON VANILLA EXTRACT
3 EGGS	1 TEASPOON LEMON EXTRACT
⅔ CUP VEGETABLE OIL	

1. Preheat oven to 350°F.

2. In a large bowl, mix together 4½ cups flour, baking powder, and nutmeg. Form a well in the center of these dry ingredients. Set aside.

3. In another bowl, whisk eggs, oil, molasses, sugar, and extracts. Pour the egg mixture into the well of dry ingredients. Mix well with a wooden spoon.

4. Turn out dough onto a well-floured surface. Knead in an additional ½ cup of flour to make a firm dough. Divide dough into four equal pieces. Roll each piece into a loaf about 12 inches long. Place loaves on a parchment-lined cookie sheet, spacing them 3 inches apart.

5. Bake for 15 to 20 minutes, or until lightly browned and tops of loaves are firm to the touch.

6. Remove cookie sheet from the oven.

7. Carefully remove loaves from cookie sheet onto wire cooling racks, using two metal spatulas. Cool.

8. Place cooled loaves on a cutting board. Using a large, sharp knife, slice diagonally into ½-inch-wide strips. Store cookies in an airtight container.

YIELDS 45 COOKIES

◆ **COMARE** ◆

ALTHOUGH COMARE LITERALLY MEANS GODMOTHER, MOST ITALIANS USE THIS WORD TO DESCRIBE A CLOSE FRIEND OR NEIGHBOR.

CAPPUCCINO BISCOTTI

This is the perfect snack for coffee lovers, with just a hint of cinnamon.
These are the ideal companion to a cup of espresso. Enjoying espresso outside in the
backyard was our nightly summer tradition. My job, as a child, was to run to three or
four neighbors and cry "caffè è pronto!" or "the coffee is ready!"

¼ POUND BUTTER, SOFTENED

1½ CUPS SUGAR

2 EGGS

2 TABLESPOONS FINELY GROUND
ESPRESSO

1 TEASPOON CINNAMON

2 TABLESPOONS COFFEE LIQUEUR

2½ CUPS FLOUR

1½ TEASPOONS BAKING POWDER

PINCH OF SALT

1 EGG, BEATEN

1. Preheat oven to 375°F.

2. Using an electric mixer, cream the butter and sugar. Add eggs, espresso, cinnamon, and coffee liqueur. Mix until well blended.

3. On low speed, add flour, baking powder, and salt and mix until just blended. Turn out dough onto a lightly floured surface and knead until well blended. The dough will be soft.

4. Divide the dough into two equal pieces. Roll each piece of dough into a loaf about 12 inches long. Place the loaves 3 inches apart on a parchment-lined cookie sheet. Brush the tops of the loaves with beaten egg.

5. Bake for 20 to 25 minutes, or until golden brown. Remove cookie sheet from the oven. Using two metal spatulas, remove the loaves from the cookie sheet onto a wire cooling rack.

6. Cool. Place cooled loaves on a cutting board. Using a sharp knife, slice loaves diagonally into ½-inch-wide strips.

7. Return the slices to the cookie sheet, in a single layer. Toast 12 to 15 minutes, or until lightly browned. Remove cookie sheet from the oven.

8. Cool toasted biscotti on a wire cooling rack. Store in an airtight container.

YIELDS 30 COOKIES

SESAME CORNMEAL BISCOTTI

These lightly sweetened biscotti are the ideal accompaniment to a traditional antipasto. The sesame seeds and cornmeal give them a subtle nutty and rustic flavor.

¼ POUND BUTTER, SOFTENED

½ CUP SUGAR

3 EGGS

1 TEASPOON VANILLA EXTRACT

1½ CUPS FLOUR

½ CUP YELLOW CORNMEAL

1½ TEASPOONS BAKING POWDER

1 CUP SESAME SEEDS

ADDITIONAL SESAME SEEDS

1. Preheat oven to 350°F.

2. Using an electric mixer, cream butter and sugar until light. Add 2 of the eggs and vanilla. Mix until well blended.

3. On low speed, gradually add flour, cornmeal, baking powder, and sesame seeds. Mix until just blended to form a soft dough.

4. Turn out dough onto a lightly floured surface. Divide dough in half. Roll into two loaves about 12 inches long. Place the loaves on a parchment-lined cookie sheet, spacing them 3 inches apart.

5. In a small bowl, beat the remaining egg with a fork. Using a pastry brush, brush the tops of the loaves with the egg and sprinkle with additional sesame seeds.

6. Bake for 20 to 25 minutes, or until golden brown.

7. Remove the cookie sheet from the oven. Using two metal spatulas, remove the loaves from the cookie sheet and place on a wire cooling rack. Cool.

8. Place cooled loaves on a cutting board. Using a sharp knife, slice the loaves diagonally into ½-inch-wide strips.

9. Return the slices to the cookie sheet in a single layer and bake for 12 to 15 minutes, or until lightly browned. Remove the cookie sheet from the oven.

10. Cool cookies on a wire cooling rack. Store in an airtight container.

YIELDS 25 COOKIES

MARSALA WINE BISCOTTI

These are one of my favorite treats. The biscotti has the sweet, slightly nutty flavor of marsala wine, which is an ideal dessert wine. Try these biscotti as a great summertime companion to a plate of fresh fruit.

1 CUP DRIED CURRANTS	2 EGGS
1 CUP MARSALA WINE	2½ CUPS FLOUR
¼ POUND BUTTER, SOFTENED	1½ TEASPOONS BAKING POWDER
1¼ CUPS SUGAR	¼ TEASPOON SALT

1. In a small mixing bowl, soak currants in marsala wine for 1 to 2 hours.

2. Drain currants and set aside soaking liquid.

3. Preheat oven to 375°F.

4. In an electric mixer, cream the butter and sugar. Add eggs and 3 tablespoons of reserved marsala. Mix until well blended.

5. On low speed, gradually add flour, baking powder, and salt. Stir in currants. Turn out dough onto a lightly floured surface. This will be a soft dough.

6. Divide the dough into three equal pieces. Roll each piece into a loaf about 12 inches long.

7. Place on parchment-lined cookie sheets, spacing them about 3 inches apart. Using a pastry brush, brush the tops of the loaves with marsala wine and sprinkle with additional sugar.

8. Bake for 20 to 25 minutes, or until golden brown.

9. Remove cookie sheet from oven.

10. Using two metal spatulas, remove the loaves from the cookie sheet onto a wire cooling rack. Cool.

11. Place cooled loaves on a cutting board. Using a sharp knife, slice loaves diagonally into ½-inch-wide strips.

12. Return slices to the cookie sheet, in a single layer. Bake for 15 to 20 minutes, or until lightly browned. Remove cookie sheet from the oven. Cool toasted biscotti on a wire cooling rack. Store in an airtight container.

YIELDS 36 COOKIES

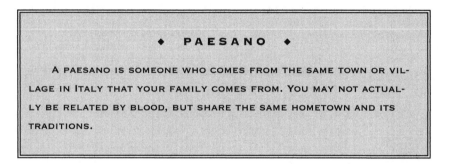

◆ **PAESANO** ◆

A PAESANO IS SOMEONE WHO COMES FROM THE SAME TOWN OR VILLAGE IN ITALY THAT YOUR FAMILY COMES FROM. YOU MAY NOT ACTUALLY BE RELATED BY BLOOD, BUT SHARE THE SAME HOMETOWN AND ITS TRADITIONS.

SUN-DRIED TOMATO BISCOTTI

*Although these savory treats are more of an appetizer or snack,
I had to include them in my collection. They are ideal appetizers served
with a sharp firm cheese, fresh grapes, and a glass of chianti.
Fresh basil and parsley are always the most flavorful,
but you can substitute dried herbs, if necessary.*

¼ POUND BUTTER, SOFTENED

1 TABLESPOON SUGAR

3 EGGS

1¾ CUPS FLOUR

½ CUP GRATED PECORINO ROMANO
CHEESE

2 GARLIC CLOVES, MINCED

2 TABLESPOONS CHOPPED FRESH
BASIL (OR 2 TEASPOONS DRIED BASIL)

1 TABLESPOON CHOPPED FRESH
PARSLEY (OR 1 TEASPOON DRIED
PARSLEY)

1 TEASPOON SALT

2 TEASPOONS BAKING POWDER

1 CUP SUN-DRIED TOMATOES,
CHOPPED (DRY TOMATOES, NOT
PACKED IN OIL)

1. Preheat oven to 350°F.

2. In an electric mixer, cream butter and sugar until blended. Add eggs. Mix well.

3. In a separate bowl, combine the flour, cheese, garlic, basil, parsley, salt, baking powder, and sun-dried tomatoes. Mix until well blended with a wooden spoon.

4. Add the flour mixture to the butter mixture. Mix on low speed just until ingredients are blended.

5. Turn out dough onto a lightly floured surface. Knead just enough to blend ingredients. Divide the dough into two equal pieces. Roll each piece into a loaf about 12 inches long. Place loaves on a parchment-lined cookie sheet, spacing them about 3 inches apart.

6. Bake for 20 to 25 minutes, or until golden brown. Remove cookie sheet from the oven. Using a metal spatula, remove loaves to a wire cooling rack.

7. When cool, slice diagonally into ½-inch-wide slices. Place these slices in a single layer on the cookie sheet. Return to the oven for 10 to 12 minutes, or until lightly browned.

8. Serve warm or cool.

YIELDS ABOUT 25 COOKIES

FRUIT BISCUITS

BISCOTTI DI FRUTTA

This is a rare recipe from my mother's side of the family. It is a traditional biscotti with glacé cherries or pineapple. You can use just about any combination of dried fruit or nuts to suit your taste.

My mom's mom, Agnes, was more a gardener than a baker, but she treated us to these biscotti with red and green cherries every Christmas. Now, if I only knew her secret for successful roses . . .

4 CUPS FLOUR	¼ CUP ORANGE JUICE
1 CUP SUGAR	2 TEASPOONS ORANGE RIND
3 TEASPOONS BAKING POWDER	¼ POUND BUTTER, MELTED
6 EGGS	4 CUPS GLACÉ CHERRIES, CHOPPED

1. Preheat oven to 375°F.

2. Place flour, sugar, and baking powder in a large bowl and mix well with a wooden spoon. Make a well in the center. Set aside.

3. In another bowl, whisk 5 of the eggs, orange juice, and orange rind. Add melted butter and cherries. Mix well.

4. Pour the egg mixture into the well. Mix with a wooden spoon. Turn out dough onto a lightly floured surface and knead until blended. Divide the dough into four equal portions. Roll each piece of dough into a 12-inch-long-loaf. Place loaves on parchment-lined cookie sheets, spacing them 3 inches apart. Lightly pat down the tops of loaves to flatten slightly.

5. In a small bowl, beat remaining egg with a fork. Brush the tops of the loaves with the beaten egg, using a pastry brush.

6. Bake until golden brown, 20 to 25 minutes. Remove cookie sheet from the oven.

7. Using two metal spatulas, remove the loaves from the cookie sheet and place on wire racks. Cool.

8. Place cooled loaves on a cutting board. Using a sharp knife, cut loaves diagonally into ½-inch-wide strips. Place strips in a single layer on the cookie sheet.

9. Return to the oven for 12 to 15 minutes, or until lightly browned. Remove cookie sheet from the oven. Cool toasted biscotti on a wire cooling rack. Store in an airtight container.

YIELDS 50 COOKIES

◆ CALZONE ◆

STRAIGHT FROM THE DICTIONARY, CALZONE MEANS TROUSERS OR PANTS. IN ITS AMERICAN CONNOTATION, IT IS A TURNOVER TYPE OF COOKIE OR PIZZA DOUGH FILLED WITH A SWEET OR SAVORY FILLING AND EITHER BAKED OR FRIED. THIS USAGE IS PROBABLY DERIVED FROM FILLING THE POCKETS OF PANTS OR TROUSERS.

PISTACHIO BISCOTTI

These cookies have a toasted nutty flavor that's not too sweet.
They're perfect as a breakfast biscotti. It is a bit time-consuming to shell your
own pistachios, but well worth the effort.
(Many specialty food shops now sell shelled pistachios.)

¼ POUND BUTTER, SOFTENED	4 CUPS FLOUR
1 CUP SUGAR	4 TEASPOONS BAKING POWDER
5 EGGS	PINCH OF SALT
1 TEASPOON VANILLA EXTRACT	1½ CUPS PISTACHIO NUTS, CHOPPED

1. Preheat oven to 350°F.

2. Using an electric mixer, cream the butter and sugar. Add 4 of the eggs and vanilla. Mix until well blended.

3. On low speed, mix in flour, baking powder, and salt to form a soft dough. Add the pistachios and mix on low speed, until just blended. Turn out dough onto a lightly floured surface. Divide the dough into three equal pieces. Roll each piece of dough into loaves about 12 inches long. Place loaves 3 inches apart on a parchment-lined cookie sheet.

4. In a small bowl, beat the remaining egg. Brush tops of loaves with the egg and sprinkle with additional sugar.

5. Bake for 20 to 25 minutes, or until golden brown. Remove cookie sheet from the oven.

6. Using two metal spatulas, carefully remove the loaves from the cookie sheet and place on a wire cooling rack. Cool.

7. Place cooled loaves on a cutting board. Using a sharp knife, slice diagonally into ½-inch-wide strips. Place in a single layer on the cookie sheet. Return to the oven for 10 to 15 minutes, or until lightly browned. Cool. Store cookies in an airtight container.

YIELDS 55 COOKIES

AMARETTO BISCOTTI
WITH ALMONDS

These biscotti are the most popular ones we sell. They have a hearty flavor and texture. Because these are baked twice using the traditional method, there are unused end portions of the loaves left over. Every time we make a batch at the bakery, everyone fights to take home the biscotti ends for munching.

½ POUND BUTTER, SOFTENED	2 CUPS SLICED ALMONDS
1½ CUPS SUGAR	6 CUPS FLOUR
6 EGGS	6 TEASPOONS BAKING POWDER
2 TEASPOONS VANILLA EXTRACT	PINCH OF SALT
2 TABLESPOONS AMARETTO LIQUEUR	

1. Preheat oven to 350°F.

2. In an electric mixer, cream the butter and sugar until light.

3. Add the eggs, vanilla, and amaretto liqueur. Mix well.

4. On low speed, mix in almonds until just blended. Add flour, baking powder, and salt. Mix on low speed until just blended. Turn out dough onto a lightly floured surface. Divide dough into five equal pieces. Roll into loaves about 12 inches long and place 3 inches apart on a parchment-lined cookie sheet.

5. Bake for 20 to 25 minutes, or until well browned.

6. Remove cookie sheet from the oven.

7. Using two metal spatulas, carefully remove the loaves from the cookie sheet onto a wire cooling rack. Cool.

8. Place cooled loaves on a cutting board. Using a sharp knife, slice diagonally into ½-inch-wide strips. Place strips in a single layer on the cookie sheet.

9. Return to the oven for about 12 to 15 minutes, or until lightly browned. Remove cookie sheet from oven. Cool toasted biscotti on a wire cooling rack. Store in an airtight container. Freeze cookies in plastic freezer bags.

YIELDS 50 COOKIES

CHOCOLATE CHIP BISCOTTI

I developed this recipe to combine the best of both worlds—New England and Italy. On my first trip to Italy, I was amazed to see how similar the houses were in the areas around Naples to the houses in my neighborhood in Waterbury, Connecticut. They were tall stone and stucco homes clustered very close together, sharing backyards and rich gardens. When people think of New England, they usually think of the Pilgrims, but the European influence is strong too.

½ POUND BUTTER, SOFTENED

½ CUP SUGAR

1¼ CUPS BROWN SUGAR

2 TEASPOONS VANILLA EXTRACT

6 EGGS

5½ CUPS FLOUR

6 TEASPOONS BAKING POWDER

½ TEASPOON SALT

2 CUPS MINI SEMISWEET CHOCOLATE CHIPS

1 CUP COARSELY CHOPPED WALNUTS, OPTIONAL

1. Preheat oven to 350°F.

2. In an electric mixer, cream the butter, sugar, and brown sugar. Add vanilla and eggs. Mix well.

3. Gradually add the flour, baking powder, and salt. Mix on low speed until just blended. Stir in chocolate chips and walnuts, if desired.

4. Turn out dough onto a lightly floured surface. Divide the dough into four equal pieces. Roll each piece into a loaf about 12 inches long. Place loaves on a parchment-lined cookie sheet, spacing them 3 inches apart. Brush the tops of the loaves with water and sprinkle with a bit of additional sugar.

5. Bake for 20 to 25 minutes, or until golden brown. Remove the cookie sheet from the oven.

6. Using two metal spatulas, remove the loaves from the cookie sheet and place on wire cooling racks. Cool. Place cooled loaves on a cutting board. Using a sharp knife, slice each loaf diagonally into ½-inch-wide slices.

7. Place slices in a single layer on the cookie sheet. Return to the oven for 12 to 15 minutes, or until lightly browned. Remove cookie sheet from the oven. Cool toasted biscotti on a wire cooling rack. Store in an airtight container.

YIELDS 45 COOKIES

◆ CAFFÈ ◆

MOST ITALIANS LOVE COFFEE. WITH THE ONSLAUGHT OF COFFEE BARS IN THE U.S., MANY TYPES OF ITALIAN COFFEES ARE GAINING WIDESPREAD ACCEPTANCE.

Espresso IS A VERY STRONG COFFEE SERVED BLACK, WITHOUT MILK. THE TRADITION OF SERVING ESPRESSO WITH A TWIST OF LEMON RIND IS AN ADOPTED AMERICAN TRADITION. ESPRESSO IS ALSO SOMETIMES SERVED WITH AN ANISETTE LIQUEUR.

Cappuccino IS ESPRESSO COFFEE TOPPED WITH FROTHY STEAMED MILK. IT IS ALSO TASTY SPRINKLED WITH A PINCH OF GROUND CINNAMON.

Caffè latte IS ALSO ESPRESSO WITH STEAMED MILK, BUT THERE IS MORE MILK THAN COFFEE IN A LATTE. CAPPUCCINO HAS MORE COFFEE AND FOAMIER MILK.

TARALLE AND BISCUITS

Taralle are traditional large ring-shaped biscuits that are boiled, and then baked. There are probably as many taralle recipes as there are Italian families in America. Our family has always made two varieties of taralle, one sweet, the other savory. The salt and pepper taralle were always served as appetizers at parties. The sweet taralle are ideal for a light dessert or a breakfast biscuit.

Because taralle are large biscuits, they always have their own tray and are never mixed in with our other cookies. They have a great crunchy exterior and an airy center. One of the original recipes from my Aunt Giulia actually included 12 tablets of Brioschi, an antacid, as an ingredient! (The acidity in the antacid tablets probably served as baking powder does—to leaven and lighten the dough.)

SWEET TARALLE

TARALLE DOLCI

These are a sweet version of the large ring-shaped biscuits. They looked so impressive when I was a child, all drenched in icing and piled high like a pyramid!

When I was growing up, our family lived in houses next to each other, with one large common backyard. I'll always remember Gemma carrying huge piles of sweet taralle from house to house. And she never dropped one!

6 EGGS	3 TO 3½ CUPS FLOUR
¼ CUP VEGETABLE OIL	PINCH OF SALT
¼ CUP SUGAR	1 TEASPOON BAKING POWDER

1. Preheat oven to 375°F.

2. Using an electric mixer, beat eggs, oil, and sugar. With a wooden spoon, mix in flour, salt, and baking powder. Turn out dough onto a lightly floured surface and knead to make a soft elastic dough. Knead for 5 to 8 minutes. If the dough is too sticky to handle, dust with additional flour.

3. Divide the dough into eight equal pieces. Roll each piece into a cylinder about 1 inch thick and 10 inches long. Form the cylinder into a ring, pressing the dough together at the ends to attach.

4. Bring a large pot of water to a boil over high heat. Two at a time, drop the rings into boiling water. When the taralle float to the top, turn over and let boil, uncovered, for 2 to 3 minutes. Remove taralle from water using two slotted spoons and drain on paper towels.

5. Place each taralle directly on oven shelf or on a parchment-lined cookie sheet. Bake 25 to 30 minutes, or until golden brown. Use a potholder or oven mitt to place taralle on a wire cooling rack. Cool. Frost with Confectioners' Frosting, vanilla or lemon (see recipe page 12). Store frosted taralle in an airtight container.

YIELDS 8 TARALLE

SALT AND BLACK PEPPER
TARALLE

These are perfect biscuits to enjoy before dinner with a glass of wine.
All of our neighborhood gatherings began with these salt and pepper taralle.
A few years back, our comare (godmother) Philomena spent an afternoon
at the bakery giving us a family taralle-making class. We had such a good time,
we wondered why we hadn't done it sooner.

6 EGGS	¼ CUP VEGETABLE OIL
2 TABLESPOONS SALT	3¼ CUPS FLOUR
1 TABLESPOON BLACK PEPPER	1 TEASPOON BAKING POWDER

1. Preheat oven to 375°F.

2. Using an electric mixer, beat the eggs, salt, pepper, and oil. With a wooden spoon, blend in 3 cups of the flour and baking powder. Turn out dough onto a lightly floured surface. Knead to make a soft elastic dough. Knead in remaining ¼ cup of flour. Knead for 5 to 8 minutes. If the dough is too sticky to handle, dust the dough with additional flour.

3. Divide the dough into eight equal pieces. Roll each piece of dough into a cylinder about 1 inch thick and 10 inches long. Form the cylinder into a ring, pressing the dough together at the ends to attach.

4. Bring a large pot of water to a boil over high heat. Two at a time, drop the rings into the boiling water. When the taralle float to the top, turn over, using two slotted spoons. Let boil, uncovered, for 2 to 3 minutes.

5. Remove from the water with the slotted spoons and drain on paper towels. Continue until all rings have been boiled and drained.

6. Place taralle directly on oven shelf, or on a parchment-lined cookie sheet. Bake for 25 to 30 minutes, or until golden brown. Use a potholder or oven mitt to remove baked taralle from the oven to wire cooling racks. Cool and serve. Store taralle in an airtight container.

YIELDS 8 TARALLE

WINE BISCUITS

BISCOTTI DI VINO

This recipe is from one of my favorite customers.
His family always enjoyed dunking these biscuits in wine while they played cards.
They are great munchies whether you're winning or losing.

2¼ TO 2½ CUPS FLOUR

2 TEASPOONS BAKING POWDER

½ CUP SUGAR

½ CUP DRY WHITE WINE

½ CUP VEGETABLE OIL

1. Preheat oven to 400°F.

2. In a large bowl, mix together all ingredients with a wooden spoon. Mix until well blended. Turn out dough onto a lightly floured surface and knead just until dough is soft and smooth.

3. Shape dough into balls the size of walnuts. Place on parchment-lined cookie sheets. Flatten the tops of the balls with your fingertips.

4. Bake for 8 to 10 minutes, until golden brown. Remove biscuits with a metal spatula onto wire racks for cooling. Store cooled biscuits in an airtight container.

YIELDS 30 BISCUITS

PEPPER BISCUITS

FRIZZELLE

*These black pepper biscuits are part of every Italian baker's recipe box.
To be sure they're crunchy, brush them with oil just before baking.*

3 EGGS	1 TABLESPOON BLACK PEPPER
½ CUP WATER	2 TABLESPOONS FENNEL SEED
½ CUP VEGETABLE OIL	3 CUPS FLOUR
1 TABLESPOON SALT	3 TEASPOONS BAKING POWDER

1. Preheat oven to 400°F.

2. In a large bowl, whisk together the eggs, water, and oil. Add salt, pepper, and fennel seed.

3. Stir in flour and baking powder, using a wooden spoon. Turn out dough onto a lightly floured surface. Knead until dough is soft and elastic. If the dough is too sticky, dust with additional flour.

4. Roll out dough into pencil-like strips. Cut into strips approximately 6 inches long. Form these strips into rings, pressing ends of dough together to adhere. Place rings on parchment-lined cookie sheets. Using a pastry brush, brush the tops of the rings with oil.

5. Bake for 15 to 20 minutes, or until golden brown. Remove the cookie sheet from the oven. Remove biscuits from the hot cookie sheets using a metal spatula. Place biscuits on a wire cooling rack. Cool.

6. Store cooled biscuits in an airtight container.

YIELDS 70 BISCUITS

ITALIAN PRETZELS

These soft biscuits are another great snack or appetizer. Try using a basketful on your dinner table instead of breadsticks or rolls. You can make them in the traditional pretzel shape, rings, or braids.

1 PACKAGE DRY YEAST	1 TEASPOON BLACK PEPPER
1 CUP WARM WATER	2 TABLESPOONS FENNEL SEED
4 CUPS FLOUR	¾ CUP VEGETABLE OIL
1 TEASPOON SALT	COARSE SALT

1. In a small bowl, combine yeast and water. Mix well using a wooden spoon.

2. In a medium-size mixing bowl, combine flour, salt, pepper, and fennel seed. Mix well.

3. Using a wooden spoon, stir yeast mixture and oil into flour. Mix until blended.

4. Turn out dough onto a lightly floured surface. Knead for 5 minutes to make a smooth, elastic dough. Place dough in a large mixing bowl. Cover bowl with plastic wrap, then a clean towel, and place in a warm spot to rise. The top of a warm stove is an ideal place. Let the dough rise until it's doubled in bulk, about 2 hours.

5. Preheat oven to 350°F.

6. Roll dough into pencil-wide strips about 10 inches long. Form into a pretzel shape or ring and place on a parchment-lined cookie sheet, spacing them about 2 inches apart. Using a pastry brush, brush the tops of the pretzels with water and sprinkle with coarse salt.

7. Bake for 20 to 25 minutes, or until golden brown.

8. Remove cookie sheet from the oven. Using a metal spatula, remove the pretzels from the cookie sheet and place on wire cooling racks. Cool. Store in an airtight container.

YIELDS 20 TO 25 PRETZELS

SWEET POPOVERS

My mother-in-law and her cousins have perfected this recipe for the perfect puff. The secret to these popovers is to beat the eggs thoroughly for a fluffy, airy center and a slightly crusty outside. To keep the crusty exterior, store unused popovers wrapped in aluminum foil. Storing in a plastic bag or airtight container will allow the popovers to soften.

9 EGGS   **2 CUPS FLOUR**

1 CUP VEGETABLE OIL

1. Preheat oven to 375°F.

2. Using an electric mixer with the whisk attachment, whip eggs and oil on high speed.

3. Gradually add flour, on low speed. Whip on high speed for 5 minutes. This will produce a thick, smooth batter.

4. Spray a mini muffin pan with nonstick coating. Using a tablespoon, fill each cup with batter.

5. Bake for 15 to 20 minutes, or until golden brown. Remove pan from the oven.

6. Carefully transfer popovers to a wire cooling rack. Repeat the spraying and filling procedure if you have only one muffin pan.

7. When cool, frost popovers with Lemon Confectioners' Frosting (see recipe page 12).

YIELDS 36 POPOVERS

PIZZELLES

*These thin, waferlike cookies are made using a specific type
of iron, similar to a waffle iron. The spaces aren't as
deep and are arranged in a snowflake pattern, but the procedure is the same: Heat the iron, drop in the batter, close
the top, and bake. If you decide to invest in one of these
irons, you're sure to get your money's worth. You can purchase them in specialty cookware shops. The newer models
are nonstick and don't require any greasing. This is great for
hassle-free baking and easy cleanup. If you have an old cast
iron model, you may have to spray the iron with a nonstick
spray after every two or three pizzelles. Many of the
older model pizzelle irons have deeper grooves than
the newer models. These deep grooves really
show off the pattern.*

*You can also make other great desserts with these pizzelles.
After they'd baked, you can sandwich two pizzelles
together with ice cream in the center. Or, while the pizzelle
is hot, you can carefully roll it into a cannoli-type shell,
or a cone. When cooled, these creations can be filled with
whipped cream, fresh fruits, or ice cream.*

*Pizzelles look impressive on their own tray, and are too
fragile to include on a tray with other varieties of cookies.
They are at their best when eaten soon after baking.*

VANILLA PIZZELLES

These are definitely my Aunt Josephine's specialty. Her secret is to use butter for the richest flavor. This recipe can easily be doubled if you need a larger number. On really humid days, the pizzelles will have a softer texture instead of the usual crunch.

3 EGGS

1 CUP SUGAR

2 TEASPOONS VANILLA EXTRACT

¼ POUND UNSALTED BUTTER, MELTED, THEN COOLED

2 CUPS FLOUR

2 TEASPOONS BAKING POWDER

1. Preheat pizzelle iron as directed by the manufacturer. (This is often as simple as plugging it in and letting it heat for 15 to 20 minutes.)

2. In an electric mixer, beat the eggs and sugar. Add extract and melted butter. On low speed, gradually add flour and baking powder to make a sticky dough.

3. Drop dough from a teaspoon onto the hot iron. If the iron you are using allows you to bake 2 pizzelles at once, drop a teaspoonful into the center of each pattern outline.

4. Close the cover of pizzelle iron and bake for 30 to 45 seconds, or until nicely browned.

5. Using two forks, remove the hot wafer from the iron and place the pizzelle flat on a parchment-lined cookie sheet. Be sure to lay the hot pizzelles in a single layer on the cookie sheet. When they are completely cool, you can stack them.

6. Dust with confectioners' sugar.

YIELDS ABOUT 30 PIZZELLES

There are many variations of this pizzelle recipe. You can use flavorings to create your own varieties. Here are a few of my favorites:

CHOCOLATE: Add ½ cup cocoa to the pizzelle dough when you are mixing in the flour.

LEMON: Substitute 2 teaspoons lemon extract for the vanilla. Add 2 tablespoons lemon rind (grated rind from 2 lemons)

ALMOND: Replace vanilla with 2 teaspoons almond extract. Reduce the amount of flour to 1¾ cups. Add ½ cup finely ground almonds.

THREE MORE FAVORITES

The final three recipes aren't exactly classified as cookies,
but are traditional small sweets that my family
has always enjoyed.

BOW TIES

These are light fried twists, dusted with confectioners' sugar. They are another Christmas family favorite, the perfect light ending to a full holiday feast. The thinner you roll the dough, the lighter and crisper the bow tie.

4 TABLESPOONS BUTTER, SOFTENED

3 EGGS

1 TEASPOON VANILLA EXTRACT

1½ TO 1¾ CUPS FLOUR

3 TEASPOONS BAKING POWDER

VEGETABLE OIL FOR FRYING

¼ TEASPOON SALT

CONFECTIONERS' SUGAR FOR DUSTING

1. In an electric mixer, beat the butter, eggs, and vanilla. On low speed, gradually add 1 cup of flour, baking powder, and salt. Turn out dough onto a well-floured surface and knead in the remaining flour. The dough should be soft and elastic. If it is too sticky, dust with additional flour.

2. Divide the dough in half. Cover the half that you are not using with plastic wrap. Using a lightly floured rolling pin, roll out the dough on a lightly floured surface as thin as you can in an oblong shape.

3. Using a pastry cutter, cut the dough into strips measuring approximately 4 inches long by 2 inches wide. With the pastry cutter, cut a ½-inch slit in the center of the strip. Take one end of the strip and pull it through the slit in the center. This will give you a bow tie. You can twist the dough into whatever interesting shapes you like.

4. Continue rolling and shaping all the dough.

5. In a large saucepan, heat 2 inches of oil over medium heat. Drop twisted bow ties into oil. Fry 3 to 4 bows at a time in a single uncrowded layer until lightly browned on each side, 1 to 2 minutes, turning with tongs or a slotted spoon. When cooked, remove the bow ties from the oil with a slotted spoon and drain on paper towels.

6. When cooled, dust with confectioners' sugar.

YIELDS ABOUT 40 BOWTIES

CHRISTMAS HONEY CLUSTERS
STRUFOLI

These treats aren't really cookies, but because they use the same dough as the bow ties, I couldn't resist including them.

Originally, these clusters were formed into shapes and allowed to harden. They became brittle like candy, and were eaten by breaking off piece after piece. My grandmother's recipe adds butter and baking powder to the traditional recipe, which softens and lightens the dough, making these treats more of a dessert than a candy.

Some people like to pick on these a few morsels at a time, but we eat them by the bowlful!

ONE RECIPE BOW TIE DOUGH (SEE PRECEDING RECIPE)

VEGETABLE OIL FOR FRYING

1 CUP HONEY

1 TABLESPOON SUGAR

1 TABLESPOON MULTICOLORED CANDIES (NONPAREILS)

1. Prepare the dough as directed for Bow Ties in step 1. You may need to knead in about ¼ cup additional flour to be sure the dough isn't sticky. If your dough is sticky, the honey clusters will stick together while frying.

2. Pull off a walnut-size piece of the dough. Roll into a long pencil-like cylinder. On a cutting board, using a sharp straight-edge knife, chop the pencil into ¼-inch pieces. Continue rolling and cutting the entire dough. Use a pancake spatula to move the dough pieces from the cutting board to a lightly floured cookie sheet in a single layer to avoid sticking.

3. In a large, deep saucepan, over medium heat, heat 2 inches of oil. Add one scoop of the dough pieces to the hot oil, stirring constantly with a slotted spoon. It is very important that you watch the oil in case it rises. If it rises and foams too much, lift the pan off the heat and stir oil. It is helpful to fry near a sink, just in case the oil bubbles over.

4. Fry the dough just until lightly browned. Remove the clusters from the oil with a slotted spoon and place them in a strainer to drain. Fry all the pieces in small batches.

5. When cool, place fried dough balls in a large mixing bowl.

6. In a small saucepan over low heat, heat the honey and sugar just until boiling. Stir constantly with a wooden spoon. Pour honey and sugar mixture over fried strufoli. Mix thoroughly with a wooden spoon. Spoon clusters into a serving bowl and sprinkle the top with nonpareils. Cover top of bowl with plastic wrap and store at room temperature.

YIELDS 14 ½-CUP SERVINGS

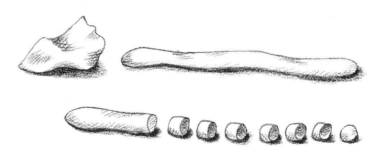

FRIED SWEET DOUGH

SFINGI FRITTELLI

These are sweet fried doughnuts with just the right amount of spice.
They make a great Sunday morning treat.

2 EGGS	¼ TEASPOON SALT
⅓ CUP SUGAR	3 TEASPOONS BAKING POWDER
½ CUP MILK	2 CUPS FLOUR
1 TEASPOON CINNAMON	VEGETABLE OIL FOR FRYING

1. Using an electric mixer, beat eggs and sugar until well blended. Add milk, cinnamon, salt, baking powder, and flour. Beat until smooth. Cover the batter with plastic wrap. Let the batter rest at room temperature for 15 to 20 minutes.

2. Heat 3 inches of oil in a large saucepan over medium heat. Drop ¾ teaspoon of batter into hot oil. Fry until golden, about 3 minutes. Remove with a slotted spoon onto paper towels. Roll in sugar. Serve warm or cooled.

YIELDS 25 FRITTELLI

COOKIE
JAR

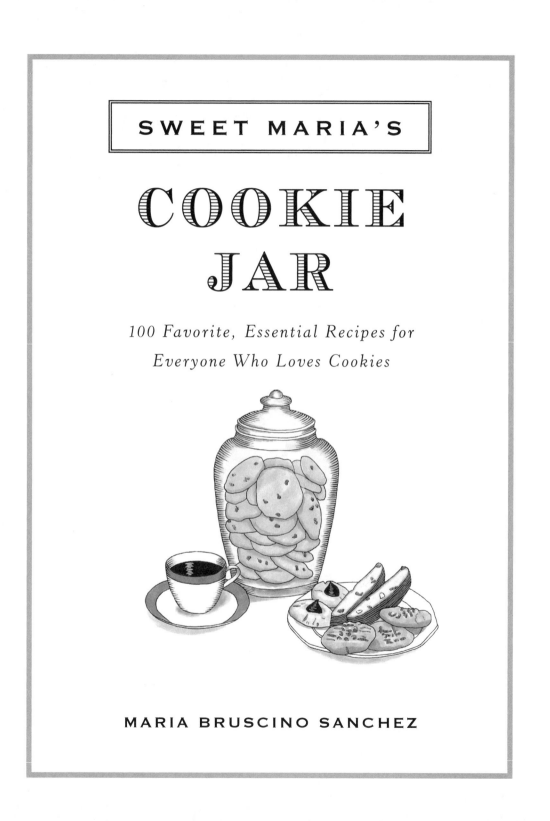

SWEET MARIA'S

COOKIE JAR

100 Favorite, Essential Recipes for
Everyone Who Loves Cookies

MARIA BRUSCINO SANCHEZ

FOR THE

SWEET MARIA STAFF,

WHO CONTINUE TO INSPIRE ME THROUGH THEIR

INSIGHT, HARD WORK, AND SENSE OF HUMOR.

CONTENTS

ACKNOWLEDGMENTS

Thanks to my agent, Carla Glasser, for her dedication, enthusiasm and for finally experiencing a mother-daughter cookie swap.

A huge thanks for my editor, Marian Lizzi, for again bringing her expertise and honesty to this, our fourth book together.

Everyone at St. Martin's, including Amelie Littell, Jennifer Reeve, Merrill Bergenfeld, Michael Stowings, Gretchen Achilles, Dorothy Rheinhardt, and photographer Anthony Loew for their tireless effort on my behalf.

As always, Mom and Dad for just about everything.

To Edgar, for being not only my encouraging husband, but a part of the Sweet Maria staff.

The Sweet Maria Staff: Aunt Dolly Mastronunzio, Aunt Babe DelGobbo, Lynn D'Aniello, Sarah Figluizzi, Maryse LeBlanc, Kaleen Overbaugh, Diana Ranganadan, Susan Tropasso, Sondra Tucci.

Thanks to my loyal customers who continue to challenge and support me.

Special thanks for sharing recipes: Mom, Aunt Babe Briotti, Sue Barron, Tom Butcher, Lynn D'Aniello, Richard Lee, Sandy Trusiewicz, and Betsy Walsh.

INTRODUCTION

Everyone loves cookies. From simple shortbreads to elegant linzers, cookies are a sweet treat that everyone enjoys. Each of us has our own personal favorite to eat and to bake. Every culture and family likes them. Whether enjoyed as a snack or dessert, or part of a simple breakfast, cookies have found a special place in our lives. I've never met a person who didn't like a cookie. For me, it's always difficult to choose a favorite. Cookies are as multiple as your moods. I adore a plain shortbread or ladyfinger along with a scoop of ice cream, a hearty biscotti as an after-dinner treat with an espresso, or a chewy chocolate chip cookie with a glass of cold milk for breakfast. When I was a kid, the cookie jar was always filled with something good, and that has never changed.

Cookies are also delightfully easy to make. They're not as intimidating or as fussy as cakes or breads. When I was growing up, cookie baking was a favorite hobby. I remember coming home from school, doing homework, and asking my Mom, "What kind should we bake tonight?" She would dutifully go to the refrigerator and take out several sticks of butter. The butter would come to room temperature while we ate supper, we'd clean the dinner mess, and then make a fresh batch. As I got older, I still found baking a relaxing hobby, even after getting a part-time job in a bakery. And it is really still a passion, although it has become my business for the last eleven years. There's nothing like rolling your sleeves up, getting flour on your nose, and eating a bit of cookie dough while you prepare a batch of cookies. Plus, when all the work is done, you have a delicious morsel or two (or more!).

Most of the cookies in this book are ones we bake at Sweet Maria's, my specialty cake and cookie shop. We bake about thirty-five flavors of cakes and about 20 (and growing!) types of cookies. We are committed to using the same fine ingredients that you use at home, although we bake in larger quantities. Fresh butter, spices, and extracts are essential for any size batch of cookies.

We've recently added an in-store cookie jar at the bakery, which we fill with the "cookie of the day." This sparks our creativity in creating new flavors and getting instant feedback on our creations from our customers. Many of the recipes here are the stars of that cookie jar.

This book is organized into sections that include All-American Cookies, International Favorites, Bakery Favorites, Chocolate Cookies and Simple Candies, Holiday Favorites, and Low-Fat, Low-Sugar, and Gluten-Free Cookies. There is also an index that organizes the cookies according to method, such as drop cookies, bar cookies, and rolled and filled cookies.

You'll find some of my family cookie recipes—some classics, others new variations of familiar favorites. With so many great cookies in the world, I've tried to give a broad selection. I've asked some of my friends to contribute their favorites and they were more than happy to share. Even customers will bring me their own cookies to show off their baking talents and family traditions. That's where the fun begins—sharing recipes and cookies. Sharing the cookies has also led to the phenomenon known as "cookie swapping," which is a fun way to share your favorite cookies with your favorite friends.

I hope this collection will become a part of your traditions and will inspire more great cookies.

So soften some butter, roll up your sleeves, and keep your cookie jar filled at all times.

INGREDIENTS

The ingredients used in this cookbook are widely available. Here's a list of some of the basics you'll need.

Flour

Unless specified in an individual recipe, all of the cookies in this book can be made with unbleached flour or all-purpose flour. These flours are readily available and are perfect in taste and texture. Cake flour is lighter in texture and may be recommended in certain recipes for very light and delicate cookies such as madeleines and tuiles.

Sugar

The sugar recommended for these cookies is fine granulated sugar.

BROWN SUGAR: Many recipes use brown sugar, which is simply granulated sugar processed with molasses for a rich flavor. You can use either light or dark brown sugar, loosely packed.

CONFECTIONERS' SUGAR: Confectioners' sugar is also known as powdered sugar or icing sugar. It is graded according to its fineness. The most readily available are 6X and 10X. You can use either in these recipes.

Eggs

Whole, grade A large eggs work the best for the recipes in this book. If you need to separate eggs, it's easier to do when they're cold.

Butter

Unsalted butter is recommended for the fullest flavor and texture. For most recipes, the butter will need to be soft enough to blend with sugar and other ingredients. Butter should hold an imprint when pressed but still retain its shape.

Shortening

Some of these recipes call for shortening. All-purpose vegetable shortening will work fine. Shortening baking sticks are now available in most supermarkets. These sticks make measuring very easy.

Oil

Unless otherwise noted, vegetable oil is preferred for these recipes. It is especially recommended for frying cookies.

Chocolate

Always use the finest and freshest chocolate available. The recipes in this book use a wide variety of chocolate; white chocolate, dark chocolate, and semisweet chocolate are the most widely used and the most readily available.

Cocoa

Because of the processing technique used to make Dutch process cocoa, it provides the fullest flavor and color for baking. It has less acidity and a rich, reddish color.

Nuts

A large variety of nuts and nut sizes are used for these cookie recipes, including almonds, hazelnuts, walnuts, cashews, peanuts, pecans, pine nuts, and pistachios. Be sure your supply of nuts is fresh. If you have a large amount, you can store nuts in a plastic bag in the freezer.

To coarsely chop nuts, use a cutting board and a sharp, straight knife. For nuts that are finely ground, pulse until desired size in a food processor.

Baking Soda and Baking Powder

Be sure that both of these leaveners are fresh. Store separately in airtight containers for freshness.

Extracts and Liqueurs

Extracts and liqueurs are used to flavor many cookies. Pure extracts and name-brand liqueurs are the best for the fullest flavor. Imitation extracts and cheap liqueurs may be less expensive, but you'll really sacrifice flavor.

Spices

Spices such as ginger, cinnamon, and cloves are used in these recipes. Be sure that your supply is fresh.

Citrus Rind

Orange and lemon rinds are used for a zesty citrus taste. When grating the rind, use a grater or zester. Be sure to avoid the pith, the white, fleshy, bitter part of the fruit.

Cream Cheese/Sour Cream

Many of the cookies have cream cheese or sour cream in their doughs. These often provide a richness and moisture that makes the cookie tender and tasty.

Food Color

You can add food color to either cookie dough or frostings. I prefer paste food colors. These are concentrated, so you only need to use a small portion. They are available in a multitude of colors and last a long time, if properly covered. Liquid food color is okay, but it will add liquid to your cookie dough or frosting.

Decorating Sugars

Colored sugars or sanding sugars are great for sprinkling on cutout cookies before they're baked or after they're frosted. They come in many different colors and can be the same texture as granulated sugar or coarser, like kosher salt.

EQUIPMENT

Much of the equipment used to make cookies are items that most people already have in their kitchens. Items such as mixing bowls, cookie sheets, cooling racks, measuring cups and spoons, spatulas and saucepans are a sampling of what you'll need.

Cookie Sheets

Sturdy, firm, clean baking sheets are an absolute necessity for cookie baking. You may use traditional sheets or the "air cushion" variety. The air cushion cookie sheets make cookies that are light in color and chewy. For crispier cookies, use a traditional cookie sheet.

Rolling Pins

You can use a marble or wood rolling pin to roll out your doughs. The choice is a personal one; use the kind you are most comfortable with.

Measuring Cups

Metal or plastic nested measuring cups are best for dry ingredients. Scoop and level off. Heat-resistant glass measuring cups with pouring spouts work best for liquid ingredients.

Parchment Paper

We consistently use parchment paper to line our cookie trays. This eliminates greasing the pan. Not only does it keep cookies from sticking or burning, but it also makes cleanup easier.

Silpat Baking Mats

These heat-resistant silicone mats are used to line cookie sheets. They are used in place of parchment paper and are washable and reusable.

Electric Mixer

A stand-up model electric mixer is a great tool. You can use a hand-held mixer for many of these recipes, but the stand-up gives you greater flexibility and efficiency. While the butter is creaming with sugar, you can tackle another task, such as preparing cookie sheets or chopping nuts.

If you're using a hand-held mixer, you may need to hand-mix the final amounts of flour in some recipes. If dough becomes stiff, stir in flour with a spatula or wooden spoon.

Wire Cooling Racks

Wire cooling racks are the best way to cool cookies after removing from the oven. The wire rack allows cool air to circulate under the cookie sheet for even cooling. Wire cooling racks are also essential for frosting cookies: Place a wire cooling rack on a parchment-lined cookie sheet. Place frosted cookies on wire rack. Any excess frosting will drip onto the parchment. For easy cleanup, just discard the parchment.

Containers

Many of the recipes call for storing baked cookies in an airtight container at room temperature. You can use cookie tins or Tupperware-type sealable containers. If the cookies are not delicate, you can also store them in plastic bags.

GENERAL TYPES OF COOKIES AND TECHNIQUES

Drop Cookies

Drop cookies are one of the easiest types to make. You simply drop the dough from a teaspoon onto a parchment-lined cookie sheet. No fussy chilling, rolling, or forming is needed. Most drop cookies spread when baked to form the cookie. If the dough is sticky, you can dust your fingers lightly with additional flour.

Rolled and Filled Cookies

Some cookies need to be rolled out with a rolling pin and cut into shapes. For most of these cookies, it's easier to chill the dough before rolling. Lightly dust your surface and rolling pin with additional flour. Too much flour will cause the cookies to become tough. Cut and fill as recipe directs.

Molded Cookies

This dough is usually broken into pieces and rolled and shaped, by hand, into a ball or crescent. If the dough is sticky, lightly dust your fingers with additional flour.

Refrigerator Cookies

This type of cookie is also called "slice and bake." The dough is rolled into a cylinder, usually about 2 inches in diameter. The dough is wrapped in plastic wrap and refrigerated 2 to 3 hours, or overnight. Remove from the refrigerator and slice dough into ½-inch slices. Place on cookie sheet and bake. This is a great cookie to have in the refrigerator or freezer for last-minute fresh baked cookies. To keep refrigerator cookies from flattening on one side, cut filled cylinder and place in a tall drinking glass. This will allow the dough to keep a round side.

Piped Cookies

This technique refers to squeezing or "piping" the dough through a pastry bag or cookie gun to achieve the desired shape. Different decorating tips and cookie-gun attachments produce a variety of shapes.

Bar Cookies

Bar cookies are an easy cookie to make. Ingredients are spread or layered in a pan, similar to a brownie. Many of the bar cookies in this collection use standard pans that are readily available, either an 8 × 8 × 2-inch baking pan, a 13 × 9-inch baking pan, or 14 × 10-inch jelly roll pan, depending on what the recipe specifies.

Many bar cookies use the "baking blind" technique, popular for making tarts. After preparing the crust in the pan, the crust is baked without filling to avoid the bottom from being soggy and undercooked. The filling is then placed on top of the hot crust and returned to the oven for additional baking.

Sandwich Cookies

Most of the sandwich cookies in this book use a chill, roll, and cut method. Be sure to keep the dough you're *not* working with chilled. This will help to keep the sizes uniform as you roll the shapes. It will be easier to match pairs when making the sandwiches. To fill, spread filling on the underside of one of the cookies. Gently press partner cookie to adhere with filling. Allow to dry completely before storing.

Biscotti

Biscotti are Italian cookies that are baked twice. The dough is shaped into loaves and baked. The loaves are then cooled, and sliced diagonally into ½-inch slices. The slices are placed in a single layer on a cookie sheet and toasted again. This produces a crunchy, hearty biscuit, ideal for dunking.

No-Bake Cookies

These are cookies that do not require an oven. Some resemble candies. They are a nice, easy way to make a sweet treat or top off a cookie tray.

Fried Cookies

Some cookies such as Guava Empanadas and Italian Fried Cookies are cooked by frying in vegetable oil. Use hot oil, 375°F., and fry until golden. Drain on absorbent paper. Fried cookies are best when served immediately.

GENERAL BAKING DIRECTIONS AND TIPS

Oven Temperature

The first step to successful cookie baking is to know your oven temperature. Use an oven thermometer or have a repairman check the calibration. If you use the oven a lot, you probably know how it performs; you can then make temperature adjustments. If you don't bake a lot, check it before you begin. Just because your oven is new, don't assume the temperature is accurate.

Mixing Methods

CREAMING METHOD: This is the most popular method for making cookie dough, and many of the recipes in this book use it. You start with either butter, margarine, or shortening (whatever the recipe directs) and beat it in an electric mixer. Adding the sugar comes next. This is the important part of the creaming method. You must beat butter and sugar until light in color and fluffy. The butter must be at room temperature for proper creaming. Eggs are usually added next, then dry ingredients just until blended. Many popular cookies, like chocolate chip, oatmeal raisin, and brownies, require this method.

SPONGE METHOD: The sponge method is similar to the process for making a sponge cake. Egg whites are beaten until stiff. Separately, butter and sugar are creamed; egg yolks and dry ingredients are added to the butter-sugar mixture. The egg whites are gently folded into the butter mixture to make a delicate batter for cookies. One cookie that is mixed by using the sponge method is the madeleine.

Baking Times

Baking times included in these recipes are approximate. Directions are also given for what the finished cookie should look like. If a recipe says 10 to 12 minutes or until golden brown and you check after 12 minutes and the cookies are still not golden brown, bake an additional 1 to 2 minutes until proper color is achieved. Some ovens may bake unevenly. If your oven does, check the cookies halfway through the suggested baking time. You may need to rotate the cookie sheet for even baking.

I love an oven door with a light and a window. It allows you to check the baking progress without opening the oven door and letting out heat.

Chopping Nuts

Whole almonds and walnut halves are used in this book, usually as a garnish for the top of a cookie. These are readily available in most supermarkets. If you need coarsely chopped nuts, use a cutting board and a sharp, straight knife. Finely chopped nuts can be done in a food processor. A few quick pulses should do the trick.

Egg Wash

Egg wash is simply a bakery term for brushing the tops of cookies with a lightly beaten egg. This adds a shine and a professional look to some cookies.

Dusting or Rolling in Confectioners' Sugar

Many cookies in this book are finished with a dusting of confectioners' sugar, also known as powdered sugar. To dust cookies, place a few tablespoons of confectioners' sugar into a small strainer. Using a spoon, stir the sugar around the strainer while holding it over the cookies. Repeat as necessary.

To coat cookies in confectioners' sugar, place sugar in a medium bowl. Add 10 to 12 cookies at a time. Using your fingers, carefully toss cookies to coat, being careful not to break them.

Dipping and Decorating with Chocolate

TO MELT CHOCOLATE: I've always found the easiest way to melt chocolate is over simmering water in a double boiler. Be sure that the water is not boiling.

To melt a small amount of chocolate, you can also use the microwave. For 8 ounces chocolate, microwave 1 to 2 minutes on high.

If you're using chocolate for decorating, drizzling, or dipping, you may want to melt 1 tablespoon of vegetable shortening in every cup of chocolate. This will create a coating chocolate that will set without the work of tempering the chocolate.

TO DRIZZLE: Place the cookies close together. Dip a fork into melted chocolate. Swing fork back and forth over cookies to drizzle with chocolate.

TO DIP: Dip half the cookie into melted chocolate. Place on a parchment-lined cookie sheet. While chocolate is still wet, sprinkle with chopped nuts or candies, as desired.

Grating Citrus Rind

The rind of citrus fruit such as lemons, oranges, and limes is a great and natural way to flavor cookies. Use a zester or grater, and be careful not to use the white pith underneath.

Vanilla Sugar

Another way to flavor cookies is to use a vanilla bean. Using a small, sharp paring knife and cut the bean in half. Using the tip of the knife, scrape the inside of the bean into sugar, using the proportion of 1 bean to ½ cup sugar. You can use vanilla sugar, instead of plain sugar and vanilla extract, to flavor cookies.

Filling and Using a Pastry Bag

Some cookies are formed using a pastry bag. This will give you professional-looking cookies at home. Here's an easy way to fill the pastry bag. Place the empty bag, tip side down, into a tall drinking glass. Fold the edges over the rim of the glass. This will give you a steady, open bag. Spoon dough into bag, being careful not to overfill it. Gather up the edges and remove from the glass. To use, simply squeeze the center of the bag, releasing the dough from the bottom. Practice will help you regulate the sizes and shapes of whatever you're piping.

Figuring Cookie Quantities

It's always hard to guesstimate how many cookies you'll need for a particular event. If the cookies are being used as favors or take-home gifts, you'll need to have one large cookie for each guest. If they are fancy cookies on a tray, a safe guess is usually 4 to 5 cookies per person. If you're serving other desserts as well, you can probably figure 2 to 3 cookies per person.

Storage

The best way to store cookies for short periods of time is at room temperature in air-tight containers. Re-sealable containers like Tupperware are ideal. It is best to keep different types of cookies in separate storage bins. This way, each cookie can keep its own true flavor. If you need to store cookies for a longer period of time, freezing is the best way. Refrigeration is fine for making dough in advance, but not for baked cookies, which will become stale more quickly in the refrigerator.

Freezing Dough

Freezing cookie dough is a great way to work ahead if you're making a large quantity of cookies. Many of the butter-based doughs, especially refrigerator cookies, are ideal for freezing. You can even take a small portion from the freezer and bake it whenever you want a few fresh-baked cookies.

Freezing Baked Cookies

An easy way to freeze cookies that are already baked is to use heavy-duty freezer plastic bags. If you are freezing cookies that need icing or dusting in sugar, freeze without the icing. Then, remove from freezer, thaw, and frost as desired.

CHAPTER 1

ALL-AMERICAN COOKIES

The cookies in this chapter include perennial favorites such as chocolate chip and oatmeal raisin. You'll find classics as well as new variations. Considering that the United States is a melting pot, many different cultures influenced all of the food we now consider American, but somehow the results seem all our own.

From traditional toll house to oatmeal raisin, maple walnut, and peanut butter, these are the cookies we rely on for comfort. They're the perfect take-along treat for school lunches, picnics, and tailgate parties.

CHOCOLATE CHIP COOKIES

This classic cookie recipe just can't be beat. It's the perfect combination of butter and chocolate; the ultimate comfort food. I like them chewy, slightly undercooked. If you prefer crunchy cookies, bake 3 to 5 minutes longer.

If we ever overbake a batch of these cookies—or burn them—my cousin Steve is very happy. He loves his Chocolate Chip Cookies burnt.

1/2 POUND BUTTER, SOFTENED	1 TEASPOON BAKING SODA
3/4 CUP SUGAR	1/2 TEASPOON SALT
3/4 CUP BROWN SUGAR	2 1/2 CUPS CHOCOLATE CHIPS
1 TEASPOON VANILLA EXTRACT	1 CUP WALNUTS, COARSELY CHOPPED (OPTIONAL)
2 EGGS	
2 1/4 CUPS FLOUR	

1. Preheat oven to 350°F.

2. In an electric mixer, on medium speed, cream the butter, sugar, and brown sugar until light. Add vanilla and eggs. Mix until well blended.

3. On low speed, add flour, baking soda, and salt. Mix just until blended.

4. Stir in chocolate chips and nuts.

5. Drop dough from a teaspoon onto a parchment-lined cookie sheet, spacing cookies 2 inches apart.

6. Bake 10 to 12 minutes or until lightly browned.

7. Remove cookie sheet from the oven. Using a metal spatula, remove cookies from the cookie sheet and place on a wire cooling rack. Cool on wire racks. Store cookies in an airtight container.

YIELD: 50 COOKIES

VARIATION: WHITE CHOCOLATE CHIP COOKIES

This is a nice variation on the traditional toll house cookie. Substitute white chocolate chips for semisweet chocolate chips.

VARIATION: LARGE COOKIES

Many people love a "mall-size" cookie. You can easily make them at home and use them to make ice cream sandwiches. Use an ice cream scoop to spoon dough onto a parchment-lined cookie sheet. Gently press the top of the cookie to flatten. Bake 12 to 15 minutes, or until lightly browned.

YIELD: 20 COOKIES

◆ "BIRTHDAY CAKE" COOKIES ◆

SOME PEOPLE LIKE TO DECORATE A COOKIE AS IF IT WERE A BIRTHDAY CAKE. THE BEST TYPE OF COOKIE FOR THIS TREAT IS A CHOCOLATE CHIP OR OATMEAL COOKIE. TO MAKE AN 8-INCH ROUND COOKIE, PLACE AN 8-INCH CAKE PAN ONTO A PARCHMENT-LINED COOKIE SHEET. TRACE THE OUTSIDE OF THE PAN WITH A PENCIL. TURN THE PARCHMENT OVER SO THAT THE PENCIL MARKS ARE ON THE UNDERSIDE. SCOOP COOKIE DOUGH INTO THE CIRCLE AND GENTLY PRESS TO FILL IN CIRCLE EVENLY WITH THE DOUGH. BAKE COOKIE UNTIL LIGHTLY BROWNED. YOU WILL NEED TO BAKE THIS A BIT LONGER THAN SMALLER COOKIES. LET COOKIE COOL COMPLETELY ON PARCHMENT PAPER. WHEN COOL, SLIP A DOILY-LINED CORRUGATED CAKE CIRCLE UNDER THE COOKIE. THIS WILL HELP TO SUPPORT THE COOKIE AND MAKES A NICE PRESENTATION. USE BUTTERCREAM FROSTING OR ROYAL ICING TO PIPE BORDERS AND WRITING ON COOKIE. CUT INTO WEDGES AND SERVE.

CHOCOLATE CHIP
ICE CREAM SANDWICHES

*These treats are the classic combination of chocolate chip
cookies and vanilla ice cream. Be sure to work quickly
so that your ice cream doesn't melt.*

20 LARGE (4-INCH-DIAMETER)
CHOCOLATE CHIP COOKIES
(SEE VARIATION, PREVIOUS
RECIPE)

ONE-HALF GALLON VANILLA ICE
CREAM

NUTS AND SPRINKLES (OPTIONAL)

1. Slightly soften ice cream in refrigerator. Place 1½ heaping scoops of ice cream onto the bottom of a cookie. Using a spatula, gently smooth ice cream to the edges of cookie. Press bottom of another cookie on top to form sandwich. Roll edges in nuts or sprinkles, if desired. Repeat until all cookies are filled.

2. Place sandwiches onto a plate or cookie sheet. Place in the freezer to harden. When firm, wrap each sandwich in plastic wrap or a cellophane bag. Store sandwiches individually wrapped in the freezer.

YIELD: 10 SANDWICHES

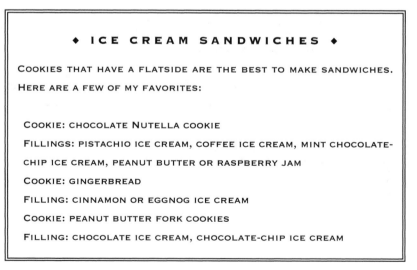

◆ ICE CREAM SANDWICHES ◆

COOKIES THAT HAVE A FLATSIDE ARE THE BEST TO MAKE SANDWICHES.
HERE ARE A FEW OF MY FAVORITES:

COOKIE: CHOCOLATE NUTELLA COOKIE
FILLINGS: PISTACHIO ICE CREAM, COFFEE ICE CREAM, MINT CHOCOLATE-
CHIP ICE CREAM, PEANUT BUTTER OR RASPBERRY JAM
COOKIE: GINGERBREAD
FILLING: CINNAMON OR EGGNOG ICE CREAM
COOKIE: PEANUT BUTTER FORK COOKIES
FILLING: CHOCOLATE ICE CREAM, CHOCOLATE-CHIP ICE CREAM

OATMEAL CRUNCHIES

*The finely chopped walnuts in this crunchy cookie
make this an ideal treat. It's one of the first
cookies I learned to bake and eat.*

¼ POUND BUTTER, SOFTENED	1 CUP FLOUR
½ CUP SUGAR	½ TEASPOON BAKING POWDER
½ CUP BROWN SUGAR	½ TEASPOON BAKING SODA
1 TEASPOON VANILLA EXTRACT	PINCH OF SALT
1 EGG	¼ CUP CHOPPED WALNUTS
¾ CUP OATS	ADDITIONAL SUGAR FOR DIPPING

1. Preheat oven to 350°F.

2. In an electric mixer on medium speed, cream butter, sugar, and brown sugar until light. Add vanilla and egg. Mix until well blended.

3. On low speed, add oats, flour, baking powder, baking soda, and salt. Mix just until blended. Stir in walnuts.

4. Roll dough into 1-inch balls. Dip tops into additional sugar. Place onto a parchment-lined cookie sheet, spacing cookies 2 inches apart.

5. Bake 10 to 12 minutes or until light brown.

6. Remove cookie sheet from the oven. Using a metal spatula, remove cookies from the cookie sheet and place on a wire cooling rack. Cool cookies on wire rack. Store cookies in an airtight container.

YIELD: 36 COOKIES

OATMEAL RAISIN

This hearty cookie is a dig-your-teeth-into kind of cookie.
A chewy combination of butter, brown sugar, oats,
and raisins, they're good for you, too.

½ POUND BUTTER, SOFTENED	1 ½ CUPS FLOUR
1 CUP BROWN SUGAR	½ TEASPOON SALT
½ CUP SUGAR	1 TEASPOON BAKING POWDER
1 TEASPOON VANILLA EXTRACT	2 CUPS OATS
2 EGGS	1 CUP RAISINS

1. Preheat oven to 350°F.

2. In an electric mixer, cream butter, brown sugar, and sugar until light. Add vanilla and eggs. Mix until well blended. On low speed, add flour, salt, and baking powder. Add oats and raisins. Mix just until blended.

3. Drop cookies from a teaspoon onto a parchment-lined cookie sheet, spacing each 2 inches apart.

4. Bake 12 to 15 minutes or until lightly browned.

5. Remove cookie sheet from the oven. Using a metal spatula, remove cookies from the cookie sheet and place on a wire cooling rack. Cool completely. Store cookies in an airtight container.

YIELD: 50 COOKIES

CHOCOLATE CHOCOLATE CHIP COOKIES

*These double chocolate treats are the perfect treat for chocolate
lovers everywhere. They're great to enjoy on their own or
sandwiched together with your favorite ice cream. For
a variation, you can substitute white chocolate chips instead
of chocolate chips, for a white polka-dot cookie.*

2½ STICKS BUTTER, SOFTENED

1½ CUPS SUGAR

2 EGGS

2 CUPS FLOUR

¾ CUP COCOA

½ TEASPOON BAKING SODA

½ TEASPOON SALT

2 CUPS CHOCOLATE CHIPS

1. Preheat oven to 350°F.

2. In an electric mixer, cream butter and sugar until light. Add eggs. Mix well. On low speed, add flour, cocoa, baking soda, and salt. Mix just until blended.

3. Stir in chocolate chips.

4. Drop from a teaspoon onto a parchment-lined cookie sheet, spacing each 2 inches apart.

5. Bake 12 to 15 minutes, or until firm. Remove cookie sheet from the oven. Cool cookies completely on parchment paper. Store in an airtight container.

YIELD: 60 COOKIES

PEANUT BUTTER FORK COOKIES

*Peanut butter is one of my favorite cookie ingredients. You can use
either chunky or smooth, depending on whether you want
a bit of crunch. They're called fork cookies because of
how you make the crisscross design on top.*

½ POUND BUTTER, SOFTENED	1½ CUPS CHUNKY PEANUT BUTTER
1 CUP BROWN SUGAR	2 CUPS FLOUR
½ CUP SUGAR	1 TEASPOON BAKING POWDER
2 EGGS	1 TEASPOON BAKING SODA

1. In an electric mixer, cream butter, brown sugar, and sugar until light. Add eggs and peanut butter. Mix until well blended.

2. On low speed, add flour, baking powder, and baking soda. Mix just until blended. Wrap dough in plastic wrap and refrigerate 4 to 5 hours or overnight.

3. Preheat oven to 375°F.

4. Roll dough into 1-inch balls. Place on a parchment-lined cookie sheet, spacing each 2 inches apart. Using your fingers, slightly flatten the tops. Dip a fork into additional flour. Press fork into the top of the cookies in a crisscross manner.

5. Bake 12 to 15 minutes or until lightly browned.

6. Remove cookie sheet from the oven. Using a metal spatula, remove cookies from the cookie sheet and place on a wire cooling rack. Cool completely. Store cookies at room temperature in an airtight container.

YIELD: 50 COOKIES

MAGIC BARS

These rich, layered bars have had many names over the years, including seven-layer bars and congo bars. Whatever you call them, they're a delicious combination of chocolate, coconut, walnuts, and sweetened condensed milk. For easier cutting, chill pan in refrigerator after baking.

¼ POUND BUTTER, MELTED AND COOLED

1½ CUPS GRAHAM CRACKER CRUMBS

1 CUP WALNUTS, COARSELY CHOPPED

1 CUP CHOCOLATE CHIPS

1½ CUPS FLAKED COCONUT

14 OUNCES SWEETENED CONDENSED MILK

1. Preheat oven to 350°F.

2. Place graham cracker crumbs in a small mixing bowl. Pour butter over crumbs. Mix well. Press into the bottom of an ungreased 13 × 9-inch baking pan. Sprinkle nuts evenly over crumbs. Sprinkle chocolate chips over nuts. Sprinkle 1 cup of the coconut over the chocolate chips.

3. With a tablespoon, drizzle the sweetened condensed milk evenly over the coconut. Sprinkle top with remaining ½ cup of coconut.

4. Bake 25 to 30 minutes or until lightly browned.

5. Remove baking pan from the oven. Cool in pan on a wire cooling rack. When completely cool, cut into squares. Store cookies in an airtight container.

YIELD: 24 COOKIES

SNICKERDOODLES

*Simple and delicious, these cookies are rolled in a mixture of cinnamon
and sugar. Since I was a child, the name has always been a mystery.
Be careful not to overbake them; they should be slightly chewy.*

½ POUND BUTTER, SOFTENED	TOPPING:
1½ CUPS SUGAR	4 TABLESPOONS SUGAR
2 EGGS	2 TEASPOONS CINNAMON
2½ CUPS FLOUR	
1 TEASPOON BAKING SODA	
½ TEASPOON SALT	

1. Preheat oven to 350°F.

2. In an electric mixer, cream butter and sugar until light. Add eggs. Mix until well blended.

3. On low speed, add flour, baking soda, and salt. Mix just until blended.

4. In a small bowl, combine 4 tablespoons sugar and cinnamon.

5. Roll dough into 1-inch balls. Roll balls in cinnamon and sugar mixture. Place onto a parchment-lined cookie sheet, spacing each cookie 2 inches apart.

6. Bake 10 to 12 minutes or until firm.

7. Remove cookie sheet from the oven. Cool cookies completely on parchment. Store cookies in an airtight container.

YIELD: 48 COOKIES

BUTTERSCOTCH DROPS

These flavorful little drop cookies are sure to satisfy your
sweet tooth. They're loaded with butterscotch drops,
one of my mom's favorite ingredients.

¼ POUND BUTTER, SOFTENED	1 ½ CUPS FLOUR
1 CUP BROWN SUGAR	2 TEASPOONS BAKING POWDER
2 EGGS	¼ TEASPOON SALT
1 TEASPOON VANILLA EXTRACT	1 ½ CUPS BUTTERSCOTCH CHIPS

1. Preheat oven to 350°F.

2. In an electric mixer, cream butter and brown sugar until light. Add eggs and vanilla. Mix until well blended.

3. On low speed, add flour, baking powder, and salt. Mix just until blended. Stir in butterscotch chips.

4. Drop dough from a teaspoon onto a parchment-lined cookie sheet, spacing each 2 inches apart.

5. Bake 10 to 12 minutes or until golden.

6. Remove cookie sheet from the oven. Using a metal spatula, remove cookies from the cookie sheet and place on a wire cooling rack. Cool completely. Store cookies in an airtight container at room temperature.

YIELD: 36 COOKIES

MAPLE WALNUT DROPS

These moist and nutty drop cookies are the perfect autumn treat.
Serve them plain or with the sweet maple icing.

1 ½ STICKS BUTTER, SOFTENED

½ CUP SUGAR

½ CUP BROWN SUGAR

2 TEASPOONS MAPLE EXTRACT

¾ CUP APPLESAUCE

1 EGG

2 CUPS FLOUR

½ TEASPOON BAKING SODA

½ TEASPOON SALT

1 ½ CUPS WALNUTS, COARSELY CHOPPED

1. Preheat oven to 350°F.

2. In an electric mixer, cream butter, sugar, and brown sugar until light. Add maple extract, applesauce, and egg. Mix until well blended.

3. On low speed, add flour, baking soda, and salt. Mix just until blended. Stir in walnuts. Dough will be soft and slightly sticky.

4. Drop dough from a teaspoon onto a parchment-lined cookie sheet, spacing each 2 inches apart.

5. Bake 10 to 12 minutes or until edges are lightly browned and tops are firm.

6. Remove cookie sheet from the oven. Using a metal spatula, remove cookies from the sheet and place on a wire cooling rack. Cool completely.

7. Serve plain or frost with maple confectioners' icing (see page 25).

YIELD: 50 COOKIES

MAPLE CONFECTIONERS' ICING

3 CUPS CONFECTIONERS' SUGAR   ¼ CUP WATER

3 TEASPOONS MAPLE EXTRACT

In an electric mixer, combine all ingredients. Mix until well blended and smooth. Using a metal spatula, frost the tops of the cookies. Place cookies on wire cooling rack, with parchment paper underneath to catch any excess frosting. Dry completely.

◆ CRUNCHY VS. CHEWY ◆

FOR MANY DROP COOKIES, YOU HAVE THE OPTION OF BAKING CHEWY COOKIES OR CRISPY COOKIES. FOR CHEWY COOKIES, SLIGHTLY UNDER-COOK; FOR CRISPY COOKIES, SLIGHTLY OVERCOOK. WHICH IS BETTER? THIS HAS BEEN A CONTINUOUS SOURCE OF DEBATE FOR EVERYONE AT SWEET MARIA'S. IT IS REALLY A PERSONAL CHOICE, BUT I MUST SAY THAT I LOVE CHEWY CHOCOLATE CHIP COOKIES.

PEANUT BUTTER KISS COOKIES

*Proudly topped with a chocolate kiss, these cookies are
my friend and accountant Lori's favorite. I'm always sure to make
her a batch for her birthday—and for tax season! Just be sure to
press the kisses in while the cookies are still warm.*

¼ POUND BUTTER, SOFTENED	1 ½ CUPS FLOUR
½ CUP SUGAR	1 TEASPOON BAKING SODA
½ CUP BROWN SUGAR	½ TEASPOON SALT
1 TEASPOON VANILLA EXTRACT	ADDITIONAL SUGAR
1 EGG	30 CHOCOLATE KISS CANDIES
½ CUP PEANUT BUTTER	

1. Preheat oven to 350°F.

2. In an electric mixer, on medium speed, cream the butter, sugar, and brown sugar until light. Add vanilla, egg, and peanut butter. Mix until well blended.

3. On low speed, add flour, baking soda, and salt. Mix just until blended.

4. Roll dough into 1-inch balls. Roll in additional sugar. Place on a parchment-lined cookie sheet, spacing each cookie 2 inches apart.

5. Bake 12 to 15 minutes, or until golden.

6. Remove cookie sheet from the oven. While cookies are hot, press bottom of chocolate kiss into cookie. Using a metal spatula, remove cookies from cookie sheet and place on a wire cooling rack. Cool completely. Be sure chocolate kiss is firmly set before storage. Store cookies in an airtight container at room temperature.

YIELD: 30 COOKIES

PIÑA COLADA COOKIES

*Enjoy a taste of the tropics with these cookies. They're
a moist combination of pineapple, rum,
coconut, and macadamia nuts.*

¼ POUND BUTTER, SOFTENED

1 CUP SUGAR

2 EGGS

2 TABLESPOONS RUM

2 CUPS FLOUR

¼ TEASPOON BAKING SODA

¼ TEASPOON SALT

½ CUP CRUSHED PINEAPPLE,
DRAINED

⅔ CUP FLAKED COCONUT

1 CUP MACADAMIA NUTS, COARSELY
CHOPPED

CONFECTIONERS' SUGAR FOR
DUSTING

1. Preheat oven to 350°F.

2. In an electric mixer, on medium speed, cream butter and sugar until light. Add eggs and rum. Mix well.

3. On low speed, add flour, baking soda, and salt. Mix just until blended. Stir in pineapple, coconut, and macadamia nuts.

4. Drop dough from a teaspoon onto a parchment-lined cookie sheet, spacing each 2 inches apart.

5. Bake 10 to 12 minutes or until lightly browned.

6. Remove cookie sheet from the oven. Using a metal spatula, remove cookies from the cookie sheet and place on a wire cooling rack. Cool completely.

7. Dust with confectioners' sugar. Store cookies in an airtight container.

YIELD: 50 COOKIES

CRANBERRY COBBLER BARS

These delicious bars are a quintessential New England dessert.
The cranberries and lemon give these bars the right amount
of zip. Try them plain or paired with a scoop
of fresh vanilla ice cream.

CRUST:

1 ½ CUPS FLOUR

1 CUP OATS

¾ CUP SUGAR

1 ½ STICKS BUTTER, MELTED AND COOLED

½ TEASPOON BAKING SODA

PINCH SALT

1 TEASPOON VANILLA EXTRACT

FILLING:

2 CUPS CRANBERRIES, FRESH OR FROZEN

GRATED RIND OF 1 LEMON

GRATED JUICE OF 1 LEMON

1. Preheat oven to 350°F.

2. In an electric mixer on low speed, combine all of the crust ingredients. Mixture will be crumbly.

3. Reserve one cup of crumb mixture. Press remaining crumb mixture into a greased 13 × 9-inch pan.

4. In a separate bowl, combine cranberries, lemon rind, and lemon juice. Spread over the top of crust mixture. Sprinkle cranberries with remaining crumb mixture.

5. Bake 30 to 35 minutes or until golden.

6. Remove pan from the oven. Place on a wire cooling rack. Cool completely. Cut into squares. Store bars in an airtight container.

YIELD: 24 SQUARES

GRANOLA COOKIE DROPS

These crunchy drops are a perfect breakfast cookie—tasty and not too sweet.
You can use store-bought granola or try our homemade recipe.

We first began making our own granola at Sweet Maria's several years ago.
It started as a way to use up a large inventory of nuts and oats.
The granola has now become so popular on its own, we never
have to worry about stocking too many nuts or oats!

1 CUP SUGAR

1/2 CUP VEGETABLE OIL

1/3 CUP MOLASSES

2 EGGS

2 CUPS FLOUR

1/2 TEASPOON BAKING SODA

1/4 TEASPOON SALT

2 1/2 CUPS GRANOLA (SEE
FOLLOWING RECIPE OR USE
STORE-BOUGHT)

1. Preheat oven to 350°F.

2. In an electric mixer on medium speed, mix sugar, oil, and molasses. Add eggs. Mix until well blended. On low speed, add flour, baking soda, and salt. Mix just until blended. Stir in granola.

3. Drop from a teaspoon onto a parchment-lined cookie sheet, spacing each cookie 2 inches apart.

4. Bake 10 to 12 minutes or until well browned.

5. Remove cookie sheet from the oven. Using a metal spatula, remove cookies from the sheet and place on a wire cooling rack. Cool completely. Store cookies at room temperature in an airtight container.

YIELD: 40 COOKIES

GRANOLA

You only need 2½ cups of granola for the cookies, but this granola is addictive, so you're sure to use the whole batch.

2 CUPS OATS	¼ CUP WHEAT GERM
½ CUP RAISINS	¼ CUP VEGETABLE OIL
¼ CUP ALMONDS, SLICED	⅓ CUP HONEY
½ CUP COCONUT	

1. Preheat oven to 350°F.

2. In an electric mixer, combine oats, raisins, almonds, coconut, and wheat germ. Mix on low speed until blended. Add oil and honey. Mix until well blended.

3. Spread granola in a thin layer on a parchment-lined cookie sheet.

4. Bake 25 to 30 minutes, or until golden brown. With a wooden spoon, stir granola every ten minutes to cook evenly.

5. Remove cookie sheet from the oven. Let granola cool on cookie sheet. When cool, break up large bunches of granola. Store in an airtight container.

YIELD: 6 CUPS

KEY WEST LIME BARS

*This variation of the classic lemon bar will make you pucker up.
I like them best chilled, served with a cup of espresso. You can
use either key limes or regular limes to make these bars.*

CRUST:

1 1/4 CUPS FLOUR

1/4 CUP SUGAR

1/4 POUND BUTTER, SOFTENED

FILLING:

1/2 CUP SUGAR

2 TABLESPOONS FLOUR

1/2 TEASPOON BAKING POWDER

2 EGGS

1/4 CUP LIME JUICE (FROM 2 LIMES)

GRATED RIND OF 2 LIMES

CONFECTIONERS' SUGAR FOR
DUSTING

1. Grease an 8 × 8 × 2-inch baking dish. Set aside.

2. Preheat oven to 350°F.

3. Prepare crust. In an electric mixer on low speed, mix flour, sugar, and butter until the mixture resembles coarse crumbs. Press mixture into prepared pan.

4. Bake 12 to 15 minutes or until crust is lightly browned.

5. Prepare filling. In another mixing bowl, with wire whisk, mix together sugar, flour, and baking powder. Add eggs, lime juice, and lime rind. Mix until well blended. Pour mixture over hot crust.

6. Bake 10 to 12 minutes or until lightly browned and firm. Remove pan from the oven. Cool cookies completely in pan on a wire cooling rack. Cover and refrigerate overnight.

7. Dust the top with confectioners' sugar. Cover pan with plastic wrap and refrigerate. Cut into squares as needed. Serve chilled.

YIELD: 20 SQUARES

LYNN'S SUNSHINE
SOUR CREAM COOKIES

These moist little drops are a perfect treat when you need a little something sweet. They are tasty plain or with the orange confectioners' glaze.

1½ STICKS BUTTER, SOFTENED	JUICE OF 1 ORANGE
1 CUP SUGAR	1 CUP SOUR CREAM
2 EGGS	2½ CUPS FLOUR
GRATED RIND OF 1 ORANGE	2 TEASPOONS BAKING POWDER

1. Preheat oven to 375°F.

2. In an electric mixer, cream butter and sugar until light. Add eggs, orange rind, orange juice, and sour cream. Mix until well blended. On low speed, add flour and baking powder. Mix just until blended.

3. Drop dough from a teaspoon onto a parchment-lined cookie sheet, spacing each 2 inches apart.

4. Bake 10 to 12 minutes or until edges begin to brown.

5. Remove cookie sheet from the oven. Using a metal spatula, remove cookies from the cookie sheet and place on a wire cooling rack. Cool completely.

6. If desired, frost with orange confectioners' glaze or serve plain. Store cookies in an airtight container.

YIELD: 50 COOKIES

ORANGE CONFECTIONERS' GLAZE

See page 60 for Confectioners' Icing. Replace water with equal amount of orange juice.

FLUFFER NUTTER BARS

*Named for everyone's favorite sandwich of peanut butter and
marshmallow fluff, this bar has a flavor-packed peanut butter crust
topped with fluff, peanuts, and chocolate chips. To help spread
the fluff, dip your knife or spatula in water.*

CRUST:

1/4 POUND BUTTER, SOFTENED

1 CUP SUGAR

1/2 CUP PEANUT BUTTER

1 EGG

1 1/4 CUPS FLOUR

2 TEASPOONS BAKING POWDER

1/2 TEASPOON SALT

TOPPING:

2 CUPS MARSHMALLOW FLUFF

1 CUP PEANUTS

1 CUP SEMISWEET CHOCOLATE CHIPS

1. Preheat oven to 350°F.

2. Prepare crust. In an electric mixer, cream butter and sugar until light. Add peanut butter and egg. Mix until well blended. On low speed, add flour, baking powder, and salt. Mix just until blended. Press crust into the bottom and slightly up the sides of an ungreased 13 × 9-inch baking pan.

3. Spoon fluff over crust, spreading to cover. Sprinkle peanuts over fluff. Sprinkle chocolate chips over peanuts.

4. Bake 15 to 20 minutes or until top is lightly browned.

5. Remove pan from the oven. Place on a wire cooling rack. Cool completely. When cool, cut into squares.

YIELD: 24 SQUARES

BASIL CHEDDAR ROUNDS

You can use any kind of cheddar in these cookies but I like extra sharp.
These savory cookies are a perfect alternative to crackers, served
with your favorite soup. Or top with a dollop of pesto for
an easy make-ahead hors d'oeuvre.

1/4 POUND BUTTER, SOFTENED

1 CUP SHREDDED CHEDDAR

3/4 CUP FLOUR

1/2 TEASPOON BAKING POWDER

1/2 TEASPOON SALT

2 TABLESPOONS FRESH BASIL, CHOPPED

1. Preheat oven to 350°F.

2. In an electric mixer, on medium speed, cream butter and cheddar until well blended. On low speed, add flour, baking powder, salt, and basil. Mix just until blended.

3. Roll dough out onto a lightly floured surface to 1/4-inch thick. Using a 1 1/2-inch round cookie cutter, cut into rounds. Place on a parchment-lined cookie sheet, spacing each 2 inches apart.

4. Bake 15 to 20 minutes or until edges begin to brown.

5. Remove cookie sheet from the oven. Using a metal spatula, remove cookies from the cookie sheet and place on a wire cooling rack. Cool completely. Store cookies refrigerated in an airtight container.

YIELD: 20 COOKIES

CHAPTER 2

INTERNATIONAL FAVORITES

The cookies in this section represent a small sampling from around the world. Many of these cookies began as a way to celebrate religious holidays and other special occasions, using the finest resources and ingredients. You'll find Cuban cookies that use the finest citrus and guava, gingerbread that uses the finest spices, and delicate madeleines that were developed by fine French culinary talents.

My grandparents are from Italy, so you will find a few Italian specialties in this section. If you'd like a more complete collection of Italian cookies, my first cookbook, *Sweet Maria's Italian Cookie Tray*, features many. This section also includes other favorites—almond cookies from Taiwan, shortbread from Scotland, and nut rolls from Eastern Europe, just to name a few. Many of my friends were happy to share their ethnic traditions and cookies that have become a part of their family celebrations. Try asking your friends to share, too.

RASPBERRY LINZERS

To make these classic Austrian sandwich cookies, you'll need a 2-inch round cookie cutter, plus a ½-inch cutter to make the inside cutout. The secret is to roll the dough thin and be sure to keep the dough you're not working with refrigerated. This will ensure that all the cookies remain the same size and will be easy to pair.

1½ STICKS BUTTER, SOFTENED

1 CUP SUGAR

2 EGGS

1 TEASPOON ALMOND EXTRACT

2¼ CUPS FLOUR

1 TEASPOON BAKING POWDER

½ TEASPOON SALT

CONFECTIONERS' SUGAR FOR DUSTING

FILLING

½ CUP RASPBERRY OR OTHER FLAVOR PRESERVES

1. In an electric mixer, cream butter and sugar until light. Add eggs and almond extract. Mix until blended. On low speed, add 2 cups flour, baking powder, and salt. Mix just until blended. Turn dough out onto a lightly floured surface. Knead in remaining ¼ cup flour to make a firm dough. Wrap dough in plastic wrap and refrigerate 2 to 3 hours or overnight.

2. Preheat oven to 350°F.

3. Roll dough out on a lightly floured surface to ⅛-inch thick. Using a 2-inch round fluted cookie cutter, cut dough into cirdes. Using a ½-inch round fluted cookie cutter, cut out the center of half of the circles. Re-roll and cut dough until you have an even number of bottoms (without hole) and tops (with hole). Place circles on a parchment-lined cookie sheet, spacing each 2 inches apart.

4. Bake 8 to 10 minutes or until edges just begin to brown.

5. Remove cookie sheet from the oven. Using a metal spatula, remove cookies from the cookie sheet and place on a wire cooling rack. Cool completely.

6. To assemble, pair cookies of similar size tops and bottoms. Dust tops with confectioners' sugar. Using a butter knife or small spatula, spread a small amount of preserves on the bottom cookie. Place a top over the preserves and press gently.

7. Dry completely. Store cookies in an airtight container.

YIELD: 36 COOKIES

SWEDISH SPICE COOKIES

Topped with a lemon glaze, these traditional Swedish spice cookies have just the right amount of spice. These are usually baked to celebrate Christmas.

1 ½ STICKS BUTTER, SOFTENED	½ TEASPOON SALT
¾ CUP SUGAR	½ TEASPOON BAKING SODA
1 EGG	½ TEASPOON NUTMEG
¼ CUP HONEY	1 TEASPOON CINNAMON
2 CUPS FLOUR	

1. Preheat oven to 350°F.

2. In an electric mixer, cream butter and sugar until light. Add egg and honey. Mix until well blended.

3. On low speed, add flour, salt, baking soda, nutmeg, and cinnamon. Mix just until blended.

4. Drop dough from a teaspoon onto a parchment-lined cookie sheet, spacing each 2 inches apart.

5. Bake 10 to 12 minutes or until light brown. Remove cookie sheet from the oven. Using a metal spatula, remove cookies from the sheet and place on a wire cooling rack. Cool completely.

6. Frost with lemon glaze. Store cookies in an airtight container.

YIELD: 35 COOKIES

LEMON GLAZE

1 CUP CONFECTIONERS' SUGAR   **1 TEASPOON LEMON RIND**

2 TABLESPOONS WATER

In a small bowl, mix all ingredients. Lightly frost the top of each cookie. Dry
completely.

BROWN SUGAR SHORTBREADS

*These simple sweet treats look great when you use a cookie stamp
to press down the tops. If you don't have a cookie stamp,
use a fork to make a crisscross design on top.*

½ POUND BUTTER, SOFTENED

¾ CUP BROWN SUGAR

1¾ TO 2 CUPS FLOUR

PINCH OF SALT

1. Preheat oven to 350°F.

2. In an electric mixer, cream butter and brown sugar until light. On low speed, add 1¾ cups flour and salt. Mix just until blended. Dough should be stiff enough to roll. If needed, add remaining ¼ cup flour.

3. Roll dough into 1-inch balls. Place on a parchment-lined cookie sheet, 2 inches apart. Use a cookie stamp or forks to flatten tops and imprint pattern.

4. Bake 12 to 15 minutes, or until lightly browned.

5. Remove cookie sheet from the oven. Using a metal spatula, remove cookies from the cookie sheet and place on a wire cooling rack. Cool completely. Store cookies at room temperature in an airtight container.

YIELD: 30 COOKIES

◆ COOKIE STAMPS ◆

COOKIE STAMPS ARE A UNIQUE WAY TO DECORATE COOKIES. THESE CERAMIC STAMPS, WITH RECESSED DETAILS, ARE PRESSED INTO THE COOKIE TO FLATTEN AND IMPRINT BEFORE BAKING. TO KEEP THE STAMP FROM STICKING TO THE COOKIE, LIGHTLY BRUSH IT WITH VEGETABLE OIL. COOKIE STAMPS WORK BEST WITH FIRM DOUGH LIKE SHORTBREAD. THEY ARE MADE IN VARIOUS DESIGNS AND CAN BE FOUND IN SPECIALTY KITCHEN SHOPS.

BRANDY SNAPS

These tasty, crispy cookies can be shaped into diplomas or cookie cups. They're easier to shape if you bake only 3 to 4 cookies at a time. Before shaping, let the cookies cool 1 to 2 minutes after removing the cookie sheet from the oven. Wrap the cookie around the handle of a wooden spoon to create a crispy cookie tube, or shape the cookie around the bottom of an upside ramekin to form a cookie cup. Fill them with whipped or ice cream for an impressive dessert.

¼ POUND BUTTER	½ CUP OATS
½ CUP BROWN SUGAR	½ CUP WALNUTS, FINELY CHOPPED
¼ CUP SUGAR	1 TABLESPOON HEAVY CREAM
½ CUP CORN SYRUP	1 TEASPOON BRANDY
⅔ CUP FLOUR	

1. Preheat oven to 350°F.

2. In a medium saucepan, over medium heat, combine butter, brown sugar, sugar, and corn syrup. Bring mixture to a boil, stirring constantly until sugars melt, about 3 minutes. Remove pan from the heat. Stir in flour, oats, walnuts, heavy cream, and brandy. Cool dough slightly.

3. Drop dough from a teaspoon onto a parchment-lined cookie sheet, spacing each 4 inches apart.

4. Bake until cookies are golden brown and bubbling has subsided, about 8 to 10 minutes. Remove cookie sheet from the oven. Let cookies cool 1 to 2 minutes.

5. Carefully shape cookie around the handle of a wooden spoon. Slide cookie off the handle and place onto a wire cooling rack. To form cookie cup, wrap hot cookie around the bottom of an upside-down ramekin. If cookies become too cool to shape, return pan to oven to reheat and shape. Cool completely. Store cookies in an airtight container.

YIELD: 30 COOKIES

ROYAL TEACAKES

These cookies have a great sconelike texture. It's the perfect match with a dollop of clotted cream and a spot of afternoon tea. When you use the cookie cutter to cut, you may get stuck cutting a raisin. That's okay—press on! Even the queen can't get enough of these casual, rustic, biscuitlike cookies.

4 TABLESPOONS BUTTER, SOFTENED	1½ TEASPOONS BAKING POWDER
4 TABLESPOONS SHORTENING	¼ TEASPOON SALT
¾ CUP SUGAR	1 CUP RAISINS
1 EGG	1 EGG WHITE FOR TOPPING
1½ CUPS FLOUR	ADDITIONAL SUGAR FOR TOPPING

1. In an electric mixer on medium speed, cream butter and shortening. Add sugar and cream until light. Add egg. Mix until well blended.

2. On low speed, add flour, baking powder, and salt. Mix just until blended. Stir in raisins.

3. Cover dough with plastic wrap and refrigerate 2 hours or overnight.

4. Preheat oven to 375°F.

5. On a lightly floured surface, roll dough out to ¼-inch thickness. Using a 1½-inch round cookie cutter, cut dough into cirdes. Reroll and cut until all dough is used.

6. Place rounds onto a parchment-lined cookie sheet, spacing each 2 inches apart.

7. In a small bowl, beat egg white with a fork. Brush the tops of each cookie with egg white and sprinkle tops with additional sugar.

8. Bake 10 to 12 minutes or until lightly browned.

9. Remove cookie sheet from the oven. Using a metal spatula, remove cookies from the cookie sheet and place on a wire cooling rack. Cool completely. Store cookies at room temperature in an airtight container.

YIELD: 36 COOKIES

HAZELNUT TUILES

These cookies are the perfect way to impress your friends and family.
They are light, curved cookies that resemble roof tiles, or "tuile" in French.
They are beautiful on their own, or as an accompaniment for ice cream.
(You can even mold the dough into cookie cups for this purpose).

These cookies are best when baked on a lightly greased cookie sheet,
not on parchment paper. They need to cling to the cookie sheet. For
best results, bake only 4 to 5 cookies at a time. This will give you time to
shape the just-baked cookies before they cool. If they should cool before
you're done shaping them, return cookie sheet to the oven for 1 to 2
more minutes. Humidity can soften these cookies, so don't attempt
to bake these on a humid day. I've also found that using a cushioned
cookie sheet allows these cookies to bake more evenly.

3 EGG WHITES

3/4 CUP SUGAR

PINCH OF SALT

1/4 POUND BUTTER, MELTED AND
COOLED

1/2 TEASPOON HAZELNUT LIQUEUR

1/2 CUP CAKE FLOUR

1/2 CUP HAZELNUTS, FINELY CHOPPED

1. Preheat oven to 375°F.

2. In an electric mixer, beat egg whites, sugar, and salt until thick. Add butter and liqueur. Mix until well blended.

3. On low speed, add flour and hazelnuts. Mix just until blended.

4. Drop from a tablespoon onto a greased cookie sheet, spacing each 5 inches apart. Using the back of the spoon, spread each into a thin circle.

5. Bake 10 to 12 minutes or until golden.

6. Remove pan from the oven. Using a metal spatula, carefully remove from the cookie sheet and lay on top of a rolling pin to form a curved cookie. (Shape on the bottom of an upside-down ramekin to form cookie cups). Cool completely. If cookies cool off before shaping, reheat cookie sheet in oven 1 to 2 minutes. Repeat with all the dough. Store cookies in an airtight container.

YIELD: 20 COOKIES

◆ HOW TO MAKE A COOKIE TRAY ◆

THE TRADITION OF MAKING COOKIE TRAYS FOR WEDDINGS, SHOWERS, AND HOLIDAYS IS STILL THRIVING. THESE TRAYS ARE A WAY TO SHOW APPRECIATION FOR THE BRIDE OR HOST. EVERY BAKER MAKES HIS OR HER SPECIALTY, AND THEY ARE POOLED TOGETHER TO MAKE LARGE TRAYS.

START WITH A FLAT TRAY OR PLATE. COVER IT WITH A DOILY, IF DESIRED. START LAYERING COOKIES, ARRANGING THEM FLAT ON THE TRAY. CONTINUE TO LAYER VARIOUS TYPES OF COOKIES, KEEPING THE FLAT, STURDY ONES ON THE BOTTOM AND THE LIGHTER, MORE DELICATE COOKIES ON TOP. BE SURE TO PAY ATTENTION TO COLOR, ALTERNATING ROWS OF CHOCOLATE, VANILLA, AND JELLY-FILLED COOKIES. WRAP IN FESTIVE CELLOPHANE AND RIBBONS.

MADELEINES

*These delicate sponge cakes are light and sweetly flavored.
The method for making them is like making a sponge cake.
The key to success is to stiffly beat the egg whites and gently fold
them into the rest of the batter. You will need to use a
shell-shaped madeleine pan. These are available in most
kitchen stores. Madeleines do not have a long shelf life, so
bake and enjoy them as soon as possible. French
writer Marcel Proust would be proud!*

1/4 POUND BUTTER, MELTED AND
COOLED

1/2 CUP CONFECTIONERS' SUGAR

2 EGGS, SEPARATED

1 TABLESPOON GRAND MARNIER OR
OTHER ORANGE LIQUEUR

2/3 CUP CAKE FLOUR

PINCH OF CREAM OF TARTAR

CONFECTIONERS' SUGAR FOR
DUSTING

1. Preheat oven to 350°F.

2. In a medium bowl, with a wire whisk, blend butter and confectioners' sugar until smooth. Add egg yolks and Grand Marnier. Mix until well blended. Gradually stir in flour. Set aside.

3. In an electric mixer with wire attachment, beat egg whites and cream of tartar until stiff.

4. Fold egg whites into the butter and sugar mixture. Fold until well blended.

5. Spray madeleine pan with nonstick baking spray. Fill molds three-quarters full with batter.

6. Bake 10 to 12 minutes or until edges begin to brown and center of cookie springs back to the touch.

7. Remove pan from the oven. Carefully unmold cookies and place on a wire cooling rack. Brush out mold. Cool mold completely before re-spraying and filling. Repeat until all batter is used.

8. Dust cooled cookies with confectioners' sugar. Store cookies at room temperature in an airtight container.

YIELD: 15 MADELEINES

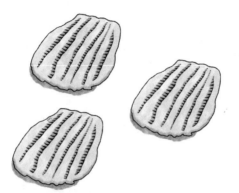

PALMIERS

The rolled layers of dough in this classic French specialty resemble palm leaves. This version, which uses cinnamon and sugar, is easy to make if you use pre-made puff pastry. You can find sheets of frozen puff pastry in just about every grocery store. Be sure to roll them on a surface lightly dusted with granulated sugar. This sugar will work into the dough as you roll and caramelize as the cookies bake.

1 SHEET OF FROZEN PUFF PASTRY, 9 × 9 INCHES

1/2 CUP SUGAR

1 TEASPOON CINNAMON

1 EGG

1. Thaw puff pastry at room temperature for 20 minutes. On a lightly sugared surface, roll dough until thin into a rectangle measuring about 10 × 17 inches.

2. In a small bowl, combine sugar and cinnamon. In another small bowl, beat egg. With a pastry brush, brush the surface of the puff pastry with the egg. Sprinkle with cinnamon mixture to cover dough. Starting at opposite ends, roll up both sides of dough to meet in the center. Brush the outside of dough with remaining egg. Sprinkle with remaining cinnamon mixture. Place on a parchment-lined cookie sheet and refrigerate 30 minutes.

3. Preheat oven to 375°F.

4. Remove pastry from the refrigerator. Using a sharp, straight knife, cut dough into 1/4-inch slices. Place cut side up on a parchment-lined cookie sheet, spacing each 3 inches apart. Bake 12 to 15 minutes, or until golden brown.

5. Remove cookie sheet from the oven. Using a metal spatula, remove cookies from the cookie sheet and place on wire cooling rack. Cool completely. Store in an airtight container.

YIELD: 24 COOKIES

RUGELACH

This traditional Jewish cookie is a rich and flavorful treat that was originally baked to celebrate Hannukah. These two versions are my favorites—raspberry almond and caramel chocolate chip. In this recipe, the dough is rolled thin into a circle like a pie crust, filled, cut into wedges, and rolled and shaped into a crescent.

CRUST:

½ POUND BUTTER, SOFTENED

1 EGG YOLK

¾ CUP SOUR CREAM

2 CUPS FLOUR

CARAMEL CHOCOLATE CHIP FILLING:

½ CUP CARAMEL ICE CREAM TOPPING

1 CUP WALNUTS, FINELY CHOPPED

½ CUP BROWN SUGAR

½ CUP CHOCOLATE CHIPS

RASPBERRY ALMOND FILLING:

1 CUP RASPBERRY PRESERVES

½ CUP SUGAR

1 CUP SLICED ALMONDS

1. Prepare crust. In an electric mixer, cream the butter. Add egg yolk and sour cream. Mix until well blended. On low speed, add flour. Mix just until blended. Turn dough out onto a lightly floured surface and knead until blended. Wrap dough in plastic wrap and refrigerate 2 to 3 hours or overnight.

2. Preheat oven to 375°F.

3. Divide dough in half. Leave unused portion of dough in refrigerator while you work with the first piece. Using a lightly floured rolling pin, roll out first half of dough until very thin, ⅛ inch thick, on a lightly floured surface.

4. Fill cookies. For caramel chocolate chip filling: Spread half the caramel ice cream topping over the dough. Sprinkle half the walnuts, brown sugar, and

chocolate chips over the caramel. For raspberry almond filling: Spread half the raspberry preserves over the dough. Sprinkle with half the sugar and sliced almonds.

5. Using a fluted pastry cutter, cut the circle into 16 wedges. Roll each wedge, starting at the wide end, toward the center of the circle. Pinch at the middle to adhere loose end of the dough. Slightly curve the cookie into a crescent shape and place seam-down on a parchment-lined cookie sheet, spacing each cookie about 2 inches apart. Repeat rolling and filling remaining dough.

6. Bake 15 to 20 minutes, or until lightly browned.

7. Remove the cookie sheet from the oven. Using a metal spatula, remove the cookies from the cookie sheet and place on a wire cooling rack. Cool completely. Store cooled cookies in an airtight container.

YIELD: 32 COOKIES

SLAVIC COLD DOUGH COOKIES

KIFFLES AND KOLACZI

These Eastern European treats have a sweet yeast dough with a unique, spongy texture. The nut rolls, or kiffles, are a favorite of my friend Tom. His mom made these for all their family gatherings. Because the dough is rolled out with a mixture of confectioners' sugar and flour, you need to work quickly because the dough becomes sticky.

CRUST:

1 PACKAGE YEAST

½ CUP WARM WATER

2 EGG YOLKS

2 CUPS FLOUR

¼ POUND BUTTER, SOFTENED

2 EGG YOLKS

½ CUP SOUR CREAM

FILLING:

2 EGG WHITES

¾ CUP SUGAR

1 ¼ CUP WALNUTS, CHOPPED

1 TEASPOON VANILLA EXTRACT

1. Dissolve yeast in warm water. Set aside.

2. Place flour in a food processor. Pulse in butter until mixture resembles coarse crumbs. Transfer to a medium bowl. Stir in egg yolks, sour cream, and yeast mixture. Turn dough out onto a lightly floured surface. Knead to make a soft, sticky dough. Divide dough into three equal pieces. Wrap in plastic wrap and refrigerate 2 to 3 hours or overnight.

3. Preheat oven to 375°F.

4. Beat egg whites until foamy. Gradually add sugar and beat until stiff. Stir in walnuts, and vanilla. Set aside.

5. Remove one-third of the dough from the refrigerator. Using a rolling pin dusted with a combination of confectioners' sugar and flour, roll dough out onto a surface that has been generously dusted with the same mixture. Roll dough very thin, like a pie crust.

6. Spread one-third of the filling on the dough. Using a pastry cutter, cut into wedges. Roll from the wide end to the center. Place on a parchment-lined cookie sheet, spacing each 2 inches apart. Be sure that seam is underneath cookie. Repeat rolling and filling remaining dough.

7. Bake 15 to 20 minutes or until well browned.

8. Remove cookie sheet from the oven. Using a metal spatula, remove cookies from the cookie sheet and place on a wire cooling rack. Cool. Store cooled cookies in an airtight container.

YIELD: 45 COOKIES

VARIATION: KOLACZI

These jelly-filled rounds use the same tasty dough as the kiffles.

1 RECIPE SLAVIC COLD DOUGH

1 CUP RASPBERRY OR APRICOT JELLY

1/2 RECIPE CONFECTIONERS' ICING (SEE PAGE 60)

1. Prepare dough and refrigerate as directed. Remove one-third of the dough from the refrigerator. Using a rolling pin that has been dusted with a combination of confectioners' sugar and flour, roll dough out ¼ inch thick. Using a 2-inch cookie cutter, cut dough into rounds. Place on a parchment-lined cookie sheet, spacing each 2 inches apart. Cover top of cookie sheet with plastic wrap. Let cookies rest 15 to 20 minutes at room temperature. Using your fingers, make a well in the middle of each cookie. Fill with raspberry jelly.

2. Bake 12 to 15 minutes or until lightly browned. Remove cookie sheet from the oven. Using a metal spatula, remove cookies from the cookie sheet and place on a wire cooling rack. Cool completely. Drizzle tops of cookies with confectioners' icing. Let dry completely. Store cookies in an airtight container.

YIELD 30 COOKIES

CUBAN CITRUS COOKIES

These zesty cookies are a big buttery treat. Their refreshing flavor comes from a generous amount of citrus rind. You can use any type of citrus; I like a combination of lemon and lime.

1/2 POUND BUTTER, SOFTENED

1 CUP SUGAR

1 TABLESPOON GRATED CITRUS RIND

2 TABLESPOONS CITRUS JUICE

1 3/4 CUPS FLOUR

1 TEASPOON BAKING POWDER

1/4 TEASPOON SALT

COARSE SANDING SUGAR TO DECORATE

1. Preheat oven to 350°F.

2. In an electric mixer, cream butter and sugar until light. Add rind and juice. Mix until well blended. On low speed, add flour, baking powder, and salt. Mix just until blended to form a stiff dough.

3. Roll dough into one-inch balls. Place on a parchment-lined cookie sheet, spacing each 2 inches apart. With the bottom of a glass, flatten cookies. Sprinkle with sanding sugar.

4. Bake 10 to 12 minutes or until edges begin to brown.

5. Remove cookie sheet from the oven. Using a metal spatula, remove cookies from the cookie sheet and place on a wire cooling rack. Cool completely. Store cookies at room temperature in an airtight container.

YIELD: 36 COOKIES

GUAVA EMPANADAS

*These sweet Cuban turnovers can be either fried or baked.
The crust is a rich, flavorful dough made with cream cheese and
the filling is guava paste, which is a concentration of guava and sugar.
It is available in Spanish specialty shops and some supermarkets.
If you can't find guava paste, any tropical fruit preserve such
as pineapple or mango would be just as delicious.*

CRUST:

1/4 POUND BUTTER, SOFTENED

3 OUNCES CREAM CHEESE

1 CUP FLOUR

FILLING:

1/2 CUP GUAVA PASTE OR FRUIT
PRESERVES

VEGETABLE OIL FOR FRYING

CONFECTIONERS' SUGAR FOR
DUSTING

1. In an electric mixer, cream the butter and cream cheese until light. On low speed, add flour. Mix just until blended. Turn dough out onto a lightly floured surface. Knead to form a stiff, not sticky dough. Wrap in plastic wrap and refrigerate 2 to 3 hours or overnight.

2. Preheat oven to 350°F. (if you're not frying them). Remove dough from the refrigerator. Roll dough out onto a lightly floured surface about ⅛-inch thick. Cut into circles using a 3-inch round cookie cutter. Place ½ teaspoon of preserves in the center of each circle. Wet the edges of circle with water. Fold dough in half. Press edges together firmly to seal. Reroll, fill, and cut remaining dough. Let rest 15 to 20 minutes. For baking, place each cookie onto a parchment-lined cookie sheet, spacing each 2 inches apart.

3. Bake 15 to 20 minutes or until edges begin to brown.

4. Remove cookie sheet from the oven. Using a metal spatula, remove cookies from the cookie sheet and place on a wire cooling rack. Cool completely. Dust with confectioners' sugar. Store unused cookies in an airtight container.

5. For frying, fry cookies in hot oil, 375°F. until lightly browned. Drain on absorbent paper. Dust with confectioners' sugar. Serve immediately.

YIELD: 20 COOKIES

MEXICAN WEDDING CAKES

These buttery cookies are loaded with chopped hazelnuts.
They are traditionally baked to celebrate a wedding,
but I like to bake and enjoy them anytime.

½ POUND BUTTER, SOFTENED

⅓ CUP CONFECTIONERS' SUGAR

1 TEASPOON HAZELNUT LIQUEUR

1½ CUPS FLOUR

1 CUP HAZELNUTS, CHOPPED

CONFECTIONERS' SUGAR FOR DUSTING

1. Preheat oven to 350°F.

2. In an electric mixer, cream butter and confectioners' sugar until light. Add hazelnut liqueur. Mix until blended. On low speed, add flour and hazelnuts. Mix just until blended.

3. Roll dough into 1-inch balls. Place cookies on a parchment-lined cookie sheet, spacing each 2 inches apart.

4. Bake 10 to 12 minutes or until lightly browned.

5. Remove cookie sheet from the oven. While cookies are warm, toss to coat in confectioners' sugar. Cool completely. Store cookies in an airtight container.

YIELD: 50 COOKIES

CHINESE ALMOND COOKIES

These almond cookies are a traditional Chinese sweet. My friend Richard,
who is from Taiwan, bakes these as part of his childhood tradition.
The egg wash on top gives these cookies a professional look.

½ POUND BUTTER, SOFTENED	1 TEASPOON BAKING POWDER
1 CUP CONFECTIONERS' SUGAR	1 TEASPOON BAKING SODA
1 EGG	½ CUP ALMONDS, SLICED
1 TEASPOON ALMOND EXTRACT	WHOLE ALMONDS (ABOUT 40)
2 CUPS FLOUR	1 EGG FOR EGG WASH

1. Preheat oven to 350°F.

2. In an electric mixer on medium speed, cream butter and confectioners' sugar until light. Add egg and almond extract. Mix until well blended.

3. On low speed, add flour, baking powder, and baking soda. Mix just until blended. Stir in sliced almonds.

4. Roll dough into 1-inch balls. If dough is too sticky to roll, dust your fingers and the dough with additional flour. Place balls onto a parchment-lined cookie sheet, spacing each 2 inches apart. Using your fingers, flatten the tops of the balls. Press a whole almond into the center of each cookie.

5. In a small bowl, beat egg. Brush tops of cookies with egg.

6. Bake 10 to 12 minutes or until edges begin to brown.

7. Remove cookie sheet from the oven. Using a metal spatula, remove cookies from the cookie sheet and place on a wire cooling rack. Cool completely. Store cookies in an airtight container at room temperature.

YIELD: 40 COOKIES

SWEET WONTONS

These Asian-inspired fried cookies use wonton wrapper as a crispy crust to two simple fillings. These wrappers are available in most supermarkets. These are best served freshly fried.

CHOCOLATE CREAM CHEESE FILLING

8 OUNCES CREAM CHEESE

¼ CUP CONFECTIONERS' SUGAR

1 CUP CHOCOLATE CHIPS

1 EGG FOR ADHERING

25 WONTON WRAPPERS, SQUARE OR ROUND

VEGETABLE OIL FOR FRYING

1. In an electric mixer, cream cream cheese and confectioners' sugar until light. Stir in chocolate chips.

2. In a small bowl, beat egg. Fill wonton wrappers with ½ teaspoon of filling. Brush edges of wrapper with beaten egg. Press to seal edges. Fill all wrappers. Cover and refrigerate 1 to 2 hours.

3. Fry in hot oil, 375°F., until golden. Drain on absorbent paper. Dust with confectioners' sugar and serve warm.

YIELD: 25 COOKIES

VARIATION: TROPICAL FRUIT FILLING

½ CUP CHOPPED DRIED TROPICAL FRUIT (DRIED PAPAYA, PINEAPPLE, BANANAS)

½ CUP COCONUT

2 TABLESPOONS SUGAR

2 TABLESPOONS HEAVY CREAM

In a medium bowl, combine all ingredients. Fill wrappers and fry as directed above.

ITALIAN DROP COOKIES

ANGINETTI

This favorite, from my first cookbook, is the cookie that most people think of when they think of Italian cookies. They're very easy to make, and can be flavored with vanilla, anise, or traditional lemon. These are a "must have" on a Sweet Maria wedding cookie tray.

3 EGGS	1/2 CUP VEGETABLE OIL
1/2 CUP MILK	3 CUPS FLOUR
2 TEASPOONS LEMON EXTRACT	8 TEASPOONS BAKING POWDER
1/2 CUP SUGAR	

1. Preheat oven to 350°F.

2. In an electric mixer on medium speed, beat eggs, milk, lemon extract, sugar and oil until well blended.

3. On low speed, add flour and baking powder. Mix just until blended. The dough should be soft and sticky.

4. Using a teaspoon, drop the dough onto a lightly greased cookie sheet, spacing the cookies 2 inches apart.

5. Bake immediately for 8 to 10 minutes or until slightly browned.

6. Remove cookie sheet from the oven. Using a metal spatula, remove cookies from the cookie sheet and place on a wire cooling rack. Cool completely.

7. Frost with confectioners' icing (see page 60).

YIELD: 50 COOKIES

CONFECTIONERS' ICING

*This versatile frosting is used for our Italian drop cookies and other recipes.
To make clean-up easier when frosting cookies, place a piece of
parchment paper under a wire cooling rack. Place frosted cookies
on the wire cooling rack. The excess frosting will drip
onto the paper, which you can simply discard.*

6 CUPS CONFECTIONERS' SUGAR   **1/2 CUP WATER**

2 TEASPOONS LEMON EXTRACT

1. In an electric mixer, on medium speed, beat all ingredients until smooth.

2. Using a metal spatula, frost the tops of the cookies. The frosting will drip down the sides and coat the cookie.

3. Dry the frosted cookies on wire cooling racks. Store in an airtight container.

YIELD: ENOUGH FOR 50 COOKIES

PIGNOLI COOKIES

These almond macaroons covered in pine nuts, along with their chocolate almond variation, are so popular at the bakery, we can't seem to make them quick enough. This dough is a bit sticky, so try dipping your fingers in water as you roll it. This will keep the dough from sticking to your fingers and will help the nuts to adhere to the cookies.

1½ POUNDS ALMOND PASTE, BROKEN
INTO PEBBLE-SIZE PIECES

1½ CUPS SUGAR

1 CUP CONFECTIONERS' SUGAR

4 EGG WHITES

2 CUPS PINE NUTS

1. Preheat oven to 350°F.

2. In an electric mixer, combine almond paste, sugar, confectioners' sugar, and egg whites on low speed until blended. Mix on medium speed for 2 minutes. This will make a sticky dough.

3. Roll dough into 1-inch balls. Roll balls in a bowl of pine nuts, pressing to adhere the nuts. Place the cookies on a parchment-lined cookie sheet, spacing them 2 inches apart. Using your fingers, press to slightly flatten the tops of the cookies.

4. Bake 15 to 20 minutes, or until golden brown.

5. Remove the cookie sheet from the oven. For easiest removal, let cookies cool completely on parchment. When cookies are completely cool, use a metal spatula to loosen them from the parchment paper. Store in an airtight container.

YIELD: 50 COOKIES

CHOCOLATE ALMOND MACAROONS

Bake these cookies alongside the pignoli nut cookies to check for doneness.

1 1/2 POUNDS ALMOND PASTE, BROKEN
INTO PEBBLE-SIZE PIECES

1/2 CUP COCOA

1 1/2 CUPS SUGAR

1 CUP CONFECTIONERS' SUGAR

4 EGG WHITES

2 CUPS ALMONDS, SLICED

1. Follow same directions as above for pignoli nut cookies. Add cocoa when you add sugars. Roll cookies in almonds instead of pine nuts.

AMARETTO BISCOTTI
WITH ALMONDS

These biscotti, from my first cookbook, are the most popular ones we make. They're perfect with a hot cup of cappuccino. They are baked using the traditional method, first forming a loaf and baking, then slicing diagonally and toasting.

½ POUND BUTTER, SOFTENED	6 CUPS FLOUR
1 ½ CUPS SUGAR	2 CUPS SLICED ALMONDS
6 EGGS	6 TEASPOONS BAKING POWDER
2 TEASPOONS VANILLA EXTRACT	PINCH OF SALT
2 TABLESPOONS AMARETTO LIQUEUR	

1. Preheat oven to 350°F.

2. In an electric mixer, cream the butter and sugar until light. Add eggs, vanilla, and amaretto liqueur. Mix well.

3. On low speed, add flour, almonds, baking powder, and salt. Mix just until blended. Turn dough out onto a lightly floured surface. Divide dough into 5 equal pieces. Roll each piece into loaves about 12 inches long. Place on a parchment-lined cookie sheet, spacing each loaf about 2 inches apart.

4. Bake 20 to 25 minutes, or until well browned. Using 2 metal spatulas, carefully remove the loaves from the cookie sheet onto a wire cooling rack. Cool.

5. Place cooled loaves on a cutting board. Using a sharp knife, slice diagonally into ½-inch-wide strips. Place strips in a single layer on cookie sheet. Return to the oven for 12 to 15 minutes, or until lightly browned.

6. Remove cookie sheet from the oven. Cool toasted biscotti on a wire cooling rack. Store in an airtight container.

YIELD: 50 COOKIES

DRIED CHERRY AND ALMOND BISCOTTI

These biscotti are made in the traditional Italian style, without fat. Because they don't have butter or any other type of fat, they harden to a crunchy cookie. Be sure to slice them while they're still warm.

1¼ TO 1¾ CUPS FLOUR

1 CUP SUGAR

2 TEASPOONS BAKING POWDER

¼ TEASPOON SALT

1 TEASPOON CINNAMON

1 CUP DRIED CHERRIES

1 CUP WHOLE ALMONDS

3 EGGS

2 TEASPOONS AMARETTO

1. Preheat oven to 350°F.

2. In a large mixing bowl, combine 1¼ cups flour, sugar, baking powder, salt, cinnamon, cherries, and almonds. In a separate bowl, beat eggs with a wire whisk. Add amaretto and mix well.

3. Pour wet ingredients into dry ingredients. Mix to form a soft dough. Turn dough out onto a floured surface. If dough is sticky, knead in an additional ¼ to ½ cup of flour. Dough should be soft but not sticky.

4. Divide dough into 3 equal pieces. Roll each piece into a loaf about 12 inches long. Place on a parchment-lined cookie sheet, spacing each 4 inches apart.

5. Bake 20 to 25 minutes or until golden brown.

6. While cookies are still warm, slice diagonally into ½-inch slices. Return cookies to the cookie sheet in a single layer. Bake 15 minutes or until well toasted.

7. Remove cookie sheet from the oven. Using a metal spatula, remove cookies and place on a wire cooling rack. Cool. Store cookies in an airtight container.

YIELD: 30 BISCOTTI

ITALIAN LOVE KNOTS

TARALLI

*These classic Italian biscuits can be shaped into an s, a knot,
or a twist. I love to eat these plain, but you can
top them with confectioners' icing*

½ POUND BUTTER, SOFTENED

¾ CUP SUGAR

¼ CUP VEGETABLE OIL

4 EGGS

½ TEASPOON VANILLA EXTRACT

2½ CUPS FLOUR

2 TEASPOONS BAKING POWDER

1. Preheat oven to 350°F.

2. In an electric mixer, cream butter and sugar until light. Add oil, eggs, and vanilla. Mix well.

3. On low speed, add 2 cups of flour and baking powder. Mix just until blended. Turn dough out onto a lightly floured surface. Knead in remaining ½ cup of flour. Knead until the dough is soft but not sticky. Cover with plastic wrap and let dough rest at room temperature 15 to 20 minutes.

4. Break off pieces of dough and roll on a lightly floured surface into small snakes, about ½ inch wide by 4 inches long. Twist or knot dough pieces, or shape into an *s*. Place on a parchment-lined cookie sheet, spacing each 2 inches apart.

5. Bake 10 to 12 minutes or until edges begin to brown.

6. Remove cookie sheet from the oven. Using a metal spatula, remove cookies from the sheet and place on a wire cooling rack. Cool completely.

7. Frost, if desired, with confectioners' icing (see page 60). Store cookies in an airtight container.

YIELD: 36 COOKIES

ITALIAN FRIED COOKIES

CENCI

There are many versions of this type of fried cookie. Every family has their favorite way to flavor and shape these fried treats. This version is light and crispy but adds a touch of cinnamon. The secret to success is to roll the dough very thin and fry in very hot oil.

3 EGGS	2 TO 2½ CUPS FLOUR
¼ CUP SUGAR	½ TEASPOON SALT
2 TABLESPOONS HEAVY CREAM	½ TEASPOON CINNAMON
2 TABLESPOONS SHORTENING, MELTED AND COOLED	VEGETABLE OIL FOR FRYING
1 TEASPOON VANILLA EXTRACT	CONFECTIONERS' SUGAR FOR DUSTING

1. In a medium mixing bowl, whisk eggs and sugar. Add heavy cream, shortening, and vanilla. Mix until well blended. Add 2 cups flour, salt, and cinnamon. Turn dough out onto a lightly floured surface. Knead to make a soft dough. If dough is too sticky, add additional flour. Wrap dough in plastic and refrigerate 2 to 3 hours or overnight.

2. Divide dough in half. Roll dough out onto a lightly floured surface until very thin. Using a fluted pastry cutter, cut dough into various sizes of triangles. Repeat with remaining dough.

3. Fry in hot oil, 375°F., until well browned. Drain on absorbent paper. Dust with confectioners' sugar and serve. Store in an airtight container.

YIELD: ABOUT 40 TRIANGLES

GORGONZOLA PEPPER BISCUITS

These savory cookies use Italian blue cheese and black pepper, a great combination. You can use any type of blue cheese you like, but gorgonzola has always been a family favorite. Pair these biscuits with grapes and wine for an easy-to-prepare appetizer. Delicioso!

1 TO 1¼ CUPS FLOUR	1 CUP GORGONZOLA, CRUMBLED
2 TEASPOONS BLACK PEPPER	4 TABLESPOONS BUTTER, SOFTENED
1 CUP WALNUTS, FINELY CHOPPED	2 EGG YOLKS

1. In a medium bowl, combine 1 cup flour, black pepper and walnuts. Using a pastry blender, cut gorgonzola and butter into flour mixture. Mix until mixture resembles coarse crumbs.

2. Using a wooden spoon, add egg yolks. Turn dough out onto a lightly floured surface. Knead in additional ¼ cup of flour to make a stiff dough. Divide dough into thirds. Shape each piece into cylinders about 10 inches long. Wrap in plastic wrap and refrigerate 2 to 3 hours or overnight.

3. Preheat oven to 375°F.

4. Remove dough from the refrigerator. Slice cylinders into ¼-inch slices. Place on a parchment-lined cookie sheet, spacing each 2 inches apart.

5. Bake 10 to 12 minutes or until edges begin to brown. Remove cookie sheet from the oven. Using a metal spatula, remove cookies from the cookie sheet and place on a wire cooling rack. Cool completely. Store cookies refrigerated, in an airtight container.

YIELD: 60 COOKIES

CHAPTER 3

BAKERY FAVORITES

This section includes many bakery staples, popular not just at Sweet Maria's but at traditional bakeries across the country—good old-fashioned favorites like sugar cookies, hermits, and cheesecake squares. This is the type of cookie I made when I started at my first bakery job.

I've also included some cookies that are a part of our popular culture—cookies like pecan sandies, vanilla sandwiches, and newtons, cookies that we love but Mom *didn't* make. Whether they are made by elves, machine, Mom, or our neighborhood bakery, they are a delicious part of our lives. Plus, they're easy enough for you to bake at home.

VANILLA SUGAR COOKIES

*These simply delicious cookies are great plain, or used as the basis for two
great variations: Stained Glass Cookies, and Black and White Cookies.
If you don't want to use a vanilla bean, you can use 1 teaspoon of
vanilla extract to flavor the cookie. Create your own shapes, sizes,
and designs by using any shape or size cookie cutter.*

½ CUP SUGAR	2 CUPS FLOUR
1 VANILLA BEAN	2 TEASPOONS BAKING POWDER
1 ¼ STICKS BUTTER, SOFTENED	½ TEASPOON SALT
2 EGGS	ADDITIONAL SUGAR FOR DUSTING

1. Place sugar in a small mixing bowl. With a small paring knife, slice the vanilla bean lengthwise. Using the tip of the knife, scrape the vanilla seeds into the sugar. Mix until sugar and vanilla are well blended. Set aside.

2. In an electric mixer, cream the butter and vanilla sugar until light. Add eggs. Mix until well blended. On low speed, add flour, baking powder, and salt. Mix just until blended.

3. Wrap dough in plastic wrap and refrigerate 2 to 3 hours, or overnight.

4. Preheat oven to 350°F.

5. Roll dough out onto a lightly floured surface to ¼-inch thickness. Using a 2½-inch cookie cutter, cut dough into rounds. Place on a parchment-lined cookie sheet, spacing each 2 inches apart. Sprinkle tops with additional sugar.

6. Bake 10 to 12 minutes or until edges are lightly browned.

7. Remove cookie sheet from the oven. Using a metal spatula, remove cookies from the sheet and place on a wire cooling rack. Cool completely. Store in an airtight container.

YIELD: 30 2½-INCH COOKIES

STAINED GLASS WINDOWS

These cookies are our basic sugar cookie gone Hollywood.
Simply use a tiny cutter to cut out shapes from inside the cookie.
Fill these shapes with crushed hard candies in various colors. As they bake,
they become translucent. They're a fun project for holiday baking with
the kids. Be sure to roll these a bit thinner than sugar cookies.

1 RECIPE VANILLA SUGAR COOKIE
DOUGH (SEE PAGE 70)

ABOUT 4 OUNCES ASSORTED HARD
CANDIES

VARIOUS COOKIE CUTTERS IN
DIFFERENT SHAPES AND SIZES

1. Prepare vanilla sugar cookie dough. Refrigerate overnight.

2. Preheat oven to 375°F.

3. In a food processor, pulse hard candy into small crystals (like coarse salt). Chop each color separately. Set aside.

4. On a lightly floured surface, roll dough out to ⅛-inch thick. Using a 3-inch cutter, cut dough into rounds. Place on a parchment-lined cookie sheet. Using smaller cutters in various patterns, cut shapes out of dough circles. Re-roll and cut scraps of dough until dough is finished.

5. Using a small spoon, fill cut-out shapes with crushed candy.

6. Bake 10 to 12 minutes or until edges are lightly browned.

7. Remove cookie sheet from the oven. Cool cookies completely on parchment sheet. Store in an airtight container.

YIELD: 36 3-INCH COOKIES

BLACK AND WHITE COOKIES

This bakery classic is a basic sugar cookie is frosted half with vanilla icing
and half with chocolate icing. Popular since the nineteen forties,
it was recently immortalized in a Seinfeld episode that focused
on race relations and how we could all get along.
"Look to the cookie. . . ." This version uses a tasty icing and a
rich chocolate ganache to coat the cookies.

1 RECIPE VANILLA SUGAR COOKIE
(SEE PAGE 70)

½ RECIPE COOKIE DECORATING
FROSTING (SEE PAGE 000)

1 RECIPE CHOCOLATE GANACHE

1. Prepare dough and bake as described on page 70 for basic vanilla sugar cookies.
   Cut dough into 2½-inch circles. Bake and cool.

2. Using a small spatula or butter knife, spread chocolate ganache onto half of the
   cookie. Refrigerate until set. Frost other half of cookie with cookie decorating
   icing. Let cookies dry at room temperature. Store in an airtight container.

YIELD: 30 2½-INCH COOKIES

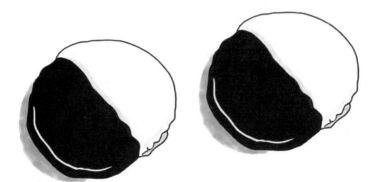

BUTTER COOKIES

These classic buttery cookies are a specialty in many bakeries, including Sweet Maria's. You can dress them up with a cherry or walnut half before baking, or dip them in melted chocolate after they're baked.

1/2 POUND BUTTER, SOFTENED

3/4 CUP SUGAR

1 EGG

1 TEASPOON VANILLA EXTRACT

2 1/2 CUPS FLOUR

1/2 TEASPOON BAKING POWDER

PINCH OF SALT

GLACÉ CHERRY HALVES, OPTIONAL

1. Preheat oven to 350°F.

2. In an electric mixer, cream the butter and sugar until really fluffy, 3 to 4 minutes. Add egg and vanilla. Mix until well blended.

3. On low speed, add flour, baking powder, and salt. Mix just until blended. Overmixing the dough will make it tough to squeeze from a pastry bag.

4. Fill a pastry bag with a large open star tip with the cookie dough. Pipe cookies onto a parchment-lined cookie sheet, spacing them 2 inches apart. If desired, place a cherry half in the center of each cookie before baking.

5. Bake 10 to 15 minutes, or until edges begin to brown.

6. Remove cookie sheet from the oven. Using a metal spatula, lift cookies off the cookie sheet and onto wire cooling racks. Cool completely. Store cookies in an airtight container.

YIELD: 40 COOKIES

Variation: Chocolate Butter Cookies

Add ½ cup cocoa when adding flour. Reduce flour to 2 cups.

> If you don't want to use a pastry bag to form cookies, you can use the following method:
>
> 1. Break off a piece of dough and roll it into a 1-inch ball. If the dough is sticky, lightly dust your fingers with flour.
> 2. Place balls on a parchment-lined cookie sheet, spacing them 2 inches apart. Press the tops of the balls to flatten.
> 3. Decorate the tops of the cookies using a fork in a criss-cross fashion. Or place a nut half or cherry in the center and bake as directed.

LEMON COCONUT MACAROONS

This lemon variation of the classic coconut macaroon has just the right amount of zip. Because they're a bit gooey, be sure to cool the cookies completely on parchment paper before removing.

3 CUPS COCONUT

2/3 CUP SWEETENED CONDENSED MILK

GRATED RIND OF 1 LEMON

GRATED JUICE OF 1 LEMON

2 EGG WHITES

1. Preheat oven to 350°F.

2. In a medium bowl combine coconut, condensed milk, rind, and juice of one lemon. With a wooden spoon, mix until blended.

3. In an electric mixer, beat egg whites until stiff. Fold into coconut mixture. Drop dough from a teaspoon onto a parchment-lined cookie sheet, spacing each 2 inches apart.

4. Bake 10 to 12 minutes or until lightly browned.

5. Remove cookie sheet from the oven. Place cookie sheet on a wire cooling rack. Cool cookies completely on parchment. Do not remove until completely cool. Store in an airtight container.

YIELD: 36 COOKIES

RASPBERRY PINWHEELS

*These refrigerator cookies have a spiral swirl of raspberry.
Rolling out the dough between 2 sheets of plastic wrap makes it
much easier to create the spiral effect. After making the "jelly roll" log,
just chill, slice, and bake. This is also the perfect cookie to make ahead.
Simply freeze cylinders of dough, and take them out of the freezer
and slice and bake whenever you want fresh cookies.*

½ POUND BUTTER, SOFTENED

1 CUP SUGAR

2 EGG YOLKS

2½ CUPS FLOUR

1 TEASPOON BAKING POWDER

¼ TEASPOON SALT

¼ CUP RASPBERRY JELLY

1. In an electric mixer, cream butter and sugar until light. Add egg yolks. Mix until well blended. On low speed, add 2¼ cups of the flour, baking powder, and salt. Mix just until blended. Dough should be stiff, not sticky.

2. Divide dough in half. Return half of dough to the mixer. On low speed, add raspberry jelly and remaining ¼ cup of flour. Mix until uniform in color.

3. Between 2 sheets of plastic, roll raspberry dough into a rectangle about 16 × 5 inches and ¼ inch thick. Remove plastic from top of dough.

4. Roll white dough the same way, to the same size, and remove plastic from top of dough. Using a pastry brush, wet the top of the raspberry dough with water. Carefully lay the white dough on top of the raspberry dough. Remove the plastic wrap from the top of the white dough. Using the plastic wrap underneath as a guide, roll the cookies lengthwise, jellyroll fashion. Cover the entire roll with plastic wrap and place seam side down on a cookie sheet. Refrigerate until firm, 2 to 3 hours or overnight.

5. Preheat oven to 375°F.

6. Remove cookie roll from the refrigerator. Using a sharp, straight knife, slice cookies into ¼-inch-thick slices. Place slices on a parchment-lined cookie sheet, spacing each 2 inches apart.

7. Bake 12 to 15 minutes or until edges begin to brown.

8. Remove cookie sheet from the oven. Using a metal spatula, remove cookies from the cookie sheet and place on a wire cooling rack. Cool completely.

YIELD: 40 COOKIES

♦ HOW TO ROLL BETWEEN SHEETS OF PLASTIC WRAP ♦

COOKIES LIKE RASPBERRY PINWHEELS AND FIG SWIRLS ARE EASY TO MANEUVER IF YOU ROLL THE DOUGH BETWEEN 2 SHEETS OF PLASTIC WRAP. PLACE DOUGH BETWEEN 2 SHEETS OF WRAP AND ROLL WITH A ROLLING PIN FROM THE CENTER OUT TO THE EDGES. FILL AND ASSEMBLE AS RECIPE DIRECTS. USING THE BOTTOM PIECE OF WRAP AS A GUIDE, ROLL DOUGH UP TIGHTLY, JELLYROLL FASHION.

CHOCOLATE ESPRESSO CHECKERBOARDS

This version of another bakery classic combines two of my favorite flavors, coffee and chocolate. The dough is just about the same as the raspberry pinwheels, but these cookies have a flavor and style all their own.

½ POUND BUTTER, SOFTENED

1 CUP SUGAR

2 EGG YOLKS

2¼ CUPS FLOUR

1 TEASPOON BAKING POWDER

¼ TEASPOON SALT

½ CUP CHOCOLATE CHIPS, MELTED

3 TEASPOONS INSTANT ESPRESSO POWDER

1. In an electric mixer, cream butter and sugar until light. Add egg yolks. Mix until well blended. On low speed, add flour, baking powder, and salt. Mix just until blended. Divide dough into 2 pieces, one slightly bigger than the other. In the smaller piece, mix in melted chocolate and instant espresso until well blended.

2. Divide white dough into 5 equal pieces. Roll each piece into a cylinder about 10 inches long. Flatten top and sides to form a square-sided rope, about ½ inch thick.

3. Divide chocolate dough into 4 equal pieces. Roll and shape these pieces the same as the white dough.

4. Stack the dough rectangles onto a piece of parchment paper. Arrange them white, chocolate, white, next to each other. Place remaining rectangles on top of these, alternating colors and stacking 3 rectangles high. Moisten each piece with water to adhere. Wrap entire cube of dough in plastic wrap and refrigerate until firm, 2 to 3 hours or overnight.

5. Preheat oven to 375°F.

6. Remove dough from the refrigerator. Using a sharp straight knife, cut the dough into ¼-inch-thick slices. Place slices on a parchment-lined cookie sheet, spacing each 2 inches apart.

7. Bake 12 to 15 minutes, or until edges just begin to brown.

8. Remove cookie sheet from the oven. Using a metal spatula, remove cookies from the cookie sheet and place them on a wire cooling rack. Cool completely. Store cookies in an airtight container.

YIELD: 24 COOKIES

RUM BALLS

*These no-bake cookies are based on an old bakery favorite that used stale
cake crumbs instead of graham cracker crumbs. You can use any type
of rum or any liqueur as long as it is high quality. These
cookies are potent—so adults only, please!*

2½ CUPS GRAHAM CRACKER CRUMBS

1 CUP CONFECTIONERS' SUGAR

½ CUP COCOA

½ CUP GLACÉ CHERRIES

½ CUP RAISINS

½ CUP WALNUTS, FINELY CHOPPED

½ CUP DARK RUM

¼ CUP CORN SYRUP

ADDITIONAL CONFECTIONERS' SUGAR
FOR COATING COOKIES

1. In a large mixing bowl, combine graham cracker crumbs, confectioners' sugar, cocoa, glacé cherries, raisins, and walnuts. Mix with a wooden spoon. Add rum and corn syrup. Mix until well blended.

2. Roll dough into 1-inch balls. Dough may be sticky to roll. Dip hands in water for easier rolling. Roll balls in confectioners' sugar.

3. Place on parchment-lined cookie sheet or plate. Refrigerate until serving.

4. Store in an airtight container in the refrigerator. Serve chilled.

YIELD: 45

SOUR CREAM CUTOUTS

We bake these cookies for just about every holiday: trees and bells for Christmas, hearts for Valentine's Day, and flags for Flag Day. The sour cream and lemon combine for a great flavor and moisture. You can use butter instead of margarine, but it will be harder to roll out, especially when chilled.

1 1/2 STICKS MARGARINE, SOFTENED	1/2 TEASPOON LEMON EXTRACT
3/4 CUP SUGAR	1/4 CUP SOUR CREAM
1 EGG	3 CUPS FLOUR
1/2 TEASPOON VANILLA EXTRACT	2 TEASPOONS BAKING POWDER

1. In an electric mixer, on medium speed, cream margarine and sugar until light. Add egg, vanilla, and lemon extract. Mix until well blended. Add sour cream. Mix well.

2. On low speed, add flour and baking powder. Mix just until blended.

3. Wrap dough in plastic wrap and refrigerate overnight.

4. Preheat oven to 350°F.

5. Divide dough in half. Keep other half in refrigerator. Roll dough to 1/4 inch thick. Cut into desired shapes. Repeat with other half of the dough. Save scraps for the end and re-roll until all dough is used.

6. Place cookies onto a parchment-lined cookie sheet, spacing each 2 inches apart.

7. Bake 10 to 12 minutes or until firm and edges are just browned.

8. Remove cookie sheet from the oven. Using a metal spatula, remove cookies from the sheet and place on a wire cooling rack. Cool completely.

9. Frost and decorate as desired.

YIELD: 30 3-INCH DAISY COOKIES

HOW TO DECORATE SOUR CREAM CUTOUTS

There are several ways to decorate sour cream cutouts, depending on what type of look you'd like, and how much time you can spend decorating. The sky is the limit for your own creativity for decorating these cookies. Here are a couple of methods:

WATER WASH AND COLORED SUGARS

The simplest way to decorate cutout cookies is to brush the tops with water, and sprinkle with colored sugars. This should be done before baking.

You can also add food coloring right to the dough for an extra burst of color. You can also marble the dough by adding food color and not blending the color totally together. This will give the cookies an interesting design and texture.

FROSTED COOKIES

To frost these cutouts we use cookie decorating frosting (see page 000). To get a smooth finish on cookies, add a bit of water to the icing so it spreads smoothly. Let cookies dry completely before piping on designs or monograms, especially if you are using another color. The colors may bleed if the base color is not completely dry.

HAND-PAINTED COOKIES

This method of decorating gives the cookies a hand-painted watercolor style. After baking, frost cookies with cookie decorating frosting (see page 00). Let cookies dry completely. Using a clean paint brush and food coloring, paint desired designs. I prefer to use paste food coloring. I will take a bit of color from the jar and place it on a small piece of aluminum foil. This will be my palette. Dip your paintbrush in water to get a lighter shade of the color you are using. You can also mix colors on this aluminum foil palette. We use this technique for springtime cookies. Frost a 4-inch round cookie with white icing. Let dry. Paint on bright yellow or red tulips with stems and leaves. For summer, we paint bright sunflowers or daisies.

PIPING FROSTING ONTO COOKIES

You can decorate cutout cookies with a pastry bag, too. We use this technique for daisies, sunflowers, and poinsettia cookies. All these flowers use the same petal flower cookie cutter, about 3" diameter. The frosting will need to be a little stiffer to hold the design you're piping. Bake cookies shaped with a daisy-type petal flower cutter. Pipe petals from the center to the edge with tip #32 for daisies, tip #67 for sunflowers, and tip #352 for poinsettias. With tip #32 for daisies, pipe a different color center into the middle of the cookie (brown for sunflower center). Use tip #3 in yellow for poinsettias. Let cookies dry completely.

You can also frost cookies, then pipe on monograms, or pipe on sports logos or college logos. These personal types of cookies make ideal favors for weddings or showers. I've done dresses and wedding cake cookies for these occasions, as well as tropical fish, ladybugs, and farm animals.

LEMON POPPY BARS

These bars have a zesty lemon topping and a tender, buttery crust. You can either grease the baking pan or line it with aluminum foil for easy removal.

CRUST:

1/4 POUND BUTTER, SOFTENED

1/2 CUP CONFECTIONERS' SUGAR

1 CUP FLOUR

1 TABLESPOON POPPY SEEDS

FILLING:

2 EGGS

1 CUP SUGAR

JUICE OF 1 LEMON

GRATED RIND OF 1 LEMON

1/2 TEASPOON BAKING POWDER

1 TABLESPOON FLOUR

CONFECTIONERS' SUGAR FOR DUSTING

1. Preheat oven to 350°F.

2. In an electric mixer, cream butter and confectioners' sugar until light. On low speed, add flour and poppy seeds. Mix just until blended.

3. Press crust into a greased 8 × 8 × 2-inch baking pan.

4. Bake 8 to 10 minutes or until edges begin to brown. Remove pan from the oven.

5. With a wire whisk, mix eggs and sugar until light. Add lemon juice, lemon rind, baking powder, and flour. Mix until smooth.

6. Pour filling over crust. Bake 10 to 12 minutes or until lightly browned and the center is set.

7. Remove pan from the oven. Cool completely in pan on wire cooling rack. Dust with confectioners' sugar. Cover pan with plastic wrap and refrigerate. Cut into squares as needed.

8. Store unused bars in the refrigerator.

YIELD: 20 SQUARES.

CLASSIC GINGERSNAPS

Gingersnaps are always in season. This recipe is the best I've ever tried, a family secret shared by my friend Betsy. Be sure to bake the cookies until evenly browned to get that gingersnap "snap." If they're undercooked, they'll still be tasty but chewy. Be sure to space them 3 inches apart because they will spread during baking.

2/3 CUP VEGETABLE OIL

1 CUP SUGAR

1 EGG

1/3 CUP MOLASSES

1 1/2 TO 1 3/4 CUPS FLOUR

1 TEASPOON CINNAMON

1 TEASPOON GINGER

1 TEASPOON SALT

2 TEASPOONS BAKING SODA

1 TEASPOON CREAM OF TARTAR

ADDITIONAL SUGAR FOR COATING COOKIES

1. Preheat oven to 350°F.

2. In an electric mixer on medium speed, beat oil and sugar. Add egg and molasses. Beat until well mixed.

3. On low speed, add flour, cinnamon, ginger, salt, baking soda, and cream of tartar. Mix just until blended.

4. Roll dough into 1-inch balls. Roll in additional sugar. Place onto a parchment-lined cookie sheet, spacing each 3 inches apart.

5. Bake 12 to 15 minutes or until well browned.

6. Remove cookie sheet from oven. Using a metal spatula, remove cookies from sheet and place on a wire cooling rack. Cool completely. Store cookies in an airtight container.

YIELD: ABOUT 30 COOKIES

PECAN SANDIES

These cookies have a truly nostalgic bakery taste. The sugar gives them their sandy texture, with just the right amount of crunch. They're easy to bake and can be made with any nut you like.

1 CUP SHORTENING	1 ½ CUPS FLOUR
1 CUP SUGAR	1 TEASPOON SALT
1 TEASPOON VANILLA EXTRACT	1 TEASPOON BAKING SODA
1 EGG	1 CUP PECANS, CHOPPED

1. In an electric mixer, cream shortening and sugar. Add vanilla and egg. Mix until well blended.

2. On low speed, add flour, salt, and baking soda. Stir in nuts.

3. Divide dough into 3 equal pieces. On a lightly floured surface, roll dough into cylinders about 12 to 14 inches long. Wrap in plastic wrap and refrigerate 2 to 3 hours or overnight.

4. Preheat oven to 350°F.

5. Remove dough from the refrigerator. Cut into ¼-inch-thick slices and place on a parchment-lined cookie sheet, spacing each 2 inches apart.

6. Bake 10 to 12 minutes or until golden brown.

7. Remove cookie sheet from the oven. Using a metal spatula, remove cookies from the cookie sheet and place on a wire cooling rack. Cool completely.

8. Store cookies in an airtight container at room temperature.

YIELD: 50 COOKIES

FIG SWIRLS

These fig-filled cookies are always a favorite.
The technique is similar to the one used for Raspberry Pinwheels.
Rolling the dough between two sheets of plastic wrap really
helps to maneuver the dough into a log.

CRUST:

1/4 POUND BUTTER, SOFTENED

1 CUP SUGAR

1 EGG

1 1/2 CUPS FLOUR

1/2 TEASPOON SALT

1/2 TEASPOON BAKING SODA

FILLING:

1/2 POUND DRIED FIGS

1/4 CUP SUGAR

1/4 CUP WATER

1/2 CUP WALNUTS, CHOPPED

1. Prepare crust. In an electric mixer, cream butter and sugar until light. Add egg. Mix until well blended. On low speed, gradually add flour, salt, and baking soda. Mix just until blended. Divide dough in half. Wrap in plastic wrap and refrigerate overnight.

2. Prepare filling. Combine all ingredients in a food processor. Pulse for 15 to 20 seconds or just until blended. Set aside.

3. Between two sheets of plastic wrap, roll out half the dough into a rectangle about 16 × 4 inches. Spread half the filling over the dough, leaving about 1/4 inch all along the edges. Roll lengthwise, jellyroll fashion, using the plastic to help you roll. Place on a parchment-lined cookie sheet. Repeat with other half of dough and filling. Cover completely with plastic wrap and refrigerate 3 to 4 hours or overnight.

4. Preheat oven to 350°F. Remove plastic wrap. Slice dough into 1/4-inch slices and place cut side up onto a parchment-lined cookie sheet.

5. Bake 10 to 12 minutes or until lightly browned.

6. Remove cookie sheet from the oven. Using a metal spatula, remove cookies from the cookie sheet and place on a wire cooling rack. Cool completely. Store cookies in an airtight container at room temperature.

YIELD: 50 COOKIES

◆ COOKIE JARS ◆

WHEN I WAS GROWING UP, WE HAD QUITE A VARIETY OF COOKIE JARS, FROM PLAIN CANISTERS TO A LARGE GREEN PEAR. MY FAVORITE WAS A BRIGHT YELLOW SMILEY FACE, THE ULTIMATE SYMBOL OF HAPPINESS FROM THE 1970S. MANY PEOPLE COLLECT COOKIE JARS, AND SOME ARE NOW WORTH A LOT OF MONEY. MY APPROACH TO COOKIE JAR COLLECTING IS TO LET PERSONAL TASTE AND STYLE BE MY GUIDE.

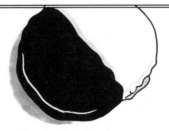

VANILLA SANDWICHES

These classic sandwich cookies are like a homemade vanilla Oreo.
They are a nostalgic treat that can very easily be made at
home. For a lemon filling variation, add the grated
rind and juice of one lemon to the filling.

DOUGH:

½ CUP SHORTENING

¼ POUND BUTTER, SOFTENED

1 CUP SUGAR

1 EGG YOLK

1 TEASPOON VANILLA EXTRACT

1¾ CUPS FLOUR

PINCH OF SALT

FILLING:

4 CUPS CONFECTIONERS' SUGAR

6 TABLESPOONS BUTTER, MELTED AND COOLED

2 TEASPOON VANILLA

6 TABLESPOONS HEAVY CREAM

1. Prepare dough. In an electric mixer, on medium speed, cream shortening and butter until well blended. Add sugar and mix until light. Add egg yolk and vanilla. Mix until blended.

2. On low speed, add flour and salt. Mix just until blended. Divide dough into two equal pieces. Wrap in plastic wrap. Refrigerate overnight.

3. Preheat oven to 350°F. Remove dough from the refrigerator. Roll dough out onto a lightly floured surface. Roll very thin, about ⅛ inch thick. Using a 2-inch round cookie cutter, cut dough into rounds. Place on a parchment-lined cookie sheet, spacing each 2 inches apart. Using a fork, prick holes in the center of the cookies. Repeat rolling and cutting remaining dough, re-rolling all the scraps at the end.

4. Bake 10 to 12 minutes or until edges just begin to brown.

5. Remove cookie sheet from the oven. Using a metal spatula, remove cookies from the cookie sheet and place on a wire cooling rack. Cool completely.

6. Prepare filling. In an electric mixer, combine confectioners' sugar, butter, vanilla, and heavy cream. Mix until well blended and smooth.

7. Assemble sandwiches. Pair off cookies to matching pairs. Using a butter knife or small spatula, spread a generous amount of frosting on the underside of one cookie. Press another matching cookie firmly together to form sandwich.

8. Continue to fill all cookies. Let dry. Store unused cookies at room temperature in an airtight container.

YIELD: 40 COOKIES

HONEY CINNAMON COOKIES

*These are hearty sugar cookies topped with cinnamon and sugar.
The honey in the dough really adds another depth of
flavor to this seemingly simple cookie.*

¾ CUP SHORTENING

½ CUP SUGAR

1 EGG

½ CUP HONEY

2¼ CUPS FLOUR

TOPPING:

3 TABLESPOONS SUGAR

2 TEASPOONS CINNAMON

½ CUP WALNUTS, FINELY CHOPPED

1. In an electric mixer, cream shortening and sugar until light. Add egg and honey. Mix until well blended. On low speed, add flour. Mix just until blended. Wrap dough in plastic wrap and refrigerate overnight.

2. Preheat oven to 350°F.

3. In a small bowl, combine sugar, cinnamon, and walnuts. Set aside.

4. Using a rolling pin, roll dough out onto a lightly floured surface, about ¼ inch thick. Using a 3-inch round cookie cutter, cut dough into circles. Place on a parchment-lined cookie sheet, spacing each 2 inches apart. Brush the tops of the cookie with water. Sprinkle generously with topping.

5. Bake 10 to 12 minutes or until edges begin to brown.

6. Remove cookie sheet from the oven. Using a metal spatula, remove cookies from the cookie sheet and place on a wire cooling rack. Cool. Store cookies in an airtight container at room temperature.

YIELD: 20 COOKIES

STRAWBERRY JELL-O
LOLLIPOP COOKIES

*These cookies are like fruity shortbreads on a stick, and perfect fun for
kids to make and take for a lunchtime treat. You can use any
flavor Jell-O—that'll give you a variety of options
for flavor and color.*

¾ CUP BUTTER, SOFTENED

½ CUP SUGAR

2 EGGS

1 PACKAGE STRAWBERRY JELL-O

1 TEASPOON BAKING POWDER

2 CUPS FLOUR

¼ TEASPOON SALT

40 4-INCH LOLLIPOP STICKS

COARSE SUGAR

1. Preheat oven to 350°F.

2. In an electric mixer, cream the butter and the sugar until light. Add eggs. Mix until well blended.

3. On low speed, add Jell-O, flour, baking powder, and salt. Mix just until well blended. Roll dough into 1-inch balls. Place on a parchment-lined cookie sheet, spacing each 2 inches apart and leaving enough space between rows for half the length of the lollipop sticks. Use a cookie stamp or bottom of a juice glass to press cookies flat, to ¼ inch thick.

4. Dip end of lollipop stick in water and insert halfway into the cookie. Lightly brush cookies with water and sprinkle on coarse sugar.

5. Bake 10 to 12 minutes or until edges begin to brown.

6. Remove cookie sheet from the oven. Using a metal spatula, remove cookies from the cookie sheet and place on a wire cooling rack. Cool completely. Wrap top cookie portion only in cellophane or colored plastic wrap. Tie tightly around the neck with a colorful ribbon.

YIELD: 40 COOKIE LOLLIPOPS

BANANA DATE NUT NEWTONS

These filled cookie rolls have a rich combination of flavors.
They're a perfect treat for any occasion and
look fantastic on cookie trays.

CRUST:

1/4 POUND BUTTER, SOFTENED

1 CUP SUGAR

2 EGGS

2 1/2 CUPS FLOUR

1/4 TEASPOON BAKING SODA

PINCH OF SALT

FILLING:

2 RIPE BANANAS

1/2 CUP SUGAR

8 OUNCES DATES, CHOPPED

1/2 CUP FLOUR

1 CUP WALNUTS

1. Prepare crust. In an electric mixer, on medium speed, cream butter and sugar until light. Add eggs. Mix until well blended. On low speed, add 2 cups flour, baking soda, and salt. Mix just until blended.

2. Turn dough out onto a lightly floured surface. Knead in remaining 1/2 cup of flour to make dough soft, but not sticky. Divide dough in half. Wrap in plastic wrap and refrigerate 4 to 5 hours or overnight.

3. Preheat oven to 350°F.

4. In a food processor, combine all filling ingredients. Pulse until almost smooth. Refrigerate filling while rolling out the crust.

5. Roll half of the dough out onto a lightly floured surface. Roll into a rectangle measuring approximately 16 × 8 inches. Cut dough into two strips measuring 16 × 4 inches. Working with one strip at a time, spoon one-quarter of the filling down the middle of the dough lengthwise (see illustration). Fold both sides over to seal.

6. Place on a parchment-lined cookie sheet, seam side down. Refrigerate 20 to 30 minutes. Remove filled cookies from the refrigerator. Cut into 1/4-inch strips.

7. Place on a parchment-lined cookie sheet, spacing each 2 inches apart. Be sure to place the seam side down. Repeat with other half of dough.

8. Bake 12 to 15 minutes or until lightly browned.

9. Remove cookie sheet from the oven. Using a metal spatula, remove cookies from the cookie sheet and place on a wire cooling rack. Cool completely.

YIELD: 36–40 COOKIES

◆ **COOKIE NAMES** ◆

I LOVE COOKIE NAMES. SO MANY OF THEM REFLECT WHAT THE COOKIE IS ALL ABOUT. THE NAMES CHEWIES, CRUNCHIES, BROWNIES, AND SANDIES REALLY DESCRIBE THE COOKIES' TEXTURES. OTHER NAMES SUCH AS DROPS, SQUARES, AND CUTOUTS ARE NAMED FOR THE TECHNIQUES USED TO MAKE THEM. COOKIE NAMES SUCH AS SNICKERDOODLES AND NEWTONS ARE STILL QUITE MYSTERIOUS.

HERMITS

*These hearty cookies were a specialty of the first bakery I
worked in, Rita's, and this recipe uses the same style, resulting in
Hermits that have a great combination of spice, nuts, and raisins.
The dough is flattened on the cookie sheet in strips,
baked, and then cut into 3-inch cookies.*

*Hermits are a New England specialty. The name refers
to leaving these cookies alone to let their spices
blend and age before eating.*

¼ POUND BUTTER, SOFTENED	1½ TEASPOONS BAKING SODA
1 CUP SUGAR	½ TEASPOON SALT
1 EGG	1½ CUPS RAISINS
⅓ CUP MOLASSES	½ CUP WALNUTS, FINELY CHOPPED
½ CUP MILK	
3 CUPS FLOUR	1 EGG FOR EGG WASH
2 TEASPOONS CINNAMON	ADDITIONAL SUGAR FOR DUSTING
1½ TEASPOONS GINGER	

1. In an electric mixer, cream butter and sugar until light. Add egg, molasses, and milk. Mix until well blended.

2. On low speed, add flour, cinnamon, ginger, baking soda, and salt. Mix just until blended. Stir in raisins and walnuts.

3. Divide dough into quarters. Wrap in plastic wrap and refrigerate dough 2 to 3 hours or overnight.

4. Preheat oven to 350°F.

5. Roll each piece of dough into a cylinder the length of a cookie sheet. Press dough into a strip 3 inches wide and ¼ inch thick on a parchment-lined cookie sheet. Space each strip 2 inches apart.

6. In a small bowl, beat egg. Using a pastry brush, brush each strip with egg and sprinkle with additional sugar.

7. Bake 15 to 20 minutes or until dark brown.

8. Remove cookie sheet from the oven. While cookies are still hot, cut into 3-inch pieces. Cool cookies on parchment. Cool completely.

9. Store cookies in an airtight container at room temperature.

YIELD: 24 COOKIES

CAPPUCCINO DROPS

*These cookies deliver a great combination of coffee
and cinnamon. They're easy to make and are a perfect
companion to a cup of hot coffee and a good book.*

½ POUND BUTTER, SOFTENED

1¼ CUPS SUGAR

3 TEASPOONS INSTANT ESPRESSO
POWDER

2 EGGS

1 TABLESPOON COFFEE LIQUEUR

2¼ CUPS FLOUR

1 TEASPOON CINNAMON

1 TEASPOON BAKING SODA

½ TEASPOON SALT

1. Preheat oven to 350°F.

2. In an electric mixer, cream butter and sugar until light. Add espresso powder, eggs, and coffee liqueur. Mix until well blended.

3. On low speed, add flour, cinnamon, baking soda, and salt. Mix just until well blended.

4. Drop dough from a teaspoon onto a parchment-lined cookie sheet, spacing each 2 inches apart.

5. Bake 10 to 12 minutes or until lightly browned.

6. Remove cookie sheet from the oven. Using a metal spatula, remove cookies and place on a wire cooling rack. Cool completely. Store cookies at room temperature in an airtight container.

YIELD: 50 COOKIES

PRUNE BARS

These delicious bars were a specialty of the first bakery
I worked in. They have a crumblike crust and
topping and a rich, flavorful center.

CRUST:

1 ½ CUPS FLOUR

1 ½ CUPS OATS

1 CUP BROWN SUGAR

1 TEASPOON BAKING SODA

1 ½ STICKS BUTTER, SOFTENED

FILLING:

12 OUNCES DRIED PRUNES

¼ CUP SUGAR

1 CUP WALNUTS, COARSELY CHOPPED

1. Preheat oven to 350°F.

2. Grease and flour or spray with nonstick baking spray a 13 × 9-inch baking pan. Set aside.

3. Prepare crust. In a medium bowl, combine flour, oats, brown sugar, and baking soda. Mix well. Add butter and cut in with a pastry cutter until mixture resembles coarse crumbs.

4. Press three-quarters of the mixture into the prepared pan. Set aside the rest of the crumb mixture.

5. Prepare filling. In a food processor, pulse prunes and sugar until coarse. Sprinkle mixture over the top of crust. Sprinkle walnuts over prune mixture. Top with remaining crumb mixture. Press the top gently.

6. Bake 25 to 30 minutes or until golden brown.

7. Remove pan from the oven. Place on a wire cooling rack. Cool in pan completely. Cover pan with plastic wrap. Store bars in pan at room temperature. Cut into squares as needed.

YIELD: 24 SQUARES

MINT SHORTBREADS

These are a special summertime refresher, although you can make them all year round if you have a supply of fresh mint. They are perfect served with your favorite ice cream (mine is chocolate).

1½ STICKS BUTTER, SOFTENED

1 CUP CONFECTIONERS' SUGAR

1⅓ CUPS FLOUR

3 TABLESPOONS CORNSTARCH

PINCH OF SALT

3 TABLESPOONS FRESH MINT, FINELY CHOPPED

ADDITIONAL SUGAR FOR SPRINKLING TOPS

1. Preheat oven to 350°F.

2. In an electric mixer, cream butter and confectioners' sugar until light. On low speed, add flour, cornstarch, salt, and mint. Mix just until blended.

3. Roll dough out onto a lightly floured surface. Roll to about a 10-inch square, about ⅛ inch thick. Using a sharp, straight knife, cut dough into 2-inch squares. Cut squares diagonally into triangles. Irregular shapes are okay.

4. Place cookies onto a parchment-lined cookie sheet, spacing each 2 inches apart. Sprinkle tops with granulated sugar.

5. Bake 10 to 12 minutes or until edges begin to brown.

6. Remove cookie sheet from the oven. Using a metal spatula, remove cookies from the cookie sheet and place on a wire cooling rack. Cool completely. Store cookies at room temperature in an airtight container.

YIELD: 30 COOKIES

BRASS CITY BARS

These cookies are named for my hometown, Waterbury, Connecticut, which was once the brass capital of the world. Waterbury today has all kinds of chips and we're all a little nuts to live here. But these bars, like the citizens here, are sweet and friendly. You can use any combination of chips in this recipe—in fact, it's a delicious way to make use of a variety of leftover chips.

CRUST:

1 CUP FLOUR

¾ CUP OATS

½ CUP SUGAR

½ TEASPOON BAKING SODA

¼ TEASPOON SALT

¼ POUND BUTTER, SOFTENED

FILLING:

½ CUP CARAMEL ICE CREAM TOPPING

½ CUP WALNUTS, CHOPPED

½ CUP PEANUT BUTTER CHIPS

½ CUP WHITE CHOCOLATE CHIPS

½ CUP CHOCOLATE CHIPS

1. Preheat oven to 350°F.

2. Prepare crust. In a food processor, combine flour, oats, sugar, baking soda, and salt. Add butter and pulse just until mixture resembles coarse crumbs. Reserve and set aside 1 cup of crust.

3. Grease an 8 × 8 × 2-inch baking pan. Press crumb mixture evenly into the bottom of the pan. Bake 10 to 12 minutes or until lightly browned.

4. Pour caramel topping over the hot crust. Evenly sprinkle nuts, peanut butter chips, white chocolate chips, and chocolate chips over the caramel. Sprinkle with remaining crust. Gently press together.

5. Bake 15 to 20 minutes or until lightly browned.

6. Remove pan from the oven. Place pan on a wire cooling rack. Cool completely. Cut into squares. Store unused cookies in an airtight container.

YIELD: 20 SQUARES

CHEESECAKE SQUARES

*These cheesecake bars can be flavored with a variety
of toppings. It's the perfect way to satisfy
a craving for cheesecake.*

CRUST:

1 ½ STICKS BUTTER, SOFTENED

½ CUP SUGAR

1 ½ CUPS FLOUR

FILLING:

8 OUNCES CREAM CHEESE

1 CUP SUGAR

¼ CUP FLOUR

4 EGGS

TOPPING:

½ CUP PINEAPPLE OR ANY FLAVOR
PRESERVE

1. Preheat oven to 350°F.

2. Prepare crust. In an electric mixer, cream butter and sugar until light. On low speed, add flour. Mix just until blended. Press dough into an ungreased 13 × 9-inch baking pan. Bake 12 to 15 minutes or until lightly browned. Remove from the oven.

3. Prepare filling. In an electric mixer, mix cream cheese and sugar until light and smooth. Add flour. Add eggs, one at a time, beating well after adding each one. Mix until smooth. Pour filling over hot crust.

4. Bake 20 to 25 minutes or until edges begin to brown and center is set.

5. Remove pan from the oven and place on a wire cooling rack. Cool completely.

6. Spread preserves evenly over filling. Refrigerate 2 to 3 hours or overnight. Cut into squares. Serve chilled. Store cookies in refrigerator.

YIELD: 24 SQUARES

ALMOND TRIANGLES

These bars are a star at Sweet Maria. The buttery crust is topped
with a sweet combination of almonds, sugar, and honey.
For easier cutting, refrigerate before slicing.

CRUST:

½ POUND BUTTER, SOFTENED

½ CUP SUGAR

1 EGG

2 CUPS FLOUR

TOPPING:

¼ POUND BUTTER

¼ CUP BROWN SUGAR

½ CUP HONEY

1½ CUPS SLICED ALMONDS

2 TABLESPOONS HEAVY CREAM

1. Preheat oven to 375°F.

2. Prepare crust. In an electric mixer, cream butter and sugar. Add egg. Mix well. On low speed, add flour and mix just until blended. Press dough into the bottom and slightly up the sides of a 14 × 10-inch greased jellyroll pan.

3. Bake 10 to 15 minutes or until lightly browned. Remove pan from the oven.

4. Prepare topping. In a medium saucepan on medium-high heat, combine butter, brown sugar, and honey. Stir often until butter melts, sugar dissolves, and mixture comes to a boil. Remove from the heat. Stir in almonds and heavy cream. Spread almond mixture on top of the crust.

5. Bake 10 to 12 minutes or until top begins to bubble and brown.

6. Remove pan from the oven. Place pan on a wire cooling rack. Cool cookies completely in pan. Refrigerate. Cut into squares. Cut squares in half, diagonally, to form triangles. Store cookies in refrigerator in an airtight container.

YIELD: 50 TRIANGLES

CHAPTER 4

CHOCOLATE COOKIES AND SIMPLE CANDIES

This chapter spotlights everyone's favorite flavor, chocolate. What flavor is better for comfort or indulgence than chocolate? Here you'll find some classics, like fudge brownies and toffee bars, as well as new creations, such as *Chocolat*-inspired chili pepper cookies and chocolate Nutella sandwiches. The cookie jar always empties quicker whenever chocolate cookies are the cookie of the day, and I hope you'll see why.

Most of the recipes in this collection use semi-sweet chocolate, milk chocolate, dark chocolate, or white chocolate. You can certainly substitute one for the other, depending on your personal preference. Chocolate is satisfying on its own or paired with great partners such as peanut butter, nuts, cherries, and orange.

A few of the recipes in this chapter are more like a candy than a cookie. Treats such as fudge and peanut butter balls are hard to classify. Whatever you call them, they are a delicious snack, and a perfect gift for that chocoholic in everyone.

FUDGE BROWNIES

Classic chocolate brownies are the ultimate treat with a glass of cold milk. These do not disappoint. Some people have trouble testing for the doneness of brownies. Using a cake tester or a toothpick, the center should have a slight crumb on it, not batter. Many consider this to be undercooked, but the brownie will continue to bake in the pan when removed from the oven.

¼ POUND BUTTER, SOFTENED	¾ CUP COCOA
2 CUPS SUGAR	1 CUP FLOUR
1 TEASPOON VANILLA EXTRACT	½ TEASPOON BAKING POWDER
4 EGGS	¼ TEASPOON SALT

1. Preheat oven to 350°F.

2. Grease a 13 × 9-inch baking pan. Set aside.

3. In an electric mixer, cream butter and sugar until light. Add vanilla. Add eggs one at a time, beating well after adding each one. Mix until well blended. On low speed, add cocoa, flour, baking powder, and salt. Beat until well blended. Pour batter into prepared pan. Using a metal spatula, spread batter evenly.

4. Bake 25 to 30 minutes or until batter begins to pull away from the sides. Check the center with a toothpick or cake tester. There should be a slight crumb, but it should not be wet in the middle.

5. Remove pan from the oven. Place on a wire cooling rack. Cool completely in pan. Cover pan with plastic wrap and store at room temperature. Cut into squares as needed or cut into squares and wrap individually in plastic wrap.

YIELD: 24 BROWNIES

TOFFEE BARS

*You can use any brand of toffee bars to make these delicious
and sweet bar cookies. The Sweet Maria staff is usually the first to
empty the cookie jar when these cookies are around!*

CRUST:

4 TABLESPOONS BUTTER, SOFTENED

½ CUP BROWN SUGAR

1 CUP FLOUR

FILLING:

¼ POUND BUTTER

¼ CUP BROWN SUGAR

1 CUP CRUSHED TOFFEE BARS

1. Preheat oven to 350°F.

2. In an electric mixer on low speed, mix butter, brown sugar, and flour. Mix until mixture resembles coarse crumbs.

3. Press crust mixture into an 8 × 8 × 2-inch baking dish.

4. In a medium saucepan, combine butter and brown sugar. Bring to a boil, stirring constantly. Pour over crust. Sprinkle with crushed toffee bars.

5. Bake 15 to 20 minutes or until lightly browned.

6. Remove pan from the oven. Cool cookies completely in pan on a wire cooling rack. Cover pan with plastic wrap and store at room temperature. Cut into squares as needed or cut into squares and wrap individually in plastic wrap.

YIELD: 20 SQUARES

CHOCOLATE NUTELLA SANDWICHES

These are grown-up double-chocolate sandwich cookies with an Italian accent. The filling is a popular Italian chocolate and hazelnut spread called Nutella. You can find it at most supermarkets and specialty food stores. These cookies are very tender, so be sure they're completely cool before assembling.

1/2 POUND BUTTER, SOFTENED

3/4 CUP SUGAR

1 1/4 CUPS FLOUR

1/2 CUP COCOA

FILLING:

1 CUP NUTELLA

1. Preheat oven to 350°F.

2. In an electric mixer, on medium speed, cream butter and sugar until light. On low speed, gradually add flour and cocoa. Mix just until well blended.

3. Roll dough into 1-inch balls. Place on a parchment-lined cookie sheet, spacing each 2 inches apart. If dough is sticky, dust your fingers with additional cocoa. Using a fork lightly dusted in cocoa, press tops of cookies to flatten.

4. Bake 12 to 15 minutes or until firm.

5. Remove cookie sheet from the oven. Using a metal spatula, remove cookies from the cookie sheet and place on a wire cooling rack. Cool completely.

6. To assemble, pair cookies of similar size tops and bottoms. Using a small metal spatula, spread some Nutella on the bottom of one cookie. Press another cookie, bottom first, to form a sandwich. Press together gently. Let dry on a wire cooling rack. Store at room temperatue.

YIELD: 14 2 1/2-INCH COOKIES

CHOCOLATE CHIP PECAN BLONDIES

Do these cookies have more fun? These pecan-packed bars are a not-so-chocolate alternative to brownies. Try them topped with your favorite ice cream and a drizzle of fudge sauce.

1½ STICKS BUTTER, SOFTENED	1¾ CUPS FLOUR
1½ CUPS BROWN SUGAR	1 TEASPOON BAKING POWDER
½ CUP SUGAR	PINCH OF SALT
2 EGGS	1 CUP CHOCOLATE CHIPS
1 TEASPOON VANILLA EXTRACT	1 CUP PECANS, COARSELY CHOPPED

1. Preheat oven to 350°F.

2. Grease a 13 × 9-inch pan. Set aside.

3. In an electric mixer, cream butter, brown sugar, and sugar until light. Add eggs and vanilla. Mix well.

4. On low speed, add flour, baking powder, and salt. Mix just until blended. Stir in chocolate chips and pecans.

5. Spread into prepared pan.

6. Bake 25 to 30 minutes. Check center with a cake tester or toothpick. There should be a slight crumb, but it should not be wet in the middle.

7. Remove pan from the oven. Place on a wire cooling rack. Cool completely in pan. Cover pan with plastic wrap and store at room temperature. Cut into squares as needed or cut into squares and wrap individually in plastic wrap.

YIELD: 24 SQUARES

CHOCOLATE ORANGE BISCOTTI

*The complementary flavors of chocolate and orange combine
to give these biscotti a rich and satisfying taste. Enjoy
them with a cup of cappuccino or hot chocolate.*

1/4 POUND BUTTER, SOFTENED	3 EGGS
3/4 CUP SUGAR	2 CUPS FLOUR
2 TEASPOONS INSTANT ESPRESSO POWDER	1/2 CUP COCOA
	3 TEASPOONS BAKING POWDER
GRATED RIND OF 1 ORANGE	PINCH OF SALT
JUICE OF 1 ORANGE	

1. Preheat oven to 375° F.

2. In an electric mixer, cream butter, sugar, and instant espresso powder.

3. Add rind, juice, and eggs. Mix until well blended.

4. On low speed, add flour, cocoa, baking powder, and salt. Mix until just blended.

5. Turn dough out onto a lightly floured surface. Divide dough into 3 equal portions. Roll dough into a cylinder. Place on a parchment-lined cookie sheet, spacing each 3 inches apart.

6. Bake 20 to 25 minutes or until firm.

7. Remove cookie sheet from the oven. Using two metal spatulas, carefully remove loaves from the hot cookie sheet onto wire cooling racks. Cool. Place cooled loaves on a cutting board. Using a sharp knife, slice the loaves diagonally into 1/2-inch-wide slices.

8. Place the slices on a cookie sheet in a single layer. Return to the oven for 12 to 15 minutes, or until lightly browned. Remove cookie sheet from the oven. Cool toasted biscotti on a wire cooling rack. Store in an airtight container.

YIELD: 24 BISCOTTI

CHOCOLATE ALMOND HEARTS

These sweet somethings are the perfect Valentine treat. Serve them plain, or dipped or drizzled in chocolate. You can enjoy them any time of the year, in any shape.

½ POUND MARGARINE, SOFTENED	½ CUP COCOA
1 CUP CONFECTIONERS' SUGAR	1½ CUPS FLOUR
2 TEASPOONS ALMOND EXTRACT	¼ TEASPOON SALT

1. In an electric mixer on medium speed, cream the margarine and confectioners' sugar until light. Add almond extract.

2. On low speed, add cocoa, flour, and salt. Mix just until well blended. Wrap dough in plastic wrap and refrigerate 2 to 3 hours or overnight.

3. Preheat oven to 350°F.

4. Roll out dough about ¼-inch thick onto a surface lightly dusted with cocoa. Using a 1½-inch heart-shaped cookie cutter, cut the dough into shapes. Place cookies onto a parchment-lined cookie sheet, spacing each 2 inches apart.

5. Bake 12 to 15 minutes or until firm.

6. Remove cookie sheet from the oven. Using a metal spatula, remove cookies from the cookie sheet and place onto a wire cooling rack. Cool completely.

7. Serve plain or dipped or drizzled with chocolate. Store cookies in an airtight container.

YIELD: 50 1½-INCH HEARTS

PEANUT BUTTER BALLS

This recipe is easily doubled or tripled if your family loves them as much as ours does. You may need to finesse the dough texture a bit. It should be firm enough to hold a round shape when rolled. Sometimes the butter or the kitchen itself will be too warm and this will cause the dough to be too soft to hold a firm round shape. If it is too warm, just add a bit more confectioners' sugar until you find the desired texture. If the dough is too dry to roll, add a bit of milk.

We always dip these in dark chocolate, but you can use milk, dark, or white chocolate to coat the treats. The fork drizzle after dipping gives the peanut butter balls a professional look.

4 TABLESPOONS BUTTER, SOFTENED	FOR DIPPING:
½ CUP SMOOTH PEANUT BUTTER	2 CUPS CHOCOLATE CHIPS
1 CUP CONFECTIONERS' SUGAR	1 TABLESPOON VEGETABLE SHORTENING

1. In an electric mixer, cream the butter and peanut butter until smooth. On low speed, add confectioners' sugar. Mix just until blended.

2. Roll dough into ½-inch balls. Place on a parchment-lined cookie sheet, spacing each 1 inch apart. Cover with plastic wrap and freeze overnight.

3. Over simmering water in a double boiler, melt chocolate chips and shortening.

4. Using a fork and spoon, dip peanut butter ball into melted chocolate. Drip off excess chocolate and place dipped ball bottom side down on a parchment-lined cookie sheet. Repeat with remaining balls.

5. Dip fork into melted chocolate. Shake fork back and forth over tops of dipped balls to drizzle. Let dry completely. Store refrigerated in an airtight container.

YIELD: 40 BALLS

AMARETTO CHEESECAKE BROWNIES

Amaretto liqueur and mascarpone cheese combine to give these brownies a touch of Italy. Buon appetito!

BROWNIE:

4 OUNCES CHOCOLATE CHIPS

¼ POUND BUTTER

3 EGGS

2 TEASPOONS AMARETTO

1 CUP SUGAR

¾ CUP FLOUR

TOPPING:

8 OUNCES MASCARPONE CHEESE, SOFTENED

½ CUP SUGAR

2 TEASPOONS AMARETTO

1 EGG

2 TABLESPOONS FLOUR

1. Preheat oven to 350°F.

2. Grease an 8 × 8 × 2-inch baking pan.

3. Over simmering water, or in microwave, melt chocolate chips and butter. Cool.

4. In an electric mixer, on medium speed, beat eggs, amaretto, and sugar. Add chocolate mixture. Mix until smooth. On low speed, add flour. Mix just until blended.

5. Prepare filling. In a another bowl, cream mascarpone and sugar. Add amaretto, egg, and flour. Mix just until blended.

6. Spread two-thirds of the brownie mixture into prepared pan. Pour filling on top of brownie mixture. Dot remaining brownie mixture on top of cheese mixture.

7. Bake 30 to 35 minutes.

8. Remove pan from the oven and place on a wire cooling rack. Cool completely. Refrigerate and cut into squares. Store bars in refrigerator.

YIELD: 20 SQUARES

SUSIE'S CHOCOLATE CHERRY BOMBS

My friend Susie is a fantastic baker. These are just one of her many chocolate specialties. Be sure to use pitted cherries, without stems.

25 WHOLE MARASCHINO CHERRIES, PLUS JUICE (16 OUNCES)

1/4 POUND MARGARINE, SOFTENED

1 CUP SUGAR

1 1/2 CUPS FLOUR

1/2 CUP COCOA

1/2 TEASPOON BAKING SODA

1/4 TEASPOON SALT

1 CUP CHOCOLATE CHIPS

COATING:

1 1/2 CUPS CHOCOLATE CHIPS

1 TABLESPOON SHORTENING

1. Preheat oven to 350°F.

2. Drain cherries and reserve juice. Blot cherries with a paper towel to dry thoroughly. Set aside cherries and juice.

3. In an electric mixer, cream margarine and sugar until light. Add 1/4 cup cherry juice. Mix until well blended.

4. On low speed, add flour, cocoa, baking soda, and salt. Mix just until blended. Stir in chocolate chips.

5. Break off a piece of dough, about a 1 1/2-inch ball. Flatten and insert cherry. Wrap dough around cherry. Roll into a ball about the size of a small golf ball. Be sure the cherry is completely covered. Place on a parchment-lined cookie sheet, spacing each about 2 inches apart.

6. Bake 15 to 20 minutes. Tops will crack. Using a metal spatula, remove cookies from the cookie sheet and place on a wire cooling rack. Cool completely.

7. Melt chocolate chips over simmering water or in microwave. Stir in 1 tablespoon shortening. Frost tops of cookies with chocolate mixture. Allow frosting to set at room temperature. Store in an airtight container.

YIELD: 25 COOKIES

CHOCOLATE CHIP PECAN PIE SQUARES

This gooey pie bar is almost too decadent to be called a cookie.
You can enjoy these bars served chilled, or slightly
warmed "à la mode" like pecan pie.

CRUST:

1½ STICKS BUTTER, SOFTENED

¼ CUP SUGAR

1 EGG

2 CUPS FLOUR

FILLING:

4 EGGS

1 CUP SUGAR

½ CUP LIGHT CORN SYRUP

3 TABLESPOONS BUTTER, MELTED

2 CUPS PECAN HALVES

1½ CUPS CHOCOLATE CHIPS

1. Preheat oven to 350°F.

2. Grease a 13 × 9-inch baking pan. Set aside.

3. Prepare crust. In an electric mixer, cream butter and sugar until light. Add egg. Mix well. On low speed, add flour. Mix just until blended. Press dough into prepared pan.

4. Bake 15 to 20 minutes or until lightly browned.

5. Prepare filling. In an electric mixer, beat eggs and sugar. Add corn syrup and butter. Mix well. Stir in pecans and chocolate chips. Pour filling over hot crust.

6. Bake 20 to 25 minutes, or until center is set.

7. Remove pan from the oven. Cool in pan on a wire cooling rack. Cut into squares. Serve with ice cream, if desired.

YIELD: 24 SQUARES

CHOCOLATE APRICOT OAT BARS

The flavor of these bars really comes to life when you toast the wheat germ first. Simply spread the wheat germ on a parchment-lined cookie sheet, and toast in the oven about 12 minutes or until lightly browned. Cool completely before using.

CRUST:

1 ½ CUPS OATS

1 CUP FLOUR

¾ CUP BROWN SUGAR

2 TABLESPOONS WHEAT GERM, TOASTED

¼ TEASPOON BAKING SODA

1 ½ STICKS BUTTER, SOFTENED

FILLING:

¾ CUP APRICOT PRESERVES

¾ CUP CHOCOLATE CHIPS

1. Preheat oven to 350°F.

2. Grease an 8 × 8 × 2-inch baking dish. Set aside.

3. In an electric mixer, combine oats, flour, brown sugar, wheat germ, and baking soda. Mix on low speed. Add butter. Continue to mix on low until mixture is crumbly.

4. Reserve 1 cup of the crumb mixture. Set aside.

5. Press remaining crumb mixture into prepared pan. Spread apricot preserves over the crust. Sprinkle chocolate chips over apricot preserves. Sprinkle with remaining crumb mixture. Press top gently.

6. Bake 20 to 25 minutes, or until golden brown.

7. Remove pan from the oven. Cool cookies in pan on a wire cooling rack. When completely cool, cut into squares. Store in an airtight container.

YIELD: 20 SQUARES

WHITE CHOCOLATE PISTACHIO BARS

These layered bars are an amazing combination of sweet and salty.
For easy cutting, refrigerate before cutting into squares.

¼ POUND BUTTER

1½ CUPS GRAHAM CRACKER CRUMBS

1½ CUPS COCONUT

1½ CUPS PISTACHIO NUTS

1½ CUPS WHITE CHOCOLATE CHIPS

14 OUNCES SWEETENED CONDENSED MILK

1. Preheat oven to 350°F.

2. Place butter in a 13 × 9-inch baking pan. Place pan in oven to melt butter, about 5 minutes. Remove pan from the oven.

3. Sprinkle graham cracker crumbs on top of melted butter. Spread evenly and press lightly.

4. Spread 1 cup of coconut over the graham cracker crumbs. Reserve ½ cup coconut. Set aside.

5. Sprinkle pistachios on top of coconut. Spread white chocolate chips over pistachios. Using a teaspoon, drizzle sweetened condensed milk over the white chocolate chips. Top with remaining coconut.

6. Bake 25 to 30 minutes or until evenly browned.

7. Remove pan from the oven. Cool pan on a wire cooling rack. Cool completely. Cut into squares and serve. Store in an airtight container.

YIELD: 24 SQUARES

CHOCOLATE BANANA BOURBON BARS

These moist bars are topped with a rich chocolate ganache topping. Chocolate and banana is a winning combination, especially in these bars.

1 1/2 STICKS BUTTER, SOFTENED	1 TEASPOON BAKING SODA
1 CUP SUGAR	1 TEASPOON BAKING POWDER
2 EGGS	1/4 TEASPOON SALT
1 CUP MASHED BANANAS (2 LARGE)	CHOCOLATE GANACHE TOPPING (PAGE 118)
2 TABLESPOONS BOURBON	
2 CUPS FLOUR	

1. Preheat oven to 350°F.

2. Grease a 13 × 9-inch baking pan. Set aside.

3. In an electric mixer, cream butter and sugar until light. Add eggs, bananas, and bourbon. Mix until well blended. On low speed, add flour, baking soda, baking powder, and salt. Mix just until blended. Spread batter evenly in prepared pan.

4. Bake 20 to 25 minutes. Check the center with a toothpick or cake tester. There should be a slight crumb, it should not be wet in the center.

5. Remove pan from the oven. Place pan on a wire cooling rack. Cool completely. Frost with chocolate ganache topping (see page 118). Store cookies in pan and cut into squares as needed.

YIELD: 24 SQUARES

CHOCOLATE GANACHE TOPPING

This frosting is perfect for all brownies.

1 CUP SEMISWEET CHOCOLATE CHIPS   1 TABLESPOON BUTTER
1/2 CUP HEAVY CREAM

1. In a food processor, pulse chips until finely ground. Place chocolate in a small mixing bowl.

2. In a small saucepan, heat the cream over medium heat. Stirring constantly, bring the cream to a boil. Pour hot cream over chocolate. Stir until chocolate is melted and color is uniform. Stir in butter. Stir until well blended.

3. Spread ganache evenly over the top of chocolate bourbon banana bars. Refrigerate to set. Cut into squares.

CHOCOLATE CHILI PEPPER COOKIES

These chocolate cookies have just a touch of heat, from adding chili powder to the dough. It is an old Mayan custom to combine chocolate with chili—and I was also inspired by the film Chocolat, *which is a chocolate lover's fantasy.*

½ POUND BUTTER, SOFTENED

½ CUP SUGAR

1 TEASPOON VANILLA EXTRACT

2 TEASPOONS CHILI POWDER

1½ CUPS FLOUR

⅓ CUP COCOA

1. Preheat oven to 350°F.

2. In an electric mixer on medium speed, cream butter and sugar until light. Add vanilla and chili powder. Mix until well blended.

3. On low speed add flour and cocoa. Mix just until blended.

4. Roll dough into 1-inch balls. If dough is sticky, dust your fingers lightly with cocoa. Place balls on a parchment-lined cookie sheet, spacing each 2 inches apart.

5. Bake 10 to 12 minutes or until firm.

6. Remove cookie sheet from the oven. Using a metal spatula, remove cookies from the cookie sheet and place on a wire cooling rack. Cool completely. Store cookies at room temperature in an airtight container.

YIELD: 24 COOKIES

RICH COFFEE TRUFFLES

*These rich little treats are full of the great combination of coffee
and chocolate. These are easy to make, a little bit messy, but ideal for
chocolate lovers everywhere. They can be served as part of
a dessert buffet or wrapped as a take-home treat. I use a small ice
cream scoop or melon baller to scoop out truffles to roll.*

1/2 CUP HEAVY CREAM

3 TABLESPOONS BUTTER

1 TABLESPOON LIGHT CORN SYRUP

1 1/2 CUPS CHOCOLATE CHIPS

2 TABLESPOONS COFFEE LIQUEUR

1 TEASPOON INSTANT ESPRESSO
POWDER

COCOA FOR COATING

1. In a small saucepan over low heat, combine heavy cream, butter, corn syrup, and chocolate. Heat over low heat, stirring constantly, until butter and chocolate melt and mixture is smooth. Remove from the heat.

2. Stir in coffee liqueur and espresso powder. Stir until blended. Transfer mixture to a bowl. Cover and refrigerate overnight.

3. Roll mixture into 1/2-inch balls. Roll in cocoa. Place on a parchment-lined tray or plate. If the mixture is sticky, dust your fingers with additional cocoa.

4. Cover truffles with plastic wrap. Refrigerate until serving.

YIELD: 40 TRUFFLES

TOASTED ALMOND WHITE CHOCOLATE TRUFFLES

These white chocolate treats are perfectly accented with toasted almonds and almond liqueur. The name "truffle" comes from the famous fungus with a similar shape—but all you'll think of is their sweet almond flavor when you eat them.

1 ½ CUPS WHITE CHOCOLATE CHIPS

½ CUP HEAVY CREAM

1 CUP ALMONDS, TOASTED AND FINELY CHOPPED

1 TABLESPOON ALMOND LIQUEUR

CONFECFIONERS' SUGAR FOR COATING

1. In a double boiler over simmering water, melt chocolate with heavy cream. Stir to blend well.

2. Remove from the heat. Stir in almonds and almond liqueur. Refrigerate until thick enough to roll into balls, about 3 to 4 hours.

3. Dust fingers with confectioners' sugar. Roll dough into ¾-inch balls. Roll in confectioners' sugar.

4. Place on a parchment-lined cookie sheet. Refrigerate until serving.

YIELD: 30 TRUFFLES

SANDY'S EASY FUDGE

This smooth fudge uses sweetened condensed milk for its sweetness and smoothness. It's an easy-to-make fudge, with no fussy candy thermometers necessary. My friend Sweet Sandy shared this family favorite.

2¼ CUPS CHOCOLATE CHIPS   PINCH OF SALT

1 CAN SWEETENED CONDENSED MILK   1 CUP WALNUTS, COARSELY CHOPPED

1 TEASPOON VANILLA EXTRACT

1. Grease an 8 × 8 × 2-inch baking dish. Set aside.

2. In a double boiler over low heat, melt chocolate chips. Stir constantly until smooth. Remove from the heat. Stir in sweetened condensed milk, vanilla, salt, and walnuts. Mix until blended.

3. Pour into prepared pan and spread evenly. Cover top of pan with plastic wrap and refrigerate until set. Cut into squares. Store fudge, covered, in refrigerator.

YIELD: 20 SQUARES

CHAPTER 5

HOLIDAY FAVORITES

The holidays are always a popular time for baking. No matter how crazy the holiday season may get, people always feel nostalgic for home-baked goods. Whether you're carrying on a family tradition or starting one of your own, baking cookies is a great way to spend time together and treat your family and friends to cookies. Today, when Milanos are made by robots, people will appreciate the time you'll spend creating and baking a special treat. Santa loves when cookies are left for him. Your loved ones will, too.

COOKIE SWAP OR EXCHANGE

You can get together with friends to bake cookies, or schedule a cookie swap or cookie exchange. Not only is this a great way to spend an afternoon or evening with friends, but it also allows you to sample a large variety of cookies—and you'll only have to bake one kind. This is how a swap works: Say you plan the event with ten friends. Each friend bakes 10 dozen of one type of cookie. At the swap, everyone takes one dozen of each type of cookie. Everyone leaves with 10 varieties of cookies. You can also include recipes for the cookies. People are choosing this option not only around the holidays, but before weddings and showers, too. This can also be a popular social event with refreshments and light sandwiches or hors d'oeuvres. I have friends that do an annual "mother-daughter" cookie swap that promotes baking and keeping up relationships. It is a good idea to ask participants what type of cookie they will be bringing. This can avoid having 2 or 3 of the same type of cookie.

GIFT-GIVING IDEAS

You can present a tray of cookies, festively wrapped and tied with a bow, as a great gift. You can also package cookies as gifts in baskets, ceramic planters, tool boxes, or handmade pottery. The container of the cookies can reflect the personality of the receiver. Plus, the recipient will have the plate, planter, or toolbox to reuse. A terrific gift!

SHIPPING COOKIES

The holidays are a good time to ship cookies to friends and relatives. Sturdy cookies work best. You should package the cookies in a tin with a tight-fitting lid. Place the tin in a sturdy crush-proof corrugated box. Cushion around the tin with crumpled newspaper and tissue paper. Ship the quickest method, either overnight or second-day service. Mark the box "perishable." This way the recipient will be sure to know to open it right away. This is especially important if they're not expecting a package of treats.

PUMPKIN PIE DROPS

*These moist drops are a perfect addition to your
Thanksgiving traditions. In fact, they'd be
welcome at any autumn gathering.*

½ POUND BUTTER, SOFTENED	1 TEASPOON BAKING SODA
1 CUP BROWN SUGAR	1 TEASPOON CINNAMON
1 EGG	¼ TEASPOON NUTMEG
1 CUP CANNED PUMPKIN	¼ TEASPOON CLOVES
2 CUPS FLOUR	CINNAMON CONFECTONER'S ICING (PAGE 126)

1. Preheat oven to 350°F.

2. In an electric mixer, on medium speed, cream butter and brown sugar until light. Add egg and pumpkin. Mix until well blended.

3. On low speed, add flour, baking soda, cinnamon, nutmeg, and cloves. Mix just until blended.

4. Drop dough from a teaspoon onto a parchment-lined cookie sheet, spacing each 2 inches apart.

5. Bake 10 to 12 minutes, or until firm.

6. Remove cookie sheet from the oven. Using a metal spatula, remove cookies from the cookie sheet and place on a wire cooling rack. Cool completely.

7. Frost with cinnamon confectioners' icing (see page 126). Place a wire cooling rack on top of a parchment-lined cookie sheet. This will catch any excess frosting and will make cleanup easier. Using a small spatula or butter knife, frost the top of the cookie. You don't have to frost the entire surface of the cookie. The frosting will naturally fall down the sides of the cookie.

8. Let frosting dry completely. Store in an airtight container at room temperature.

YIELD: 50 COOKIES

CINNAMON CONFECTIONERS' ICING

3 CUPS CONFECTIONERS' SUGAR   **¹/₂ CUP WATER**

1 TEASPOON CINNAMON

In an electric mixer, combine all ingredients. Mix until well blended and smooth.

GINGERBREAD COOKIES

*This versatile dough can be used to make cookies or gingerbread houses.
It is functional and delicious, especially for the holidays. At Sweet
Maria's we make an equal amount of ginger men and ginger
women. The women are always more fun to decorate,
with flowers in their hair and lacy skirts.*

½ POUND MARGARINE, SOFTENED	1½ TEASPOONS GINGER
1½ CUPS SUGAR	1½ TEASPOONS CINNAMON
2 EGGS	3 TEASPOONS BAKING SODA
½ CUP MOLASSES	3½ CUPS FLOUR

1. In an electric mixer, cream margarine and sugar until light. Add eggs and molasses. Mix until well blended. Add ginger, cinnamon, baking soda, and flour. Mix on low speed just until blended. Wrap dough in plastic and refrigerate overnight.

2. Preheat oven to 350°F.

3. Roll dough out onto a lightly floured surface, about ⅛-inch thick. Using a cookie cutter, cut dough into desired shapes. Place cookies onto a parchment-lined cookie sheet, spacing each about 2 inches apart.

4. Bake 8 to 10 minutes or until evenly browned.

5. Remove cookie sheet from the oven. Using a metal spatula, remove cookies from the cookie sheet and place on a wire cooling rack. Cool completely.

6. Decorate, if desired, with cookie decorating frosting (*see* page 000), using a pastry bag fitted with tip #5 (large writing tip). For small details, use tip #3.

YIELD: ABOUT 40 FLOWER COOKIES (3-INCH FLOWER CUTTER)
OR 20 GINGERPEOPLE (6 INCHES TALL)

COOKIE DECORATING FROSTING

This frosting is used to decorate gingerbread cookies, sour cream cutouts, and other sugar cookies. It is also called royal icing, and it will air-dry overnight. This makes it the ideal frosting to use when making cookies for individually wrapped gifts. After the icing dries, wrap your creations in cellophane bags and tie with a festive ribbon.

This icing is very flexible. You can add whatever extract and/or food colorings you prefer. There is also flexibility in its texture. To decorate cookies piped from a pastry bag or to assemble a gingerbread house, the frosting needs to be stiff. You may need to add more confectioners' sugar. To get a smooth, glossy surface on a cookie, water must be added to make a soft frosting. Do not refrigerate cookies decorated with this frosting. The frosting will melt. Let frosted cookies air-dry and store in airtight containers at room temperature.

4 CUPS CONFECTIONERS' SUGAR

1/2 TEASPOON LEMON EXTRACT (OR OTHER FLAVORING)

3 TABLESPOONS WATER

1/2 TEASPOON CREAM OF TARTAR

2 EGG WHITES

FOOD COLORING (OPTIONAL)

Combine all ingredients in an electric mixer. Mix on low speed until blended. Whip on high speed 2 to 3 minutes or until shiny and smooth. Add food coloring, if desired. Store in an airtight container.

YIELD: ABOUT 2 CUPS

ORANGE PFEFFERNÜSSE

*A new twist on an old holiday favorite, these "pepper balls"
have a zesty orange flavor. This German favorite is a
great cookie with which to celebrate the season.*

2½ CUPS FLOUR

½ TEASPOON BAKING SODA

½ TEASPOON SALT

¼ TEASPOON BLACK PEPPER

½ TEASPOON BAKING POWDER

1 TEASPOON CINNAMON

1 CUP HONEY

1 EGG

GRATED RIND OF ONE ORANGE

4 TABLESPOONS BUTTER, MELTED AND COOLED

CONFECTIONERS' SUGAR FOR COATING

1. Preheat oven to 350°F.

2. In a medium bowl, combine flour, baking soda, salt, black pepper, baking powder, and cinnamon. With a wooden spoon, mix until blended.

3. Add honey, egg, rind, and butter. Stir until well blended.

4. Roll dough into 1-inch balls and place on a parchment-lined cookie sheet, spacing each 2 inches apart.

5. Bake 12 to 15 minutes or until golden brown.

6. Remove cookie sheet from the oven. Carefully roll warm cookies in confectioners sugar. Cool completely.

YIELD: 40 COOKIES

FRUITCAKE SQUARES

*Forget all the old jokes about fruitcake. These colorful and tasty bars
are an easy way to brighten up a holiday table. Be sure to use a combination
of red and green cherries for the fullest color. You can also substitute
holiday favorites such as citron or candied pineapple.*

1½ STICKS BUTTER, SOFTENED

1 CUP SUGAR

1 TEASPOON VANILLA EXTRACT

4 EGGS

1¼ CUPS FLOUR

2 CUPS GLACÉ CHERRIES
(RED AND GREEN)

2 CUPS CHOPPED WALNUTS

CONFECTIONERS' SUGAR FOR
DUSTING

1. Preheat oven to 350°F.

2. Grease a 13 × 9-inch baking pan.

3. In an electric mixer on medium speed, cream butter and sugar until light. Add
   vanilla and eggs. Mix until well blended. On low speed, add flour, cherries, and
   nuts. Spread dough into prepared pan.

5. Bake 25 to 30 minutes or until lightly browned.

6. Remove pan from the oven. Let cool completely on a wire cooling rack.

7. Dust with confectioners' sugar. Cut into squares. Store in an airtight container
   at room temperature.

YIELD: 24 SQUARES

THUMBPRINT COOKIES

Nothing says home-baked like these jelly-filled cookies. Roll them in coconut or chopped walnuts and fill them with your favorite flavors. Mine is plum, from our very own plum tree.

½ POUND BUTTER, SOFTENED

½ CUP SUGAR

2 EGGS, SEPARATED

2 TEASPOONS VANILLA EXTRACT

2 CUPS FLOUR

½ TEASPOON SALT

2 CUPS FINELY CHOPPED WALNUTS OR COCONUT

¾ CUP JELLY

1. Preheat oven to 350°F.

2. In an electric mixer, cream the butter and sugar until light. Add the egg yolks and vanilla. Mix until well blended. On low speed, gradually add flour and salt. Mix just until blended to form a soft dough.

3. Roll dough into 1-inch balls.

4. In a small bowl, beat egg whites with a fork until fluffy. Place chopped nuts or coconut in another small bowl.

5. Dip balls into egg whites and then roll in nuts (or coconut). Coat thoroughly. Place balls on a parchment-lined cookie sheet, spacing each 2 inches apart.

6. Using your fingers, press the tops of the balls to flatten slightly. With your index finger, make a hole in the center of each cookie.

7. Spoon ½ teaspoon of jelly into each hole.

8. Bake for 15 to 20 minutes, or until lightly browned.

9. Remove cookie sheet from the oven. Using a metal spatula, remove cookies and place on a wire cooling rack. Cool. Store in an airtight container.

YIELD: 35 COOKIES

CINNAMON LACE COOKIES

These are crispy, flavorful cookies. I love them plain or sandwiched together with melted chocolate.

1 1/2 CUPS CHOPPED WALNUTS

1/2 CUP FLOUR

1/2 TEASPOON CINNAMON

1/2 STICK BUTTER

3/4 CUP SUGAR

3/4 CUP HEAVY CREAM

1. Preheat oven to 350°F.

2. In a medium bowl, combine walnuts, flour, and cinnamon. Set aside.

3. In a small saucepan, on medium heat, combine butter, sugar, and heavy cream. Stir until butter melts and mixture comes to a boil. Pour over dry ingredients. Stir until well blended. Let cool slightly.

4. Using a heaping teaspoon, drop dough onto a parchment-lined cookie sheet, 4 inches apart. Using the back of the teaspoon, spread into 2-inch-diameter circles.

5. Bake 10 to 12 minutes or until edges begin to brown.

6. Remove cookie sheet from the oven. Using a metal spatula, remove cookies from the cookie sheet and place on a wire cooling rack. Cool completely. Store cookies in an airtight container.

YIELD: 30 COOKIES

◆ LACE COOKIE DESSERTS ◆

TO MAKE AN IMPRESSIVE DESSERT, SANDWICH TWO OR THREE LACE COOKIES WITH WHIPPED CREAM AND SLICED STRAWBERRIES IN BETWEEN. THIS WILL MAKE THE PERFECT FINALE TO ANY MEAL.

CRANBERRY APRICOT COCONUT BALLS

*These brightly colored no-bake treats are a pretty addition to
cookie trays and delicious to eat. They're another simple, no-bake
cookie that's perfect for today's busy lifestyle.*

1 CUP DRIED CRANBERRIES, CHOPPED	1 1/2 CUPS COCONUT, TOASTED
1 CUP DRIED APRICOTS, CHOPPED	2/3 CUP SWEETENED CONDENSED MILK

1. In a medium bowl, combine cranberries, apricots, and ½ cup coconut. With a wooden spoon, mix until well blended. Stir in condensed milk. Refrigerate dough 1 hour.

2. Remove dough from the refrigerator. Roll dough into ½-inch balls. Dough may be sticky. Dip fingers in water so that dough does not stick to hands. Roll balls in remaining coconut. Place on a parchment-lined cookie sheet. Refrigerate until serving.

3. Store cookies in an airtight container in refrigerator.

YIELD: 30 COOKIES

◆ HOW TO TOAST COCONUT ◆

TO TOAST COCONUT, SPREAD A THIN LAYER OF COCONUT ON A
PARCHMENT-LINED COOKIE SHEET. BAKE AT 350° 10 TO 12 MINUTES,
STIRRING OCCASIONALLY, TO TOAST UNTIL LIGHTLY BROWNED. LET COOL
BEFORE USING.

GUMDROP COOKIES

Colorful gumdrop cookies are perfect for all your holiday cookie trays.
Kids especially love to make and eat them. For a tasty variation,
substitute 2½ cups M&M candies instead of the gumdrops.
They'll be festive and delicious either way.

½ POUND BUTTER, SOFTENED	2 CUPS FLOUR
1 CUP SUGAR	½ TEASPOON BAKING SODA
1 TEASPOON VANILLA EXTRACT	2 CUPS GUMDROPS
2 EGGS	

1. Preheat oven to 350°F.

2. In an electric mixer, cream butter and sugar until light. Add vanilla and eggs. Mix until well blended. On low speed, add flour and baking soda. Mix just until blended. Stir in gumdrops.

3. Drop dough from a teaspoon onto a parchment-lined cookie sheet, spacing each 2 inches apart.

4. Bake 12 to 15 minutes or until edges begin to brown.

5. Remove cookie sheet from the oven. Using a metal spatula, remove cookies from the cookie sheet and place on a wire cooling rack. Cool.

6. Store cookies in an airtight container at room temperature.

YIELD: 40 COOKIES

WREATH COOKIES

These cookies are great to bake with kids. They'll love to decorate them with colored coconut and cherries. You can also make a variation for Easter that forms the dough into Easter baskets.

¼ POUND BUTTER, SOFTENED

½ CUP SUGAR

1 TEASPOON VANILLA EXTRACT

1 EGG

2 CUPS FLOUR

½ CUP MARASCHINO CHERRIES, CHOPPED

½ CUP COCONUT

1. Preheat oven to 350°F.

2. In an electric mixer, cream butter and sugar until light. Add vanilla and egg. Mix until well blended. On low speed, add flour. Mix just until blended. Stir in cherries and coconut.

3. Break off a piece of dough. Roll on a lightly floured surface into a pencil-thick strip about 6 inches long. Form strip into a ring and press edges together to seal. Roll and shape remaining dough. Place rings onto a parchment-lined cookie sheet, spacing each 2 inches apart.

4. Bake 12 to 15 minutes or until lightly browned.

5. Remove baking sheet from the oven. Using a metal spatula, remove cookies from the cookie sheet and place on a wire cooling rack. Cool completely, frost, and decorate (see page 136).

YIELD: 30 COOKIES

WREATH FROSTING

2 CUPS CONFECTIONERS' SUGAR

¼ CUP OR A BIT LESS WATER

1–1 ½ CUPS COCONUT, COLORED GREEN

ABOUT 30 PIECES OF CHOPPED GLACÉ CHERRIES

Mix confectioners' sugar with water until smooth. Frost tops of cookie with wreath frosting. While frosting is still wet, sprinkle with green coconut and glacé cherries, as desired. Let dry completely. Store cookies in an airtight container.

VARIATION: EASTER BASKETS

Make tighter rings while shaping dough so that there is a smaller hole. Frost cookies with wreath frosting. Sprinkle with green coconut and place jelly beans in frosting. Let dry. Store cookies in an airtight container.

◆ HOW TO COLOR COCONUT ◆

PLACE 2 CUPS OF COCONUT IN A MEDIUM BOWL. ADD 2 TO 3 DROPS OF LIQUID FOOD COLORING. TOSS WITH YOUR FINGERS OR A WOODEN SPOON TO ACHIEVE DESIRED COLOR. IT'S ALWAYS EASIER TO START WITH LESS COLOR AND GRADUALLY ADD MORE. IF YOU'RE USING PASTE FOOD COLORS, ADD WATER TO PASTE COLOR, THEN ADD TO COCONUT.

DATE NUT BALLS

These are delicious no-bake cookies that use Rice Crispie cereal for a crunchy partner to dates and walnuts. This recipe can be easily doubled. Make a double batch, and share some with your Secret Santa.

¼ POUND BUTTER

½ CUP SUGAR

1 TEASPOON VANILLA EXTRACT

1 EGG

1 CUP DATES, CHOPPED

2 CUPS PUFFED RICE CEREAL

1 CUP WALNUTS, FINELY CHOPPED

1. In a medium saucepan over medium low heat, melt butter. Add sugar, vanilla, egg, and dates. Stir constantly 3 to 4 minutes or until egg is cooked and mixture is slightly thickened.

2. Remove pan from the heat. Stir in puffed rice cereal and walnuts. Mix until well blended. Set aside to cool.

3. When cool, roll into 1-inch balls. If dough is sticky, dip fingers in water and then roll. Place cookies on a parchment-lined cookie sheet. Refrigerate until serving. Store cookies in an airtight container in refrigerator.

YIELD: 30 COOKIES

AUNT BABE'S PECAN TASSIES

These little nut tarts are a special treat for any occasion. They can be a bit labor intensive, so be sure to savor every bite when someone gives you a tray of tassies. Press the dough into a miniature muffin pan to form the crust. A tart shaper can be used to form crust into the pan (these are available at most kitchen shops). If you have only one pan, be sure to let it cool before filling it again.

CRUST:

3 OUNCES CREAM CHEESE, ROOM TEMPERATURE

¼ POUND BUTTER, SOFTENED

1 CUP FLOUR

FILLING:

1 EGG

¾ CUP BROWN SUGAR

1 TABLESPOON BUTTER, MELTED AND COOLED

½ TEASPOON VANILLA EXTRACT

¼ CUP PECANS, FINELY CHOPPED

24 PECAN HALVES

1. Prepare crust. In an electric mixer, cream cream cheese and butter until fluffy. On low speed, add flour. Mix just until blended. Wrap dough in plastic wrap and refrigerate 2 to 3 hours or overnight.

2. Preheat oven to 350°F.

3. Prepare filling. In a medium mixing bowl, beat egg, brown sugar, butter, and vanilla. Mix until well blended. Stir in chopped pecans. Set aside.

4. Roll dough into 1-inch balls. Press ball into a greased mini muffin pan. Line pan on the bottom and sides. Using a teaspoon, fill the muffin cups with filling. Top with pecan half.

5. Bake 20 to 25 minutes or until edges begin to brown.

6. Remove pan from the oven. Cool in pan on a wire rack. Repeat with remaining dough and filling. Store in an airtight container.

YIELD: 24 TASSIES

VARIATION:

LEMON PISTACHIO TASSIES

This variation uses the same crust as the pecan tassies, but has a zesty lemon filling containing pistachios.

FILLING:

1 EGG

¾ CUP SUGAR

1 TABLESPOON BUTTER, MELTED AND COOLED

GRATED RIND OF 1 LEMON

½ CUP PISTACHIOS, FINELY CHOPPED

Follow same directions for making Pecan Tassies.

EGGNOG COOKIES

*These moist and simple drop cookies really capture the
flavor of Christmas. After frosting, be sure to sprinkle the tops
with nutmeg while the frosting is still wet.*

¼ POUND BUTTER, SOFTENED	1½ CUPS FLOUR
½ CUP SUGAR	½ TEASPOON BAKING POWDER
1 EGG	½ TEASPOON SODA
½ CUP EGGNOG	PINCH OF SALT
	EGGNOG FROSTING (PAGE 141)

1. Preheat oven to 350°F.

2. In an electric mixer, cream butter and sugar until light. Add egg and eggnog. Mix until well blended. On low speed, add flour, baking powder, baking soda, and salt. Mix just until blended. Dough will be soft and a little sticky.

3. Drop dough from a teaspoon onto a parchment-lined cookie sheet, spacing each 2 inches apart.

4. Bake 10 to 12 minutes or until edges begin to brown.

5. Remove cookie sheet from the oven. Using a metal spatula, remove cookies from the sheet and place on a wire cooling rack. Cool completely. Frost with eggnog frosting, page 141. Sprinkle with nutmeg.

YIELD: 36 COOKIES

EGGNOG FROSTING

This frosting is the perfect accent for the eggnog cookies.

3 CUPS CONFECTIONERS' SUGAR

1/4 CUP PLUS 2 TABLESPOONS
EGGNOG

3 TABLESPOONS RUM

1. In an electric mixer, combine all ingredients. Mix until smooth.

2. Place a wire cooling rack on top of a parchment-lined cookie sheet. This will catch any excess frosting and will make cleanup easier. Using a metal spatula, frost the top of the cookies. Frosting will drizzle down the cookies. Sprinkle tops with nutmeg. Let dry.

PERSIMMON COOKIES

These tasty spice cookies have the unique addition of pureed persimmon. A popular fruit found at the holiday table, served in a fruit assortment or in holiday desserts, persimmons are a sure sign that autumn has arrived. Persimmons need to be completely soft before using. To puree the persimmon, remove skin and cut into cubes. Pulse in food processor 1 to 2 minutes.

1/4 POUND BUTTER, SOFTENED	1/2 TEASPOON BAKING POWDER
1 CUP BROWN SUGAR	1/4 TEASPOON SALT
1 EGG	1 TEASPOON CINNAMON
1 TEASPOON VANILLA EXTRACT	1 CUP PURÉED PERSIMMON
1 1/2 CUPS FLOUR	1 CUP WALNUTS, CHOPPED
1/2 TEASPOON BAKING SODA	

1. Preheat oven to 350°F.

2. In an electric mixer, cream butter and brown sugar until light. Add egg and vanilla. Mix well. On low speed, add flour, baking soda, baking powder, salt, and cinnamon. Mix just until blended. Stir in persimmon and walnuts.

3. Drop from a rounded teaspoon onto a parchment-lined cookie sheet, spacing each 2 inches apart.

4. Bake 10 to 12 minutes, or until firm.

5. Remove cookie sheet from the oven. Using a metal spatula, remove cookies from the cookie sheet and place on a wire cooling rack. Cool completely. Store cookies in an airtight container.

YIELD: 45 COOKIES

CHAPTER 6

LOW-FAT, LOW-SUGAR, AND GLUTEN-FREE COOKIES

This section addresses the special dietary needs of cookie lovers. For what they may lack in fat, sugar, or gluten, these cookies certainly aren't lacking in flavor.

Low fat: Our low-fat cookies use egg whites and sugar and include the meringues in this chapter. Other low-fat recipes in this book are Pignoli and Chocolate Almond Macaroons.

Low sugar: Low-sugar cookies use apples and plum purées for a natural sugar that is easy to absorb and a healthy portion of oats.

Gluten free: Those who are allergic to gluten can enjoy my Pignoli or Chocolate Almond Macaroons, Lemon Coconut Macaroons, and Peanut Butter Balls—in addition to the gluten-free cookies in this chapter. This chapter also includes a tasty dog biscuit. After all, *everyone* loves cookies.

APRICOT DATE OATMEAL CHEWS

*These chewy, low-fat cookies are moist and tasty, thanks
to applesauce and a healthy combination of dried
apricots, dates, and oatmeal.*

¼ POUND MARGARINE, SOFTENED

½ CUP BROWN SUGAR

2 EGG WHITES

½ CUP APPLESAUCE

1½ CUPS FLOUR

1 TEASPOON BAKING SODA

¼ TEASPOON SALT

2½ CUPS OATS

1 CUP DRIED APRICOTS, COARSELY CHOPPED

1 CUP DATES, COARSELY CHOPPED

1. Preheat oven to 350°F.

2. In an electric mixer, cream margarine and brown sugar until light. Add egg whites and applesauce. Mix until well blended. On low speed, add flour, baking soda, and salt. Mix just until blended. Stir in oats, apricots, and dates.

3. Drop dough from a teaspoon onto a parchment-lined cookie sheet, spacing each 2 inches apart.

4. Bake 12 to 15 minutes, or until lightly browned.

5. Remove cookie sheet from the oven. Using a metal spatula, remove cookies from the cookie sheet and place on a wire cooling rack. Cool. Store cookies at room temperature in an airtight container.

YIELD: 55 COOKIES

CHOCOLATE CLOVE LESS-FAT COOKIES

*This spicy chocolate cookie is the perfect treat
for the low-fat crowd. It'll satisfy anyone's craving
for a chewy chocolate cookie.*

1 ¼ CUPS FLOUR	½ TEASPOON SALT
½ CUP SUGAR	½ TEASPOON CLOVES
½ CUP COCOA	½ CUP LIGHT CORN SYRUP
½ TEASPOON BAKING SODA	3 EGG WHITES

1. Preheat oven to 350°F.

2. In an electric mixer, combine flour, sugar, cocoa, baking soda, salt, and cloves. Mix until uniform. Add corn syrup and egg whites. Mix just until blended. Dough will be sticky. Drop dough from a teaspoon onto a parchment-lined cookie sheet, spacing each 2 inches apart.

3. Bake 8 to 10 minutes or until set. Do not overbake.

4. Remove cookie sheet from the oven. Cool cookies completely on parchment. Store cookies in an airtight container.

YIELD: 30 COOKIES

WINTER AND
SUMMER MERINGUES

*These cookies are the perfect treat for anyone who has a gluten allergy.
Here are two variations, Lime for a spring and summer treat, or
Maple Spice for cold weather. This recipe uses a pastry bag, without a tip,
to form the dough into small kisses. If you don't want to use a pastry bag,
you can spoon the dough onto the cookie sheet.*

LIME MERINGUES

*Be sure to clean the whip well to be sure all
the grated rind is added to the batter.*

4 EGG WHITES	GRATED RIND OF 2 LIMES
1 ¼ CUPS SUGAR	JUICE OF 2 LIMES

1. Preheat oven to 225°F.

2. In an electric mixer, with wire whip, beat egg whites at high speed. Gradually add sugar in a steady stream as you beat egg whites. Add grated rind and juice. Beat until stiff and glossy, about 5 minutes.

3. Using a pastry bag, pipe small kisses onto a parchment-lined cookie sheet. You can pipe cookies close together because they won't spread.

4. Bake 1½ hours or until dry.

5. Remove cookie sheet from the oven. Cool cookies completely on parchment. Store cookies in an airtight container.

YIELD: 70 SMALL MERINGUES

MAPLE SPICE MERINGUES

*A spicy combination of maple and cinnamon make these
cookies a cold-weather treat. Perfect by the
fire with a steaming hot cocoa.*

4 EGG WHITES	1 TEASPOON MAPLE EXTRACT
1 CUP SUGAR	1 TEASPOON CINNAMON

1. Preheat oven to 225°F.

2. In an electric mixer, with wire whip, beat egg whites at high speed. Gradually add sugar as you beat the egg whites. Add maple extract and cinnamon. Beat until stiff and glossy, about 5 minutes.

3. Using a pastry bag, pipe small kisses onto a parchment-lined cookie sheet. You can pipe them close together because they won't spread.

4. Bake 1½ hours or until dry.

5. Remove cookie sheet from the oven. Cool cookies completely on parchment. Store cookies in an airtight container.

YIELD: 70 SMALL MERINGUES

CASHEW CHEWIES

*This cookie is a delicious treat made with simple cashew butter.
I almost hate to categorize it—although the recipe is
gluten free, this cookie is yummy
for anyone to enjoy.*

2 CUPS WHOLE CASHEWS

1/4 CUP VEGETABLE OIL

1 CUP BROWN SUGAR

1 EGG

1 TEASPOON VANILLA EXTRACT

1. Preheat oven to 350°F.

2. In a food processor, grind cashews until fine. Add oil in a slow stream while grinding, to form a paste similar in texture to chunky peanut butter. This should yield one cup of cashew butter.

3. In an electric mixer, cream cashew butter and brown sugar. Add egg and vanilla and mix until well blended.

4. Drop dough from a teaspoon onto a parchment-lined cookie sheet, spacing each 2 inches apart.

5. Bake 10 to 12 minutes or until browned.

6. Remove cookie sheet from the oven. Let cookies cool completely on parchment paper. After cooling, remove cookies from the cookie sheet, using a metal spatula. Store cookies in an airtight container.

YIELD: 24 COOKIES

APPLE CINNAMON SUGAR FREES

A chunky, chewy cookie loaded with flavor,
this recipe uses apples and raisins as a natural sweetener.

1 1/2 CUPS RAISINS	1 TEASPOON CINNAMON
3/4 CUP APPLE, CHOPPED	1 TEASPOON VANILLA EXTRACT
1 CUP WATER	2 EGGS, BEATEN
1/2 CUP BUTTER	1 CUP OATS
1 CUP FLOUR	1/2 CUP WALNUTS, FINELY CHOPPED
1 TEASPOON BAKING SODA	

1. In a medium saucepan, combine raisins, apple, and water. Bring to a boil, over medium heat, and boil 3 to 4 minutes. Remove saucepan from the heat. Stir in butter until melted. Set aside to cool.

2. In a medium mixing bowl, combine flour, baking soda, and cinnamon. Mix until blended. Add vanilla, eggs, oats, walnuts, and cooled raisin mixture. Stir until blended. Cover bowl and refrigerate overnight.

3. Preheat oven to 350°F.

4. Drop dough from a teaspoon onto a parchment-lined cookie sheet, spacing each 2 inches apart.

5. Bake 10 to 12 minutes, or until lightly browned.

6. Remove cookie sheet from the oven. Using a metal spatula, remove cookies from the cookie sheet and place on a wire cooling rack. Cool completely. Store cookies in an airtight container.

YIELD: 45 COOKIES

BOW WOW BISCUITS

Labs, pugs, and shepherds agree—these treats are really yummy.
This newest addition to our Sweet Maria menu keeps them
howling for more. We've tried to make these biscuits various shapes
but found the traditional dog bone shape to be the
easiest for most dogs to eat.

2 BOUILLON CUBES, CHICKEN OR BEEF

1/4 POUND MARGARINE, CUT INTO CUBES

1 EGG, SLIGHTLY BEATEN

2 TEASPOONS SUGAR

1/2 CUP POWDERED MILK

3 TO 31/2 CUPS WHOLE WHEAT FLOUR

1/2 TEASPOON SALT

1. Preheat oven to 350°F.

2. Dissolve bouillon cubes in 1 cup of boiling water. Place margarine in a large mixing bowl. Pour hot dissolved bouillon over margarine. Stir to melt margarine. Add egg, sugar, powdered milk, 3 cups flour, and salt. Mix until blended.

3. Turn dough out onto a lightly floured surface. Knead in remaining 1/2 cup flour to make a firm, not sticky dough.

4. Roll dough to 1/2 inch thick. Cut into shapes. Place on a parchment-lined cookie sheet. You can place them close together. They won't spread.

5. Bake 35 to 40 minutes, or until browned and dry. Remove cookie sheet from the oven. Using a metal spatula, remove cookies from the cookie sheet and place on a wire cooling rack. Cool completely.

6. Store biscuits in an airtight container at room temperature.

YIELD: 20 DOG BONE–SHAPE BISCUITS (41/2 INCHES LONG)

Sweet Maria's
CAKE
KITCHEN

Sweet Maria's

CAKE

KITCHEN

Casual and Creative Recipes for Layer,
Loaf, and Bundt Cakes

MARIA BRUSCINO SANCHEZ

FOR MY CUSTOMERS,
WHO CONTINUE TO ENCOURAGE
AND CHALLENGE ME

CONTENTS

ACKNOWLEDGMENTS

Many thanks to my agent, Carla Glasser, for everything.

To my editor, Marian Lizzi, and everyone at St. Martin's whose expertise has made my cookbook career an enjoyable experience.

To Mom, Dad, and Edgar for their love and patience.

To the Sweet Maria's staff for their support and encouragement.

And to Tony, Louise, and Helen, who were the first to nurture my fascination with cakes.

INTRODUCTION

At Sweet Maria's, just about every cake order marks a birthday, a homecoming, a new baby, the union of two people, or some other celebration. It's great to be part of such a happy business, creating cakes that make someone feel special, even if it's simply to say "I love you," "TGIF," or "Happy Spring."

Today's cake has evolved from being a mere dessert to being the centerpiece of a party. At Sweet Maria's we have many requests for unusual shapes, colors, and inscriptions that either blend with or are the theme of the party. I've actually had a few customers pick out their cake first and then plan their theme and decorations around the cake.

Many people are intimidated by the thought of baking their own cakes, and not without reason. Cake baking is a science, exact in its measurements, unforgiving when it comes to miscalculations. In cooking or cookie baking, there is less that can go wrong. There are a lot of variables in cake baking: accurate measurement, fresh ingredients, the right oven temperature. But don't let that deter you. With a few tips and attention to detail you can bake and enjoy successful cakes.

This book offers a selection of some of my personal favorites and some of our biggest-selling cakes. It includes butter-based cakes as well as lighter sponge-type cakes. In Connecticut, where Sweet Maria's is located, there seems to be a regional preference for whipped cream–frosted cakes, so I've included a number of them. These cakes are usually paired with fresh fruit and offer a less sweet alternative to traditional buttercream cakes. Buttercreams are rich and sweet and are commonly used on birthday and wedding cakes. I've included these as well.

Most of the cakes in this book are made the same way we prepare them at Sweet Maria's. Of course, we bake much larger batches of both cake and frosting.

Sometimes the quality of ingredients available to bakeries is much higher than that available to the customer. For example, pasteurized heavy cream, which is the freshest, is available to us in large quantities directly through a dairy. The same dairy will sell heavy cream to a supermarket. However, they will sell them only ultra-pasteurized cream, because it has a longer shelf life. In this respect, the cakes you make may differ from those made at our bakery.

The other way they may differ is in the number of layers in the layer cakes. Most cakes frosted with whipped cream made at the bakery are three layers. We slice two layers in half horizontally to make four thin layers. We use three layers for one cake and save the odd piece for use in another cake. When you're baking at home, this would be wasteful, so I've made many of the cakes in this book into four-layer versions for the home baker.

When I was a child, my mom made all our special-occasion cakes. Every birthday, she'd make a devil's food cake with chocolate pudding frosting. It didn't have any fancy decorations—just a few swirls in the frosting. But it's always been my favorite. I hope the cakes in this book help bring the same sweet pleasure to your home.

BEFORE YOU BEGIN

INGREDIENTS

It is important that your cake ingredients are at room temperature. This is the only way for all the elements to blend together successfully. This makes cake baking a planned event: You must get organized and let the refrigerated ingredients come to room temperature before mixing. This usually takes two to three hours.

FLOUR: Cake flour is the best flour to use for most cake baking. It produces a light texture. Other flours have more gluten, which will toughen the cake. All–purpose flour and unbleached flour contain more gluten than cake flour, strengthening the batter. This type of heavier, denser batter is used primarily in fruitcakes. The higher gluten is needed to hold up the fruit and nuts and to keep them from sinking to the bottom of the cake.

SUGAR: Extra-fine granulated sugar is used in the cake recipes in this book. It provides a great flavor, and it blends well with butters and shortenings.

BROWN SUGAR: Brown sugar is sugar that has been processed with molasses for a rich flavor. You can use light brown or dark brown sugar depending on your personal preference, unless a particular type has been specified. When measuring brown sugar, spoon sugar into a measuring cup and lightly pack it into cup with the back of a spoon or with your fingers.

CONFECTIONERS' SUGAR: Confectioners' sugar is very fine powdered sugar that has a bit of cornstarch added to prevent sticking. Because of its fine texture, it blends well with other ingredients to produce smooth icings and glazes.

BUTTER: Unsalted butter is used in these recipes. It offers the fullest and freshest flavor. It's easier to add salt to your recipe as needed instead of assuming there's enough in salted butter. You can substitute margarine or shortening in these recipes, but you'll be sacrificing the fresh, full flavor of butter.

VEGETABLE SHORTENING AND VEGETABLE OIL: Whenever shortening is called for in these recipes, use vegetable shortening. Vegetable shortening provides a smooth texture. It can be used to grease cake pans if you're going to grease and flour them to prevent the cake from sticking in the pan.

When a recipe calls for oil, use a vegetable oil. Olive oil is very expensive and often too heavy for most cake baking.

EXTRACTS: Be sure to use pure extracts in all your baking. You can really taste the difference compared with cheaper flavorings. You can keep your frostings white by using a clear extract.

EGGS: Whole, large grade A eggs are recommended for these recipes. If you need to separate eggs, it's easier to do when they are cold. Then let the eggs come to room temperature before using.

BAKING POWDER AND BAKING SODA: These are two leavening agents that are commonly used in cake baking. Be sure that your supply is fresh for best results. Store unused baking powder and baking soda in airtight containers.

MILK AND BUTTERMILK: When a recipe calls for milk, use whole Grade A milk. Don't substitute low-fat or nonfat milk. You'll be compromising the texture and flavor of your cake.

Years ago, buttermilk was the liquid that was left after churning butter. Today it is made by adding a bacteria to whole milk to produce a slightly sour taste. It adds a richer flavor to many of our cakes.

SPICES: There are several common spices used in this cookbook. They include cinnamon, nutmeg, ginger, and cloves. These are readily available in supermarkets, already ground. Just be sure your supply of spices is fresh. If your spice jars have been opened for more than six months, you should replace them with a new supply.

FRUITS AND VEGETABLES: This book includes some cakes that require fresh fruits or vegetables. Try to take advantage of local produce and use the seasonal specialties of your area. Strawberries, raspberries, and blueberries are best when they're fresh and in season, but a good alternative is "IQF" berries. These are berries that are "individually quick frozen" separately, then frozen together. This allows the whole berry to thaw whole instead of the pieces and juice that come with other types of frozen fruits.

Every baker has his or her favorite variety of apples. Use your favorite or try Empire or Cortland. These are firm and flavorful for most baking purposes.

Pears are gaining in popularity for baking purposes and rightly so. Bosc pears bake wonderfully and are available just about all year.

CHOCOLATE: Always use the finest and freshest chocolate available. Most of these recipes use semisweet bars or semisweet chocolate chips that are available in most supermarkets.

COCOA: Many bakers will debate the best type of cocoa. I've found that Dutch-processed cocoa can't be beat for a full rich flavor and color.

CITRUS RIND AND JUICE: A great way to flavor cakes is by using the rind and juice of citrus fruit such as lemons, limes, and oranges. This adds a much more pungent and natural flavor than any extract. It's easier to squeeze the fruits for juice if they are at room temperature. To grate the rind, use a zester or four-sided grater. Just be sure to avoid the bitter white pith underneath the rind.

WHIPPED CREAM: Heavy cream is recommended for whipped cream frosting. It has a higher butterfat content than whipping cream or light cream, so it whips up the stiffest and has the richest flavor. Pasteurized heavy cream is the freshest-tasting cream, but is usually hard to find. Most supermarkets stock ultra-pasteurized cream that will work in most recipes.

MASCARPONE: This is a soft Italian cheese similar to cream cheese in texture. It is the basis for the Italian dessert tiramisù.

CREAM CHEESE: Any brand of cream cheese will work in these recipes. Be sure it is softened to room temperature for the easiest blending. Neufchatel cheese is a natural low-calorie alternative to cream cheese. It has a lower milkfat content than traditional cream cheese, and it makes a fine substitute.

YOGURT AND SOUR CREAM: Both yogurt and sour cream are added for flavor and moisture in some of the cakes in this book.

NUTS: A wide variety of nuts is used in this book, including walnuts, pecans, and almonds. In many of the recipes you can interchange the types of nuts (e.g., if the recipe calls for almonds, change to hazelnuts). If you have a large amount of nuts that you need to store, place in a plastic bag and freeze for later use.

Freshly chopping nuts helps to bring out their natural flavors and oils. This book uses various sizes of nuts.

For finely chopped, use a food processor. For coarsely chopped, use a long knife and cutting board.

Roasting nuts and coconut helps to draw out their natural oils and flavor. Lay the measured amount of nuts or coconut on a clean parchment-lined cookie sheet. Spread in a single layer. Bake in the oven at 350°F for 5 to 8 minutes, or until lightly browned. Let cool before using.

EQUIPMENT

It is very important to have the right tools for cake baking. The wrong size pan or cheap foil layer cake pans can ruin the best batters.

LAYER CAKE PANS: If you are using round layer cake pans, use the ones with straight sides, two inches deep. For layer cakes, you only need the pan to be the same height as the finished cake will be. Disposable foil pans are not recommended for layer cake baking.

LOAF PANS: Loaf pans come in many sizes, the most common are 10 x 6 x 2½ inches and 8 x 4 x 3 inches. Foil pans are fine for loaf pans and are especially practical for wrapping and gift giving. Mini loaf pans make a unique individual dessert. These pans usually come in a set of six pans, 4½ x 2½ x 1½ inches each.

BUNDT AND TUBE PANS: Tube pans are round, tall pans that have a center column. Bundt was originally the brand name for a fancier fluted tube pan. Now any fluted tube pan is referred to as a Bundt pan, regardless of the manufacturer. The most common sizes are 9 x 4 inches and 10 x 4 inches. Mini Bundtlette pans (4 x 2 inches) are also available and make ideal individual desserts. Tube pans are commonly found in 9 x 4 inch or 10 x 4 inch sizes. Some tube pans have feet that make them ideal to invert foam-style cakes for cooling.

PARCHMENT PAPER: Lining loaf and layer pans with parchment prevents the cake from sticking to the pan and produces straighter bottoms and cake sides. It also makes cleaning up easier. Cut parchment into circles to fit the appropriate size pan (e.g., 8- or 9-inch round). Then cut parchment into 2-inch-wide strips. I usually cut a bunch of strips in various sizes just to have them handy. Spray the cake pans with nonstick spray, then line the bottom of the pan with the circle of parchment. Use the strips to adhere to the sides of the pan. This also eliminates the messy task of greasing and flouring pans.

When using a tube pan for butter-based cakes, you can cut the parchment to adhere around the inner tube. When spraying, try to hold the pan and spray over the sink. This helps to eliminate messy overspray. If you're using foil loaf pans and are giving them as gifts, in the pan, you don't need to line the pan with parchment. Just grease and flour, or spray with nonstick spray.

For fluted Bundt pans that can't be lined with parchment, carefully grease with vegetable shortening, being sure you grease every crevice. Dust with flour to coat pan. This will prevent the cake from sticking. Spread shortening over inside of pans using your fingers or a pastry brush.

When baking chocolate cakes, dust the greased pan with cocoa instead of flour to avoid any white blotches on the cake. If you absolutely hate to grease and flour, you can use a nonstick cooking spray. I've found this method to have irregular results, whereas the traditional method of greasing and flouring is virtually foolproof.

MIXING BOWLS AND UTENSILS: You will need the usual types of mixing bowls, rubber spatulas, cake testers, measuring cups, and spoons that are normally found in most kitchens.

ELECTRIC MIXERS: Hand-held electric mixers will work fine, but a stand-up mixer is a great tool to have. This allows you to walk away from the mixer while butter is creaming, for example, and do another task like prepare cake pans.

You'll need a hand-held mixer to make our Seven-Minute Frosting. This frosting is mixed in a double boiler over boiling water, so it would be impossible to use a stand-up mixer.

DOUBLE BOILERS: These are pots that fit together, with one pot in another. The lower pot holds water that either simmers or boils to gently cook whatever is in the upper pot. If you don't have a double boiler, you can carefully use a saucepan filled with water as the bottom, and a stainless steel bowl that fits over the top.

WIRE COOLING RACKS: These are necessary to cool cakes properly. They allow air to circulate around and underneath the cake to cool it completely. Wire racks are also great while glazing the top of a cake with confectioners' frosting. Place a piece of parchment or waxed paper under the wire rack to catch any excess frosting that drips off.

OVENS: The recipes in this book are timed using a moderate oven, either gas or electric. If you are using a convection oven, your baking times will be less than the recommended times. Please consult your owner's manual for more specific baking times.

I don't suggest going out and purchasing a new oven, but oven doors with windows and ovens with lights are ideal for anxious cake bakers. This allows you to glimpse the progress of baking without actually opening the oven and disturbing the baking process. You can cause the cake to fall if you open the oven door too soon and let cold air in.

Be sure to check your oven temperature. Many bakers assume their ovens work fine because they cook roasts and casseroles well. Remember that cakes are sensitive and need the proper heat to generate volume. Use an oven thermometer to check for accurate temperatures. These are inexpensive and can give you an accurate reading. If the oven temperature is too low or high, call a repairman to make the proper adjustments.

GENERAL INFORMATION AND TECHNIQUES

Room-Temperature Ingredients

I stress once again that all the cake ingredients should be at room temperature. This is the only way to ensure that all of the elements will blend together successfully and smoothly. A good way to start is to read through the recipe first so that you understand all the directions. Then organize your ingredients according to mixing order to be sure you don't forget anything. Also, prepare your pans before you begin mixing so that you can get the cakes in the oven as soon as they're mixed.

Mixing Methods

There are several methods for blending ingredients together. One is the creaming method. This is commonly used for butter cakes. The butter or shortening is creamed first, then the sugar is gradually added and blended until light. Eggs are added one at a time. It's important to the volume and structure of the cake that one egg is well incorporated before adding the next egg. After the eggs and extracts are added, the dry ingredients are added. Usually all the dry ingredients (flour, baking powder, salt, etc.) are combined together. They are either added slowly or added alternately with some type of liquid (such as milk, buttermilk, or sour cream). It's important not to overmix at this point. If overbeaten, the cake can become dry and tough. Blend just until smooth and pour into the prepared pan.

Foam Cake Mixing

This technique is used primarily with angel food and sponge-type cakes. With sponge cakes, the egg whites and yolks are separated. The yolks are beaten with sugar until thick and uniformly yellow. In another bowl, the whites are whipped until stiff but not dry. Flour is added to the yolk mixture. The yolks are then carefully folded into the egg white mixture using a rubber spatula. The batter is poured into an ungreased pan. The angel food technique is the same as above, without the yolk stage.

How to Fold in Beaten Egg Whites

It's important to have a light hand while folding. Using a rubber spatula, with small wrist turning strokes, add air as you incorporate ingredients. Be sure to scrape the bottom of the bowl with your turning strokes.

How to Tell When a Cake Is Done

The traditional method of checking for doneness is to stick a cake tester into the center of the cake. When the tester comes out clean, the cake is done. Sometimes, however, when a tester comes out clean, the cake ends up overdone because it will continue cooking in the pan. I've found it best to remove a cake when the tester comes out with a small crumb. Not batter, just a fine crumb.

Cooling Cakes

Most butter-based cakes should be cooled in the pan, on wire cooling racks, after removal from the oven. Most cakes at this point are too fragile to be turned out of the pans; they will break. After cooling in the pan for 5 to 10 minutes, remove cake from the hot pan, carefully flipping the cake bottom side down on the wire cooling rack. If you leave the cake top side down on the cooling rack, it can split. You can easily flip the cake bottom side down by using another wire rack to turn it.

Continue cooling for 15 to 20 minutes on cooling rack. If you are going to frost the cake, leave it on the rack until fully cool. Otherwise, when almost cool, wrap in foil, then plastic. Store at room temperature overnight or freeze for later use.

Angel food and sponge cakes are baked in tube pans. They need to be inverted for proper cooling. Many older models of tube pans will have feet extending from the top of the pan. If you have a pan with feet, simply turn it upside down and let the cake stand on a clean counter or table until cool. If your tube pan does not have feet, you can invert the pan onto the neck of a soda bottle. Although it may look precarious, this method will hold the cake firmly on top of the bottle and it will hang there and cool successfully. To remove sponge cakes from the pan, use a long, sharp knife. Run the knife around the sides of the tube pan. Loosen the inside cone. Run the knife around the inside cone and underneath the bottom of the cake.

Frosting

Frost cakes only when completely cool. There will be less breakage and crumbs if the cake is frosted the day after baking. If unfrosted cake layers have been frozen, thaw them first, then frost.

Dusting with Confectioners' Sugar

To dust a cake or cake slice with confectioners' sugar, place a few tablespoons of powdered sugar in a small dry strainer. Hold the strainer over the cake and with a teaspoon stir the sugar over the cake in the desired amount.

Storage

Wrap unfrosted cake in foil, then plastic. Freeze up to two months. Thaw cake in the refrigerator before serving or frosting.

Store cakes frosted with a buttercream icing in the refrigerator for two to three days. Once a cake has been frosted with a buttercream frosting, it is sealed. Bring to room temperature before serving.

Cakes frosted with whipped cream can stay refrigerated for one to two days. Whipped cream is a more porous frosting, so it doesn't have the sealing capabilities of buttercream. Keep whipped cream cakes away from odors in the refrigerator. The cream will absorb odors.

Shipping

Unfrosted loaf and Bundt cakes can be shipped through the mail, but layer cakes with frosting are not recommended for shipping. If you need to ship a cake, be sure to use a heavy corrugated cardboard shipping box. Wrap the cake in plastic to secure freshness, and perhaps use a cookie tin or wrap with some cellophane and ribbon. Be sure to properly cushion the cake with newspaper or tissue paper. Use the quickest service possible to ship perishable food items.

Determining Serving Quantities

Many of these recipes for layer cakes are for either 8- or 9-inch cakes. These cakes serve 10 to 12, and 12 to 15 respectively. If you're having a larger party, I recommend making two different types of cakes—perhaps one chocolate and one another flavor.

The number of servings will vary with loaf and tube pans. Although they are standard-size pans, the type of cake will dictate the number of servings. A dense fruit-filled butter cake should be cut into thin pieces. Because these types of cakes are rich, they will yield more servings than a light, plain angel food cake.

Baking for Company

When baking or cooking for guests, it is less stressful to prepare a recipe that you've already tried. This way you know if you like the cake and what to expect for preparation time. It's also a good idea to prepare as many elements ahead of time as possible. For example, if you are having a party on a Saturday night, bake your cake and make your filling on Friday. Make your frosting and assemble the cake on Saturday morning.

How to Whip Cream

If you're whipping the cream to use as a dollop on a slice of cake, you don't need to beat until very stiff. Stiff whipped cream is necessary only if you're filling and frosting a layer cake.

Chill the mixing bowl and beaters for 10 to 15 minutes before whipping cream. Use a fresh heavy cream. Whip with an electric mixer using wire whisk attachment. Whip at high speed until medium peaks form, about 2 minutes. Add granulated sugar and continue whipping another 30 seconds, or until stiff. Use immediately.

BASIC CAKE DECORATING TIPS AND EQUIPMENT

Here are a few basic items that are great for decorating cakes.

Pastry Bags and Tips

Don't be intimidated by a pastry bag. It's a great tool to use to assemble and decorate layer cakes. If you're just starting to use a pastry bag, I recommend using the flexible plastic reusable type. These are pliable, easy to use, and easy to clean. Some of the older cloth pastry bags absorb greasy frostings, are hard to dry, and can become stiff with age. The only decorating tip you may need for the cakes in this book is the basic star tip, usually numbered 32 by most manufacturers. We won't spend a lot of time on decorating techniques—just enough to assemble your layer cake and perhaps make a simple shell border.

Spatulas and Combs

Straight metal spatulas are recommended for frosting cakes. Try to find the length that you are most comfortable with. I prefer a wooden-handled 6 x 3-inch version. Metal scrapers, found in most kitchen shops, are another great tool to help you smooth the sides of your layer cakes. You can also purchase, quite inexpensively, a triangular cake comb that will give your sides a ribbed effect. Just hold the comb against the sides of your cake as you turn the cake on your turntable.

Turntables

Professional cake decorators use a turntable to spin cakes around for easier decorating. You can use the same technique at home by using a lazy susan to turn your cake as you frost it.

Cake Bases

A flat, sturdy plate can serve as the base for your decorated cake. If you are bringing the cake somewhere and don't want to worry about getting your plate back, use a cardboard cake circle. These corrugated cardboard circles can be purchased at specialty kitchen or party shops. Use a cardboard base that is at least two inches larger than your cake. For exceptionally heavy or large cakes, double or triple the cardboard thickness.

A nice way to present your cake is to use a doily on top of your cake base. Use a bit of buttercream to adhere the doily to the cake base and to adhere the cake to the doily to prevent any slipping of your cake.

To keep your doily clean as you decorate, place a piece of cellophane or plastic wrap over the entire doily surface. Then place the bottom cake layer on the plastic or cellophane. After decorating, carefully cut away the excess plastic, leaving the clean doily.

Frosting

The easiest way to frost a layer cake is to start from the top. Pile some frosting on top of your filled layer cake. Working from the center, spread the frosting to the edges with your metal spatula. Work the frosting onto the sides of the cake, covering all areas. It's always best to pile on more frosting. Be generous. After you get the frosting on, you can eliminate the excess with your spatula, metal scraper, or comb. If you're working with a dense frosting like a buttercream, it's a good idea to have a bowl of hot water nearby. You can dip your spatula, scraper, and/or comb into the water to help spread the frosting and help to release it from the spatula.

For fancy smooth finishes with buttercream icings, it's best to apply two coats of frosting. The first coat is called the crumb coat. This is a thin layer that you apply without worrying about crumbs in the frosting. Refrigerate the crumb-coated cake for about 30 minutes, or until hard to the touch. Now you can apply the crumb-free finish coat of frosting to the cake.

Whipped cream frostings are easier to spread than buttercream frostings and require only one coat. It is important that you use the whipped cream immediately after whipping it. Frost quickly to be sure that the frosting stays firm.

Filling a Pastry Bag

An easy way to fill a pastry bag is to place the tip side down in a tall drinking glass. Fold the top edges of the bag down around the outside of the glass. Spoon your frosting into the open bag, being careful not to overfill it. Gather up the top edges and remove from the glass. To use, simply squeeze and add pressure to the center of the bag. This will release the frosting through the tip.

Making a Dam

For many loose fillings such as custards and lemon curd, you will need to make a frosting dam to hold the filling in. Using a pastry bag fitted with a basic star tip (or no tip at all), simply pipe a line of frosting around the perimeter of the layer of cake. Spoon your filling inside the frosting outline and place the top layer of cake on top.

Piping a Shell Border

A shell border is a basic border for the top and bottom of a layer cake, made with a pastry bag and, most often, an open star tip (#32). Practice on a flat surface, such as a parchment-lined cookie sheet. You can then scrape up frosting, refill the pastry bag, and practice again. You can use a top and bottom border to frame your cakes or just a top border.

Covering Your Mistakes

One of the easiest things to do when decorating is to cover your mistakes. With many of the cakes in this book, you don't have to be fussy about frosting the cake sides and tops. While the frosting is still wet, cover the frosting with chopped nuts, coconut, or colored sprinkles. This is an easy way to get a professional look without the headaches of professional cake decorating. Garnish generously with sliced fruit or chocolate pieces, candy, or fresh, nonpoisonous, unsprayed flowers and herbs. These are simple elegant ways to garnish a cake. Remember that your cake doesn't need to have a structured, store-bought look. A natural, simple home-baked look is more appetizing and shows that you've spent the time and energy to produce something of your own.

Other Enhancements

If you don't want to decorate your cake, decorate around it. Pretty platters, doilies, candles, tablecloths, and floral arrangements can all enhance the presentation of your desserts.

LOAF AND BUNDT CAKES

LOAF AND BUNDT CAKE TIPS

Loaf and Bundt cakes are a great place to start cake baking. These are simple cakes that can be garnished and glazed to make a perfect dessert or a perfect brunch accompaniment. The loaf cakes in this collection include fine-textured butter cakes, fruitcakes, and coffee cakes. A lot of these cakes have long cooking times because of their height. But you can put the cake in the oven and almost forget about it while you do something else.

Try to follow the recipe for pan-size requirements, otherwise your baking times and servings will be different. These recipes are flexible so that if you want to use two loaf pans instead of one Bundt pan, you can. Just be sure to adjust your baking time. Two smaller loaf pans will bake quicker than one Bundt pan. These types of cakes freeze best without any dusting or frosting. Simply wrap in foil, then plastic, and freeze. Thaw, frost, and enjoy.

BASIC POUND CAKE

This is a classic and should be a part of every baker's repertoire. It offers great flexibility; you can pair it with almost any frosting or garnish. The name "pound cake" comes from the original measurements used to make this cake: one pound of butter, one pound of sugar, one pound of eggs, and one pound of flour.

½ POUND BUTTER, SOFTENED	2 CUPS CAKE FLOUR
1½ CUPS SUGAR	1 TEASPOON BAKING POWDER
1 TEASPOON VANILLA EXTRACT	PINCH OF SALT
4 EGGS	CONFECTIONERS' SUGAR FOR DUSTING

1. Preheat oven to 350°F.

2. Grease and flour or line a 10 x 6 x 2½-inch loaf pan with parchment paper. Set aside.

3. In an electric mixer, cream butter on medium speed. Gradually add sugar and beat until light in color.

4. Add vanilla. Scrape down the sides of the mixing bowl to be sure mixture is well blended. Add eggs, one at a time, beating well after each egg.

5. On low speed, blend in flour, baking powder, and salt just until blended.

6. Pour batter into prepared pan. Bake for 50 to 55 minutes, or until a tester comes out with a fine crumb.

7. Remove pan from the oven and place on wire cooling rack. Let cool in pan for 10 minutes. Carefully remove cake from the pan and continue to cool on wire rack until cool. Remove and discard parchment.

8. Dust the top with confectioners' sugar and serve. Store unused cake wrapped in plastic wrap at room temperature or freeze for later use.

YIELD: ONE LARGE LOAF, ABOUT 12 SLICES

ALMOND POUND CAKE

This family recipe is a popular variation of the Basic Pound Cake, accented by a rich burst of almond. My dad loves this cake topped with Strawberries in Vermouth (page 59) and a dollop of whipped cream.

12 TABLESPOONS BUTTER, SOFTENED

¾ CUP ALMOND PASTE

1 CUP SUGAR

4 EGGS

1 TEASPOON VANILLA EXTRACT

2 CUPS CAKE FLOUR

2 TEASPOONS BAKING POWDER

1 TEASPOON SALT

¾ CUP MILK

1. Preheat oven to 350°F.

2. Grease and flour or line a 10 x 6 x 2½-inch loaf pan with parchment paper. Set aside.

3. In an electric mixer on medium speed, cream the butter. Add almond paste and mix until smooth. Gradually add sugar and beat until light in color.

4. Add eggs, one at a time, mixing well after each egg. Add vanilla.

5. In a small bowl, combine flour, baking powder, and salt. Add this mixture alternately with the milk, beginning and ending with the flour mixture. Mix just until blended.

6. Pour batter into prepared pan. Bake for 55 to 60 minutes, or until a tester comes out with a fine crumb.

7. Remove cake from the oven and cool in pan on wire cooling rack for 10 to 15 minutes.

8. Carefully remove cake from the pan and continue to cool on wire cooling rack. When cool, serve or wrap in foil. Store at room temperature or wrap in foil and plastic, then freeze.

This cake can also be used for the Frozen Almond Strawberry Cake (page 103).

YIELD: ONE LARGE LOAF, ABOUT 12 SLICES

PUMPKIN RAISIN CAKE

This is a moist and spicy autumn favorite that's not too sweet. It's ideal served plain,
alongside a savory soup, or topped with Cream Cheese Frosting (page 122)
for a true New England dessert.

3 EGGS	1½ TEASPOONS BAKING POWDER
1¼ CUPS SUGAR	1½ TEASPOONS CINNAMON
1½ CUPS CANNED PUMPKIN	1 TEASPOON SALT
1¼ CUPS VEGETABLE OIL	1 TEASPOON BAKING SODA
1½ CUPS UNBLEACHED FLOUR	1¼ CUPS RAISINS

1. Preheat oven to 350°F.

2. Grease and flour or line a 10 x 6 x 2½-inch loaf pan with parchment paper.

3. In an electric mixer, mix eggs, sugar, pumpkin, and oil on medium speed until well blended, 2 to 3 minutes.

4. On low speed, gradually add flour, baking powder, cinnamon, salt, and baking soda. Mix just until smooth. Stir in raisins.

5. Pour batter evenly into prepared pan.

6. Bake for 45 to 50 minutes, or until a tester comes out with a fine crumb. Remove pan from the oven and place on wire cooling rack. Cool cake in pan for 10 to 15 minutes.

7. Carefully remove cake from the pan and place on wire cooling rack. Remove and discard parchment.

8. Store at room temperature, wrapped in foil or a plastic bag. Or freeze for later use.

YIELD: ONE LARGE LOAF, ABOUT 12 SLICES

DOT'S ZUCCHINI WALNUT CAKE

This favorite breakfast cake was made by a friend's mom who always baked a batch to take along on family trips. She'd bake one with nuts and one without, to suit everyone in her family. Try a lightly toasted slice with butter or cream cheese.

3 EGGS

1 CUP VEGETABLE OIL

2 CUPS SUGAR

2 TEASPOONS VANILLA EXTRACT

3 CUPS FINELY CHOPPED OR GRATED ZUCCHINI

2 CUPS ALL-PURPOSE FLOUR

¼ TEASPOON BAKING POWDER

1 TEASPOON BAKING SODA

2 TEASPOONS CINNAMON

¼ TEASPOON SALT

1 CUP WALNUTS, COARSELY CHOPPED

1. Preheat oven to 350°F.

2. Grease and flour or line a 10 x 6 x 2½-inch loaf pan with parchment paper. Set aside.

3. In an electric mixer on medium speed, beat eggs. Add oil, sugar, and vanilla and beat until light. Add zucchini.

4. On low speed, gradually add flour, baking powder, baking soda, cinnamon, and salt. Mix just until blended. Stir in walnuts.

5. Pour batter into prepared pan.

6. Bake for 1 hour and 15 to 20 minutes, or until a tester comes out with a fine crumb.

7. Remove pan from the oven. Cool in pan on a wire cooling rack for 10 to 15 minutes. Carefully remove cake from the pan and continue to cool on wire rack. Remove and discard parchment.

YIELD: ONE LARGE LOAF, ABOUT 12 SLICES

RUSTIC APPLE CAKE

This apple and cinnamon cake is a hearty dessert for any occasion. It's great served slightly warm with a scoop of vanilla ice cream. Be sure to line the tube pan with parchment. The apples can get a little sticky without it.

1½ CUPS PLUS 2 TABLESPOONS SUGAR

2 TEASPOONS CINNAMON

1 CUP CHOPPED WALNUTS, OPTIONAL

6 EGGS

½ CUP VEGETABLE OIL

4 TABLESPOONS LEMON JUICE

GRATED RIND OF 1 LEMON

1 TEASPOON VANILLA EXTRACT

2 CUPS ALL-PURPOSE FLOUR

2 TEASPOONS BAKING POWDER

4 APPLES, CORED, PEELED, AND THINLY SLICED (ABOUT 4 CUPS)

1. Preheat oven to 350°F.

2. Grease and flour or line a 10-inch tube pan with parchment paper. Set aside.

3. In a small bowl, combine 2 tablespoons sugar, cinnamon, and walnuts. Set aside.

4. In an electric mixer on medium speed, mix eggs, 1½ cups sugar, oil, lemon juice, lemon rind, and vanilla. On low speed, add flour and baking powder. Mix until batter is smooth.

5. Pour half the batter into prepared pan. Spread half the apple slices over batter. Sprinkle with half the cinnamon and sugar mixture. Pour remaining batter over apples. Spread the remaining apple slices on top and sprinkle with remaining cinnamon and sugar.

6. Bake for 60 to 65 minutes, or until a tester comes out with a fine crumb. Remove pan from the oven and cool in pan on wire cooling rack. Be sure that this cake is very cool before you remove it from the pan.

YIELD: ONE 10-INCH CAKE, ABOUT 25 SLICES

CITRUS YOGURT CAKE

This light and zesty cake is ideal for summer picnics and parties. This is my favorite version, using a combination of lemons and limes. You can use either one or the other, or try using oranges.

½ POUND BUTTER, SOFTENED	1 CUP PLAIN YOGURT
2 CUPS SUGAR	2¼ CUPS CAKE FLOUR
3 EGGS	½ TEASPOON BAKING SODA
GRATED RIND OF 2 LEMONS	¼ TEASPOON SALT
GRATED RIND OF 2 LIMES	JUICE OF 2 LIMES
JUICE OF 2 LEMONS	CONFECTIONERS' SUGAR FOR DUSTING

1. Preheat oven to 350°F.

2. Grease and flour or line two 8 x 4 x 3-inch loaf pans with parchment paper. Set aside.

3. In an electric mixer on medium speed, cream butter. Add sugar gradually and beat until light in color.

4. Add eggs, one at a time, beating well after adding each one. Add lemon and lime rind and lemon juice. Add yogurt and blend well.

5. On low speed, add flour, baking soda, and salt. Mix just until blended. Pour batter into prepared pans. Spread batter evenly in pans.

6. Bake for 55 to 60 minutes, or until a tester comes out with a fine crumb.

7. Remove from the oven. Pour lime juice over the hot cakes. Cool cakes in pans for 20 to 25 minutes. Carefully remove cakes from the pans and continue to cool on wire cooling racks. Cool completely. Remove and discard parchment.

8. Dust with confectioners' sugar or Confectioners' Glaze (page 54) and serve.

YIELD: TWO SMALL LOAVES, ABOUT 12 SLICES EACH

BLUEBERRY BANANA CAKE

This tasty breakfast cake uses mashed bananas for the perfect complement to fresh blueberries. Try a slice with your morning coffee or a hot herbal tea. If fresh blueberries are not available, frozen ones will work just as well.

¼ POUND BUTTER, SOFTENED	PINCH OF SALT
2 CUPS PLUS 1 TABLESPOON SUGAR	1½ TEASPOONS BAKING POWDER
3 EGGS	½ CUP MILK
½ CUP MASHED BANANAS (1½ MEDIUM BANANAS)	2 CUPS FRESH OR FROZEN BLUEBERRIES
3 CUPS PLUS 1 TABLESPOON ALL-PURPOSE FLOUR	

1. Preheat oven to 350°F.

2. Grease and flour a 9-inch fluted Bundt pan. Set aside.

3. In an electric mixer on medium speed, cream the butter. Gradually add sugar. Add eggs, one at a time, beating well after each one. Add mashed bananas.

4. In a separate bowl, mix flour, salt, and baking powder. Add flour mixture to the butter mixture alternately with the milk, starting and ending with the flour mixture. Mix until just blended and smooth.

5. In a separate bowl, mix blueberries with 1 tablespoon flour and 1 tablespoon sugar to coat. Stir coated blueberries into batter. Pour into prepared pan.

6. Bake for 60 to 65 minutes, or until a tester comes out with a fine crumb. Remove cake from oven and place on wire cooling rack. Cool cake in pan for 15 to 20 minutes. Remove cake from pan and continue to cool, right side up, on cooling rack.

YIELD: ONE 9-INCH CAKE, ABOUT 20 SLICES

APRICOT NUT CAKE

This dense butter cake accented with dried apricots updates a classic family fruitcake recipe. For this cake, and most fruitcakes, coat the fruit and nuts with flour before adding to your batter. This will keep them from sinking to the bottom of the cake.

1½ CUPS PECANS, COARSELY CHOPPED

1½ CUPS DRIED APRICOTS, COARSELY CHOPPED

3½ CUPS CAKE FLOUR

½ POUND BUTTER, SOFTENED

2 CUPS SUGAR

2 TEASPOONS VANILLA EXTRACT

4 EGGS

1 TEASPOON BAKING SODA

1½ CUPS SOUR CREAM

CONFECTIONERS' SUGAR FOR DUSTING

GLAZE:

¼ CUP RUM

½ CUP ORANGE JUICE

1. Preheat oven to 350°F.

2. Grease and flour or line two 10 x 6 x 2½-inch loaf pans with parchment paper. Set aside.

3. Combine nuts and apricots in a small bowl. Toss them with 3 tablespoons of the flour. Coat well. Set aside.

4. In an electric mixer on medium speed, cream butter and sugar until light in color. Add vanilla. Add eggs, one at a time, mixing well after each egg. Scrape down the sides of the bowl.

5. Combine flour and baking soda. Add flour mixture to the butter mixture, gradually at low speed, alternating with the sour cream. Start and end with the flour mixture. Mix just until blended.

6. Stir in nuts and apricots. Spoon batter equally into prepared loaf pans.

7. Bake for 50 to 55 minutes, or until a tester comes out with a fine crumb. Remove pans from the oven. Place on wire cooling racks.

8. In a small cup, mix together rum and orange juice. Pour evenly over the hot cakes. Cool cakes in pans for 15 to 20 minutes. Remove cakes from the pans and

continue cooling the cakes on wire racks until cool. Remove and discard parchment. Dust with confectioners' sugar before serving, or freeze.

YIELD: TWO LARGE LOAVES, ABOUT 12 SLICES EACH

◆ **DECORATING AND SERVING LOAF AND** ◆
BUNDT CAKES

THROUGHOUT THE BOOK I'VE MADE SERVING SUGGESTIONS, PAIRING CAKES WITH GARNISHES. THESE ARE MERELY SUGGESTIONS. FEEL FREE TO MAKE UP YOUR OWN COMBINATIONS. YOU CAN ALSO SIMPLY DUST THE TOP WITH CONFECTIONERS' SUGAR, USE A GLAZE DRIZZLED OVER THE TOP, OR TOP A SLICE OF CAKE WITH A SCOOP OF ICE CREAM OR WHIPPED CREAM AND FRESH FRUIT.

A NICE SIMPLE WAY TO SERVE A PIECE OF CAKE IS TO SPREAD A FRUIT SAUCE ON THE PLATE, TOP WITH A SLICE OF CAKE, AND ADD ANOTHER DRIZZLE OF SAUCE ON TOP. DRIZZLE BY DIPPING A FORK INTO A FRUIT OR FUDGE SAUCE, THEN SHAKE THE SAUCE ONTO THE CAKE.

CRANBERRY NUT BUNDT CAKE

Cranberries, dates, and walnuts make the perfect combination for holiday gatherings. This is the first of many recipes given to me by my mother-in-law. She easily doubles this recipe and makes extra cakes that are ideal holiday gifts for teachers or neighbors.

2 EGGS

1 CUP SUGAR

¾ CUP VEGETABLE OIL

2½ CUPS ALL-PURPOSE FLOUR

1 TEASPOON BAKING POWDER

1 TEASPOON BAKING SODA

1 CUP BUTTERMILK

1 CUP WHOLE CRANBERRIES, FRESH OR FROZEN

1 CUP CHOPPED DATES

1 CUP WALNUTS, COARSELY CHOPPED

CONFECTIONERS' SUGAR FOR DUSTING

GLAZE:

¼ CUP ORANGE JUICE

¼ CUP WHISKEY

1. Preheat oven to 350°F.

2. Grease and flour a 9-inch Bundt pan. Set aside.

3. In an electric mixer on medium speed, mix eggs, sugar, and oil. In a separate bowl, blend flour, baking powder, and baking soda. Gradually add the flour mixture, alternately with the buttermilk, on low speed. Start and end with the flour mixture. Mix just until blended.

4. Fold in cranberries, dates, and walnuts. Pour batter into prepared pan. Bake for 25 to 30 minutes, or until a tester comes out with a fine crumb. Remove cake from the oven and place on wire cooling rack. Mix orange juice and whiskey and pour over hot cake.

5. Cool cake in pan for 10 to 15 minutes. Carefully remove cake from the pan and continue cooling on wire cooling rack. Dust with confectioners' sugar or frost with Confectioners' Glaze (page 54).

YIELD: ONE 9-INCH CAKE, ABOUT 20 SLICES

PECAN DATE BOURBON CAKE

This nut-and-date-studded cake has a subtle orange flavor. The bourbon orange juice glaze keeps it fresh and moist for days. It's an ideal cake to bake and give for that perfect thank you.

12 TABLESPOONS BUTTER, SOFTENED	½ TEASPOON SALT
1½ CUPS SUGAR	1½ TEASPOONS BAKING SODA
1 TEASPOON VANILLA EXTRACT	1½ CUPS BUTTERMILK
1 TABLESPOON GRATED ORANGE RIND	1 CUP PECANS, COARSELY CHOPPED
3 EGGS	1 CUP DATES, CHOPPED
3 CUPS CAKE FLOUR	CONFECTIONERS' SUGAR FOR DUSTING

GLAZE:

¼ CUP ORANGE JUICE	2 TABLESPOONS BOURBON

1. Preheat oven to 350°F.

2. Grease and flour a 9-inch Bundt pan. Set aside.

3. In an electric mixer on medium speeed, cream the butter. Gradually add sugar and beat until light in color. Add vanilla and orange rind. Beat until blended. Add eggs, one at a time, beating well after adding each one.

4. Combine flour, salt, and baking soda in a separate bowl. Add flour mixture to the butter mixture alternately with the buttermilk. Begin and end with the flour mixture. Mix until smooth. Stir in pecans and dates. Pour batter into prepared pan.

5. Bake for 40 to 45 minutes, or until a tester comes out with a fine crumb. Remove cake from the oven. Cool cake in pan on wire rack. While cake is hot, mix orange juice and bourbon and pour over the cake. Cool in pan for 10 to 15 minutes. Remove cake from the pan. Continue to cool on wire rack until cool.

6. Dust top with confectioners' sugar and serve.

YIELD: ONE 9-INCH CAKE, ABOUT 20 SLICES

COCONUT POUND CAKE

This moist and sweet cake is great served plain or topped with a spoonful of crushed pineapple and a dollop of whipped cream for a piña colada dessert.

½ POUND UNSALTED BUTTER	1 TEASPOON BAKING POWDER
2 CUPS SUGAR	¼ TEASPOON SALT
1 TEASPOON VANILLA EXTRACT	1 CUP MILK
4 EGGS	1½ CUPS SHREDDED COCONUT
2½ CUPS CAKE FLOUR	

1. Preheat oven to 350°F.

2. Grease and flour or line two 8 x 4 x 3-inch loaf pans with parchment paper. Set aside.

3. In an electric mixer on medium speed, cream the butter. Gradually add the sugar and beat until light in color. Add vanilla. Add eggs, one at a time, beating well after each egg.

4. In a small bowl, combine flour, baking powder, and salt. On low speed, add to the butter mixture alternately with the milk. Start and end with the flour mixture. Mix just until blended. Stir in coconut. Pour batter into prepared pans.

5. Bake for 55 to 60 minutes, or until a tester comes out with a fine crumb. Remove cakes from the oven and cool on wire cooling racks for 10 to 15 minutes. If you're using foil pans, continue cooling the cakes completely in the pans. If you're using a traditional cake pan, carefully remove the cakes from the pan and continue to cool on wire cooling racks until completely cool.

YIELD: TWO LOAVES, ABOUT 12 SLICES EACH

HOLIDAY FRUITCAKE

This recipe is one of my mom's holiday specialties. Use a combination of red and green cherries for a festive Christmas look. Save a slice for Santa.

8 OUNCES CREAM CHEESE, SOFTENED	1½ TEASPOONS BAKING POWDER
½ POUND BUTTER	2 CUPS GLACÉ CHERRY HALVES
1½ CUPS SUGAR	2 CUPS WALNUTS, COARSELY CHOPPED
1 TEASPOON VANILLA EXTRACT	½ CUP CHOPPED DATES
4 EGGS	½ CUP RAISINS
2 CUPS PLUS 3 TABLESPOONS ALL-PURPOSE FLOUR	¼ CUP WHISKEY
	CONFECTIONERS' SUGAR FOR DUSTING

1. Preheat oven to 325°F.

2. Grease and flour a 9-inch Bundt pan. Set aside.

3. In an electric mixer on medium speed, cream the cream cheese until fluffy, about 3 minutes. Add butter. Beat until smooth. Gradually add sugar and beat until light.

4. Add vanilla. Add eggs, one at a time, beating well after each one. On low speed, gradually add 2 cups flour and baking powder. Mix just until blended.

5. In a medium mixing bowl, combine cherries, nuts, dates, and raisins. Toss with 3 tablespoons of flour to coat. Fold fruit and nut mixture into batter. Pour batter into prepared pan.

6. Bake for 55 to 60 minutes, or until a tester comes out with a fine crumb. Remove pan from the oven and place on a wire cooling rack. Pour whiskey evenly over the hot cake. Cool cake in pan for 10 to 15 minutes. Carefully remove from pan and continue to cool on wire cooling rack. Store at room temperature wrapped in foil, or freeze. Dust with confectioners' sugar or frost with Confectioners' Glaze (page 54) before serving.

YIELD: ONE 9-INCH CAKE, ABOUT 25 SLICES

CARIBBEAN FRUITCAKE

This dark, rich fruitcake is full of flavor from rum-soaked fruit. This type of
fruitcake originated in the islands, where spices, molasses,
and rum were plentiful.

2 CUPS RAISINS	2 CUPS DARK BROWN SUGAR
1 CUP DATES, CHOPPED	5 EGGS
1 CAN CRUSHED PINEAPPLE, WITH JUICE	2 CUPS ALL-PURPOSE FLOUR
	2 TEASPOONS BAKING POWDER
1 CUP SLICED ALMONDS	1½ TEASPOONS ALLSPICE
1 CUP CURRANTS	PINCH OF SALT
½ CUP DARK RUM	CONFECTIONERS' SUGAR FOR DUSTING
½ POUND BUTTER, SOFTENED	

1. In a medium mixing bowl combine raisins, dates, pineapple, almonds, currants, and rum. Let soak for 1 to 2 hours at room temperature.

2. Preheat oven to 350°F.

3. Grease and flour or line a 10-inch tube pan with parchment paper. Set aside.

4. In an electric mixer on medium speed, cream the butter. Gradually add the brown sugar and beat until light in color. Add eggs, one at a time, beating well after each egg.

5. On low speed, gradually add the flour, baking powder, allspice, and salt. Mix just until blended. Fold in fruit mixture. Pour batter into prepared pan.

6. Bake for 60 to 65 minutes, or until a tester comes out with a fine crumb. Remove cake from the oven and place on wire cooling rack. Cool cake in pan for 20 to 25 minutes. Carefully remove cake from the pan and continue to cool on wire rack. Store at room temperature wrapped in foil, or freeze. Dust with confectioners' sugar before serving.

YIELD: ONE 10-INCH CAKE, ABOUT 30 SLICES

CHOCOLATE MAYONNAISE CAKE

This cake combines one of my least favorite things, mayonnaise, with one of my favorite things, chocolate. It may sound like an odd match, but since mayonnaise is basically eggs and oil, it's the perfect secret ingredient for making this light, moist cake. It works with a number of toppings. Try it with a spoonful of Raspberry Sauce (page 58), ice cream, and fresh berries.

2 CUPS CAKE FLOUR	¼ TEASPOON SALT
1½ CUPS SUGAR	1 CUP COLD BREWED COFFEE
2 TEASPOONS BAKING SODA	1 CUP MAYONNAISE
½ CUP COCOA	1 TEASPOON VANILLA EXTRACT

1. Preheat oven to 350°F.

2. Grease and flour or line a 10 x 6 x 2½-inch loaf pan with parchment paper. Set aside.

3. In an electric mixer on low speed, blend flour, sugar, baking soda, cocoa, and salt. Add coffee, mayonnaise, and vanilla. Beat until smooth and well blended, about 2 minutes.

4. Pour batter into prepared pan. Bake for 25 to 30 minutes, or until a tester comes out with a fine crumb. Remove cake from the oven and cool in pan on wire cooling rack for 10 to 15 minutes.

5. Carefully remove cake from the pan and continue to cool top side up on wire cooling rack. Remove and discard parchment.

6. Serve, or wrap in foil and store at room temperature, or freeze.

YIELD: ONE LARGE LOAF, ABOUT 12 SLICES

NEW ENGLAND MAPLE
WALNUT CAKE

Top this cake with a dollop of whipped cream or a scoop of ice cream and a drizzle of maple syrup. It's the perfect way to conclude an autumn feast.

½ POUND PLUS 4 TABLESPOONS
BUTTER, SOFTENED

1½ CUPS SUGAR

½ CUP BROWN SUGAR

1½ TEASPOONS MAPLE EXTRACT

6 EGGS

2¼ CUPS CAKE FLOUR

2 TEASPOONS BAKING POWDER

½ TEASPOON SALT

1¼ CUPS CHOPPED WALNUTS

1. Preheat oven to 350°F.

2. Grease and flour or line a 10-inch tube pan with parchment paper. Set aside.

3. In an electric mixer on medium speed, cream butter. Add sugar and brown sugar gradually and beat until light in color. Add maple extract.

4. Add eggs, one at a time, beating well after adding each one.

5. On low speed, add flour, baking powder, and salt mix just until ingredients are incorporated. Scrape down the mixing bowl to be sure batter is well mixed.

6. Fold in walnuts.

7. Pour batter into prepared tube pan. Bake for 50 to 55 minutes, or until a tester comes out with a fine crumb. Remove pan from the oven. Let cake cool in pan on wire rack for 10 to 15 minutes. Carefully remove cake from pan and let cool completely on wire rack.

8. Frost with Maple Glaze (page 56) and serve.

YIELD: ONE 10-INCH CAKE, ABOUT 25 SLICES

PISTACHIO CAKE

This hearty and flavorful loaf cake is the ideal companion to a cup of fresh brewed coffee. Its light-green color makes it a natural for St. Patrick's Day.

½ POUND BUTTER

1¼ CUPS SUGAR

4 EGGS

½ TEASPOON PISTACHIO EXTRACT
(OPTIONAL)

1¾ CUPS ALL-PURPOSE FLOUR

1 TEASPOON BAKING POWDER

1 CUP CHOPPED PISTACHIOS, TOASTED

CONFECTIONERS' SUGAR FOR DUSTING

1. Preheat oven to 350°F.

2. Grease and flour or line a 10 x 6 x 2½-inch loaf pan with parchment paper. Set aside.

3. In an electric mixer on medium speed, cream the butter. Add the sugar and beat until light in color. Add the eggs, one at a time, beating well after adding each one. Add pistachio extract.

4. On low speed, gradually add the flour and baking powder. Mix just until blended. Stir in pistachios.

5. Bake for 55 to 60 minutes, or until a tester comes out with a fine crumb. Remove pan from the oven. Cool cake in pan on wire cooling rack for 10 to 15 minutes. Remove cake from the pan and continue to cool cake on wire rack. Remove and discard parchment. Dust top of cake with confectioners' sugar and serve.

YIELD: ONE LARGE LOAF, ABOUT 12 SLICES

CLASSIC SPONGE CAKE

This cake has always been a family favorite. Dress it up with a fancy filling or serve it sliced with fresh berries for the perfect summer dessert. Be sure to use a tube pan with a removable bottom.

7 EGG WHITES, AT ROOM
TEMPERATURE

1½ CUPS SUGAR

½ TEASPOON CREAM OF TARTAR

½ TEASPOON SALT

7 EGG YOLKS

1 TEASPOON VANILLA EXTRACT

1½ CUPS CAKE FLOUR

¼ CUP COLD WATER

1. Preheat oven to 325°F.

2. In an electric mixer with wire whisk attachment, beat egg whites, ¼ cup of the sugar, cream of tartar, and salt. Start on medium speed, then use high speed until very stiff peaks form, 3 to 4 minutes.

3. In a separate bowl, with an electric mixer on medium speed, beat egg yolks, 1¼ cups sugar, and vanilla. Beat until light in color, 2 to 3 minutes.

4. Add flour and water to egg mixture alternately. Start and end with the flour. Mix just until blended.

5. Using a rubber spatula, fold egg yolk mixture into egg whites. When blended, spoon batter into an ungreased 10-inch tube pan with removable bottom. Spread batter evenly.

6. Bake for 60 to 65 minutes, or until top is golden brown. Remove pan from the oven.

7. Invert tube pan to cool cake, about 1 hour.

8. When cool, carefully remove cake from the pan. Use a sharp knife to loosen the outside of the cake from the sides of the pan.

YIELD: ONE 10-INCH CAKE, APPROXIMATELY 20 SLICES

FOR VARIATIONS AND FILLINGS SEE:

Cannoli Cake, page 69

Tiramisù Cake, page 92

Josephine & Napoleon Cake, page 110

Holiday Eggnog Cake, page 78

◆ **CAKE MYTH #1** ◆

WHEN WE WERE YOUNG, MY MOM ALWAYS TOLD US NOT TO JUMP
AROUND NEAR THE OVEN WHILE A CAKE WAS BAKING. WE WERE ALWAYS
TOLD OUR MOVEMENT WOULD CAUSE THE CAKE TO FALL. WHAT AN EX-
CUSE TO GET CHILDREN TO BEHAVE! ALTHOUGH MOVEMENT AROUND THE
OVEN SHOULDN'T MAKE A DIFFERENCE, DON'T OPEN THE OVEN DURING
THE FIRST PART OF BAKING. THIS SUDDEN CHANGE IN TEMPERATURE CAN
CAUSE THE CAKE TO FALL.

CHOCOLATE SPONGE CAKE

This variation of the Classic Sponge Cake is a real winner. It is delicious served plain, or with fresh fruit for a perfect summer dessert. You can get creative, too, by substituting this chocolate sponge in layer cake recipes that use a plain sponge. The sky's the limit!

7 EGG WHITES, AT ROOM
TEMPERATURE

1½ CUPS SUGAR

½ TEASPOON CREAM OF TARTAR

½ TEASPOON SALT

7 EGG YOLKS

1 TEASPOON VANILLA EXTRACT

1 CUP CAKE FLOUR

½ CUP COCOA

¼ CUP WATER

1. Preheat oven to 325°F.

2. In an electric mixer with wire whisk attachment, beat egg whites, ¼ cup of the sugar, cream of tartar, and salt. Start on medium speed and then increase to high speed until very stiff peaks form, 3 to 4 minutes.

3. In a separate bowl, with an electric mixer on medium speed, beat egg yolks, 1¼ cups sugar, and vanilla. Beat until light in color, 2 to 3 minutes.

4. In a small bowl, combine flour and cocoa. Add this mixture alternately with the water to the egg yolk mixture. Start and end with the flour. Mix just until blended.

5. Using a rubber spatula, fold yolk mixture into egg whites. When thoroughly blended, spoon batter into an ungreased 10-inch tube pan with removable bottom. Spread batter evenly.

6. Bake for 60 to 65 minutes. Remove pan from the oven.

7. Invert tube pan to cool cake for about 1 hour.

8. When cool, use a sharp knife to loosen the cake from the pan.

YIELD: ONE 10-INCH CAKE, ABOUT 20 SLICES

CHOCOLATE ALMOND ANGEL FOOD CAKE

This is a new twist on the classic angel food cake. Angel food cakes have always been popular for their light texture and have always been a great fat-free choice for dessert. For a low-fat filled Mocha Cake, see page 114.

¾ CUPS CAKE FLOUR

4 TABLESPOONS COCOA

1¼ CUPS SUGAR

10 EGG WHITES

¼ TEASPOON SALT

1 TEASPOON CREAM OF TARTAR

1 TEASPOON ALMOND EXTRACT

CONFECTIONERS' SUGAR FOR DUSTING

1. Preheat oven to 325°F.

2. In a small bowl, combine flour, cocoa, and ¼ cup of the sugar. Set aside

3. In an electric mixer with wire whisk attachment, beat egg whites and salt. When foamy, add cream of tartar. Whip until stiff peaks form.

4. Add remaining sugar gradually, 2 tablespoons at a time. Mix until blended.

5. Fold in almond extract. Carefully fold flour mixture into egg white mixture just until ingredients are incorporated.

6. Pour batter onto an ungreased 10-inch tube pan. Bake for 40 to 45 minutes. Remove pan from oven. Invert cake to cool pan for about 1 hour. Carefully remove cake from pan.

7. Dust with confectioners' sugar and serve.

YIELD: ONE 10-INCH CAKE, ABOUT 15 SLICES

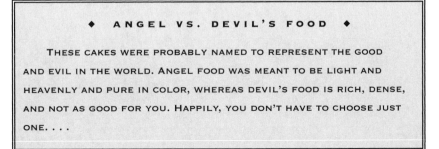

◆ ANGEL VS. DEVIL'S FOOD ◆

THESE CAKES WERE PROBABLY NAMED TO REPRESENT THE GOOD AND EVIL IN THE WORLD. ANGEL FOOD WAS MEANT TO BE LIGHT AND HEAVENLY AND PURE IN COLOR, WHEREAS DEVIL'S FOOD IS RICH, DENSE, AND NOT AS GOOD FOR YOU. HAPPILY, YOU DON'T HAVE TO CHOOSE JUST ONE. . . .

CAPPUCCINO CHIFFON CAKE

This light and fluffy cake has a nice coffee flavor with a hint of cinnamon. You can dust the top with confectioners' sugar, or try a slice with a scoop of coffee ice cream and a drizzle of hot fudge sauce.

6 EGGS, SEPARATED	2 TEASPOONS COFFEE LIQUEUR
½ TEASPOON CREAM OF TARTAR	2¼ CUPS CAKE FLOUR
1¼ CUPS SUGAR	3 TEASPOONS BAKING POWDER
¾ CUPS COOLED BREWED ESPRESSO	2 TEASPOONS CINNAMON
½ CUP VEGETABLE OIL	

1. Preheat oven to 325°F.

2. In an electric mixer with wire attachment, beat egg whites, cream of tartar, and ½ cup of the sugar until stiff peaks form. Set aside.

3. In an electric mixer on medium speed, beat egg yolks. Gradually add remaining sugar. Add espresso, vegetable oil, and coffee liqueur. On low speed, gradually add the flour, baking powder, and cinnamon. Mix until smooth. Using a rubber spatula, carefully fold flour mixture into egg whites. Pour batter into an ungreased 10-inch tube pan.

4. Bake for 50 to 55 minutes, or until a tester comes out clean. Remove cake from the oven. Invert cake to cool for about 1 hour. When completely cool, carefully remove cake from the pan. Using a sharp knife, loosen cake from around the sides and center of the pan.

YIELD: ONE 10-INCH CAKE, ABOUT 20 SLICES

APPLESAUCE CAKE

This is another personal favorite. It's easy to make and is just as popular eaten for breakfast, an afternoon snack, or dessert after a potluck supper.

4 TABLESPOONS BUTTER, SOFTENED	1¼ CUPS ALL-PURPOSE FLOUR
½ CUP SUGAR	1 TEASPOON BAKING SODA
1 EGG	½ TEASPOON BAKING POWDER
1 TEASPOON VANILLA EXTRACT	½ TEASPOON CINNAMON
1 CUP CHUNKY APPLESAUCE	

1. Preheat oven to 350°F.

2. Grease and flour or line an 8 x 4 x 3-inch loaf pan with parchment paper. Set aside.

3. In an electric mixer on medium speed, cream the butter. Add the sugar and beat until light. Add the egg, vanilla, and applesauce. Beat until well blended.

4. On low speed, gradually add the flour, baking soda, baking powder, and cinnamon. Mix just until blended. Pour batter into prepared pan.

5. Bake for 45 to 50 minutes, or until a tester comes out with a fine crumb. Remove pan from the oven. Cool cake in pan on wire rack for 10 to 15 minutes. Remove cake from the pan and continue to cool on wire rack.

YIELD: ONE SMALL LOAF, ABOUT 10 SLICES

ORANGE PLUM CAKE

This cake has a tender texture and combines fresh and dried fruit. The tart dried plums add a nice contrast to the sweetness of the orange. Perfect for breakfast or afternoon tea.

¼ POUND PLUS 3 TABLESPOONS BUTTER, SOFTENED

1 CUP CONFECTIONERS' SUGAR

2 EGGS

½ TEASPOON VANILLA EXTRACT

1 CUP CAKE FLOUR

½ TEASPOON BAKING POWDER

GRATED RIND OF 1 ORANGE

1 ORANGE, PEELED AND CUT INTO SMALL PIECES

1 CUP DRIED PLUMS, COARSELY CHOPPED

CONFECTIONERS' SUGAR FOR DUSTING

1. Preheat oven to 350°F.

2. Grease and flour or line a 10 x 6 x 2½-inch loaf pan with parchment paper. Set aside.

3. In an electric mixer on medium speed, cream the butter and confectioners' sugar until blended. Scrape down the sides of the bowl with a rubber spatula.

4. Add the eggs, one at a time, beating well after each egg. Add vanilla.

5. On low speed, gradually add the flour, baking powder, and orange rind. Mix just until blended.

6. Stir in orange pieces and plums. Spoon batter into prepared pan.

7. Bake for 50 to 55 minutes, or until a tester comes out with a fine crumb. Remove pan from the oven.

8. Cool cake in pan on wire rack for 10 to 15 minutes. Remove from the pan. Continue cooling cake on wire rack until cool. Remove and discard parchment. Dust the top with confectioners' sugar.

9. Store cake at room temperature, wrapped in aluminum foil or plastic wrap. Or freeze for later use.

YIELD: ONE LARGE LOAF, ABOUT 12 SLICES

CHOCOLATE MINT CAKE

This cake has a subtle chocolate flavor, accented with fresh mint, which is usually available year-round in most supermarkets. Our local herb farm also has a nice chocolate mint plant that works wonderfully in this recipe.

½ POUND BUTTER

3 CUPS SUGAR

3 TABLESPOONS INSTANT COFFEE

2 TEASPOONS COFFEE LIQUEUR

3 EGGS

3 CUPS CAKE FLOUR

2 TEASPOONS BAKING POWDER

¼ TEASPOON SALT

1 CUP COCOA

1¾ CUPS BUTTERMILK

2 TABLESPOONS FRESH MINT LEAVES

1. Preheat oven to 350°F.

2. Grease and flour or line a 10-inch tube pan with parchment paper. Set aside.

3. In an electric mixer on medium speed, cream the butter. Gradually add the sugar and beat until light in color. Add coffee and liqueur. Add the eggs, one at a time, beating well after adding each one.

4. In a medium bowl, combine flour, baking powder, salt, and cocoa. Add this flour mixture to the butter mixture alternately with the buttermilk, beginning and ending with the flour mixture. Stir in mint leaves. Mix just until blended. Pour batter into prepared pan.

5. Bake for 1 hour and 10 minutes, or until a tester comes out with a fine crumb. Remove cake from the oven and cool in pan on wire cooling rack for 10 to 15 minutes.

6. Carefully remove cake from the pan and continue to cool on wire rack. Remove and discard parchment. Serve, or store at room temperature in foil.

YIELD: ONE 10-INCH CAKE, ABOUT 25 SLICES

FIG COFFEE CAKE

Another family favorite—a delicious butter cake accented by a rich fig-and-raspberry filling. This recipe makes two large loaf cakes, one to serve now, another for the freezer or a friend.

FILLING:

12 OUNCES DRIED FIGS	2 TABLESPOONS GRAND MARNIER
½ CUP SUGAR	½ CUP CHOPPED WALNUTS
1 TEASPOON CINNAMON	½ CUP RASPBERRY PRESERVES

CAKE:

½ POUND BUTTER, SOFTENED	3 CUPS ALL-PURPOSE FLOUR
3 CUPS SUGAR	¼ TEASPOON BAKING SODA
2 TEASPOONS VANILLA EXTRACT	1 CUP SOUR CREAM
6 EGGS	

1. Place figs in a medium saucepan. Cover with water. Boil, uncovered, on high heat until tender, about 10 minutes. Drain.

2. Pour figs into food processor and process until finely chopped. Place in a small bowl. Stir in sugar, cinnamon, Grand Marnier, nuts, and raspberry preserves. Set aside.

3. Preheat oven to 350°F. Grease and flour or line two 10 x 6 x 2½-inch loaf pans with baking parchment. Set aside.

4. In an electric mixer on medium speed, cream butter. Add sugar and beat until light. Add vanilla. Add the eggs, one at a time, beating well after each egg.

5. Combine flour and baking soda. On low speed, add flour mixture to the butter mixture alternately with sour cream. Start and end with the flour mixture. Mix just until blended.

6. Pour half the batter into prepared pans. Spread half the filling over the batter. Pour remaining batter evenly over two cakes. Spoon remaining filling evenly over two cakes. Bake for 75 to 80 minutes, or until a tester comes out with a fine crumb. Remove pans from the oven.

7. Place on wire cooling rack and cool cakes in pans for 15 to 20 minutes. Carefully remove cakes from the pans and place on wire cooling rack to cool. Remove and discard parchment.

YIELD: TWO LARGE LOAVES, ABOUT 12 SLICES EACH

◆ **COFFEE CAKES** ◆

THIS TERM ORIGINALLY REFERRED TO CAKES THAT WERE MADE WITH YEAST, SIMILAR TO A DANISH ROLL. TODAY, IT'S USED TO INCLUDE ANY TYPE OF RICH CAKE FILLED WITH FRUIT, NUTS, OR CHEESE.

CINNAMON SOUR CREAM CAKE

This is truly one of my all-time favorites. The cinnamon-and-sugar filling is perfect anywhere and anytime—breakfasts, picnics, or lunches. Plus, baking this cake makes the whole house smell good.

FILLING:

½ CUP SUGAR

½ CUP WALNUTS, FINELY CHOPPED

2 TEASPOONS CINNAMON

CAKE:

¼ POUND BUTTER, SOFTENED

1 CUP SUGAR

3 EGGS

1 CUP SOUR CREAM

1 TEASPOON ALMOND EXTRACT

1 TEASPOON VANILLA EXTRACT

3 CUPS CAKE FLOUR

3 TEASPOONS BAKING POWDER

1 TEASPOON BAKING SODA

½ TEASPOON SALT

1. Preheat oven to 350°F.

2. Grease and flour or line a 10-inch tube pan with parchment paper. Set aside.

3. For the filling, combine sugar, cinnamon, and walnuts in a small bowl. Set aside.

4. Using an electric mixer on medium speed, cream the butter and sugar until light in color. Add eggs, one at a time, beating well after adding each egg. Add sour cream and almond and vanilla extracts.

5. On low speed, gradually add flour, baking powder, baking soda, and salt. Mix just until blended.

6. Spread half the batter in the prepared tube pan. Sprinkle the batter with three quarters of the filling mixture. Spread remaining batter on top of filling. Sprinkle top of cake with remaining filling.

7. Bake for 50 to 60 minutes, or until a tester comes out with a fine crumb. Remove pan from the oven. Place on a wire cooling rack. Cool cake in pan for 10 to 15 minutes. Carefully remove cake from the pan and continue cooling on wire rack. Remove and discard parchment.

8. Slice and serve warm, or cool completely and wrap in foil. Store at room temperature.

YIELD: ONE 10-INCH CAKE, ABOUT 20 SLICES

SPECKLED CHIP POUND CAKE

This cake combines the best white and dark chocolate flavors with chopped walnuts. It is ideal served slightly warm with ice cream and a drizzle of chocolate sauce.

¾ CUP WHITE CHOCOLATE CHIPS	3 EGGS
¾ CUP SEMISWEET CHOCOLATE CHIPS	2½ CUPS ALL-PURPOSE FLOUR
1 CUP WALNUTS, FINELY CHOPPED	½ TEASPOON BAKING SODA
½ POUND BUTTER, SOFTENED	¼ TEASPOON SALT
2 CUPS SUGAR	1 CUP BUTTERMILK
1 TEASPOON VANILLA EXTRACT	

1. Preheat oven to 350°F.

2. Grease and flour a 10-inch Bundt pan. Set aside.

3. In a food processor, pulse chocolate chips and nuts until very fine. Set aside.

4. In an electric mixer on medium speed, cream the butter. Gradually add the sugar and beat until light in color. Add vanilla. Add eggs, one at a time, beating well after adding each egg. Mix until well blended.

5. In a small bowl, combine flour, baking soda, and salt. On low speed, add flour mixture, alternately with buttermilk. Start and end with the flour mixture. Mix just until blended.

6. Stir in chocolate chips and nuts until well blended. Pour batter into prepared pan.

7. Bake for 60 to 65 minutes, or until a tester comes out with a fine crumb. Remove pan from the oven. Cool in pan on wire cooling rack for 10 to 15 minutes. Carefully remove cake from the pan and continue cooling on wire rack, fluted side up, until cool. Drizzle with Chocolate Glaze (page 55) and serve with a scoop of ice cream.

YIELD: ONE 10-INCH CAKE, 20 TO 25 SLICES

SWEET POTATO CAKE

Sweet potatoes or yams can be used interchangeably in this and many recipes. Sweet potatoes are not really related to the potato family but are members of the root vegetable family. They have always been a popular ingredient in Southern cooking and add a nice flavor and texture to this cake.

4 EGGS	2 TEASPOONS BAKING POWDER
2 CUPS SUGAR	2 TEASPOONS CINNAMON
1¼ CUP VEGETABLE OIL	½ TEASPOON CLOVES
1 TEASPOON VANILLA EXTRACT	2 CUPS GRATED SWEET POTATO
3 CUPS ALL-PURPOSE FLOUR	1 CUP WALNUTS, COARSELY CHOPPED
2 TEASPOONS BAKING SODA	

1. Preheat oven to 350°F.

2. Grease and flour or line a 10-inch tube pan with parchment paper. Set aside.

3. In an electric mixer on medium speed, blend together eggs, sugar, oil, and vanilla. Mix until well blended. On low speed, gradually add flour, baking soda, baking powder, cinnamon and cloves. Mix just until blended and smooth. Stir in sweet potato and walnuts.

4. Pour into prepared pan and bake for 55 to 60 minutes. Remove from the oven and place on wire cooling rack. Cool in pan for 10 to 15 minutes. Remove cake from the pan and continue cooling on wire rack until completely cool. Remove and discard parchment.

5. Frost with Maple Glaze (page 56) and serve.

YIELD: ONE 10-INCH CAKE, 20 TO 25 SLICES

PEAR, NUT & RAISIN LOAF

This twist on a traditional pound cake spotlights the growing popularity of pears. Bosc pears are the best for flavor and texture in baking, and they're available year-round. This moist cake, loaded with pears, raisins, and walnuts, is perfectly appropriate at breakfast or at the dinner table with assorted breads, or as dessert, topped with ice cream.

2 BOSC PEARS	¼ TEASPOON SALT
¼ POUND BUTTER, SOFTENED	1 TEASPOON CINNAMON
1½ CUPS SUGAR	1 TEASPOON NUTMEG
1 TEASPOON VANILLA EXTRACT	2 PEARS, PEELED, CORED, AND DICED
4 EGGS	(ABOUT 1½ CUPS)
2½ CUPS CAKE FLOUR	1 CUP RAISINS
1 TEASPOON BAKING POWDER	1 CUP CHOPPED WALNUTS

1. Peel and core the two Bosc pears and cut into ½-inch slices. Put pears in a small saucepan and cover with water. Boil, uncovered, over high heat for 15 to 20 minutes, or until tender. Drain. Purée in a food processor until the consistency of applesauce. You should have 1 cup. Set aside.

2. Preheat oven to 350°F.

3. Grease and flour or line a 10 x 6 x 2½-inch loaf pan with parchment paper. Set aside.

4. In an electric mixer on medium speed, cream the butter. Gradually add the sugar, beating until light in color. Add the 1 cup pear purée and vanilla. Mix until blended.

5. Add eggs, one at a time, beating well after adding each one.

6. On low speed, gradually add flour, baking powder, salt, cinnamon, and nutmeg. Mix just until blended. Stir in diced pears, raisins, and nuts. Pour batter into prepared pan.

7. Bake for 55 to 60 minutes, or until a tester comes out with a fine crumb. Remove cake from the oven and cool in a pan on wire cooling rack for 10 to 15 minutes.

8. Carefully remove the cake from the pan and continue to cool on wire cooling rack. Remove and discard parchment. Serve slightly warm or wrap in foil and store at room temperature.

YIELD: ONE LARGE LOAF, ABOUT 12 SLICES

LEMON ROSEMARY CAKE

This cake has an unusual texture because of the cornmeal added to the flour.
It is a slightly sweet cake, accented by fresh rosemary,
that is nice with a summer soup or salad.

¼ POUND PLUS 3 TABLESPOONS
BUTTER, SOFTENED

1½ CUPS SUGAR

4 EGGS

2 CUPS CAKE FLOUR

½ CUP YELLOW CORNMEAL

½ TEASPOON SALT

2 TEASPOONS BAKING POWDER

½ CUP WHITE WINE

GRATED RIND OF 1 LEMON

2 TABLESPOONS MINCED ROSEMARY

GLAZE:

¼ CUP WHITE WINE

JUICE OF 1 LEMON

1. Preheat oven to 325°F.

2. Grease and flour or line a 10 x 6 x 2½-inch loaf pan with parchment paper. Set aside.

3. In an electric mixer on medium speed, cream butter. Gradually add sugar and beat until light in color. Add eggs, one at a time, beating well after adding each one.

4. On low speed, add flour, cornmeal, salt, and baking powder. Mix just until blended. Add wine. Stir in lemon rind and rosemary. Pour batter into prepared pan.

5. Bake for 60 to 65 minutes, or until a tester comes out with a fine crumb. Remove cake from the oven and cool on wire cooling rack.

6. In a small bowl, stir together wine and lemon juice. Pour evenly over the top of the cake. Cool in pan on wire cooling rack for 10 to 15 minutes. Carefully remove the cake from the pan and continue to cool on wire rack. Remove and discard parchment. Serve when cool, or wrap in foil for storage at room temperature or freezing.

YIELD: ONE LARGE LOAF, ABOUT 12 SLICES

LESS-GUILT ORANGE CAKE

Margarine replaces some of the fat of butter in this lightly flavored cake. Egg whites add volume, and orange rind provides a subtle orange flavor, for a cake with a little less guilt. It's the perfect companion to a glass of iced herbal tea on a summer day.

4 EGG WHITES

¼ POUND MARGARINE, SOFTENED

1 CUP SUGAR

4 TABLESPOONS ORANGE JUICE

1 TABLESPOON GRATED ORANGE RIND

1 TEASPOON VANILLA EXTRACT

1½ CUPS CAKE FLOUR

2 TEASPOONS BAKING POWDER

½ TEASPOON SALT

¾ CUP BUTTERMILK

CONFECTIONERS' SUGAR FOR DUSTING

1. Preheat oven to 350°F.

2. Grease and flour or line a 10 x 6 x 2½-inch loaf pan with parchment paper. Set aside.

3. In an electric mixer, with a wire whisk, whip egg whites until stiff. Set aside.

4. With an electric mixer on medium speed, blend margarine and sugar until light in color. Add 2 tablespoons of the orange juice, rind, and vanilla. Blend well.

5. In a small bowl, combine flour, baking powder, and salt. Add to margarine mixture alternately with buttermilk. Mix just until blended. Fold batter mixture into the beaten egg whites. Pour into prepared pan.

6. Bake for 45 to 50 minutes, or until a tester comes out with a fine crumb. Remove cake from the oven and place on wire cooling rack. Pour 2 tablespoons of orange juice on top of baked cake. Cool cake in pan for 10 to 15 minutes. Remove cake from pan and continue to cool on wire cooling rack until completely cool. Remove and discard parchment.

7. Dust with confectioners' sugar and serve topped with fresh fruit.

YIELD: ONE LARGE LOAF, ABOUT 12 SLICES

MINI CHOCOLATE MOCHA LOAVES

These tiny chocolate-coated cakes make great individual desserts, served alone or on a plate with Raspberry Sauce (page 58). We originally created them as wedding favors. They were miniature monogrammed versions of the wedding cake that made the perfect take-home treat. For these cakes you will need miniature loaf pans. They are usually sold in sets of six and measure 4 x 2 x 1½ inches each.

ONE RECIPE DEVIL'S FOOD LAYER CAKE
(PAGE 67)

ONE RECIPE CHOCOLATE GANACHE
(PAGE 123)

ONE RECIPE MOCHA MOUSSE FILLING
(PAGE 82)

1. Preheat oven to 350°F.

2. Prepare cake batter according to directions. Grease and flour mini loaf pans. Fill pans halfway with batter. Bake for 12 to 15 minutes, or until done.

3. Remove pans from the oven. Carefully remove cakes from the pans and place on wire cooling rack. To reuse the pans, be sure to clean in between uses. If the pans are not cleaned properly after baking the first batch, the second batch of cakes may stick and become difficult to remove.

4. Grease and flour pans and repeat, filling pans halfway with remaining batter. Bake until done. Cool cakes completely on wire cooling rack.

5. Prepare Mocha Mousse.

6. Fill a pastry bag, fitted with an open star tip, with mocha mousse. Push the tip of the pastry bag into the bottom of the cake at 3 intervals. Squeeze pastry bag gently to release the filling into the cake. Be careful not to push the tip too far in or squeeze too much filling or you might break the cake. Re-fill the pastry bag as necessary and fill all 12 cakes.

7. Place filled cakes, bottoms down, on a wire rack. Use a clean piece of parchment or waxed paper under the wire rack to catch any excess ganache.

8. Prepare ganache. Let cool until lukewarm.

9. Using a tablespoon, pour ganache over mini loaves, one at a time. Use the back of the spoon or a metal spatula to smooth ganache over the top and onto the sides of the cake. Glaze all the cakes with ganache.

10. Refrigerate cakes until set. Let cakes come to room temperature before serving.

YIELD: TWELVE MINIATURE LOAVES, ABOUT 12 SERVINGS

◆ **BAKERY STORIES** ◆

AT SWEET MARIA'S, WE'VE MADE QUITE A FEW INTERESTING CAKES. SOME OF THE MOST MEMORABLE ARE: A CAKE THAT REPLICATES A TERRA-COTTA POT, WITH FLOWERS; A FOOD-COLORING-PAINTED MING BOWL; A MOUNTAIN RANGE WEDDING CAKE, COMPLETE WITH SNOW-CAPPED TOPS; CAKES SHAPED LIKE A PLATFORM SHOE, A SMALL PIANO, A JEWELRY BOX, TACKY SUNGLASSES; AND NUMEROUS OTHER HOLIDAY AND WEDDING CREATIONS. WE'VE ALSO DONE DIVORCE CAKES, "WILL YOU MARRY ME?" CAKES, AND CAKES FOR DOG BIRTHDAYS. OUR CAKES ARE AS VARIED AND UNIQUE AS OUR CUSTOMERS ARE.

CONFECTIONERS' GLAZE

Besides being perfect for loaf and Bundt cakes, this basic glaze can be used on cookies, layer cakes, or danish pastries. You can substitute almost any flavor extract, including vanilla or almond, to make a variety of confectioners' glazes.

3 CUPS CONFECTIONERS' SUGAR   ¼ CUP WATER

1 TEASPOON LEMON EXTRACT

Using an electric mixer, blend sugar, lemon extract, and water until blended. Beat on medium speed until smooth. Use a metal spatula to spread on the top of the cake. Place cake on wire rack, set on clean parchment to allow for easy cleanup of excess icing. Use immediately or cover and store at room temperature for later use.

YIELD: ENOUGH TO GLAZE THE TOP OF ONE 10-INCH TUBE CAKE OR 2 LARGE LOAVES

CHOCOLATE CONFECTIONERS' GLAZE

A rich glaze ideal to drizzle over the top of a pound cake.

1½ CUPS CONFECTIONERS' SUGAR   **¼ CUP WATER**

¼ CUP COCOA

Using an electric mixer, blend sugar, cocoa, and water together until blended. Beat on medium speed until smooth. Use a metal spatula to spread glaze over the top of the cake. Use immediately.

YIELD: ENOUGH TO GLAZE THE TOP OF A 10-INCH TUBE CAKE OR TWO LARGE LOAVES

MAPLE GLAZE

*This glaze is great on some of our spicier cakes. Try it drizzled over
the New England Maple Walnut Cake, Sweet Potato Cake,
or Pear, Nut & Raisin Loaf.*

1½ CUPS CONFECTIONERS' SUGAR   ½ CUP MAPLE SYRUP

In an electric mixer, blend confectioners' sugar and maple syrup until blended
and smooth. Use a metal spatula to spread glaze over the top of the cake. Use immediately.

YIELD: ENOUGH TO GLAZE THE TOP OF A 10-INCH TUBE CAKE OR TWO LARGE LOAVES

WHIPPED CREAM

Sometimes the best garnish for a slice of cake is a dollop of whipped cream. If you're using the cream this way, it doesn't need to be as stiff as if you were frosting a layer cake.

1 CUP HEAVY CREAM　　　　　　**2 TABLESPOONS SUGAR**

In an electric mixer with wire whip attachment, beat cream into peaks, about 2 minutes. Whisk in sugar. Beat until stiff, about another 30 seconds. Use immediately.

YIELD: 2 CUPS

RASPBERRY SAUCE

This sauce is the perfect partner to any chocolate or lemon cake.

2 CUPS FROZEN (SLIGHTLY THAWED)   **1 CUP CONFECTIONERS' SUGAR**
OR FRESH RASPBERRIES

Place berries and sugar in a food processor. Process until puréed and almost smooth. Use immediately or refrigerate in an airtight container.

YIELD: 1½ CUPS

STRAWBERRIES IN VERMOUTH

This is one of my grandmother's specialties. It's ideal simply spooned over a slice of sponge cake or on top of a slice of pound cake with ice cream.

1 QUART FRESH STRAWBERRIES,
CLEANED, HULLED, AND SLICED

1 CUP SWEET VERMOUTH

½ CUP SUGAR

1. Place berries in a small mixing bowl. Pour vermouth over strawberries and sprinkle with sugar. Stir with a rubber spatula.

2. Cover and refrigerate overnight. Serve chilled, spooned over cake and ice cream.

YIELD: ABOUT 15 ½-CUP SERVINGS TO USE IMMEDIATELY OR FREEZE

LAYER CAKES

LAYER CAKE TIPS

All of these layer cakes have three elements: cake, filling, and frosting. Read through each recipe before you start so that you can have a good idea when to make each element. Many of the cakes can be baked one day in advance. Custard fillings and buttercream frostings are best made one day ahead. Whipped cream and seven-minute frostings need to be whipped right before assembly of your cake.
They cannot be saved and used later.

How to Slice Cakes Horizontally to Fill Them

If you're making a two-layer cake, be sure to level off the tops of the layers by carefully slicing with a long sharp serrated knife. With one hand on the top, use a slow sawing motion to be sure you can control the knife and not slice your hand. If you don't level off the tops of your layers, you will have a rounded cake top, which is more likely to crack.

To slice two layers into four layers, use the same motion to split the layer as you would to slice off the top. If the layers are thin and fragile, use a wire cooling rack or cake circle to help move the layer during assembly.

Adhering Cakes to Plates

It is very important that you properly adhere your cake to its serving plate or cake circle. If the cake is not secure, it may slide off the plate. If you're using a buttercream frosting, use a dab of frosting to act as glue—it works quite well. Place a dab of frosting on the plate or cake circle. Gently press a doily to adhere to plate. Place another dab of frosting on the doily. Gently press the bottom cake layer onto this dab. If you're making a whipped cream–frosted cake, it's a good idea to use a bit of buttercream or confectioners' icing for this purpose.

Frosting and Garnishing

Many of these cakes use simple swirled frostings that are spread with a metal spatula. I've tried to make this book "decorator friendly" by showing easy ways to cover cakes and garnish for a pretty presentation.

WHITE LAYER CAKE

This is a versatile cake with a light texture and flavor. It works with any number of frostings, fresh fruit, and whipped cream or a sweet buttercream. This recipe uses only egg whites. If you're making the Lemon Curd Filling (page 80), you can use the yolks for that.

2½ CUPS CAKE FLOUR

1½ CUPS SUGAR

3 TEASPOONS BAKING POWDER

½ TEASPOON SALT

¼ POUND PLUS 3 TABLESPOONS BUTTER, SOFTENED

5 EGG WHITES

1 CUP MILK

1 TEASPOON VANILLA EXTRACT

1. Preheat oven to 350°F.

2. Grease and flour or line two 8-inch round cake pans with parchment paper. Set aside.

3. In an electric mixer on low speed, blend flour, sugar, baking powder, and salt until mixed. Add butter and mix until butter is uniformly blended.

4. In a separate bowl, mix egg whites, milk, and vanilla with a wire whisk.

5. Add egg mixture to flour mixture. Mix on medium speed for 1 minute.

6. Scrape down the sides of the mixing bowl. Continue to beat at medium-high speed for another minute, until batter is blended and smooth.

7. Pour batter evenly into prepared pans. Bake for 25 to 30 minutes, or until a tester comes out with a fine crumb.

8. Remove pans from the oven and cool the cakes in pans on wire cooling racks for 5 to 10 minutes. Carefully remove the cakes from the pans and continue to cool on wire racks. Remove and discard parchment.

YIELD: TWO 8-INCH ROUND LAYERS OR 20 CUPCAKES

POPPYSEED CAKE
Add ¼ cup poppyseeds to batter.

ALMOND CAKE
Replace vanilla with 1 teaspoon almond extract.

◆ OTHER VARIATIONS ◆

MOST OF THE SERVING SUGGESTIONS IN THIS BOOK ARE JUST THAT—SUGGESTIONS. FEEL FREE TO MAKE YOUR OWN COMBINATIONS USING THE BASICS IN THIS BOOK. HERE ARE A FEW VARIATIONS TO HELP YOU GET STARTED:

ALMOND POUND CAKE DRIZZLED WITH RASPBERRY SAUCE.

PUMPKIN RAISIN CAKE OR SWEET POTATO CAKE WITH A DOLLOP OF SPICED WHIPPED CREAM FROSTING.

CHOCOLATE ALMOND ANGEL FOOD CAKE WITH FRESH BERRIES AND WHIPPED CREAM.

SPECKLED POUND CAKE SERVED WARM WITH A SCOOP OF ICE CREAM.

CITRUS YOGURT CAKE WITH FRESH BERRIES AND RASPBERRY SAUCE.

A BOSTON CREME CAKE: YELLOW LAYER CAKE, VANILLA CUSTARD FILLING, AND CHOCOLATE FROSTING.

CHIP & ERNIE'S CAKE USING WHITE CHOCOLATE CHIPS AND BUTTER-CREAM FROSTING.

BANANA SOUR CREAM CAKE WITH CREAM CHEESE FROSTING.

DEVIL'S FOOD CAKE WITH SEVEN-MINUTE FROSTING COVERED WITH COCONUT.

BANANA SOUR CREAM CAKE WITH MOCHA MOUSSE FILLING AND GANACHE.

TRY APRICOT PRESERVES INSTEAD OF RASPBERRY IN THE HAZELNUT CAKE.

YELLOW LAYER CAKE

This flexible recipe is the basis for many of the layer cake variations included in this chapter. By beating the egg whites separately, then folding them into the batter, you get a very light and flavorful cake.

4 EGGS, SEPARATED

½ POUND BUTTER, SOFTENED

2 CUPS SUGAR

1 TEASPOON VANILLA EXTRACT

2½ CUPS CAKE FLOUR

2 TEASPOONS BAKING POWDER

¼ TEASPOON SALT

1 CUP MILK

1. Preheat oven to 350°F.

2. Grease and flour or line two 9-inch round cake pans with parchment paper. Set aside.

3. In an electric mixer with wire whisk attachment, beat egg whites until soft but not dry. Set aside.

4. In an electric mixer on medium speed, cream the butter. Gradually add sugar and beat until light in color. Add vanilla. Add egg yolks, one at a time, beating well after adding each one.

5. In another bowl, combine flour, baking powder, and salt. Add the flour mixture to the butter mixture alternately with the milk. Begin and end with flour mixture. Mix until batter is smooth.

6. Carefully fold flour mixture into egg whites.

7. Pour batter into prepared pans. Bake for 25 to 30 minutes, or until a tester comes out with a fine crumb. Remove pans from the oven and place on a wire cooling rack. Cool cakes in pans for 5 to 10 minutes. Carefully remove cakes from the pans and continue to cool on wire racks. Remove and discard parchment before decorating.

8. When cool, frost as desired or wrap in foil and freeze.

YIELD: TWO 9-INCH ROUND LAYERS OR 24 CUPCAKES

DEVIL'S FOOD LAYER CAKE

This amazing cake can't be beat for moistness or flavor. It is also very flexible. You can use this recipe for our chocolate layer cakes or for our Mini Chocolate Mocha Loaves.

1 CUP COCOA	1 TEASPOON SALT
1 CUP BOILING WATER	2 EGGS
2 CUPS FLOUR	1 CUP BUTTERMILK
1¾ CUPS SUGAR	½ CUP VEGETABLE OIL
1½ TEASPOONS BAKING SODA	2 TEASPOONS VANILLA EXTRACT
2 TEASPOONS BAKING POWDER	

1. In a small bowl, pour boiling water over cocoa. Set aside to cool.

2. Preheat oven to 350°F.

3. Grease and flour or line two 9-inch round cake pans with parchment paper. Set aside.

4. In an electric mixer, combine flour, sugar, baking soda, baking powder, and salt. Mix on low speed until mixed.

5. Add eggs and cocoa mixture and blend on low speed 1 minute. Scrape down the sides and bottom of mixing bowl.

6. Add buttermilk, oil, and vanilla. Beat on low speed 1 minute. Scrape down bowl. Beat on medium speed for 1 to 2 minutes, or until smooth. Pour batter evenly into prepared pans.

7. Bake for 20 to 25 minutes, or until a tester comes out with a fine crumb. Remove pans from the oven and place on wire cooling racks. Cool cakes in pans for 5 to 10 minutes. Carefully remove cakes from the pans and place on wire cooling racks.

8. Cool completely before frosting. Remove and discard parchment before decorating. Store unfrosted layers wrapped in foil, then plastic, in the freezer.

YIELD: TWO 9-INCH ROUND LAYERS, 12 MINI LOAF CAKES, OR 24 CUPCAKES

CHOCOLATE STRAWBERRY VALENTINE CAKE

This heart-shaped devil's food cake is filled with a light strawberry cream filling. It's the perfect ending to a romantic dinner. Or for a great Valentine surprise, bake one and deliver it to your sweetheart at work.

TWO 9-INCH HEART-SHAPED LAYERS DEVIL'S FOOD CAKE (PAGE 67)

1 RECIPE CHOCOLATE BUTTERCREAM (PAGE 120)

1 RECIPE STRAWBERRY CREAM FILLING (RECIPE FOLLOWS)

GARNISH: CHOCOLATE-DIPPED STRAW-BERRIES

STRAWBERRY CREAM FILLING

2 CUPS HEAVY CREAM

1 CUP STRAWBERRY PRESERVES

In an electric mixer with wire whisk attachment, whip cream until almost stiff. Add preserves and whip on high speed until stiff. Use immediately.

ASSEMBLY:

1. Make cake layers and chocolate buttercream frosting. Set frosting aside at room temperature in an airtight container or in a bowl covered with plastic wrap.

2. Make strawberry cream filling.

3. Level off tops of the cake layers. Slice each layer horizontally to give you 4 thin layers. Adhere one layer, cut side up, on a serving plate or doily-covered cake circle. Using a pastry bag filled with chocolate buttercream frosting, pipe an outline around the outside of the layer. Fill with a thin layer of the strawberry cream. Repeat with 2 layers and filling until entire cake is filled. Place last layer, cut side down, on top. Refrigerate cake for 10 to 15 minutes.

4. Frost the outside of the cake with remaining chocolate buttercream frosting. Using a metal spatula, start at the top and spread the frosting to cover the sides of the cake. If desired, pipe a border along the bottom edge of the cake. Garnish with chocolate-dipped strawberries or fresh flowers. Refrigerate cake. Serve at room temperature.

YIELD: ONE 4-LAYER 9-INCH HEART-SHAPED CAKE, 15 TO 18 SERVINGS

CANNOLI CAKE

This three-layer cake pays tribute to the classic Italian pastry. It's a light sponge cake with a sweetened ricotta cheese filling, sprinkled with a few chocolate chips. It makes a perfect dessert after a traditional Italian pasta supper, with a cup of espresso.

1 CLASSIC SPONGE CAKE (BAKED IN A10-INCH TUBE PAN (PAGE 34)

1 RECIPE CANNOLI FILLING (RECIPE FOLLOWS)

1 RECIPE WHIPPED CREAM FROSTING (PAGE 122)

GARNISH: ¼ CUP MINI CHOCOLATE CHIPS

CANNOLI FILLING

3 CUPS WHOLE MILK RICOTTA

½ CUP SUGAR

2 TEASPOONS LEMON EXTRACT

½ CUP MINI CHOCOLATE CHIPS

Combine ricotta, sugar, and lemon extract in a mixing bowl. Stir with a rubber spatula until blended. Stir in chocolate chips. Use immediately or store refrigerated in an airtight container.

ASSEMBLY:

1. Cut sponge cake into thirds, horizontally. Place the bottom layer, cut side up, on a serving dish or doily-covered cake circle.

2. Spread half the filling over the bottom layer of cake. Place middle layer on top of the filled bottom layer. Spread remaining filling over this layer and top with third layer, cut side down. Refrigerate until set, 15 to 20 minutes.

3. Make whipped cream frosting.

4. Frost the top and sides of the cakes with whipped cream frosting. Using a metal spatula, start at the top and continue to spread frosting down to cover cake sides. To garnish, sprinkle the top with chocolate chips.

5. Refrigerate until serving. Serve chilled.

YIELD: ONE 3-LAYER 10-INCH CAKE, ABOUT 25 SLICES

SOUTH BEACH POPPYSEED CAKE

This poppyseed cake accented with a fresh lime filling was inspired by the Florida sun. I usually bake one in winter and sip on an iced cappuccino to chase away the winter blues. The tart filling is the perfect partner to this poppyseed cake or a plain white cake.

TWO 8-INCH LAYERS POPPYSEED CAKE
(PAGE 65)

1 RECIPE LIME FILLING (RECIPE
FOLLOWS)

1 RECIPE LIME SEVEN-MINUTE
FROSTING (PAGE 124)

GARNISH: 1 TEASPOON POPPYSEEDS,
GRATED LIME RIND

LIME FILLING

¾ CUP SUGAR

2 TABLESPOONS CORNSTARCH

PINCH OF SALT

1 TABLESPOON GRATED LIME RIND

⅓ CUP LIME JUICE

½ CUP WATER

1 EGG, LIGHTLY BEATEN

1 TABLESPOON BUTTER

In a double boiler over simmering water, combine all ingredients. Cook, whisking constantly, until mixture thickens, 5 to 6 minutes. Remove from the heat. Cool. Cover with plastic wrap and refrigerate until ready to use.

ASSEMBLY:

1. Prepare all the ingredients.

2. Cut layers horizontally in half so you have 4 thin layers of cake. Place one layer cut side up on a cake plate or doily-covered cake circle. Using a pastry bag filled with frosting, pipe an outline of frosting along the outer edge of the layer. Spread a quarter of the chilled lime filing into frosting outline and over bottom layer of cake. Repeat the layering of cake and filling until cake is completed. Place top layer, cut side down, for final layer. The filling layers will be thin because they're very tart and rich.

3. Frost the outside of the cake with remaining frosting. Using a metal spatula start from the top and continue to spread on the sides of the cake. Lightly pull spatula away, creating small peaks. Garnish top with a sprinkle of grated lime rind and poppyseeds.

4. Refrigerate cake. Serve cake at room temperature.

YIELD: ONE 4-LAYER 8-INCH CAKE, 12 TO 15 SERVINGS

◆ **S E R V E A T R O O M T E M P E R A T U R E** ◆

MANY OF THESE CAKES NEED TO BE REFRIGERATED TO STAY FRESH. HOWEVER, MOST DO TASTE BETTER WHEN SERVED AT ROOM TEMPERA- TURE. REMOVE YOUR CAKE FROM THE REFRIGERATOR 1 TO 2 HOURS BE- FORE SERVING SO THAT FROSTINGS CAN SOFTEN AND FLAVORS WILL BE AT THEIR PEAK.

ICE BOX LAYER CAKE

This layer cake version of the classic ice box cake combines a rich yellow butter cake, custard filling, sliced bananas, and graham cracker crumbs. A new classic! The custard makes a great filling for many classic layer cakes.

TWO 9-INCH LAYERS YELLOW CAKE
(PAGE 66)

1 RECIPE VANILLA CUSTARD FILLING
(RECIPE FOLLOWS)

1 RECIPE WHIPPED CREAM FROSTING
(PAGE 122)

1 LARGE BANANA, SLICED

1 CUP GRAHAM CRACKER CRUMBS

GARNISH: 1 BANANA, SLICED

VANILLA CUSTARD FILLING

2 TABLESPOONS CORNSTARCH

PINCH OF SALT

⅓ CUP SUGAR

1 CUP HEAVY CREAM

3 EGGS

1 TABLESPOON BUTTER

1 TEASPOON VANILLA EXTRACT

1. In a double boiler over boiling water, combine cornstarch, salt, sugar, cream and eggs. Whisk constantly until mixture is thickened, about 5 minutes.

2. Remove from the heat. Stir in butter and vanilla. Cool. Cover with plastic and refrigerate.

ASSEMBLY:

1. Prepare all the ingredients.

2. Level off tops of yellow layer cakes. Place one layer, cut side up, on a serving plate or doily-covered cake circle. Using a pastry bag filled with about one-third of the whipped cream frosting, pipe an outline along the perimeter of the layer. Spoon and lightly spread the vanilla custard into the center of the cake. Arrange slices of banana in the custard.

3. Place the other layer, cut side down, on top of the bananas and custard. Press lightly. Frost the outside of the cake with remaining whipped cream, using a metal spatula and swirling motions. Start at the top and continue to spread frosting to cover sides. Don't worry if you have spots of cake showing through.

4. Place graham cracker crumbs in a flat plate. With one hand holding the cake underneath, use the other hand to cover the cake completely with crumbs. Hold the cake over the plate of crumbs so any excess will fall back into plate. Be sure to adhere crumbs while the frosting is fresh.

5. Refrigerate until serving. Just before serving, arrange banana slices on top of the cake. Serve chilled.

YIELD: ONE 2-LAYER 9-INCH CAKE, 12 TO 15 SERVINGS

◆ **PASTRY TIPS** ◆

THERE ARE MANY TYPES OF TIPS FOR PASTRY BAGS THAT ARE USED IN CAKE DECORATING. SOME OF THE MORE BASIC ONES TO ADD TO YOUR COLLECTION ARE: TIP #3, THE PERFECT WIDTH FOR WRITING ON CAKES AND MAKING POLKA DOTS; TIP #32 OR ANY OF THE OPEN STAR TIPS, WHICH ARE IDEAL FOR MAKING TOP AND BOTTOM BORDERS FOR YOUR CAKES. THE OPEN STAR TIPS ARE ALSO USED WHEN MAKING A DAM TO FILL LAYERS.

AMARETTO APPLE CAKE

This selection from our bakery menu is a Sweet Maria specialty. The baked apple filling is generously spiced with cinnamon and sugar, making this the perfect alternative to apple pie. (The filling is also a great dessert on its own, spooned over ice cream or pound cake.)

TWO 9-INCH ROUND YELLOW CAKE
LAYERS (PAGE 66)

½ CUP AMARETTO LIQUEUR

1 RECIPE CREAM CHEESE FROSTING
(PAGE 122)

1 RECIPE APPLE FILLING (RECIPE
FOLLOWS)

2 CUPS SLICED ALMONDS, TOASTED

APPLE FILLING

4 MEDIUM APPLES, PEELED, CORED,
AND CUT INTO ¼-INCH SLICES (ABOUT
4 CUPS)

½ CUP BROWN SUGAR

3 TEASPOONS CINNAMON

½ CUP WATER

Place apple slices in a small baking dish. Sprinkle with sugar and cinnamon. Pour water over apples and stir with a wooden spoon. Bake at 350°F for 20 to 25 minutes, or until apples are tender. Cool before using.

ASSEMBLY:

1. Prepare all the ingredients.

2. Level off the tops of yellow cake layers. Place one layer, cut side up, onto a serving plate or doily-covered cake circle. Using a pastry brush, brush the cake with about half the amaretto.

3. Spread a thin layer of cream cheese frosting on the cake. Using a pastry bag, pipe an outline along the outer edge of the layer. Spoon apple filling into center. Brush the cut side of other layer with remaining amaretto and place, cut side down, on top of apple filling. Press down lightly.

4. Frost the outside of the cake with remaining cream cheese frosting. Using a metal spatula, start at the top and continue to spread frosting covering the sides of the cake. Don't worry if the sides are imperfect and show crumbs. While the frosting is fresh, cover the sides and top with toasted almonds. Put the almonds on a flat

plate. Hold the cake underneath the plate with one hand. Use the other hand to adhere almonds to the sides of the cake. Hold the cake over the plate of almonds so any excess almonds will fall back onto the plate. Refrigerate. Serve cake at room temperature.

YIELD: ONE 2-LAYER 9-INCH CAKE, 12 TO 15 SERVINGS

CHOCOLATE MANDARIN
ORANGE CAKE

This is our Devil's Food Cake, drizzled with Grand Marnier and filled with chocolate cream and mandarin oranges. The deep chocolate ganache coating makes it an ideal groom's cake. An old tradition, a groom's cake is usually a rich chocolate, and is often shaped into the symbol of a sport or hobby that the groom enjoys. Some recent ones that we've created are pool tables, tennis racquets, and grand pianos.

TWO 9-INCH LAYERS DEVIL'S FOOD
CAKE (PAGE 67)

¼ CUP GRAND MARNIER

1 RECIPE CHOCOLATE BUTTERCREAM
(PAGE 120)

1 RECIPE CHOCOLATE GANACHE
(PAGE 123)

1 RECIPE CHOCOLATE CREAM FILLING
(RECIPE FOLLOWS)

2½ CUPS MANDARIN ORANGES

GARNISH: CHOCOLATE-DIPPED
MANDARIN ORANGES

CHOCOLATE CREAM FILLING

2 CUPS HEAVY CREAM

½ CUP COCOA

½ CUP SUGAR

1. In an electric mixer with wire whip attachment, beat cream and cocoa on high speed until soft peaks form. Scrape down the sides of the bowl with a rubber spatula.

2. Add sugar and whip on high speed until stiff. Use immediately.

YIELD: 3 CUPS

ASSEMBLY:

1. Make chocolate buttercream. Set aside at room temperature in an airtight container or a bowl covered with plastic wrap.

2. Make chocolate ganache. Set aside to thicken.

3. Level off the tops of both layers of cake. Slice each layer in half horizontally to give you 4 thin layers. Place one layer, cut side up, on a 9-inch cake circle. Brush

with Grand Marnier. Using a pastry bag filled with chocolate buttercream, pipe an outline along the perimeter of the layer. Spoon and spread one-third of the chocolate cream filling into the center. Arrange one-third of the mandarin oranges on top of the chocolate cream. Place another cake layer on top of the filled layer.

4. Continue to brush and fill the layers until the cake is completely filled. Place top layer cut side down. Refrigerate the cake to set, 10 to 15 minutes.

5. Frost the outside of the cake with a thin layer of chocolate buttercream. Place the frosted cake on a wire rack. Place a clean sheet of parchment paper or waxed paper under the rack to catch any excess ganache. Carefully pour ganache over the top of the frosted cake. Use a metal spatula to help guide the ganache over the sides of the cake. Refrigerate cake.

6. When ganache is set or firm to the touch, adhere cake to serving plate or a doily-covered large cake circle.

7. Garnish with chocolate-dipped mandarin oranges. Refrigerate cake. Serve at room temperature.

YIELD: ONE 4-LAYER 9-INCH CAKE, 15 TO 18 SERVINGS

HOLIDAY EGGNOG CAKE

This cake has become a welcome addition to our family's traditional Italian Christmas Eve dessert buffet. The whipped cream, laced with cinnamon and nutmeg, is the perfect accent for this cake. Top it with fresh mint leaves and berries for a festive touch.

1 CLASSIC SPONGE CAKE (BAKED IN A 10-INCH TUBE PAN (PAGE 34)

1 CUP RUM

2 RECIPES VANILLA CUSTARD FILLING (PAGE 72)

1 RECIPE SPICED WHIPPED CREAM FROSTING (RECIPE FOLLOWS)

GARNISH: FRESH MINT AND BERRIES

SPICED WHIPPED CREAM FROSTING

2 CUPS HEAVY CREAM

¼ CUP SUGAR

1 TEASPOON CINNAMON

½ TEASPOON NUTMEG

In an electric mixer with wire whip attachment, beat cream until peaks form, about 2 minutes. Add sugar, cinnamon, and nutmeg and whip until stiff, about another 30 seconds. Use immediately.

ASSEMBLY:

1. Prepare all the ingredients except whipped cream.

2. Cut sponge cake into fourths, horizontally. Place the bottom layer, cut side up, on a serving dish or doily-covered cake circle. Sprinkle with ⅓ cup rum. Spread one-third of the vanilla custard onto cake. Place next layer on top of custard. Continue to fill the layers in the same manner. Place top layer cut side down.

3. Refrigerate the filled cake while making the whipped cream.

4. With a metal spatula, frost the top and sides of the cake with the spiced whipped cream. If desired, use a pastry bag to pipe a border along the top edge of the cake.

5. Refrigerate until serving. Garnish with fresh mint leaves and berries. Serve chilled.

YIELD: ONE 4-LAYER 10-INCH CAKE, ABOUT 25 SERVINGS

ITALIAN RUM CAKE

Use plain white whipped cream to frost the cake instead of spiced whipped cream and cover the sides of the cake with sliced toasted almonds. Pipe a shell border around the top edge of the cake.

TOASTED LEMON SNOWBALL CAKE

Totally covered with toasted coconut, this white layer cake is filled with a flavor-packed lemon filling.

TWO 8-INCH LAYERS WHITE CAKE (PAGE 64)

1 RECIPE LEMON CURD FILLING (RECIPE FOLLOWS)

1 RECIPE LEMON SEVEN-MINUTE FROSTING (PAGE 124)

2 CUPS TOASTED COCONUT

GARNISH: GRATED LEMON RIND

LEMON CURD FILLING

1 CUP SUGAR

1 TABLESPOON CORNSTARCH

5 EGG YOLKS

¼ CUP LEMON JUICE

1 TABLESPOON GRATED LEMON RIND

¼ POUND BUTTER

Place sugar and cornstarch in a medium saucepan. Stir until blended. Add egg yolks and whisk with a wire whisk until blended. Add lemon juice, rind, and butter. Whisk constantly over medium-low heat until thickened and bright yellow, 8 to 10 minutes. Do not boil. Cover with plastic wrap and refrigerate.

ASSEMBLY:

1. Prepare all the ingredients.

2. Level the tops of cakes. Place one layer, cut side up, on a serving plate or doily-covered cake circle. Using a pastry bag filled with frosting, pipe an outline of frosting around the perimeter of the layer. Spread the filling into outline and over cake layer. Place top layer, cut side down, on top of filled layer.

3. Frost the outside of the cake with remaining seven-minute frosting. Using a metal spatula, spread the icing starting at the top and spreading down around the sides. While the frosting is wet, cover the sides and top of cake with toasted coconut. Place coconut in a flat plate. Hold the cake underneath with one hand. Use the other hand to adhere coconut to the sides and top of cake. Hold the cake over the plate so that any excess coconut will fall back onto the plate. Be sure to adhere the coconut while the frosting is wet.

4. Refrigerate cake. Garnish with grated lemon rind. Serve at room temperature.

YIELD: ONE 2-LAYER 8-INCH CAKE, 10 TO 12 SERVINGS

♦ LAYERS OR TIERS ♦

A LOT OF PEOPLE CONFUSE CAKE LAYERS WITH CAKE TIERS. TRY TO THINK OF LAYERS AS THE INTERIOR PART OF THE CAKE, THE PARTS OF THE CAKE THAT SANDWICH AND HOLD THE FILLINGS. TIERS ARE THE FINISHED FROSTED CAKES STACKED ONE ON TOP OF THE OTHER IN DESCENDING HEIGHT, LIKE A WEDDING CAKE.

BLACK & TAN CAKE

This cake combines our classic Yellow Layer Cake, mocha mousse filling, and a dark chocolate ganache coating. A rich indulgence for a special occasion, especially with a glass of champagne.

TWO 9-INCH YELLOW CAKE LAYERS
(PAGE 66)

1 RECIPE CHOCOLATE BUTTERCREAM
(PAGE 121)

1 RECIPE MOCHA MOUSSE FILLING
(RECIPE FOLLOWS)

1 RECIPE CHOCOLATE GANACHE
(PAGE 123)

MOCHA MOUSSE FILLING

2 CUPS HEAVY CREAM

3½ TABLESPOONS COCOA

1 TEASPOON INSTANT ESPRESSO

½ CUP SUGAR

Combine heavy cream, cocoa, espresso, and sugar. With an electric mixer with the wire whisk attachment, whip on high speed until soft peaks form, about 2 minutes. Scrape down the sides and bottom of the mixing bowl using a rubber spatula. This will ensure that your ingredients are well mixed. Continue whipping on high speed until stiff. Use immediately.

YIELD: 3 CUPS

ASSEMBLY:

1. Prepare all the ingredients except the ganache.

2. Level the tops of the cake layers. Cut layers horizontally in half to give you 4 thin layers. Place one layer, cut side up, on a serving plate or doily-covered cake circle. Using a pastry bag filled with chocolate buttercream, pipe an outline of frosting around the outer edge of the layer. Spread one-third of the mocha mousse filling into the outline. Place another layer on top of the filled layer. Continue to fill the layers in the same manner. Place the top layer cut side down. Refrigerate cake to set, 10 to 15 minutes.

3. Use a thin layer of chocolate buttercream frosting to coat the cake. Thin the frosting with water to help it spread. Using a metal spatula, start at the top and continue to spread frosting onto the sides of the cake. Set aside.

4. Prepare ganache.

5. Place frosted cake on a wire cooling rack with a clean piece of parchment or waxed paper underneath. Pour ganache over the top of the cake. Guide the glaze down the sides of the cake with a metal spatula. Smooth sides and top with a spatula. Refrigerate. Serve at room temperature.

YIELD: ONE 4-LAYER 9-INCH CAKE, 15 TO 18 SERVINGS

TOASTED ALMOND CAKE

This cake is bursting with almond flavor. It is great served alone or with a splash of Raspberry Sauce (page 58) poured over each piece. Enjoy it with a sip of a cordial, such as amaretto or Chambord.

TWO 8-INCH LAYERS WHITE ALMOND
CAKE (PAGE 65)

1 RECIPE ALMOND SEVEN-MINUTE
FROSTING (PAGE 124)

1½ CUPS SLIVERED ALMONDS,
TOASTED

ASSEMBLY:

1. Make cake and frosting.

2. Level off the tops of both cake layers. Slice each layer in half horizontally to give you 4 thin layers. Place one layer, cut side up, on a serving plate or doily-covered cake circle.

3. Using a pastry bag filled with frosting, pipe an outline of frosting around the perimeter of the layer. Spread a thin layer of frosting inside the outline. Place another layer on top of frosting. Continue to layer until completely filled. Place the top layer cut side down.

4. Frost the outside of the cake with the remaining frosting. Start at the top and continue to spread frosting to cover the sides of the cake. Place almonds in a flat dish. With one hand holding the cake underneath, use the other hand to cover the cake with almonds. Hold the cake over the plate, letting the excess nuts fall back into the plate. Be sure to adhere almonds while the frosting is fresh.

5. Refrigerate. Serve at room temperature.

YIELD: ONE 4-LAYER 8-INCH CAKE, 12 TO 15 SERVINGS

TURTLE CAKE

This chocolate, caramel, and peanut concoction is based on the popular chocolate candy called "Turtles." It pairs our Devil's Food Cake with a gooey caramel center and peanuts. Make it for your favorite chocoholic's birthday.

TWO 9-INCH LAYERS DEVIL'S FOOD
CAKE (PAGE 67)

1 RECIPE CHOCOLATE BUTTERCREAM
(PAGE 121)

½ CUP CARAMEL ICE CREAM TOPPING

½ CUP UNSALTED PEANUTS

GARNISH: 3 TABLESPOONS CARAMEL
TOPPING, PEANUTS

ASSEMBLY:

1. Make cake and buttercream frosting.

2. Level off the tops of cake layers. Place one layer, cut side up, on a serving plate or a doily-covered cake circle. Using a pastry bag filled with chocolate buttercream, pipe an outline of frosting around the perimeter of the layer. Spoon and spread the caramel topping into the center of the cake. Sprinkle peanuts on top of the caramel.

3. Place the other layer, cut side down, on top of the caramel. Refrigerate cake to set, 10 to 15 minutes.

4. Frost the outside of the cake with remaining chocolate buttercream, using a metal spatula to smooth. Start at the top of the cake and continue to spread to cover the sides. If desired, pipe a shell border along the edge of the top of the cake.

5. Using a fork, drizzle caramel in zigzags over the top of the cake. Sprinkle with peanuts. Refrigerate until serving. Serve at room temperature.

YIELD: ONE 2-LAYER 9-INCH CAKE, 12 TO 15 SERVINGS

CRAN-RASPBERRY CAKE

Meet someone special under the mistletoe with a piece of this cake and a glass of holiday eggnog. A favorite from our holiday selections, it has a tart fruit filling and a light whipped cream frosting.

TWO 9-INCH YELLOW CAKE LAYERS
(PAGE 66)

1 RECIPE WHIPPED CREAM FROSTING
(PAGE 122)

1 RECIPE CRAN-RASPBERRY FILLING
(RECIPE FOLLOWS)

1½ CUPS TOASTED CHOPPED WALNUTS

GARNISH: CRANBERRIES AND RASP-
BERRIES

CRAN-RASPBERRY FILLING

3 CUPS CRANBERRIES, FRESH OR
FROZEN

¼ CUP SUGAR

¼ CUP WATER

3 CUPS RASPBERRIES, FRESH OR
FROZEN

1. Rinse cranberries. Place in a small saucepan. Add sugar and water. Over medium heat, boil for 3 to 4 minutes, or until tender, stirring occasionally. Remove from the heat. Cool.

2. When cool, place in a medium mixing bowl. Stir in raspberries. Set aside.

ASSEMBLY:

1. Prepare all the ingredients.

2. Level the tops of two cake layers. Cut layers horizontally to give you 4 thin layers. Place one layer, cut side up, on a cake plate or doily-covered cake circle. Spread a thin layer of whipped cream over the cake. Using a pastry bag filled with whipped cream, pipe an outline around the outer edge of the layer. Fill the outline with one third of the filling. Repeat layering cake with filling until cake is filled. Place top layer cut side down.

3. Frost outside of cake with remaining whipped cream. Using a metal spatula, start at the top of the cake and continue to spread frosting onto the sides of the cake. Cover sides and top of cake with toasted walnuts. Place walnuts in a flat plate. Holding the cake from underneath with one hand, use the other hand to adhere nuts to top and sides of cake. Hold the cake over the plate of nuts so any excess

nuts will fall back onto the plate. Refrigerate cake. Garnish with fresh cranberries and raspberries. Refrigerate again. Serve chilled.

YIELD: ONE 4-LAYER 9-INCH CAKE, 15 TO 18 SERVINGS

CONNECTICUT SPICE CAKE

This flavorful cake pays tribute to my home state, also known as the Nutmeg State. It is a spiced version of our classic Yellow Layer Cake that is perfect for an autumn birthday cake or a non-pumpkin addition to your Thanksgiving desserts.

TWO 9-INCH LAYERS SPICE CAKE

1 RECIPE CREAM CHEESE FROSTING
(PAGE 122)

GARNISH: SPRINKLE OF CINNAMON
AND NUTMEG

SPICE CAKE

4 EGGS, SEPARATED

½ POUND BUTTER, SOFTENED

2 CUPS SUGAR

1 TEASPOON VANILLA EXTRACT

2½ CUPS CAKE FLOUR

2 TEASPOONS BAKING POWDER

¼ TEASPOON SALT

1½ TEASPOONS NUTMEG

3 TEASPOONS CINNAMON

1 TEASPOON GROUND CLOVES

1 CUP BUTTERMILK

1. Preheat oven to 350°F.

2. Grease and flour or line two 9-inch cake pans with parchment paper. Set aside.

3. In an electric mixer with wire whisk attachment, beat egg whites until stiff but not dry. Set aside.

4. In an electric mixer on medium speed, cream the butter. Gradually add the sugar and beat until light in color. Add vanilla. Add egg yolks, one at a time, beating well after adding each one.

5. In another bowl, combine flour, baking powder, salt, nutmeg, cinnamon, and cloves. Add to the egg yolk mixture alternately with the buttermilk. Begin and end with flour mixture. Mix until batter is smooth.

6. Carefully fold mixture into egg whites.

7. Pour batter into prepared pans. Bake for 25 to 30 minutes, or until a tester comes out with a fine crumb. Remove cakes from the oven. Cool cakes in pans on wire

cooling rack for 10 to 15 minutes. Remove cakes from the pans and continue to cool on wire racks. Remove and discard parchment.

YIELD: TWO 9-INCH CAKE LAYERS

ASSEMBLY:

1. Make the cake and cream cheese frosting.

2. Level the tops of the cakes. Place one layer, cut side up, on a serving plate or doily-covered cake circle. Spread a layer of frosting over cake. Place other layer, cut side down, on top.

3. Frost the outside of the cake, using the remaining cream cheese frosting. Using a metal spatula, start at the top of the cake and continue to spread to cover sides. Refrigerate cake. Sprinkle the top with cinnamon and nutmeg. Serve at room temperature.

YIELD: ONE 2-LAYER 9-INCH CAKE, 12 TO 15 SERVINGS

THE ELVIS CAKE

This chocolate, peanut butter, and banana combo was inspired by the King's favorite sandwich. I try to make one every January 8, Elvis's birthday.

TWO 9-INCH LAYERS DEVIL'S FOOD
CAKE (PAGE 67)

1 RECIPE WHIPPED CREAM FROSTING
(PAGE 122)

1 CUP SMOOTH PEANUT BUTTER

1 LARGE BANANA

GARNISH: 1 TEASPOON PEANUT
BUTTER, 1 BANANA, SLICED, SPRINKLE
OF COCOA

ASSEMBLY:

1. Level off the tops of the two chocolate layers. Place one cake, cut side up, on a serving plate or doily-covered cake circle. Spread a thin layer of whipped cream over the layer. Drop spoonfuls of peanut butter on top of the thin cream layer. Slice banana and arrange in the center of the cake. Place the other layer, cut side down, on top of the peanut butter and bananas. Press gently.

2. Frost the cake with remaining whipped cream frosting, using a metal spatula with swirling strokes. Start at the top and continue to spread down the sides of the cake. Refrigerate cake. Top with a spoonful of peanut butter, slices of banana, and a dusting of cocoa. Serve chilled.

YIELD: ONE 2-LAYER 9-INCH CAKE, 12 TO 15 SERVINGS

CRANBERRY PEAR CAKE

This layer cake spotlights a tasty combination of pears, cranberries, and cinnamon. Try this perfect winter pick-me-up with a mug of hot mulled cider.

TWO 9-INCH LAYERS YELLOW CAKE
(PAGE 66)

1 RECIPE CREAM CHEESE FROSTING
(PAGE 122)

1 RECIPE PEAR CRANBERRY FILLING
(RECIPE FOLLOWS)

PEAR CRANBERRY FILLING

4 BOSC PEARS, PEELED, CORED, AND
SLICED (3 CUPS)

½ CUP SUGAR

¼ CUP WATER

1 CUP FRESH CRANBERRIES

Place sliced pears in a small baking dish. Stir in sugar and water. Bake at 350°F for 20 to 25 minutes, or until just beginning to get tender. Add cranberries to the pan. Continue baking for 10 to 15 minutes, or until tender. Cool before using.

ASSEMBLY:

1. Prepare all the ingredients.

2. Level off the tops of cake layers. Place one layer, cut side up, on a serving plate or doily-covered cake circle.

3. Spread a thin layer of cream cheese frosting on the cake. Using a pastry bag filled with cream cheese frosting, pipe an outline around the perimeter of the layer. Spoon and spread filling into the center. Reserve about ½ cup filling for the top of the cake. Place the other layer, cut side down, on top of the filling. Press down gently.

4. Frost the outside of the cake with remaining cream cheese frosting. Using a metal spatula, start at the top and continue to spread frosting covering the sides of the cake.

5. Spoon remaining filling in the center of the top of the cake. If desired, pipe a shell border around the filling. Refrigerate. Serve cake at room temperature.

YIELD: ONE 2-LAYER 9-INCH CAKE, 12 TO 15 SERVINGS

TIRAMISÙ CAKE

This cake is a great way to dress up the Classic Sponge Cake. It is a rich dessert based on the traditional Italian dessert that literally means "pick me up." Any type of coffee complements this cake, but a cup of espresso is definitely my favorite.

1 RECIPE CLASSIC SPONGE CAKE
(BAKED IN 10-INCH TUBE PAN,
PAGE 34)

2 CUPS STRONGLY BREWED COFFEE
OR ESPRESSO, COOLED

1 RECIPE TIRAMISÙ FILLING (RECIPE
FOLLOWS)

3 TEASPOONS CINNAMON

1 RECIPE WHIPPED CREAM FROSTING
(PAGE 122)

GARNISH: CHOCOLATE SHAVINGS AND
A SPRINKLE OF CINNAMON

TIRAMISÙ FILLING

1 CUP HEAVY CREAM

1 POUND MASCARPONE CHEESE,
SOFTENED

½ CUP SUGAR

2 TABLESPOONS COFFEE LIQUEUR

In an electric mixer with wire whisk attachment, whip heavy cream until stiff, 2 to 3 minutes. Add mascarpone cheese, sugar, and liqueur and mix until well blended. Use immediately or refrigerate in an airtight container.

ASSEMBLY:

1. Cut sponge cake into thirds, horizontally. Place the bottom layer, cut side up, onto serving dish or doily-covered cake circle. Pour coffee over all the cake layers to soak the sponge evenly.

2. Divide the filling into thirds. Spread one-third of the filling over coffee-soaked bottom layer. Sprinkle with 1 teaspoon of cinnamon. Repeat with other layer, placing the coffee-soaked layer carefully. Spread remaining filling on top of the layer. Sprinkle with cinnamon.

3. Chill filled cake while preparing whipped cream.

4. Using a metal spatula, frost the top and sides of the cake with whipped cream frosting. Start at the top and continue to spread to cover sides. If desired, use a pastry bag to pipe a border along the top of the cake.

5. Refrigerate. Garnish with chocolate shavings and a sprinkle of cinnamon. Serve chilled.

YIELD: ONE 3-LAYER 10-INCH CAKE, 20 TO 25 SERVINGS

◆ WEDDING CAKES ◆

THE TRADITION OF CAKES AT WEDDINGS BEGAN LONG AGO. THERE ARE MANY STORIES AND SUPERSTITIONS ABOUT EARLY WEDDING CAKES. IN MEDIEVAL TIMES, GUESTS WOULD BRING SMALL BREADS OR CAKES TO THE RECEPTION. THE WHEAT-BASED GIFTS WERE A SYMBOL OF FERTILITY FOR THE HAPPY COUPLE. THESE SMALL CAKES WERE STACKED ONE ON TOP OF THE OTHER, AND THE BRIDE AND GROOM WOULD KISS OVER THE TOP FOR GOOD LUCK. A FRENCH CHEF DECIDED TO FROST THE CAKES, AND THUS TIERED WEDDING CAKES WERE CREATED. TODAY, THE BRIDE AND GROOM CUT THEIR FIRST SLICE TO ENSURE THEIR HAPPINESS. IT WOULD BE BAD LUCK IF ANYONE ELSE WERE TO CUT IT.

WHITE CHOCOLATE GANACHE WEDDING CAKE

This two-tier wedding cake is a vision in swirled white chocolate. The 6-inch and 10-inch cakes are just right for an intimate celebration. It's not hard to make; just think of it as making two separate cakes. It helps to get organized and to be sure you have all the necessary ingredients and special supplies.

I love the natural and swirled look to this frosting. It looks quite striking adorned with fresh pansies. I always plant a good supply of various colors just in case a bride chooses this design.

1½ RECIPES BUTTERCREAM FROSTING (PAGE 120)

1 RECIPE APRICOT CREAM FILLING (RECIPE FOLLOWS)

1 RECIPE WHITE CHOCOLATE GANACHE (RECIPE FOLLOWS)

GARNISH: FRESH FLOWERS (NONTOXIC, UNSPRAYED)

SPECIAL SUPPLIES:

6-INCH ROUND CAKE PAN, 3 INCHES DEEP

TWO 10-INCH ROUND CAKE PANS, 2 INCHES DEEP

ONE 6-INCH AND ONE 10-INCH ROUND FOAM CORE BOARDS

ONE 14-INCH ROUND ½-INCH-THICK PLYWOOD FOR BASE (OR STURDY CAKE PLATTER, IF NOT TRANSPORTING)

THREE ¼-INCH WOODEN DOWEL RODS CUT INTO 4 PIECES FOR BOTTOM TIER

SHEARS

HAMMER

WHITE CAKE FOR WEDDING CAKE

Please note: The following recipe doubles the White Layer Cake recipe on page 64. If you don't have a mixer large enough, mix the batter in two separate batches.

5 CUPS CAKE FLOUR

3 CUPS SUGAR

6 TEASPOONS BAKING POWDER

1 TEASPOON SALT

½ POUND PLUS 5⅓ TABLESPOONS BUTTER

10 EGG WHITES

2 CUPS MILK

2 TEASPOONS VANILLA EXTRACT

1. Preheat oven to 350°F.

2. Grease and flour or line two 10-inch and one 6-inch cake pans with baking parchment. Set aside.

3. In an electric mixer on low speed, blend flour, sugar, baking powder, and salt until mixed. Add butter and mix until butter is uniformly blended.

4. In a separate bowl, mix egg whites, milk, and vanilla with a wire whisk.

5. Add egg mixture to flour mixture. Mix on medium speed for 2 minutes.

6. Scrape down the sides of the mixing bowl. Continue to beat on medium-high for 2 minutes, or until batter is blended and smooth.

7. Pour batter into prepared pans. Fill the 6-inch pan halfway. Then pour remaining batter evenly into the two 10-inch pans.

8. Bake for 30 to 35 minutes for 10-inch layers and an additional 5 to 6 minutes for 6-inch cake.

9. Remove cakes from the oven and cool in pans on wire rack 10 to 15 minutes. Remove cakes from the pans and continue to cool on wire racks. Remove and discard parchment.

APRICOT CREAM FILLING

2 CUPS HEAVY CREAM   **1 CUP APRICOT PRESERVES**

In an electric mixer with wire whisk attachment, beat cream until almost stiff. Add apricot preserves and whip until stiff. Use immediately.

WHITE CHOCOLATE GANACHE

1¾ POUND WHITE CHOCOLATE, FINELY   1¼ CUPS HEAVY CREAM
CHOPPED

Place finely chopped chocolate in a medium mixing bowl. Heat cream over medium heat until just boiling. Pour hot cream over chocolate and stir until smooth. Refrigerate for 15 to 20 minutes, or until thick enough to spread.

ASSEMBLY (see page 125):

1. Level off the tops of all the cake layers. Slice the 6-inch tier horizontally into 4 thin layers. Slice each of the 10-inch layers in half, to give you 4 thin layers.

2. Adhere one layer of the 6-inch cake onto a 6-inch foam core board. Using a pastry bag filled with buttercream frosting, pipe an outline around the outer edge of the layer. Spread a thin layer of apricot cream in the center. Place another layer on top of the filling. Repeat filling cake until complete. Place the top layer, cut side down, on the filling. Refrigerate.

3. Adhere a layer of 10-inch cake onto a 10-inch foam core board. Repeat the filling process the same as the 6-inch layer. Refrigerate both tiers for 10 to 15 minutes.

4. Frost both cakes with a thin layer of buttercream. Using a metal spatula, start from the top and continue to spread the frosting over the sides of the cake. It doesn't need to be totally smooth and perfect. Refrigerate cakes until set, 10 to 15 minutes.

5. When ganache is ready, place both cakes on a wire rack. Using a metal spatula in large swirling motions, spread the ganache. Start at the top and continue to spread and swirl over the sides. Reserve about ¾ cup of the ganache to touch up the cake after assembly. Refrigerate the cakes to set for 10 to 15 minutes.

6. Place bottom 10-inch tier on a sturdy plywood base, or a heavy tray. Use a 6-inch cake circle or cake pan to mark the area where the smaller tier will go. You can center the cake in the traditional manner or place it slightly off center. Use a toothpick or cake tester to trace the outline of the 6 inches in the appropriate spot.

7. Cut 3 dowel rods into 4 pieces 1/16 inch higher than the cake. Insert dowels, evenly spaced, into the interior of the outline. Carefully place the 6-inch cake onto the dowel rods. Sharpen the end of one longer dowel rod. Use a hammer to drive this dowel through the center of the 6-inch cake to the bottom base. This will secure your cake. Use shears to cut the top of the dowel even with the top of the cake.

8. Use the remaining ganache to cover any gaps between layers and to cover the dowel rod hole on top. Refrigerate cake until serving. Decorate as desired with a cascade of fresh flowers or fruit.

YIELD: 60 TO 65 WEDDING CAKE SLICES

◆ WEDDING CAKE TIPS ◆

Transporting Your Wedding Cake

If you need to transport this wedding cake, try to find a cake box that measures the same size as the bottom base. If the base is 10-inches round, use a box that is 10-inches square. This way the cake will fit tightly with nowhere to move. Tear the cover off the box; you won't be able to use it. You can leave the cake uncovered or lightly cover it with a sheet of plastic wrap or cellophane. Place the box onto a towel positioned in a flat trunk or hatchback vehicle. *Do not place the cake on the seat of a car.* It needs to be flat. Be aware of the temperature. If you are traveling a long distance in the summer with a white chocolate coated cake, the trunk may become too hot. The ideal situation is an air-conditioned four-wheel drive vehicle or the floor of a van.

Serving Your Wedding Cake

If you are cutting the wedding cake yourself, instead of having a caterer do it, unassemble the cake first. Place a metal spatula underneath the foam board of the top tier. Use both hands to grab underneath the cake and pull it off the dowel rods. Discard all dowel rods. Slice the cake as shown on page 101. For best results. Use a clean, long serrated knife. Clean the knife periodically and use a slow sawing motion.

Planning and Preparing

If you decide to take on the responsibility of making a wedding cake, make it easy on yourself by doing a few tasks in advance. You can make your buttercream frosting in advance. And you can bake your layers in advance and freeze. Just be sure both cake and frosting are at room temperature before assembly.

Decorating with Fresh Flowers

Fresh flowers are a beautiful and simple way to decorate cakes. But don't use toxic flowers or flowers sprayed with pesticide. Lightly rinse flowers under water and gently pat dry. If they are edible flowers, cut stems and place directly onto the cake in a desired fashion—either cascading down the front or grouped in small clusters around the cake. If the flowers are being used for decoration only, place a small amount of plastic wrap or clear cellophane underneath the flowers.

CARROT BLUEBERRY CAKE

This cake is easy to make and very flexible. You can substitute pineapple or raspberries

for the blueberries, or make a more traditional carrot cake with raisins and walnuts.

Either grate the carrots using a four-sided grater or chop them in a food processor.

You can also use this recipe to make two loaf cakes.

TWO 8-INCH LAYERS CARROT
BLUEBERRY CAKE

1 RECIPE CREAM CHEESE FROSTING
(PAGE 122)

GARNISH: GRATED CARROTS,
BLUEBERRIES, AND A SPRINKLE OF
CINNAMON

CARROT BLUEBERRY CAKE

2 CUPS ALL-PURPOSE FLOUR

½ CUP SUGAR

1 CUP BROWN SUGAR

1¼ CUPS OIL

¼ CUP ORANGE JUICE

4 EGGS

2 TEASPOONS BAKING SODA

2 TEASPOONS CINNAMON

1 TEASPOON SALT

1 TEASPOON VANILLA EXTRACT

2 CUPS GRATED CARROTS

1 CUP FROZEN BLUEBERRIES, THAWED

1. Preheat oven to 350°F.

2. Grease and flour or line two 8-inch cake pans with parchment paper. Set aside.

3. In an electric mixer, combine all ingredients except carrots and blueberries. Beat until well blended, about 2 minutes on medium speed. Scrape down the sides and bottom of the bowl to be sure all ingredients are incorporated. Beat until light in color, 2 to 3 minutes.

4. Stir in carrots and blueberries. Pour batter into prepared pans.

5. Bake for 35 to 40 minutes, or until a tester comes out with a fine crumb. Remove pans from the oven. Cool cakes in pans on wire cooling racks for 10 to 15 minutes. Carefully remove cakes from the pans and continue to cool on wire cooling racks. Remove and discard parchment.

ASSEMBLY:

1. Make cake and cream cheese frosting.

2. Level off tops of cake layers. Place one layer, cut side up, on a cake plate or doily-covered cake circle. Spread a layer of frosting over the cake layer. Place other layer, cut side down, onto bottom layer. Using a metal spatula, frost the outside of the cake with remaining cream cheese frosting. Start at the top and continue to spread frosting onto the sides of the cake. Refrigerate cake. Garnish with grated carrots, blueberries, and a sprinkle of cinnamon. Serve at room temperature.

YIELD: ONE 2-LAYER 8-INCH CAKE, 10 TO 12 SERVINGS

VARIATIONS:

CARROT RASPBERRY CAKE
Substitute 1 cup frozen raspberries for the blueberries.

TRADITIONAL CARROT CAKE
Omit frozen blueberries. Add ¾ cup walnut halves, ½ cup raisins, and ¼ cup chocolate chips in step 4.

LOAF CAKES
Pour batter into two 8 x 4 x 3-inch loaf pans. Bake for 50 to 55 minutes.

◆ **FIRST BIRTHDAYS** ◆

FOR A CHILD'S FIRST BIRTHDAY, MANY PEOPLE ORDER A SMALL 6-INCH ROUND CAKE FOR THE GUEST OF HONOR ALONG WITH A LARGER CAKE FOR THE REST OF THE GUESTS. THIS SMALL CAKE IS FOR THE ONE-YEAR-OLD TO HAVE ALL TO HIMSELF, TO EAT, TO PLAY WITH, OR TO JUST MAKE A MESS.

BANANA SOUR CREAM CAKE

This banana cake is accented by rich chocolate buttercream frosting. It is exceptionally moist and tastes great for days. You can add walnuts if you'd like a traditional banana nut cake. Try a slice with an ice cold glass of milk.

TWO 9-INCH BANANA SOUR CREAM
CAKE LAYERS

GARNISH: 1 BANANA, SLICED

1 RECIPE CHOCOLATE BUTTERCREAM
(PAGE 121)

BANANA SOUR CREAM CAKE

¼ POUND BUTTER, SOFTENED

1 CUP SUGAR

½ CUP BROWN SUGAR

1 TEASPOON VANILLA EXTRACT

3 EGGS

2 CUPS CAKE FLOUR

1 TEASPOON BAKING POWDER

1 TEASPOON BAKING SODA

½ TEASPOON SALT

¾ CUP SOUR CREAM

2 CUPS MASHED BANANAS (2 TO 3
MEDIUM BANANAS)

1. Preheat oven to 350°F.

2. Grease and flour or line two 9-inch cake pans with parchment paper. Set aside.

3. In an electric mixer on medium speed, cream the butter. Gradually add sugar and brown sugar and mix until light. Add vanilla. Add eggs, one at a time, beating well after each one.

4. In a medium bowl, combine flour, baking powder, baking soda, and salt. In another small bowl, combine sour cream and mashed bananas. Pour each of these mixtures alternately into the butter mixture. Begin and end with flour mixture. Mix until blended.

5. Pour batter evenly into prepared pans. Bake for 20 to 25 minutes, or until a tester comes out with a fine crumb.

6. Remove pans from the oven and place on wire cooling racks. Cool in pans for 10 to 15 minutes. Carefully remove cakes from the pans and continue to cool on wire racks. Remove and discard parchment. Cool completely.

ASSEMBLY:

1. Make cake and chocolate buttercream.

2. Level off the tops of cake layers. Place one layer, cut side up, on a serving plate or doily-covered cake circle. Spread a layer of frosting onto the cake layer. Place other layer, cut side down, on top of the bottom layer. Frost the cake with remaining frosting.

3. Using a metal spatula, start at the top and continue to spread frosting onto the sides of the cake. Refrigerate. Garnish with sliced banana before serving. Serve at room temperature.

YIELD: ONE 2-LAYER 9-INCH CAKE, 12 TO 15 SERVINGS

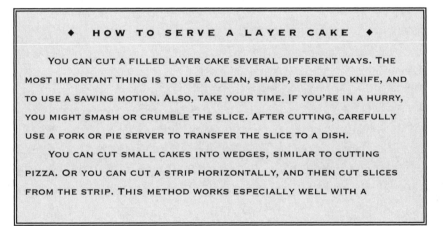

◆ **HOW TO SERVE A LAYER CAKE** ◆

YOU CAN CUT A FILLED LAYER CAKE SEVERAL DIFFERENT WAYS. THE MOST IMPORTANT THING IS TO USE A CLEAN, SHARP, SERRATED KNIFE, AND TO USE A SAWING MOTION. ALSO, TAKE YOUR TIME. IF YOU'RE IN A HURRY, YOU MIGHT SMASH OR CRUMBLE THE SLICE. AFTER CUTTING, CAREFULLY USE A FORK OR PIE SERVER TO TRANSFER THE SLICE TO A DISH.

YOU CAN CUT SMALL CAKES INTO WEDGES, SIMILAR TO CUTTING PIZZA. OR YOU CAN CUT A STRIP HORIZONTALLY, AND THEN CUT SLICES FROM THE STRIP. THIS METHOD WORKS ESPECIALLY WELL WITH A

VERY BERRY
WHIPPED CREAM CAKE

Accented by fresh fruit, this cake is our most popular whipped cream cake. It's especially popular for Fourth of July parties. Not only is it a great, refreshing summer dessert, it proudly displays our red, white, and blue.

TWO 8-INCH WHITE CAKE LAYERS
(PAGE 64)

1 RECIPE WHIPPED CREAM FROSTING
(PAGE 122)

1 CUP FRESH OR FROZEN
BLUEBERRIES

1 CUP FRESH OR FROZEN
RASPBERRIES

1 CUP FRESH STRAWBERRIES,
CLEANED, HULLED, AND SLICED

ASSEMBLY:

1. Make cake and whipped cream frosting.

2. Mix all berries together in a small bowl. Set aside.

3. Level the tops of the cakes. Slice both layers of cake in half horizontally, giving you 4 thin layers. Place one piece of cake, cut side up, on a serving plate or doily-covered cake circle. Spread a thin layer of whipped cream on the layer. Arrange one-third of the berry mixture over the cream. Repeat spreading cream and arranging berries until the cake is completely filled. Place top layer cut side down.

4. Using a metal spatula, frost the top and sides of the cake with remaining whipped cream. Garnish with berries.

5. Refrigerate until serving. Serve chilled.

YIELD: ONE 4-LAYER 8-INCH CAKE, 15 TO 18 SERVINGS

FROZEN ALMOND
STRAWBERRY CAKE

Use our classic Almond Pound Cake to create this frozen dessert. It's a great make-ahead dessert—you can leave it in the freezer for up to 2 months and have a fabulous dessert for unexpected guests.

1 ALMOND POUND CAKE (PAGE 18)

1 QUART STRAWBERRY ICE CREAM, SLIGHTLY SOFTENED

1 CUP CLEANED, HULLED, AND SLICED STRAWBERRIES

2 TABLESPOONS AMARETTO LIQUEUR

½ CUP SUGAR

½ CUP HEAVY CREAM

½ CUP SLICED ALMONDS

CONFECTIONERS' SUGAR FOR DUSTING

1. Line a large loaf pan (10 x 6 x 2½ inches) with plastic wrap. Leave enough wrap to cover loaf pan.

2. Cut pound cake lengthwise into 6 pieces. Line the prepared pan with slices of cake—one slice on the bottom, one slice on each long side of the pan. Split one slice to line the short ends of the pans.

3. In a large mixing bowl, quickly combine ice cream, strawberries, amaretto, sugar, heavy cream, and almonds. Stir with a wooden spoon until blended.

4. Spread half the ice cream mixture into the pan. Cover with a slice of cake. Spread remaining ice cream mixture on top of the cake and place the last slice of cake on top. Cover well with plastic wrap.

5. Freeze for 4 to 5 hours or overnight.

6. Thaw slightly before serving. Dust with confectioners' sugar. Using a sharp knife, slice into ½-inch pieces.

YIELD: ONE LARGE FILLED LOAF, ABOUT 12 SERVINGS

GINGERBREAD

This cake is so tasty you won't want to wait for Christmas to make it. It really does work year-round—I've even done a wedding cake in April with gingerbread. (It was a very traditional three-tier round cake with simple frosting draping, or swags, around the sides, and topped with a cluster of pale pink frosting roses.)

This cake is very flexible and tastes great with either Cream Cheese Frosting or Spiced Whipped Cream Frosting. To garnish the cake, use gingersnap crumbs to cover the cake, a sprinkle of orange rind, and cinnamon.

TWO 8-INCH GINGERBREAD CAKE LAYERS

1 RECIPE CREAM CHEESE FROSTING (PAGE 122)

OR

1 RECIPE SPICED WHIPPED CREAM FROSTING (PAGE 78)

1 CUP GINGERSNAP CRUMBS

GARNISH: GRATED ORANGE RIND AND A SPRINKLE OF CINNAMON

GINGERBREAD CAKE

12 TABLESPOONS BUTTER, MELTED

1 CUP MOLASSES

1 CUP BROWN SUGAR

1½ CUPS BUTTERMILK

3 EGGS

3 CUPS UNBLEACHED FLOUR

1 TEASPOON BAKING SODA

¼ TEASPOON SALT

3 TEASPOONS GROUND GINGER

1½ TEASPOONS CINNAMON

½ TEASPOON NUTMEG

1. Preheat oven to 350°F. Grease and flour or line two 8-inch cake pans with parchment paper.

2. In an electric mixer on medium speed, beat butter, molasses, brown sugar, buttermilk, and eggs.

3. Add dry ingredients and mix just until blended. Batter will be slightly lumpy. Do not overmix. Pour batter evenly into prepared pans. Bake for 30 to 35 minutes, or until a tester comes out with a fine crumb. Remove pans from the oven. Let cakes cool in pans on wire cooling racks for 10 to 15 minutes. Carefully re-

move cakes from the pans and turn bottom side down on racks to cool. Remove and discard parchment.

ASSEMBLY:

1. Make cake and whipped cream or cream cheese frosting.

2. Level off the tops of cake layers. Place one layer, cut side up, on a cake plate or doily-covered cake circle. Spread some frosting on the bottom layer. Place other layer, cut side down, onto bottom layer.

3. Using a metal spatula, frost the outside of the cake with remaining frosting. Start from the top and continue to spread frosting onto the sides of the cake. Cover cake with crushed gingersnap crumbs. Place crumbs onto a flat plate. Hold the cake underneath with one hand. Use the other hand to adhere crumbs to the sides and top of the cake. Be sure to hold the cake over the plate of crumbs so that excess crumbs will fall back onto plate. Refrigerate cake. Garnish with grated orange rind and a sprinkle of cinnamon. Serve cake at room temperature.

YIELD: ONE 2-LAYER 8-INCH CAKE, 10 TO 12 SERVINGS

CHIP & ERNIE'S CAKE

This is a favorite from the Sweet Maria's menu. It's especially popular for children's birthday parties. A variation of our Yellow Layer Cake, it is made with chocolate chips and a rich chocolate icing. Be sure to line the cake pan with parchment. This will prevent the chocolate chips from sticking to the pan.

TWO 9-INCH CHOCOLATE CHIP CAKE LAYERS

GARNISH: CHOCOLATE CHIPS

1 RECIPE CHOCOLATE BUTTERCREAM (PAGE 121)

CHOCOLATE CHIP CAKE

4 EGGS, SEPARATED

½ POUND BUTTER, SOFTENED

1 CUP SUGAR

1 CUP BROWN SUGAR

1 TEASPOON VANILLA EXTRACT

2½ CUPS ALL-PURPOSE FLOUR

2 TEASPOONS BAKING POWDER

¼ TEASPOON SALT

1 CUP BUTTERMILK

1½ CUPS SEMISWEET CHOCOLATE CHIPS

1. Preheat oven to 350°F.

2. Grease and line two 9-inch cake pans with parchment paper. Set aside.

3. In an electric mixer with wire whisk attachment, beat egg whites until stiff but not dry. Set aside.

4. In an electric mixer on medium speed, cream the butter. Gradually add the sugar and brown sugar and beat until light. Add vanilla. Add egg yolks, one at a time, beating well after each egg.

5. Combine flour, baking powder, and salt. Add to the butter mixture alternately with buttermilk. Begin and end with the flour mixture. Mix just until blended. Fold egg whites into flour mixture. Fold in chocolate chips.

6. Pour batter into prepared pans. Bake for 25 to 30 minutes, or until a tester comes out with a fine crumb.

7. Remove pan from the oven and place on wire cooling rack. Cool cakes in pans for 8 to 10 minutes. Carefully remove cakes from the pans and continue to cool on wire rack. Remove and discard parchment.

ASSEMBLY:

1. Make cake and chocolate buttercream.

2. Level tops of baked layers. Adhere one layer to a cake plate or doily-covered cake circle, cut side up. Spread some frosting in the center of the layer. Place the other layer on top, cut side down.

3. Starting at the top, frost top of cake with metal spatula, using large swirling motions. Continue to frost sides, covering the entire cake. Use a little of water to help to thin and spread the frosting. Refrigerate cake. Garnish with chocolate chips. Serve at room temperature.

YIELD: ONE 2-LAYER 9-INCH CAKE, 12 TO 15 SERVINGS

RUM RAISIN BANANA TRIFLE

If you're still intimidated by assembling and decorating a layer cake, use this traditional dessert to have your cake and eat it too. It's the ideal solution to broken cakes—it can be made from any thin layers accumulated from leveling off the tops of cake layers, no matter what flavor. I try to recycle these "scraps" for a casual family dessert I call "cake in a bowl."

FOUR 8- OR 9-INCH PIECES OF CAKE, ANY FLAVOR, SLICED VERY THIN

½ CUP DARK RUM

ONE RECIPE VANILLA CUSTARD FILLING (PAGE 72)

4 BANANAS, SLICED

1 CUP RAISINS

1 CUP LARGE WALNUT PIECES

ONE RECIPE CHOCOLATE CREAM FILLING (PAGE 76)

ONE RECIPE WHIPPED CREAM FROSTING (PAGE 122)

ASSEMBLY:

1. Place one layer of cake in a 3-quart trifle bowl. Drizzle the cake layer with rum. Spread half of the vanilla custard over the cake layer. Arrange bananas, raisins, and nuts over the top. Continue layering, alternating chocolate and vanilla filling, until the trifle bowl is filled. Spread whipped cream on top. If desired, pipe a design with a star tip on top. Garnish with raisins and walnut halves.

2. Refrigerate until serving. Serve chilled.

YIELD: 15 TO 18 SERVINGS

VARIATIONS:

If you have less cake than 4 pieces, use a smaller bowl and only one type of custard filling.

You can substitute any type of cake, custard, liqueur, fruit, or nuts you happen to have in your kitchen.

LEMON RASPBERRY WHIPPED CREAM CAKE

This popular cake combines two of my favorite flavors. It started as a "cake of the month" and soon became part of our regular menu. It's perfect for a bridal luncheon or tea.

TWO 8-INCH LAYERS WHITE LAYER CAKE (PAGE 64)

1 RECIPE LEMON DRIZZLE (RECIPE FOLLOWS)

1 RECIPE WHIPPED CREAM FROSTING (PAGE 122)

3 CUPS FRESH OR INDIVIDUALLY QUICK-FROZEN (IQF) RASPBERRIES

GARNISH: RASPBERRIES AND GRATED LEMON RIND

LEMON DRIZZLE

¼ CUP WATER

2 TABLESPOONS LEMON EXTRACT

Mix together in a small cup.

ASSEMBLY:

1. Prepare all the ingredients.

2. Level the tops of the cakes. Slice both cake layers in half horizontally, giving you 4 thin layers. Place one piece of cake, cut side up, on a serving plate or doily-covered cake circle. Using a pastry brush, brush the cake with lemon drizzle. Spread a thin layer of whipped cream frosting on the layer. Arrange 1 cup of berries over the cream. Place another layer on top of the berries. Repeat brushing, spreading whipped cream, and arranging berries until the cake is completely filled. Place the last layer cut side down.

3. Using a metal spatula, frost the top and sides of cake with remaining whipped cream. Garnish with raspberries and lemon rind.

4. Refrigerate until serving. Serve chilled.

YIELD: ONE 4-LAYER 8-INCH CAKE, 15 TO 18 SERVINGS

JOSEPHINE & NAPOLEON CAKE

This cake has a unique combination of sponge cake and puff pastry—the flaky dough that is the basis for the napoleon pastry—and a combination of vanilla and chocolate custard fillings. It may seem like a lot of steps, but it's well worth the effort. The best way to approach it is to bake your sponge cake first. While it's in the oven, make the custards and refrigerate them. Then make the puff pastry circles. Assemble later, or the next day.

½ RECIPE SPONGE CAKE

2 RECIPES VANILLA CUSTARD FILLING
(PAGE 72)

1 RECIPE CHOCOLATE CUSTARD
FILLING (RECIPE FOLLOWS)

TWO 10-INCH CIRCLES OF PUFF
PASTRY, BAKED (RECIPE FOLLOWS)

CONFECTIONERS' SUGAR FOR DUSTING

TO MAKE HALF THE SPONGE CAKE

Be aware that the cake will come only halfway up the sides of the pan and that the cooking time will be a little less than the full recipe.

4 EGG WHITES

½ CUP PLUS 2 TABLESPOONS SUGAR

¼ TEASPOON CREAM OF TARTAR

¼ TEASPOON SALT

4 EGG YOLKS

½ TEASPOON VANILLA EXTRACT

¾ CUP CAKE FLOUR

2 TABLESPOONS COLD WATER

1. Preheat oven to 325°F.

2. In an electric mixer with wire whisk attachment, beat egg whites, 2 tablespoons of sugar, cream of tartar, and salt. Start on medium speed, then use high speed until very stiff peaks form, 3 to 4 minutes. Set aside.

3. In a separate bowl, with an electric mixer on medium speed, beat the egg yolks, ½ cup of sugar, and vanilla. Beat until light in color, 2 to 3 minutes.

4. Alternate adding flour and water to egg yolk mixture. Begin and end with flour. Mix just until blended.

5. Using a rubber spatula, fold egg yolk mixture into beaten whites. When blended, spoon batter into a 10-inch ungreased tube pan with removable bottom.

6. Bake for 30 minutes, or until top is golden brown. Remove pan from the oven. Invert cake and cool in pan for about 1 hour.

7. When cool, carefully remove the cake from the pan. Use a sharp straight knife to loosen the outside of the cake from the pan. Remove inside of pan. Run knife along the bottom and around inside of center column to remove.

CHOCOLATE CUSTARD FILLING

2 TABLESPOONS CORNSTARCH	3 EGGS
PINCH OF SALT	3 TABLESPOONS COCOA
⅓ CUP SUGAR	1 TABLESPOON BUTTER
1 CUP HEAVY CREAM	1 TEASPOON VANILLA EXTRACT

1. In a double boiler over boiling water, combine cornstarch, salt, sugar, cream, eggs, and cocoa. Whisk constantly until mixture is thickened, about 5 minutes.

2. Remove from the heat. Stir in butter and vanilla. Cool. Cover with plastic wrap and refrigerate.

TO MAKE PUFF PASTRY CIRCLES:

1 PACKAGE (2 SHEETS) FROZEN PUFF
PASTRY

1. Preheat oven to 375°F.

2. Follow the directions on the box and thaw slightly. Carefully unroll the sheets. Cut both sheets into two 10-inch circles. Make a hole, about 2 inches in diameter, in the center, using a cookie cutter. This will line up with the center hole in your sponge cake when you assemble the layers.

3. Place each circle separately onto a parchment-lined cookie sheet. Bake until lightly browned, 12 to 15 minutes.

4. Cool on cookie sheet.

5. Insteaad of discarding unused portions of puff pastry, sprinkle unused portions with cinnamon and sugar and bake. These are great snacks.

ASSEMBLY:

1. Slice the sponge cake in half horizontally. Place the bottom layer, cut side up, on a cake plate or doily-covered cake circle. Spread half the vanilla custard over sponge cake layer. Top with a circle of baked puff pastry. Spread the chocolate custard on top of the puff pastry. Top with the sponge cake layer. Repeat spreading another layer of vanilla custard and top with the last layer of puff pastry.

2. Refrigerate until serving. Dust with confectioners' sugar just before serving. Serve chilled. Use a sharp serrated knife with a slow sawing motion to cut cake into slices.

YIELD: ONE 4-LAYER 10-INCH CAKE, ABOUT 25 SERVINGS

PIÑA COLADA CAKE

This pineapple, rum, and coconut cake is very popular at Sweet Maria's.
People order it for special occasions or for an everyday dessert.
(We sometimes call it "the Booze Cruise.")

TWO 9-INCH YELLOW CAKE LAYERS
(PAGE 66)

½ CUP RUM

1 RECIPE WHIPPED CREAM FROSTING
(PAGE 122)

3 CUPS CRUSHED PINEAPPLE, DRAINED

2 CUPS SHREDDED COCONUT

ASSEMBLY:

1. Make cake and whipped cream frosting.

2. Level off the tops of cake layers. Slice each layer in half horizontally to give you 4 thin layers. Place one layer, cut side up, on a serving plate or doily-covered cake circle. Using a pastry brush, brush the layer with rum. Spread a thin layer of whipped cream frosting over the cake. Using a pastry bag filled with whipped cream frosting, pipe an outline around the edge of the layer. Fill in the layer with 1 cup crushed pineapple. Place another layer on top of the filling. Repeat brushing with rum and filling all layers until cake is filled. Place top layer cut side down.

3. Frost the outside of the cake using the remaining whipped cream frosting. Start at the top and continue to spread to cover sides.

4. Place coconut in a flat plate. With one hand holding the cake underneath, use the other hand to adhere coconut to the top and sides of cake. Hold the cake over the plate. Let any excess coconut fall back onto the plate. Refrigerate until serving. Serve chilled.

YIELD: ONE 4-LAYER 9-INCH CAKE, 15 TO 18 SERVINGS

LESS-FAT MOCHA CAKE

This cake uses a chocolate angel food cake as its base. It is accented by a tasty mocha filling that actually tastes better the day after it's assembled. Fill the center hole with fresh berries or grapes to garnish your dessert. Enjoy with a glass of sparkling cider.

ONE 10-INCH CHOCOLATE ALMOND ANGEL FOOD CAKE (PAGE 37)

1 RECIPE LOW-FAT MOCHA FILLING (RECIPE FOLLOWS)

CONFECTIONERS' SUGAR FOR DUSTING

GARNISH: ASSORTED GRAPES OR BERRIES

LOW-FAT MOCHA FILLING

1 POUND NEUFCHÂTEL CHEESE, SOFTENED

2 TEASPOONS INSTANT COFFEE

1 TEASPOON ALMOND EXTRACT

2 TABLESPOONS COCOA

½ CUP CONFECTIONERS' SUGAR

In an electric mixer on medium-high speed, whip cheese until light and fluffy, 3 to 5 minutes. Add coffee, almond extract, and cocoa. Beat until blended. Add confectioners' sugar and beat until blended. Use immediately or refrigerate in an airtight container overnight.

ASSEMBLY:

1. Slice angel food cake horizontally into 3 pieces. Place bottom layer, cut side up, on a cake plate or doily-covered cake circle. Spread half the mocha filling over the cake layer. Top with next layer of cake. Spread remaining filling on top of this layer. Top with last layer of cake, cut side down. Chill until serving.

2. Before serving, dust with confectioners' sugar and garnish with berries and/or grapes in the center and around cake. Serve chilled.

YIELD: ONE 3-LAYER 10-INCH CAKE, 18 TO 20 SERVINGS

BROWN DERBY CAKE

This cake was a specialty of the first bakery I worked in. It's a mound of delicious chocolate cake, filled with fresh strawberries and bananas and topped with whipped cream. It is fun to frost because you use your hands to spread the cream into a rounded top.

TWO 9-INCH DEVIL'S FOOD CAKE LAYERS (PAGE 67)	2 CUPS WASHED, HULLED, AND SLICED FRESH STRAWBERRIES
1 RECIPE WHIPPED CREAM FROSTING (RECIPE FOLLOWS)	CHOCOLATE CAKE CRUMBS (MADE FROM EXTRA LAYER)
2 BANANAS SLICED	

WHIPPED CREAM FROSTING FOR DERBY CAKE

3 CUPS HEAVY CREAM	½ CUP SUGAR

In an electric mixer with wire whisk attachment, whip cream on high speed until peaks form, about 2 minutes. Add sugar. Continue to whip until stiff, another 30 seconds. Use immediately.

ASSEMBLY:

1. Cut cake layers in half horizontally so that you have 4 thin layers. Place one layer, cut side up, on a 9-inch cake circle. A circle will work easier for handling than a cake plate. Spread a thin layer of whipped cream frosting over the cake. Slice a banana in half lengthwise and place along the outer edge of the layer. Fill the center with half of the sliced strawberries. Top with another layer of chocolate cake. Repeat, spreading whipped cream, placing banana around the edge, and filling the center with remaining strawberries. Top with the third layer of cake. Chill.

2. With remaining cake layer, make crumbs: Rub the cake layer onto a grater, creating chocolate cake crumbs. Place crumbs in a pie plate or flat dish.

3. Remove chilled cake from the refrigerator. Holding the cake underneath with one hand, spread a large rounded mound of whipped cream on top of the cake with the other hand. Spread cream to cover layers and create a mound on top. Still holding the cake from the bottom, evenly spread cake crumbs all over mound to cover. Some of the white cream will show through.

4. Place the cake on a cake plate or larger doily-covered cake circle.

5. Refrigerate until serving. Serve chilled.

YIELD: ONE 3-LAYER 9-INCH CAKE, 15 TO 20 SERVINGS

HAZELNUT CAKE

This cake is a nut-lover's dream come true. In this versatile recipe you can use any type of nut you prefer: almonds or hazelnuts, or a combination of both, work great. Filled with a rich chocolate ganache and raspberry preserves and frosted with a hazelnut buttercream, it's so rich it should be eaten one sliver at a time.

TWO 8-INCH ROUND LAYERS HAZELNUT
CAKE

GANACHE FILLING (RECIPE FOLLOWS)

1 RECIPE HAZELNUT BUTTERCREAM
(RECIPE FOLLOWS)

¼ CUP RASPBERRY PRESERVES

GARNISH: FRESH RASPBERRIES,
HAZELNUTS, AND MINT LEAVES

HAZELNUT CAKE

3 EGGS

2 CUPS SUGAR

1 CUP VEGETABLE OIL

1 CUP MILK

3 TEASPOONS HAZELNUT LIQUEUR

2 CUPS CAKE FLOUR

1 TEASPOON BAKING POWDER

¼ CUP HAZELNUTS, FINELY CHOPPED

1. Preheat oven to 350°F. Grease and flour or line two 8-inch round cake pans with parchment paper.

2. In an electric mixer, blend eggs, sugar, oil, milk, and liqueur. Add flour and baking powder. Mix until smooth. Stir in nuts.

3. Pour batter evenly into prepared pans. Bake for 25 to 30 minutes, or until a tester comes out with a fine crumb. Remove pans from the oven. Cool cakes in pans on wire racks for 10 to 15 minutes.

4. Carefully remove cakes from pans and set on wire cooling racks to cool completely. Remove and discard parchment.

GANACHE FILLING

4 OUNCES FINELY CHOPPED
SEMISWEET CHOCOLATE

¼ CUP HEAVY CREAM

1. Place finely chopped chocolate in a small bowl.

2. In a small saucepan over medium-low heat, heat cream until just about boiling. Remove from the stove and pour over chocolate. Stir until well blended and smooth. Let cool at room temperature, then chill until thickened, the consistency of pudding.

HAZELNUT BUTTERCREAM

½ POUND BUTTER, SOFTENED

6 CUPS CONFECTIONERS' SUGAR

1 TEASPOON VANILLA EXTRACT

¼ CUP HAZELNUTS, FINELY CHOPPED

2 EGG WHITES

1. In an electric mixer on low speed, cream the butter with 4 cups of confectioners' sugar. Add vanilla. Gradually add remaining 2 cups of confectioners' sugar, hazelnuts, and egg whites. Beat on high speed until light in color and texture, about 5 minutes.

2. Use immediately or place in an airtight container and refrigerate. Bring frosting to room temperature before using. Thin with a few teaspoons of water for easy spreading.

ASSEMBLY:

1. Slice hazelnut layers in half horizontally, to give you 4 thin layers of cake. Place one layer, cut side up, on a cake plate or doily-covered cake circle. Using hazelnut buttercream, pipe a dam around the outer edge of the layer. Fill the dam with half the ganache. Top with another layer of cake. Make a dam along the outer edge of the layer. Fill this dam with raspberry preserves. Top with another layer of cake. Pipe a buttercream dam along the edge of the layer. Fill this dam with remaining ganache. Top the cake with the last layer of cake, cut side down. Press lightly and refrigerate until set, 15 to 20 minutes.

2. Frost the outside of the cake with hazelnut buttercream. Using a metal spatula, start at the top and continue to spread frosting to cover the sides of the cake. Refrigerate cake. Garnish with fresh raspberries, hazelnuts, and mint leaves. Serve cake at room temperature.

YIELD: ONE 4-LAYER 8-INCH CAKE, 12 TO 15 SERVINGS

CHOCOLATE CREAM–FILLED CUPCAKES AND LEMON CUPCAKES

These tasty little cakes show off how versatile our basic cake recipes are. The chocolate cream–filled cupcakes are an updated version of the cupcakes our moms packed into our lunchboxes. The lemon cupcakes are a special treat—white cakes filled with lemon curd, perfect for afternoon tea.

CHOCOLATE CREAM–FILLED CUPCAKES

24 DEVIL'S FOOD CUPCAKES (PAGE 67)

½ RECIPE BUTTERCREAM FROSTING
(PAGE 120)

1 RECIPE CHOCOLATE GANACHE
(PAGE 123)

ASSEMBLY:

1. Prepare all the ingredients.

2. Fill a pastry bag with buttercream frosting. Carefully insert the tip of the pastry bag into the cupcake. Squeeze the bag and release frosting into the center of the cupcake. Repeat until all cupcakes are filled.

3. Use a spatula to spread ganache onto the tops of the cupcakes. With buttercream frosting, pipe a small star design on top of each cupcake. Refrigerate until serving. Serve at room temperature.

YIELD: 24 CUPCAKES

LEMON CUPCAKES

20 WHITE LAYER CAKE CUPCAKES
(PAGE 64)

1 RECIPE LEMON CURD FILLING
(PAGE 80)
CONFECTIONERS' SUGAR FOR DUSTING

ASSEMBLY:

1. Using a paring knife, scoop out the top of the cupcakes, about ½ inch deep. Set tops aside.

2. Using a teaspoon, fill cupcake bottoms with lemon curd filling. If the filling sticks to your fingers, dip your fingers in water to help release the filling from the teaspoon. Place tops back on top of filling. Press gently. Dust tops with confectioners' sugar. Refrigerate. Serve at room temperature.

YIELD: 20 CUPCAKES

BUTTERCREAM FROSTING

This is a rich, traditional frosting suitable for any occasion. If you want to do fancier decorating, be sure to make 1½ recipes or double the recipe for additional frosting.

½ POUND BUTTER, SOFTENED   1 TEASPOON VANILLA EXTRACT

6 CUPS CONFECTIONERS' SUGAR   2 EGG WHITES

1. In an electric mixer on low speed, cream the butter and 4 cups of the confectioners' sugar. Add vanilla. Gradually add the remaining 2 cups of confectioners' sugar and egg whites. Scrape down the sides of the bowl.

2. Beat on high speed until light in color and texture, about 5 minutes.

3. Use immediately or cover in an airtight container and refrigerate. Bring frosting to room temperature before using. If necessary, thin with a few teaspoons of water for easier spreading.

YIELD: ENOUGH TO FILL, FROST, AND PIPE TOP AND BOTTOM BORDERS AROUND A TWO-LAYER 9-INCH ROUND CAKE

CHOCOLATE BUTTERCREAM FROSTING

This rich frosting is perfect on our Banana Sour Cream Cake, Chip & Ernie's Cake, Turtle Cake, or Chocolate Strawberry Valentine Cake.

½ POUND BUTTER, SOFTENED

1 CUP COCOA

6 CUPS CONFECTIONERS' SUGAR

½ CUP COLD BREWED COFFEE

1. In an electric mixer, cream the butter. Add cocoa and 4 cups of the confectioners' sugar. Beat on low speed until blended. Add remaining confectioners' sugar and coffee. Beat on medium high for 3 to 4 minutes, or until smooth and well blended.

2. Use immediately or store refrigerated in an airtight container. Bring frosting to room temperature before using. If necessary, thin with a few teaspoons of water for easier spreading.

YIELD: ENOUGH TO FILL AND FROST A TWO-LAYER 9-INCH ROUND CAKE

◆ CAKE DECORATING PRACTICE ◆

A GOOD WAY TO PRACTICE BORDERS IS TO PIPE THEM ONTO A COOKIE SHEET LINED WITH WAXED PAPER. AFTER PIPING A FEW ROWS, SCRAPE UP THE FROSTING AND REPEAT AGAIN. PRACTICE WILL REALLY HELP YOU REGULATE THE AMOUNT OF PRESSURE NEEDED TO ADD TO THE BAG TO GET A BORDER OF THE DESIRED SIZE. YOU CAN ALSO PRACTICE ALONG THE EDGE OF A CAKE PAN, TURNED UPSIDE DOWN. OR YOU CAN ALWAYS JUST BAKE A CAKE—AND REWARD YOURSELF WITH A SLICE AT THE END OF THE PRACTICE SESSION.

WHIPPED CREAM FROSTING

This fresh and versatile frosting is the perfect complement to cakes filled with fresh fruit or custard fillings. Our version is slightly sweetened. If you prefer a sweeter cream, just increase the sugar.

2 CUPS HEAVY CREAM   **¼ CUP SUGAR**

In an electric mixer with wire whisk attachment, beat cream into peaks, 2 to 3 minutes. Add sugar and whip until stiff. Use immediately.

YIELD: 4 CUPS, ENOUGH TO FILL AND FROST A TWO-LAYER 9-INCH POUND CAKE

CREAM CHEESE FROSTING

This rich and flavorful frosting complements spicier cakes like carrot, spice cake, amaretto, apple, and gingerbread.

16 OUNCES CREAM CHEESE,   **6 CUPS CONFECTIONERS' SUGAR**
SOFTENED

¼ POUND BUTTER, SOFTENED

1. In an electric mixer, blend together cream cheese and butter. Whip on medium-high speed for 3 to 4 minutes, or until fluffy.

2. On low speed, gradually add confectioners' sugar until well blended and smooth. Use immediately or store, refrigerated, in an airtight container. Let frosting come to room temperature before using.

YIELD: ENOUGH TO FILL AND FROST A TWO-LAYER 9-INCH ROUND CAKE

CHOCOLATE GANACHE

This rich chocolate glaze is poured over a chocolate frosted cake for a dark, smooth appearance and a rich flavor. Be sure that your chocolate is finely ground. The finer the chocolate, the easier it will blend with the hot cream. It works best when used to coat a cake that has a thin base coat of chocolate buttercream frosting.

8 OUNCES SEMISWEET CHOCOLATE   ½ CUP HEAVY CREAM

1. Process chocolate in food processor until finely ground.

2. Place processed chocolate in a medium mixing bowl.

3. Heat heavy cream in a small saucepan over medium heat. Heat until just about boiling, stirring constantly with a wooden spoon. Pour hot cream over chocolate and stir until well blended and smooth. Cool to lukewarm before using. Store refrigerated in an airtight container. To reheat, heat in a double boiler over simmering water. Stir until smooth.

YIELD: ENOUGH TO COVER ONE 9-INCH LAYER CAKE, 12 MINI LOAF CAKES, OR 24 CUPCAKES

LEMON OR LIME
SEVEN-MINUTE FROSTING

*This frosting gets its name from the amount of time you need to whip it. It has a light
meringue quality and looks great when simply "stippled" into small peaks with a metal
spatula. The pure white mounds of frosting always remind me of big fluffy clouds.
Be careful—it's easy to get distracted when whipping this frosting.
I suggest setting a timer before you begin.
Adding lemon or lime juice to this recipe instead of the traditional water gives the
frosting a flavor burst that complements the cakes and fillings it's paired with.*

1½ CUPS SUGAR

⅓ CUP LEMON OR LIME JUICE

2 EGG WHITES

¼ TEASPOON CREAM OF TARTAR

¼ TEASPOON SALT

1. Combine sugar, lemon or lime juice, egg whites, cream of tartar, and salt in the
   top of a double boiler. Beat with an electric mixer until blended. Continue mixing on high speed over boiling water until stiff peaks form, 7 to 10 minutes.

2. Remove frosting from the water and continue beating until cool and thick
   enough to spread, another 4 to 5 minutes. Use immediately.

YIELD: ENOUGH FROSTING TO COVER A 9-INCH LAYER CAKE

VARIATION:

ALMOND SEVEN-MINUTE FROSTING
Omit lemon or lime juice and add 1½ teaspoons almond extract.

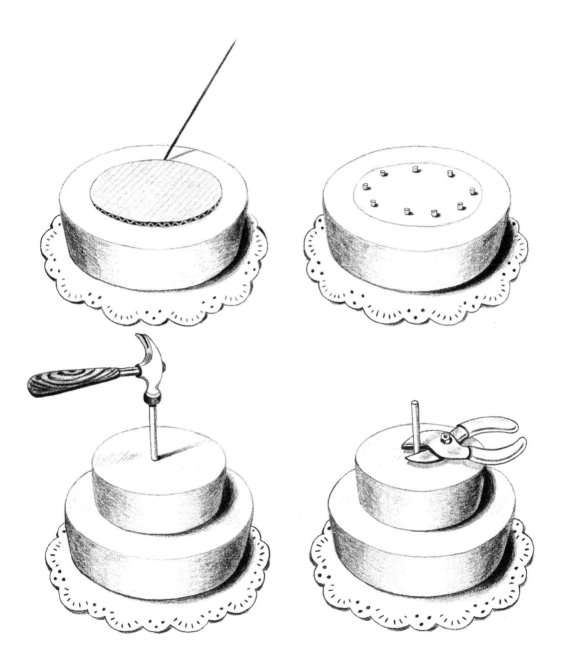

Sweet Maria's

ITALIAN
DESSERTS

Sweet Maria's

ITALIAN DESSERTS

Classic and Casual Recipes for Cookies, Cakes, Pastry, and Other Favorites

MARIA BRUSCINO SANCHEZ

FOR EDGAR

WHO SHARES MY PASSION

FOR ALL THINGS ITALIAN

CONTENTS

ACKNOWLEDGMENTS

Thanks to Carla Glasser, my agent, for her generous encouragement;
Many thanks to my editor Marian Lizzi for her enthusiastic guidance;
For everyone at St. Martin's, thanks for your support and expertise;
Mille grazie to my parents for their constant faith in all my endeavors;
To the Sweet Maria's staff for their dedication, honesty, and humor:
Angela, Aunt Babe, Aunt Dolly, Gloria,
Joanne, Maryse, Sarah, Susan, and Vinny;
And especially to Grandma Bruscino, Aunt Giulia, Philomena, Gemma,
and all their families, for giving me an inspiring childhood and heritage.

INTRODUCTION

Italian desserts are as varied and delicious as Italy itself, and the journey of sweets from Italy to America has been a long and welcome one. Italian food has become one of the most popular cuisines in America not just for its fabulous flavor but for its simplicity. Italian-American homes are filled with a large variety of wonderful aromas, meat sauce, fried eggplant, and steamed artichokes. Fresh bread, amaretti, and roasted chestnuts also fill the air.

Growing up in an American Italian home, we didn't eat dessert on a daily basis. A simple everyday Italian dessert is a piece of fruit, a slice of cheese, and a handful of nuts. Sure, there was always a biscotti in the cookie jar for snacks, but the real cakes, pies, and puddings were reserved for Sundays and other holiday celebrations. Sunday dinners and holidays meant all the generations coming together to share a meal, and a special dessert, which is typical both in Italian and Italian-American homes.

Many traditional Italian desserts, such as pannetone and rice pies, are made to celebrate important Roman Catholic holidays, such as Christmas and Easter. The ingredients themselves—ricotta cheese, rice, flour, and spices—are staples of Italian life. Fresh ingredients are a vital part to all Italian cooking, especially desserts. The flexibility of Italian cooks to substitute one fruit or nut for another based on availability is something to be admired. My mom always talks about "making do" with what you have. This philosophy is a creative way to cook. All the ingredients used in this book are readily available in most supermarkets, and you can also "make do" as you wish.

This book is a collection of various Italian sweets. Cookies have always been a part of family functions, and are perhaps the best-known Italian desserts. Every baker has his or her specialty. In our family, we would all bake one batch of our favorite and then pool them all together to create spectacular trays for weddings and showers. These cookies also make a great snack throughout the day and even at breakfast.

Italian cakes and pies are casual and delicious. They are not heavily iced and decorated as American layer cakes are. Italians are also known for their pastry such as cannoli and pasticiotta. While these are often purchased at a favorite bakery, I've included these recipes for those who would like to try them. Other classic desserts, such as tiramisù and panna cotta, are delicious and easy to prepare.

Some of the traditional family recipes in this book were handed down as "a handful of this" and "a handful of that." Luckily, my mom and I followed my grandmother around the kitchen with a measuring cup, insisting she measure her handfuls. It was a nuisance then, three women in one kitchen, but I'm sure she would be proud to share her rice pie recipe and the others presented here.

This collection is not a region-by-region account of traditional desserts. Traditions and food vary widely throughout Italy. My family is Neapolitan and Abruzzese and my husband's family is Sicilian, so many of the recipes reflect these regions. Some of these recipes are classics that I've updated or recipes that are inspired by traveling through Italy. Many are favorites enjoyed by my customers at Sweet Maria's Bakery, where Italian-Americans and others purchase desserts that range from traditional to contemporary.

The sights, food, and spirit of Italy and its people are truly enlightening. I hope you'll enjoy making these sweets, as well as eating them, and will be encouraged to preserve your own family traditions through great food and delicious desserts.

INGREDIENTS

Flour

It's very important that you use the right type of flour for each cake, cookie, bread, and pie. Each recipe will specify the best type of flour to be used, but here are general guidelines:

CAKES: Cake flour works best for delicate fine-crumb layer cakes and sponge cakes. This flour is generally lighter and "less strong" than all-purpose flour. It will give your cakes a fine texture. In contrast, some of the cakes in this book are rustic, casual cakes that are generally filled with nuts and dried fruit. These use all-purpose flour. All-purpose flour will give your batter a bit more strength to hold up the fruit and nuts. Otherwise, the fruit and nuts will sink to the bottom of the cake.

PIES AND TARTS: All-purpose or unbleached flour is fine for most of the crusts used in this book. A basic *pasta frolla,* or sweet crust recipe, is used for many of the tarts and pies.

COOKIES: All-purpose or unbleached flour is used for many of the cookies and biscuits.

BREADS: You can use all-purpose or unbleached flour for the sweet bread recipes.

Sugar

SUPERFINE GRANULATED SUGAR: Best for all of these recipes, it has a nice fine grain that allows it to blend well with other ingredients.

CONFECTIONERS' SUGAR: This very finely processed sugar with a bit of cornstarch added to prevent any clumping is used for many icings and glazes. It is graded according to how fine it is ground. "10-x" is the most widely found confectioners' sugar.

BROWN SUGAR: Regular granulated sugar that has been processed with molasses. It adds a particularly rich flavor to your baked goods.

Eggs

Whenever eggs are used in a recipe, they are Grade A large eggs. For cake baking it is important to use eggs that are brought to room temperature. If you need to separate eggs, it's easier to do when they are cold, so consider doing this ahead of time.

Butter

Fresh unsalted butter really can't be beat for flavor and texture. Using unsalted allows you to control the amount of salt in the recipe.

Vegetable Oil

Many of these Italian treats are fried pastries. Use a vegetable oil for any frying. Olive oil is not only expensive, but a bit too flavorful for most of these sweets.

Vegetable Shortening

If shortening is called for, use an all-vegetable shortening. To melt shortening, place in a small saucepan over low heat. Stir until melted. Or microwave on low until melted. Let cool before adding to other ingredients.

Nuts

Many common nuts are used in these recipes, such as almonds, walnuts, hazelnuts, and chestnuts. If pine nuts (pignoli) and pistachio nuts are hard to find, try an Italian or Middle Eastern import shop. If you purchase a large quantity, you can store the leftover nuts in the freezer. Simply wrap in heavy-duty plastic freezer bags. Chop the nuts right before you begin a recipe.

Toasting the nuts brings out their natural oils and flavors. Simply place desired amount of nuts in a single layer on a parchment-lined cookie sheet. Bake at 350°F for 5 to 8 minutes, or until lightly browned. Let cool before using.

To coarsely chop nuts, use a cutting board and a sharp straight knife.

To finely chop nuts, use a food processor and pulse to desired fineness. Nuts should resemble coarse salt.

Baking Powder and Baking Soda

Be sure to use a fresh supply of both baking powder and baking soda in all your baking. Store unused portions in airtight containers at room temperature.

Yeast

For the sweet bread recipes in this book, use an active dry yeast, available in most supermarkets. Because dry yeast needs warmth and moisture to activate its leavening power, many of the recipes direct you to dissolve the yeast in lukewarm water before adding it to the dough. Water that is too hot will kill the yeast and water that is too cold will not activate it. Store unused unopened yeast packages in the refrigerator.

Spices

Italian desserts use spices such as cinnamon, nutmeg, and ground cloves. Most of these spices are available in supermarkets. Be sure your supply is fresh to provide the fullest flavor.

Extracts and Liqueurs

Pure extracts and high-quality liqueurs and wines add flavor to your desserts. If you want the best result, don't skimp with imitation flavors. Some common flavors include vanilla, marsala wine, amaretto, and rum.

Fruit Rinds

Abundant in Italy and full of fresh flavor, the rinds of citrus fruit such as lemons and oranges are very popular in Italian desserts. To grate the rind, use a zester or four-sided grater. Be sure to avoid the bitter white pith underneath the rind. To juice citrus fruits, start with the fruit at room temperature.

Fruit

Many types of fruit are used in these desserts, including apples, pears, figs, plums, assorted berries, and cherries. Every baker has his or her favorite; I generally use McIntosh or Granny Smith apples, Bosc for pears, and a variety of berries. With so much produce available year-round these days, it's easy to find a good assortment. If you can't find fresh raspberries or blueberries, try using an "IQF" product. These are berries that are "individually quick frozen" separately, then frozen together. The whole berry can be thawed and added to the dessert without breaking into pieces. The fruit can also provide a bit of juice as it thaws.

Chocolate and Cocoa

Both semisweet baking bars and cocoa are used to flavor the chocolate desserts in this book. Be sure to use the freshest, highest-quality chocolate available. Dutch process cocoa provides a rich chocolate flavor and color.

Cheese

Served with fruit, cheese is an Italian dessert in itself, so it's no surprise there are many Italian desserts that feature cheese. Some of the favorites are:

MASCARPONE: This soft Italian cheese is like cream cheese and is best known for its use in tiramisù.

RICOTTA: This soft cheese with a slightly sweet flavor is used in classic Italian desserts such as cannoli, Easter pies, and cheesecakes. Use fresh whole milk ricotta, not the low-fat kind made from skim milk. You may need to experiment with different brands of ricotta. The moisture content will vary among manufacturers. Try to use a firm, less watery brand, if available.

Heavy Cream

Use heavy cream when making whipped cream for a frosting or a garnish. This rich cream has the highest percentage of butterfat. Pasteurized cream is the freshest-tasting cream but is usually hard to find. Ultra-pasteurized cream, the most widely available heavy cream, works fine in these recipes.

When using whipped cream for a cake frosting, be sure to whip it until stiff, as the recipe directs. To garnish a slice of cake or pie with a dollop of cream, it can be a little less stiff.

EQUIPMENT

Many of the tools you'll need for these recipes are the usual spatulas, knives, mixing bowls, and rolling pins that most of us have on hand. Here are a few other things you may need.

Mixers

There are two types of mixers a well-equipped kitchen should have: Hand-held mixers are ideal when you need to beat ingredients over the top of a double boiler. A stand-up mixer is the best choice for most other situations because you can walk away and do another task while the mixer mixes.

Parchment

Baking parchment is a vital tool for baking. You can find it in most supermarkets or gourmet kitchen and party shops. Use it to line cookie sheets as well as cake pans. It eliminates messy greasing of pans and makes cleanup easy. For cake pans, cut parchment into circles to fit the bottom of the pan you're using. Cut 2-inch-wide strips of parchment. Spray the cake pan with a nonstick spray, then line the bottom of the pan with the circle and place the strips of parchment along the sides. Line layer-cake pans as well as loaf pans, tube pans, and springform pans in the same way.

Cookie Sheets

Use sturdy, straight, clean sheets for cookie baking.

Cake Pans

Use sturdy straight-sided pans for cake baking. These include loaf pans and tube pans. Disposable foil pans are not recommended. Springform pans are used for several of the cakes in this book. Popular for cheesecakes, they have a removable bottom and spring mechanism that allows you to remove the cake from the pan without breaking it. If you're taking the cake to a party and don't want to use the metal bottom plate, cut a circle of corrugated cardboard to fit the bottom of the pan. Cover with foil and press into place as a disposable pan bottom.

Tart and Pie Pans

Many of the tarts in this book use a 9-inch round tart pan with removable bottom. This makes serving easy and creates a professional presentation. For pies, these recipes use a 9-inch round deep-dish pie pan. I like the glass Pyrex pans so I can check out the bottom crust.

Ovens

The recipes in this book are timed in a conventional oven, either gas or electric. If you are using a convection oven your baking time will be less.

Because baking is very sensitive, it's important to check your oven temperature. Invest in an inexpensive oven thermometer to be sure your temperature is accurate. You may need to call a repairman just to make an adjustment.

Although I don't recommend going out to buy a new oven, I love my glass oven door and oven lights. I always like to see how the baking is progressing without opening the door, which would allow the heat to escape; this can cause breads and cakes to collapse.

Cannoli Tubes

These are hollow metal rods, about 6 inches long, that are used to form the shell of the cannoli. You can find these at many specialty kitchen shops. The dough is wrapped around the rod, secured with egg white, and deep fried. After cooling, grab the rod with your fingertips and gently twist and pull to remove the shell. Reuse as necessary.

Fluted Pastry Cutter

This tool is similar to a pizza cutter but provides a small scalloped edge to many of the desserts in this book. You can use a pizza cutter or sharp straight knife instead, but you won't have the fancy edge.

Wire Cooling Racks

Every baker should have a few wire cooling racks. Place hot baked goods on the racks to cool. This allows air to circulate underneath to cool evenly and completely. Use wire racks to frost cookies and sweet breads. Just place a sheet of parchment or wax paper underneath to catch any excess frosting.

Double Boiler

A double boiler is used to melt chocolate slowly or cook delicate custards over simmering water. If you don't have a double boiler, use a saucepan filled with water as your bottom, and a wide-mouthed stainless steel bowl on top.

BASIC BAKING TECHNIQUES

Each recipe will give you tips on mixing, baking, and storing your desserts. Here are just a few guidelines about some of the commonly used terms you'll see throughout the book.

Making a "Well"

I use this technique often. When dry ingredients are combined in a bowl, make a mound, and with a wooden spoon make a hole on top of the mound. This is your "well." In a separate bowl, mix the wet ingredients. Pour these into the well and mix together.

Turning Out Dough

I use this technique when the dough gets too heavy for hand mixing or electric mixing. Simply empty contents of mixing bowl onto a lightly floured surface such as your counter or table. Knead together with your hands to form a soft dough.

Folding the Egg Whites

For many cake batters, the egg whites are whipped separately until stiff. Use small, light-handed strokes, with a rubber spatula, to turn whites into other batter. This will blend air into the batter. Be sure to scrape the bottom of the bowl so that all batter is incorporated evenly.

Filling a Pastry Bag

Pastry bags are used for a few cookie recipes in this book. An easy way to fill a pastry bag is to place the bag tip side down in a tall drinking glass. Fold the top edges over the sides of the glass. This will allow the bag to stay open while you spoon batter or frosting into the bag. Be careful not to overfill. Gather up edges of bag and remove from glass. Squeeze and add desired pressure to the middle of the bag to release frosting or batter from the tip.

Dusting and Rolling in Confectioners' Sugar

Many Italian cakes and pastries have a simple dusting of powdered sugar as a garnish. Place a few tablespoons of confectioners' sugar in a small dry strainer. Hold the strainer over the cake or pastry. With a teaspoon, stir the sugar to dust.

To coat cookies with confectioners' sugar, place a small amount of sugar in a medium-size mixing bowl. Place 10 to 12 cookies at a time in the sugar. Use two spoons or your hands to carefully toss and coat the cookies, being sure not to break them.

Baking Desserts for Company

Entertaining can be stressful. When baking or cooking for company, try to use a recipe you're familiar with and that you've made before. This eliminates some of the stress. Try a dry run a week or two ahead of your scheduled party to make sure you're comfortable with the recipe.

Many of the desserts in this book, especially the cakes, have several components, many of which can be made ahead. If you're having company on a Saturday evening, bake the cake and make the fillings on Friday. Assemble on Saturday morning and serve on Saturday night.

A Few Tips on Frying

Several of the desserts in this book are delicious fried pastries. To make them properly, it's important that the oil be medium hot. If it becomes too hot, the pastries will be too brown on the outside and raw on the inside. If the oil is not hot enough, the pastries will turn out soggy and pale. To turn pastries in oil, use two forks or a slotted spoon. To remove pastries from oil, use a slotted spoon and place on absorbent paper to drain. Fried pastries taste best when they're freshly fried.

COOKIES

Because cookies are so vital to Italian-American celebrations, they are a large part of this book. Cookie trays are found at most parties, and certain types of cookies are baked for specific occasions such as weddings, Christmas, and Easter. Even when most people say they don't have room for dessert, they usually make room for a cookie.

Italian cookies are generally plain biscuits, enjoyed throughout the year, ideal for dessert with fruit or ice cream, or a simple snack or breakfast. Cookies that are baked for specific holidays, like Christmas and Easter, are usually richer and fancier, using dried fruit, nuts, and raisins.

Italian cookies traditionally have less fat than American cookies. This makes them more like biscuits and harder in texture. I've included some of these cookies as well as variations that are more like American cookies with a bit more butter. Here are a few tips on the types of cookies that follow.

Drop Cookies

These are the easiest type of cookie to make. After mixing the dough, simply use a teaspoon to drop the dough onto a parchment-lined cookie sheet.

Rolled Cookies

This is another simple cookie, formed by rolling the dough into balls. If the dough is a bit sticky, dust your fingers lightly with flour.

Rolled and Filled Cookies

These cookies are rolled with a rolling pin. For most of them, the dough should be chilled first for easier rolling. You can usually make the dough ahead and refrigerate overnight. Finish the filling (usually jelly, nuts, and spices) and bake the next day.

When you're rolling and cutting dough, save all your scraps to roll at the end. By adding scraps to the fresh dough you can toughen it. While rolling, store unused portion of dough in the refrigerator to keep chilled.

When using cookie cutters, dust them lightly with flour to eliminate sticking.

Biscotti

These are popular Italian cookies that are baked twice. The dough is formed into long thin loaves and baked. After cooling, the loaves are diagonally sliced into ½-inch slices. They are baked again for a toasted crunchy cookie.

Bar Cookies

Bar cookies are another easy-to-make cookie and look great on a cookie tray. The dough is pressed into a baking pan, baked, cooled, and cut into squares or strips. You can also cut them into triangles, strips, or diamond shapes.

JELLY AND NUT CRESCENTS

These are a fancy holiday treat that can be made with any flavor jelly.
I love them with raspberry filling for the holidays, not just for their flavor
but for the way they dress up a holiday cookie tray.

CRUST:

¼ POUND BUTTER, SOFTENED	1 EGG YOLK
3 OUNCES CREAM CHEESE, SOFTENED	1 CUP FLOUR

FILLING:

½ CUP BROWN SUGAR	½ TEASPOON CINNAMON
1 CUP WALNUTS, FINELY CHOPPED	¾ CUP JELLY, ANY FLAVOR

1. In an electric mixer, cream the butter and cream cheese until light and fluffy. Add yolk. Mix until well blended. Gradually add flour on low speed. Turn out dough onto a lightly floured surface.

2. Knead until well blended. Divide dough in half. Wrap in plastic and refrigerate for 2 to 3 hours or overnight.

3. Preheat oven to 375°F.

4. In a small bowl, mix brown sugar, walnuts, and cinnamon. Set aside.

5. Using a lightly floured rolling pin and surface, roll out one half of dough until ⅛ inch thick. Spread half the jelly onto dough in a thin layer. Sprinkle with half the sugar and cinnamon mixture.

6. Using a fluted pastry cutter, cut the dough into 12 wedges.

7. Roll each edge, starting at the wide end, toward the center of the circle. Place on a parchment-lined cookie sheet and slightly curve each cookie into a crescent. Space cookies about 2 inches apart. Repeat rolling and filling with remaining dough.

8. Bake for 15 to 20 minutes, or until golden brown.

9. Remove the cookie sheet from the oven. Using a metal spatula, place cookies on a wire cooling rack. Cool. Store cookies in an airtight container.

YIELD: 24 COOKIES

EGG YOLK BISCUITS

These biscuits are perfect for breakfast or a snack. This version is a plain vanilla cookie brushed with egg yolk before baking. The recipe is also flexible: You can flavor the dough with lemon, orange, or almond instead of vanilla extract. Because these cookies are sturdy, use them for the bottom layer of your cookie tray.

½ POUND BUTTER	2½ CUPS FLOUR
1 CUP SUGAR	1 TEASPOON BAKING POWDER
3 EGG YOLKS	2 TABLESPOONS MILK
2 TEASPOONS VANILLA	

1. In an electric mixer, cream butter and sugar until light. Add 2 egg yolks and vanilla. Beat until well mixed. On low speed, add flour, baking powder, and milk. Mix just until blended. Turn out dough onto a lightly floured surface. Knead until smooth. Wrap in plastic wrap and refrigerate for 2 to 3 hours or overnight.

2. Preheat oven to 350°F.

3. Roll out dough on a lightly floured surface until ¼ inch thick. Using a cookie cutter or rim of a juice glass, cut into circles about 2½ inches in diameter.

4. Place cookies on a parchment-lined cookie sheet, spacing them 2 inches apart.

5. Brush tops of cookies with remaining egg yolk and sprinkle with sugar.

6. Bake for 15 to 20 minutes, or until lightly browned.

7. Remove cookie sheet from the oven. Using a metal spatula, remove cookies from the cookie sheet and place on wire cooling rack. Cool.

8. Store unused cookies in an airtight container.

YIELD: 24 COOKIES

ORANGE DROP COOKIES

ANGINETTI D'ARANCIA

These light and flavorful cookies are always a favorite. This recipe uses a fresh orange flavor, a nice variation on the traditional lemon version. They are quite tasty topped with an orange confectioners' icing. After the icing is dry, stack these cookies in a large mound on top of a tiered cake plate for a fabulous wedding or shower sweet.

¼ POUND BUTTER, SOFTENED	GRATED RIND OF 1 ORANGE
½ CUP SUGAR	3 CUPS FLOUR
3 EGGS	3 TEASPOONS BAKING POWDER
½ CUP ORANGE JUICE	

1. Preheat oven to 350°F.

2. In an electric mixer, cream the butter and sugar until light. Add eggs, orange juice, and orange rind. Mix until well blended.

3. On low speed, gradually add the flour and baking powder. Mix just until blended.

4. Using a teaspoon, drop rounded teaspoons onto a lightly greased cookie sheet, spacing each cookie about 2 inches apart.

5. Bake for 8 to 10 minutes, or until lightly browned.

6. Remove from the oven. Using a metal spatula, remove cookies from the sheet onto a wire cooling rack. Cool completely. Frost with orange confectioners' icing (see following recipe).

YIELD: ABOUT 50 COOKIES

ORANGE CONFECTIONERS' ICING

This versatile icing can be made with almost any flavor. Simply substitute water for orange juice and add 2 teaspoons of extract. This version really accents the orange flavor of the anginetti.

6 CUPS CONFECTIONERS' SUGAR   ¾ CUP ORANGE JUICE

GRATED RIND OF 1 ORANGE

1. In an electric mixer on medium speed, beat all ingredients until smooth.

2. Using a metal spatula, frost the tops of the cookies. The frosting will drip down the sides of the cookie. Dry the frosted cookies on a wire cooling rack. Place a sheet of parchment or wax paper underneath cooling rack to catch excess frosting. Store in an airtight container.

YIELD: ENOUGH FOR 50 COOKIES

LENTEN BISCUITS

QUARESIMALI

These plain biscuits are usually baked during the Lenten season. Because they use the traditional method of biscotti baking, without fat, be sure to slice them while they're still warm. If you let them cool first, they'll be too hard to slice.

2 CUPS FLOUR	1 CUP SLICED ALMONDS
½ CUP BROWN SUGAR	2 TEASPOONS CINNAMON
1 TEASPOON BAKING POWDER	3 EGGS
PINCH OF SALT	¼ CUP MILK

1. Preheat oven to 375°F.

2. In a large bowl, combine flour, brown sugar, baking powder, salt, almonds, and cinnamon. Make a well in the center. Set aside.

3. In a separate bowl, mix eggs and milk with a wire whisk. Add the egg mixture to the well. Stir with a wooden spoon. Turn out dough onto a lightly floured surface and knead until dough is blended.

4. Divide dough in half. Roll into two loaves, about 12 inches long. Place the loaves on a parchment-lined cookie sheet, spacing them 3 inches apart.

5. Bake for 20 to 25 minutes, or until golden brown.

6. Remove cookie sheet from the oven.

7. Carefully remove hot loaves from the cookie sheet and place on a cutting board. While still warm, cut the loaves diagonally into ½-inch-wide slices.

8. Place slices in a single layer on a cookie sheet. Return to the oven for 15 to 20 minutes, or until lightly browned. Remove cookie sheet from the oven. Cool toasted biscotti on wire cooling rack. Store in an airtight container.

YIELD: 24 COOKIES

ALMOND MERINGUES

These crunchy dry biscuits are sometimes called "forgotten cookies," because they bake in the oven for a long time at a slow temperature. They are a treat served alone, or piled with berries and whipped cream. You can make them any size, but I prefer these sweet little kisses formed with a pastry bag.

4 EGG WHITES
1¼ CUPS SUGAR

½ TEASPOON ALMOND EXTRACT

1. Preheat oven to 225°F.

2. In an electric mixer with whisk attachment, beat egg whites until soft peaks form. Gradually add sugar and almond extract. Beat until stiff.

3. Fill a pastry bag (without a tip) with half the meringue dough. Pipe small kisses onto a parchment-lined cookie sheet. You can pipe them close together because they don't spread when baking. Refill pastry bag with remaining dough and pipe until finished.

4. Bake for 1½ hours, or until dry.

5. Remove cookies from the oven. Cool meringues on parchment. When cool, carefully remove from parchment with a metal spatula. Store unused meringues in plastic wrap at room temperature.

YIELD: ABOUT 50 SMALL COOKIES

VARIATION: COCOA ALMOND MERINGUES

Enjoy these cookies on their own or use them festively to cover our
Mandarin Orange Meringue Cake (see page 72).

4 EGG WHITES

1 CUP SUGAR

3 TABLESPOONS COCOA

½ TEASPOON ALMOND EXTRACT

Follow directions for almond meringues, beating in cocoa after sugar. Bake at 225°F for 1½ hours, or until dry.

◆ **HOW TO MAKE A COOKIE TRAY** ◆

START WITH A FLAT AND STURDY PLATE OR BASKET. LINE WITH A DOILY. START STACKING COOKIES, PLACING THE MORE DURABLE COOKIES, SUCH AS BISCOTTI, ON THE BOTTOM OF THE TRAY. CONTINUE TO STACK A VARIETY OF FLAVORS IN DECREASING ORDER TO FORM A PYRAMID. PLACE FRAGILE JELLY-FILLED COOKIES ON TOP. WRAP IN CELLOPHANE AND TIE WITH RIBBONS.

SWEET SPICE COOKIES

These tasty little drop cookies are loaded with chocolate chips, nuts, and cinnamon—
a delicious combination and one of my favorite take-to-school lunch treats.

½ POUND BUTTER, SOFTENED

1 CUP BROWN SUGAR

3 EGGS

2 CUPS FLOUR

1 TEASPOON BAKING SODA

PINCH OF SALT

1 TEASPOON CINNAMON

2 CUPS CHOPPED WALNUTS

1 CUP CHOCOLATE CHIPS

1. Preheat oven to 350°F.

2. In an electric mixer, cream butter and brown sugar until light. Add eggs. Mix until well blended. On low speed, gradually add flour, baking soda, salt, and cinnamon. Mix just until blended.

3. Stir in nuts and chocolate chips.

4. Using a teaspoon, drop dough onto a parchment-lined cookie sheet, spacing each cookie about 2 inches apart.

5. Bake for 12 to 15 minutes, or until golden brown. Remove cookie sheet from the oven. Using a metal spatula, remove cookies from cookie sheet and place on a wire cooling rack. Cool completely. Store unused cookies in an airtight container.

YIELD: 50 COOKIES

RICOTTA DROP COOKIES

BISCOTTI DI RICOTTA

*These moist cookie drops combine two popular flavors for Italian desserts,
ricotta and lemon. This combination is especially popular in the Neapolitan region,
where both ingredients are plentiful. It's hard to travel anywhere in southern
Italy without seeing endless groves of citrus trees.*

¼ POUND BUTTER, SOFTENED

1 CUP SUGAR

1 EGG

¼ CUP RICOTTA

GRATED RIND OF 1 LEMON

2 CUPS FLOUR

½ TEASPOON BAKING SODA

PINCH OF SALT

1. Preheat oven to 350°F.

2. In an electric mixer, cream butter and sugar until light. Add egg, ricotta, and lemon rind. Mix until well blended. On low speed, add flour, baking soda, and salt. Mix just until blended.

3. Drop dough from a rounded teaspoon onto a parchment-lined cookie sheet, spacing each cookie about 2 inches apart.

4. Bake for 10 to 15 minutes, or until lightly browned. Remove cookie sheet from the oven. Use a metal spatula to transfer cookies to a wire cooling rack. Cool completely.

5. Dust with confectioners' sugar. Serve cooled. Store unused cookies in an airtight container.

YIELD: 30 COOKIES

FIG AND WALNUT BISCOTTI

Perfect dunked in wine or espresso, these hearty biscuits have a shiny professional look from the beaten egg brushed on top. Because they stay fresh for so long, they're the perfect cookie to bake and keep in the cookie jar.

1½ CUPS FLOUR

2 TEASPOONS BAKING POWDER

1 CUP SUGAR

2 TEASPOONS CINNAMON

½ TEASPOON SALT

⅔ CUP WALNUT HALVES

⅔ CUP COARSELY CHOPPED DRIED FIGS

2 EGGS

2 TEASPOONS VANILLA

1 EGG FOR EGG WASH

1. Preheat oven to 375°F.

2. In a large bowl, combine flour, baking powder, sugar, cinnamon, salt, walnuts, and figs. Stir until blended. Make a well in the center.

3. In a separate bowl, mix the 2 eggs and vanilla with a wire whisk. Add the eggs to the well. Stir with a wooden spoon. Turn out dough onto a lightly floured surface. Knead until dough is blended.

4. Divide dough in half. Roll into two loaves, about 12 inches long. Place the loaves on a parchment-lined cookie sheet, spacing them 3 inches apart.

5. In a small bowl, beat remaining egg with a fork. Using a pastry brush, brush the beaten egg on top of the loaves.

6. Bake for 20 to 25 minutes, or until golden brown.

7. Remove from the oven.

8. Carefully remove hot loaves from the cookie sheet and place on a cutting board. While warm, slice the loaves diagonally into ½-inch-wide slices.

(Continued)

9. Place slices in a single layer on the cookie sheet. Return to oven for 15 to 20 minutes, or until lightly browned. Remove cookie sheet from the oven. Cool toasted biscotti on wire cooling rack. Store in an airtight container.

YIELD: ABOUT 25 COOKIES

ORANGE CLOVE BISCOTTI

These biscotti are a classic pairing of citrus and spice. They are one of the first cookies I learned to bake with my mom. They're perfect partners to a tall glass of iced cappuccino or a few scoops of chocolate ice cream.

¼ POUND BUTTER, SOFTENED	2½ CUPS FLOUR
1 CUP SUGAR	1½ TEASPOONS BAKING POWDER
2 EGGS	1½ TEASPOONS GROUND CLOVES
GRATED RIND OF 2 ORANGES	
JUICE OF 1 ORANGE	

1. Preheat oven to 350°F.

2. In an electric mixer, cream the butter and sugar until light. Add eggs, orange rind, and orange juice. Mix until well blended. On low speed, add flour, baking powder, and cloves. Mix just until blended.

3. Turn out dough onto a lightly floured surface. Divide dough into thirds. Roll into three loaves, about 12 inches long. Place on a parchment-lined cookie sheet, spacing each 3 inches apart.

4. Bake for 20 to 25 minutes, or until lightly browned.

5. Remove cookie sheet from the oven. Using two metal spatulas, carefully place loaves on wire cooling racks. Cool.

6. Place cooled loaves on a cutting board. Using a large sharp knife, cut diagonally into ½-inch slices.

7. Place slices on the cookie sheet in a single layer. Bake for 12 to 15 minutes, or until lightly browned. Remove cookies from the oven. Cool toasted biscotti on wire cooling racks. Store in an airtight container.

YIELD: 30 COOKIES

MOLASSES NUT SLICES

These cookies have a rich molasses flavor, perfect with a glass of cold milk. They are so easy to make—just roll into loaves, refrigerate, cut, and bake. When I was a child, these cookies always reminded me of slices of pepperoni.

½ POUND BUTTER, SOFTENED	2 CUPS FLOUR
½ CUP SUGAR	1 TEASPOON BAKING POWDER
2 TABLESPOONS MOLASSES	¾ CUP CHOPPED WALNUTS
1 EGG	

1. In an electric mixer, cream butter and sugar until light. Add molasses and egg. Blend until well mixed. On low speed, gradually add flour, baking powder, and nuts. Turn out dough onto a lightly floured surface.

2. Divide dough in half. Roll each piece into a cylinder about 1½ inches wide. Wrap in plastic wrap and refrigerate for 2 to 3 hours or overnight.

3. Preheat oven to 375°F.

4. Place dough cylinders on a cutting board. Cut dough into slices about ½ inch wide. Place on parchment-lined cookie sheet, spacing each 2 inches apart.

5. Bake for 15 to 20 minutes, or until lightly browned. Remove from the oven.

6. Use a metal spatula to remove cookies to a wire cooling rack. Cool completely.

7. Store in an airtight container.

YIELD: 40 COOKIES

AMARETTI

These classic Italian almond macaroons are very popular. To roll the cookies
more easily, dip your fingers into a bowl of water. This will prevent
the dough from sticking to your hands.
In Sicily, amaretti cookies are formed into mounds with a crater on top,
dusted with confectioners' sugar, and baked, so that they resemble
Mount Etna. My version is shaped in the more traditional cookie manner,
but is dusted with confectioners' sugar too.

½ POUND ALMOND PASTE, BROKEN
INTO SMALL PIECES

½ CUP SUGAR

¼ CUP FLOUR

½ CUP CONFECTIONERS' SUGAR

1 EGG

ADDITIONAL CONFECTIONERS' SUGAR
TO GARNISH

1. Preheat oven to 350°F.

2. In an electric mixer, combine almond paste, sugar, flour, and confectioners' sugar. Mix on low speed until blended. Add egg. Mix on low speed for 2 minutes. This will make a sticky dough.

3. Roll dough into 1-inch balls. Place on parchment-lined cookie sheet, spacing them 2 inches apart. Using your fingers, press down the tops gently to flatten slightly. Dust the tops of cookies with additional confectioners' sugar.

4. Bake for 15 to 20 minutes, or until golden brown. Remove the cookie sheet from the oven. Let cookies cool completely on parchment for easiest removal. When cookies are completely cooled, use a metal spatula to loosen them from the parchment. Store in an airtight container.

YIELD: 20 COOKIES

CHOCOLATE HAZELNUT BISCOTTI

BISCOTTI DI CIOCCOLATA CON NOCI

Chocolate lovers adore these rich biscotti with toasted hazelnuts. For the richest flavor, use a Dutch process cocoa and freshly toasted hazelnuts.

¼ POUND BUTTER, SOFTENED

¾ CUP SUGAR

2 TABLESPOONS HAZELNUT LIQUEUR

2 EGGS

2 CUPS FLOUR

½ CUP COCOA, PREFERABLY DUTCH PROCESS

2 TEASPOONS BAKING POWDER

¾ CUP HAZELNUTS, CHOPPED AND TOASTED

1. Preheat oven to 350°F.

2. In an electric mixer, cream butter and sugar until light. Add hazelnut liqueur and eggs. Mix until well blended.

3. On low speed, gradually add flour, cocoa, and baking powder. Stir in hazelnuts.

4. Divide dough in half. Shape the dough into two loaves about 10 inches long. Place on a parchment-lined cookie sheet, spacing them 3 inches apart.

5. Bake for 20 to 25 minutes, until tops of loaves are firm. Remove cookie sheet from the oven.

6. Using two metal spatulas, carefully remove loaves from hot cookie sheet onto wire racks. Cool. Place cooled loaves on cutting board. Using a sharp knife, cut the loaves diagonally into ½-inch-wide slices.

7. Place the slices on the cookie sheet in a single layer. Return to the oven for 12 to 15 minutes. Remove cookie sheet from the oven. Cool toasted biscotti on a wire cooling rack. Store cooled cookies in an airtight container.

YIELD: 24 BISCOTTI

LADY'S KISSES

BACI DI DAMA

These petite sandwich cookies are delicately flavored with an almond and chocolate filling. When using the pastry bag, try to make all the cookies the same size. This will make it easier to pair them with the filling.

COOKIE:

½ POUND BUTTER, SOFTENED	1 TEASPOON ALMOND EXTRACT
¾ CUP CONFECTIONERS' SUGAR	1½ CUPS FLOUR
1 EGG	PINCH OF SALT

FILLING:

½ CUP ALMONDS, FINELY GROUND	1 CUP CHOCOLATE CHIPS
1 TABLESPOON ALMOND PASTE	

1. Preheat oven to 350°F.

2. In an electric mixer, cream the butter and confectioners' sugar. Add egg and almond extract. Mix well. On low speed, gradually add the flour and salt. Mix just until blended.

3. Using a pastry bag without a tip (coupler only), pipe 1-inch circles onto a parchment-lined cookie sheet, spacing cookies 2 inches apart.

4. Bake for 8 to 10 minutes, or until the edges of cookies begin to brown. Remove cookie sheet from the oven. Cool cookies on parchment.

5. Place almonds and almond paste in a food processor. Pulse until finely ground. Set aside.

6. Melt chocolate chips.

7. Using a butter knife, spread a thin layer of chocolate on the flat side of only 6 to 8 cookies at a time. Otherwise the chocolate will dry before you sandwich them. Dip

(Continued)

one chocolate side into almond mixture and press together with another flat sided cookie.

8. Repeat spreading and dipping in almond mixture until all cookies are matched.

YIELD: 30 COOKIES

♦ **ALMOND PASTE** ♦

THIS IS A POPULAR ITALIAN CONFECTION THAT IS MADE FROM ALMONDS AND SUGAR. IT IS MASHED INTO A PASTE THAT IS USED FOR AMARETTI COOKIES. IT IS ALSO USED FOR MAKING MARZIPAN.

SICILIAN PISTACHIO BISCOTTI

These salty snacks are studded with pistachios. They're a great warm-weather snack or appetizer with a cold beer. Try to find pistachios that are already shelled. Whenever I buy pistachios in the shell, I barely have enough left after shelling. Suddenly everyone in the bakery wants to help shell them, just so they can sneak a few to munch on.

¼ POUND BUTTER, SOFTENED

¼ CUP SUGAR

1 TABLESPOON MARSALA WINE

2 EGGS

2 CUPS FLOUR

1½ CUPS COARSELY CHOPPED PISTA-CHIOS

1. Preheat oven to 350°F.

2. In an electric mixer, cream the butter and sugar. Add marsala and eggs. Mix until well blended. Add flour.

3. Roll dough into ¾-inch balls. Roll balls in water and then in pistachios to coat them. Place on a parchment-lined cookie sheet, spacing 2 inches apart. Flatten the tops slightly with your finger.

4. Bake for 20 to 25 minutes, or until golden brown.

5. Remove cookie sheet from the oven. Using a metal spatula, remove the cookies from the cookie sheet and place on a wire cooling rack. Cool. Store cookies in an airtight container.

YIELD: 24 COOKIES

VANILLA BISCOTTI

Using a vanilla bean to flavor these biscotti really gives it a rich natural taste. I love to wrap these cookies in small plastic bags and tie with festive ribbons. They are a great little make-ahead gift or shower favor.

1 CUP SUGAR	2 CUPS FLOUR
1 VANILLA BEAN	1 TEASPOON BAKING POWDER
¼ POUND BUTTER, SOFTENED	PINCH OF SALT
2 EGGS	

1. Preheat oven to 350°F.

2. Place sugar in a small bowl. Slice vanilla bean in half with a paring knife. Using the tip of the knife, scrape the vanilla into the sugar. Mix until well blended.

3. In an electric mixer, cream butter and vanilla sugar until light. Add eggs. Mix until well blended. On low speed, gradually add flour, baking powder, and salt.

4. Turn out dough onto a lightly floured surface. Divide dough in half. Roll each half into a cylinder about 12 inches long. Place cylinders on parchment-lined cookie sheet, spacing 3 inches apart.

5. Bake for 20 to 25 minutes, or until golden brown. Remove cookie sheet from the oven. Using two metal spatulas, carefully remove loaves from the cookie sheet and place on wire cooling racks. Cool. Place cooled loaves on a cutting board. Using a sharp knife, cut the loaves diagonally into ½-inch slices.

6. Place the slices on the cookie sheet in a single layer. Return to the oven for 12 to 15 minutes. Cool toasted biscotti on wire cooling rack. Store cooled cookies in an airtight container.

YIELD: 24 COOKIES

VENETIANS

These bar cookies are a staple for most Italian bakeries. Their bright red, white, and green colors will brighten up any cookie tray. The colors remind us of the Italian flag or the vibrant colors of Murano glass in Venice.

6 EGGS, SEPARATED

1½ CUPS SUGAR

¼ TEASPOON CREAM OF TARTAR

1 POUND BUTTER, SOFTENED

1 TEASPOON ALMOND EXTRACT

12 OUNCES ALMOND PASTE

3 CUPS FLOUR

¼ TEASPOON SALT

2 CUPS APRICOT PRESERVES

2 CUPS SEMISWEET CHOCOLATE CHIPS

1. Preheat oven to 350°F.

2. Grease and line three 15 x 10-inch cookie sheets, with sides, with parchment. Grease parchment. Set aside.

3. In an electric mixer with wire whisk, beat egg whites, ½ cup sugar, and cream of tartar until stiff, 2 to 3 minutes. Set aside.

4. In an electric mixer, cream the butter and remaining 1 cup of sugar. Add egg yolks and almond extract. Break up almond paste into small pieces. Add and mix until well blended and smooth. Add flour and salt. Mix until well blended.

5. With wire whisk attachment, fold in egg white mixture.

6. Divide dough into three equal portions. Add a few drops of red food coloring to one and a few drops of green coloring to another. Leave one dough natural color.

7. Evenly spread each dough into prepared pans. Each layer will be thin.

8. Bake each batter for 15 minutes or until the edges begin to brown. Remove pans from the oven.

9. Cool on wire cooling rack.

10. Remove and discard parchment. Place the green layer on a parchment-lined

(Continued)

cookie sheet. Spread one cup of apricot preserves over the green layer. Slide yellow layer of cake on top of the preserves. Spread remaining cup of preserves over yellow layer. Slide the red layer over the preserves. Cover with plastic wrap. Weigh down with a cutting board on top. Refrigerate overnight.

11. Melt 1 cup of chocolate chips. Spread in a thin layer over the top of the red layer. Let set until dry. Flip cake over onto parchment. Melt remaining cup of chocolate chips. Spread over green layer. Let set.

12. Using a serrated knife, trim edges. Cut into 1-inch squares.

YIELD: ABOUT 80 COOKIES

♦ BOMBONIERE ♦

ITALIAN BRIDAL SHOWERS AND WEDDINGS OFTEN FEATURE FAVORS COMPRISED OF SMALL BOXES OR BAGS FILLED WITH FANCY CANDIES OR COOKIES. A TRADITIONAL BOMBONIERA IS A SMALL CLUSTER OF CANDY-COATED ALMONDS WRAPPED IN TUILLE AND TIED WITH MONOGRAMMED RIBBON.

CHOCOLATE CALZONES

These chocolate- and walnut-filled pockets are deep-fried and delicious. Many people are familiar with calzones that use pizza dough to encase cheese and other toppings. This sweet calzone uses the same technique—a round piece of chocolate dough that encloses a delicious chocolate and nut filling.

DOUGH:

¼ POUND BUTTER, SOFTENED	¼ CUP SOUR CREAM
¼ CUP COCOA	¾ CUP FLOUR

FILLING:

¾ CUP CHOPPED WALNUTS	½ CUP SEMISWEET CHOCOLATE CHIPS
½ CUP SUGAR	¼ CUP HEAVY CREAM
VEGETABLE OIL FOR FRYING	

1. In an electric mixer, cream butter until light. Add cocoa and sour cream. Mix until well blended. Add flour. Mix until just blended. Turn out dough onto a lightly floured surface. Knead until well blended. Wrap in plastic wrap and refrigerate for 2 to 3 hours or overnight.

2. In a medium saucepan, combine all filling ingredients. Heat on medium, stirring constantly until chocolate is melted. Set aside to cool.

3. Roll out dough on a lightly floured surface until ⅛ inch thick. Using a 3-inch-round cookie cutter or the rim of a juice glass, cut dough into circles. Place ½ teaspoon of filling in the center of each circle. Brush edges of circle with water. Fold dough over to form a turnover. Seal edges with a fork. Fill all the dough and let calzones rest for 15 to 20 minutes before frying.

4. Heat about 3 inches of vegetable oil over medium-high heat.

5. Deep-fry calzones in preheated oil until lightly browned. Remove from oil with a slotted spoon. Drain on absorbent paper. Dust with confectioners' sugar and serve warm or cool.

YIELD: 20 CALZONES

ITALIAN RING BISCUITS
CIAMBELLE

*These slightly sweet ring-shaped taralle are perfect for breakfast, a snack,
or for appetizers. Be sure to bake them until they are golden brown
and they'll stay crunchy for days.*

¼ CUP SUGAR	½ CUP WHITE WINE
½ CUP OIL	1¾ CUPS FLOUR

1. Preheat oven to 350°F.

2. In a medium mixing bowl, whisk together sugar, oil, and wine. Stir in flour. Turn out dough onto a lightly floured surface. Knead until well blended.

3. Roll dough into pencil-size pieces, about 5 inches long. Form into a ring and pinch ends together. Place on a parchment-lined cookie sheet, spacing each ring about 2 inches apart.

4. Bake for 25 to 30 minutes, or until golden brown.

5. Remove cookie sheet from the oven. Place cookies on wire cooling rack. Cool completely. Store unused ciambelle in plastic wrap at room temperature.

YIELD: 25 CIAMBELLE

ITALIAN LADYFINGERS
SAVOIARDI

These biscuits are thicker and crunchier than the ladyfingers most Americans know. They're hard on the outside yet spongy inside to absorb the espresso used to soak them while making tiramisù (see recipe page 141).

3 EGGS, SEPARATED	⅓ CUP FLOUR
½ TEASPOON CREAM OF TARTAR	½ CUP CORNSTARCH
8 TABLESPOONS SUGAR	4 TABLESPOONS WATER

1. Preheat oven to 350°F.

2. In an electric mixer with wire whisk attachment, whip egg whites and cream of tartar until stiff. Add 4 tablespoons of sugar. Whip until stiff. Set aside.

3. In an electric mixer, beat egg yolks and remaining 4 tablespoons sugar. Mix until light in color. Gradually add flour and cornstarch. Add water and mix until well blended.

4. Using a rubber spatula and small wrist-turning strokes, fold egg whites into yolk mixture. Batter will be light like a sponge cake batter. Spoon batter into a pastry bag without a tip. Pipe 5-inch strips onto a parchment-lined cookie sheet. You can pipe these cookies close together. If they spread while baking you can break apart after they cool.

5. Bake for 25 to 30 minutes, or until golden brown. Remove cookie sheet from the oven.

6. Cool cookies on parchment. When completely cool, carefully remove from parchment. Store unused cookies in a plastic bag at room temperature.

YIELD: 20 LADYFINGERS

APRICOT ORANGE BARS

These bars are easy to make and look great on a cookie tray. Try cutting them into squares, diamonds, or triangles. If you're stacking these cookies on a tray, try to keep them on top so they won't crumble.

CRUST:

¾ CUP FLOUR

½ CUP SEMOLINA FLOUR

½ CUP SUGAR

¼ POUND BUTTER, SOFTENED

FILLING:

1 CUP DRIED APRICOTS, CHOPPED

GRATED RIND OF 1 ORANGE

JUICE OF 1 ORANGE

1 CUP WATER

1. In a medium saucepan, combine all filling ingredients. Boil over low heat for 20 to 30 minutes, until apricots are tender and liquid is reduced. Set aside.

2. Preheat oven to 375°F.

3. Grease an 8-inch square cake pan. Set aside.

4. In a medium mixing bowl, combine flour, semolina flour, and sugar. Mix well. Using a pastry blender or two knives, cut butter into dry ingredients until mixture resembles coarse crumbs. Press half the crust mixture into the prepared pan. Spread filling on top of crust. Lightly press remaining crumb mixture evenly over the filling.

5. Bake for 30 to 35 minutes, or until lightly browned.

6. Remove pan from the oven. Place on wire cooling rack. Cool completely. Cut into 1-inch squares. Store unused cookies in an airtight container.

YIELD: 42 COOKIES

ALMOND BARS

These bars have a buttery crust topped with sliced almonds. Almonds are one of the most popular nuts used in Italian cooking. My mom and aunts fight to bring home from the bakery any extra toasted almonds to use in their string beans for dinner.

CRUST:

¾ CUP FLOUR

¼ CUP SUGAR

¼ POUND BUTTER, SOFTENED

TOPPING:

2 EGGS

1 CUP SUGAR

2 TABLESPOONS AMARETTO

2 TABLESPOONS FLOUR

1 TEASPOON BAKING POWDER

1½ CUPS ALMONDS, SLICED

1. Preheat oven to 375°F.

2. Grease an 8-inch square cake pan. Set aside.

3. In a medium mixing bowl, combine flour and sugar. Using a pastry blender or two knives, cut butter into flour mixture until mixture resembles coarse crumbs. Press crumb mixture into prepared pan. Bake for 10 to 15 minutes, or until lightly browned.

4. Remove crust from the oven. Place on wire cooling rack. Prepare filling.

5. In another bowl, whisk eggs and sugar until thick. Blend in amaretto. Add flour, baking powder, and almonds. Mix until well blended.

6. Pour egg mixture on top of the prepared crust. Spread evenly.

7. Bake for 20 to 25 minutes, or until lightly browned.

8. Remove pan from the oven and place on wire cooling rack. Cool completely. Cut into 1-inch squares. Store unused cookies in an airtight container.

YIELD: 42 COOKIES

◆ A Taste of Italy ◆

One of my favorite times to visit Rome is around March 19, the feast day of Saint Joseph. One of my favorite pastry shops, near the Via Condotti, makes incredible zeppole di San Giuseppe, a delicious fried cruller filled with pastry cream. This is a fresh and fabulous treat that I can never re-create at home. Just before we were to leave for the airport on our most recent visit, my dad and I ran from the hotel to the pastry shop, just to have a final taste. I ordered, paid, and cradled my pretty package of three zeppole. I guess I didn't cradle the bundle well enough. In our mad dash back to the hotel, I heard a small thump and realized my precious package had slipped from my hands and onto the street. *O Dio!* My dad and I stared down in disbelief. We scooped them up, brought them back to the hotel room, and dusted off our zeppole. We salvaged a few small bites each. This was a real taste of Italy!

CAKES

Italian cakes are different from the ones that we make in America. They are generally more casual, single layer cakes that are richly flavored with nuts, fruits, and chocolate. Cakes are usually served plain, with a dusting of powdered sugar or with a dollop of whipped cream on top. There aren't many fussy frostings and elaborate decorations. Many of the fancier cakes, reserved for holidays, are sponge cakes with fresh fruit and a simple swirled sweetened whipped cream frosting. They are not like American layer cakes with fancy buttercream piping. Other cakes or tortes, as they are called, resemble what we would call a pie. However you classify them, they're delicious.

Mixing Tips

Start by having ingredients at room temperature. This is a vital point for cake baking. For butter-based cakes this insures that the butter blends easily with sugar and eggs. For foam-type cakes, like sponge cakes, room temperature egg whites will yield the most volume.

For cheesecakes, room temperature cheese and eggs are important for maximum volume.

Testing for Doneness

Many of these cakes are made of thick layers and require long baking times. These are great to prepare and put in the oven, then relax or do another task during the baking time. Use a cake tester, inserted into the center of the cake, to test for doneness. The tester should have a fine crumb, not batter, when removed. If you wait until the tester comes out clean, you might overbake the cake. Remember, the cake will continue to bake in the pan after it's removed.

Decorating

As I've previously mentioned, Italian cakes are more casual than American cakes. The decorating is so easy you may not even need a pastry bag. A simple dusting of confectioners' sugar or cocoa (for chocolate cakes) is enough for many of these rustic cakes. Dusting to form a pattern is easy and limited only by your creativity.

To make a diagonal pattern on a 9-inch cake:

Cut ½-inch-wide strips of baking parchment approximately 9 inches long. Place strips diagonally, ½ inch apart on top of cake. Place another set of parchment strips on the opposite diagonal, again about ½ inch apart. Be sure some of the cake is showing. Dust confectioners' sugar over the top. Carefully remove parchment strips to reveal design. You can use the same technique with a lace doily or any other type of stencil you choose.

Whipped Cream Frosted Cakes

Many of these sponge-based cakes use a stiff whipped cream frosting. Use a metal spatula to spread cream where desired. Use small swirled strokes to create a home-style look.

Covering Sides of Cakes with Nuts

An easy way to cover any frosting mistakes and create a professional-looking cake is to cover the cake with toasted nuts or coconut. Place nuts or coconut on a flat plate. Hold the cake from the bottom, with one hand. Use the other hand to press nuts or coconut onto the sides of the cake. Hold the cake over the plate to catch any excess that falls away.

Dusting with Confectioners' Sugar

To dust a cake or cake slice with confectioners' sugar, place a few tablespoons of powdered sugar in a small dry strainer. Hold the strainer over the cake and with a tea-spoon stir the sugar over the cake in the desired amount.

SICILIAN CASSATA

There are many variations of this traditional Sicilian dessert, including a frozen version. Most Sicilian pastry shops have fancy marzipan-covered cassata with candied fruit. My favorite combination is still this classic pound cake filled with an orange ricotta filling and covered with a rich chocolate glaze. You can also serve this tasty, versatile cake with just a sprinkle of confectioners' sugar. Serve a generous slice with a cup of espresso for any special occasion.

POUND CAKE:

2 CUPS CAKE FLOUR

1 CUP SUGAR

1 TEASPOON BAKING POWDER

PINCH OF SALT

1½ STICKS BUTTER, SOFTENED

3 EGGS

¼ CUP MILK

SWEET RICOTTA FILLING:

2 CUPS RICOTTA

½ CUP SUGAR

GRATED RIND OF 1 ORANGE

CHOCOLATE GLAZE:

1½ CUPS SEMISWEET CHOCOLATE CHIPS

¼ POUND COLD BUTTER

1. Preheat oven to 350°F.

2. Grease and flour or line an 8 x 4-inch loaf pan with baking parchment. Set aside.

3. In an electric mixer, combine flour, sugar, baking powder, and salt. On low speed, add butter and mix until well blended. Add eggs and milk. Mix on medium speed until smooth, about 2 minutes.

4. Pour into prepared pan. Bake for 50 to 55 minutes, or until done.

5. Remove pan from the oven and place on a wire cooling rack. Let cool in pan for

10 minutes. Carefully remove cake from the pan and continue to cool on wire cooling rack. Remove and discard parchment. Cool completely before assembling cassata or wrap cake in plastic wrap. Store at room temperature overnight or freeze for later use.

6. In a small bowl, combine ricotta, sugar, and rind. Mix well with a wooden spoon. Refrigerate if not using immediately.

7. In a small saucepan, over low heat, stir chocolate chips with a wooden spoon until melted. Remove from the heat.

8. Stir in butter until smooth. Refrigerate to thicken glaze for frosting consistency.

9. To reheat, heat in a double boiler over simmering water.

10. Slice pound cake horizontally into 3 even layers. Place top layer cut side up on a serving plate or doily-covered cake circle.

11. Spread half the ricotta filling over cake, spreading to the edges. Place next layer of cake on top. Spread remaining filling on top of this layer. Top with last layer of cake.

12. Cover with plastic wrap and refrigerate until set, 2 to 3 hours or overnight. Do not attempt to frost when cassata is this fresh. It needs to be firm.

13. When cassata is set, use a metal spatula to spread chocolate glaze on top and sides of cassata. Garnish with candied orange rind. Refrigerate until serving. Serve chilled.

YIELD: ONE 3-LAYER 8 X 4 CAKE, ABOUT 12 SERVINGS

SPONGE CAKE

PANE DI SPAGNA

This classic sponge cake is the basis for many famous Italian desserts such as Zuppa Inglese and Neapolitan Cake. The key to this family classic is simple: beat your egg whites until firm and carefully fold into the yolk mixture for a light, fluffy, and foolproof sponge. Baked in an ungreased tube pan, the cake will naturally cling to the sides and middle tube and will rise beautifully.

7 EGG WHITES, AT ROOM TEMPERATURE	7 EGG YOLKS
1½ CUPS SUGAR	1 TEASPOON VANILLA EXTRACT
½ TEASPOON CREAM OF TARTAR	1½ CUPS CAKE FLOUR
½ TEASPOON SALT	¼ CUP COLD WATER

1. Preheat oven to 325°F.

2. In an electric mixer with wire whisk attachment, beat egg whites, ¼ cup sugar, cream of tartar, and salt. Start on medium speed, then use high speed until very stiff peaks form, 3 to 4 minutes.

3. In a separate bowl, on medium speed, beat egg yolks, remaining 1¼ cups sugar, and vanilla. Beat until light in color, 2 to 3 minutes.

4. Add flour and water alternately to egg mixture. Start and end with the flour. Mix just until blended.

5. Using a rubber spatula, fold egg yolk mixture into whites. When blended, spoon batter into an ungreased 10-inch tube pan with removable bottom. Spread batter evenly.

6. Bake for 60 to 65 minutes, or until top is golden brown. Remove pan from the oven.

7. Invert tube pan to cool cake, about 1 hour.

8. When cool, carefully remove the cake from the pan. Use a sharp knife to loosen the outside of the cake from the sides of the pan.

YIELD: ONE 10-INCH CAKE, ABOUT 20 SLICES

NUT CAKE

TORTE DI NOCI

This cake is perfect for nut lovers and has a simple garnish of confectioners' sugar. Dust the entire surface of the cake or use strips of parchment to create an interesting design. For the cake itself, you can use any type of nut or any combination of nuts. Try my favorite, walnuts and hazelnuts.

3 EGGS

2 CUPS SUGAR

1 CUP OIL

3 TEASPOONS AMARETTO OR OTHER NUT LIQUEUR

2 CUPS CAKE FLOUR

1 TEASPOON BAKING POWDER

1 CUP MILK

½ CUP WALNUTS, FINELY CHOPPED

½ CUP HAZELNUTS, FINELY CHOPPED

GLAZE:

½ CUP AMARETTO OR OTHER NUT LIQUEUR

1. Preheat oven to 350°F.

2. Grease and flour or line a 9 x 3-inch springform pan with baking parchment. Set aside.

3. In an electric mixer on medium-high speed, beat eggs. Gradually add sugar and beat until light in color and thick in texture. Add oil and liqueur. Beat until well blended.

4. In a small bowl, mix together flour and baking powder. Add the flour mixture alternately with the milk to the egg mixture, beginning and ending with the flour mixture.

5. Stir in walnuts and hazelnuts.

6. Pour batter into prepared pan. Bake for 1 hour and 35 to 40 minutes, or until done.

(Continued)

7. Remove from the oven. Cool cake in pan on wire cooling rack for 15 to 20 minutes. Remove cake from the pan. Using a long serrated knife, carefully cut the top of the cake to level it and remove a crust that will form during baking. Pour amaretto over cake. Turn cake upside down and finish cooling on wire rack. The bottom will become the flat top of the cake. Remove and discard parchment. Dust with confectioners' sugar or cocoa.

YIELD: ONE 9-INCH ROUND CAKE, ABOUT 15 SLICES

BLACK CAKE WITH CHESTNUT CREAM

TORTE DI NERO CON CREMA DI CASTAGNA

A rich flourless chocolate cake accented with a scoop of chestnut cream is my solution for satisfying chocolate lovers everywhere. This cake is amazingly versatile—try pairing it with an orange or raspberry sauce. It's so rich it can be served chilled, in slivers.

2 POUNDS SEMISWEET CHOCOLATE, CHOPPED

¼ POUND UNSALTED BUTTER

8 EGGS

CHESTNUT CREAM (SEE FOLLOWING RECIPE)

1. Preheat oven to 350°F.

2. Grease and line a 9 x 2-inch round cake pan with baking parchment. Set aside.

3. Over simmering water or in a double boiler, melt chocolate and butter over low heat. Remove from the heat.

4. Using an electric mixer, add eggs, two at a time, beating well after adding. Beat until smooth.

5. Pour into prepared pan. Place pan on a sheet cake pan. Carefully add water to the sheet pan. Place pans in oven and bake for 25 to 30 minutes, or until just firm in the center.

6. Remove from oven. Cool cake in pan on wire rack. Refrigerate 2 to 3 hours or overnight. Use a small paring knife to loosen the edges of the cake from the pan. Invert onto a plate and remove pan. Discard parchment.

7. Store cake in refrigerator until slicing. Pipe chestnut cream onto a slice of cake or spoon it over.

YIELD: ONE 9-INCH ROUND CAKE, ABOUT 25 SERVINGS

CHESTNUT CREAM
CREMA DI CASTAGNA

This chestnut cream is the perfect accent for our rich chocolate cake.
It also makes a perfect not too sweet dessert all on its own. Spoon into
a martini glass and top with a cherry.

1 CUP HEAVY CREAM	1 RECIPE CHESTNUT PURÉE (SEE FOL-LOWING RECIPE), OR 8 OUNCES CANNED PURÉE
¼ CUP SUGAR	
1 TABLESPOON DARK RUM	

1. In an electric mixer with wire whisk, beat heavy cream until soft peaks form. Add sugar and rum. Add chestnut purée (at room temperature).

2. Whip until stiff peaks form. Pipe onto a slice of cake to garnish or spoon onto slice and serve.

YIELD: ABOUT 2 CUPS

CHESTNUT PURÉE

Chestnut purée is hard to find in specialty shops, but you can make your own.
If you find it, substitute an 8-ounce can in the chestnut cream recipe.

1 POUND CHESTNUTS, SLIT	6 TABLESPOONS HEAVY CREAM

1. Place chestnuts in a medium saucepan. Cover with water and boil on medium high for 20 to 25 minutes. Remove pan from the stove. Drain.

2. Cool chestnuts slightly. Peel outer shell as well as the inner skin. If chestnuts break, that's OK.

3. Return shelled chestnuts to medium saucepan. Cover with water. Simmer over low heat until tender, 20 to 25 minutes. Drain.

4. Purée in a food processor until smooth, adding heavy cream. Let cool. At this point you can refrigerate the purée overnight in an airtight container and complete chestnut cream the next day.

POLENTA CAKE

This cornmeal cake is a variation of our classic sponge cake. To make the cornmeal extra fine, process for 2 minutes in a food processor. It's perfect on its own or as the basis for our Sour Cherry Cake (see following recipe).

7 EGG WHITES, AT ROOM TEMPERATURE	1 TEASPOON VANILLA EXTRACT
1¾ CUPS SUGAR	¾ CUP ALL-PURPOSE FLOUR
½ TEASPOON CREAM OF TARTAR	¾ CUP FINE YELLOW CORNMEAL
½ TEASPOON SALT	¼ CUP COLD WATER
7 EGG YOLKS	

1. Preheat oven to 325°F.

2. In an electric mixer with wire whisk attachment, beat egg whites, ¼ cup of sugar, cream of tartar, and salt. Start on medium speed, then use high speed until very stiff peaks form, 3 to 4 minutes.

3. In a separate bowl, with an electric mixer on medium speed, beat egg yolks, remaining 1½ cups sugar, and vanilla. Beat until light in color, 2 to 3 minutes.

4. In a small bowl, mix together flour and cornmeal. Add flour mixture and water alternately to egg mixture. Start and end with the flour mixture. Mix just until blended.

5. Using a rubber spatula, fold egg yolk mixture into egg whites. When blended, spoon batter into an ungreased 10-inch tube pan with removable bottom. Spread batter evenly.

6. Bake for 60 to 65 minutes, or until top is golden brown. Remove pan from the oven.

7. Invert tube pan to cool cake, about 1 hour.

8. When cool, carefully remove cake from the pan. Use a sharp knife to loosen the outside of the cake from the sides of the pan.

YIELD: ONE 10-INCH CAKE, ABOUT 20 SLICES

SOUR CHERRY CAKE

This rustic cake combines the interesting texture of our polenta cake with a rich sour cherry filling. These cherries really aren't sour, just a bit tart and not too sweet. The perfect complement to a fine Italian feast. Allow 15 to 20 minutes longer for double recipe of filling to become thickened.

1 RECIPE POLENTA CAKE (SEE PRE-CEDING RECIPE)

1 RECIPE WHIPPED CREAM FROSTING (SEE FOLLOWING RECIPE)

2 RECIPES SOUR CHERRY FILLING (SEE PAGE 95)

1. Cut polenta cake horizontally into thirds. Place the bottom layer, top-side up, on a serving plate or doily-covered cake circle. Spread a thin layer of whipped cream frosting over the cake. Place half the cherry filling on top of the cream.

2. Place middle layer of cake on top of cherry filling. Repeat layering whipped cream, cherry filling, and cake. Reserve 3 teaspoons of filling to garnish the cake. Pour any excess juice from the cherry filling over the top of the cake to soak.

3. Using a metal spatula, frost the top and sides of the cake with whipped cream frosting. Dot the top with remaining cherry filling. Sprinkle with cocoa to garnish. Refrigerate until serving. Serve chilled.

YIELD: ONE 3-LAYER 10-INCH CAKE, ABOUT 25 SERVINGS

WHIPPED CREAM FROSTING

*This fresh, not-too-sweet frosting is the perfect way to frost
or garnish your baked goods.*

2 CUPS HEAVY CREAM **½ CUP SUGAR**

In an electric mixer with wire whisk attachment, beat cream into peaks, 2 to 3 minutes. Add sugar and whip until stiff. Use immediately.

YIELD: 4 CUPS, ENOUGH TO FILL AND FROST A 3-LAYER 10-INCH CAKE

CAPRI CHOCOLATE CAKE
TORTE CAPRESE

This tasty cake originated on the Isle of Capri, one of my favorite spots in the world, home to the famous Blue Grotto. On a recent visit, I was in awe of this limestone cave that reflects the light to show an unbelievable shade of blue water. I was really afraid to get in the small rowboat to enter the grotto, but when I heard Giuseppe, our rower, singing "Volare," I knew everything would be fine.

8 EGGS, SEPARATED

¾ CUP SUGAR

¼ POUND BUTTER, SOFTENED

10 OUNCES SEMISWEET CHOCOLATE, MELTED

½ CUP FLOUR

1½ CUPS WALNUTS, FINELY CHOPPED

1. Preheat oven to 350°F.

2. Grease and line a 9 x 3-inch springform pan with baking parchment. Set aside.

3. In an electric mixer with wire whisk attachment, beat egg whites until stiff. Gradually add ¼ cup of sugar as you are beating. Set aside.

4. In electric mixer, on medium speed, cream the butter. Add remaining ½ cup sugar and beat until light. Add egg yolks, one at a time, beating well after adding each one. Add melted chocolate. Beat 2 minutes for a smooth batter, being sure to scrape the bottom and sides of the mixing bowl with a rubber spatula.

5. Stir in flour and walnuts.

6. Carefully fold egg whites into chocolate batter. Pour batter into prepared pan, smoothing the top evenly.

7. Bake for 1 hour and 15 to 20 minutes, or until done.

8. Remove cake from the oven and cool in pan on wire rack for 15 to 20 minutes. Remove cake from the pan. Use a long serrated knife to level off the top of the cake and remove a crust that may form during baking. Turn cake upside down.

(Continued)

Remove and discard parchment. Continue to cool cake on wire cooling rack. The bottom of the cake will become the flat top of the cake. Dust top with confectioners' sugar or cocoa and serve.

YIELD: ONE 9-INCH ROUND CAKE, ABOUT 20 SERVINGS

ITALIAN FRUITCAKE

TORTE DI FRUTTA SECCA

This fruitcake is one of my mom's Christmas specialties. Her original recipe used milk, which I've replaced with a generous amount of sour cream. This adds a nice flavor and moisture to the cake. This recipe yields three small loaf cakes, making it a perfect gift for yourself and two of your friends.

½ POUND BUTTER, SOFTENED

2 CUPS SUGAR

4 EGGS

2 TABLESPOONS MARSALA

3 CUPS CAKE FLOUR

1 TEASPOON BAKING SODA

1½ CUPS SOUR CREAM

GRATED RIND OF 1 ORANGE

GRATED RIND OF 1 LEMON

1 CUP GLACÉ CHERRIES, HALVED

1 CUP DRIED APRICOTS, COARSELY CHOPPED

2 CUPS WALNUTS, COARSELY CHOPPED

SOAKING GLAZE:

½ CUP MARSALA

JUICE OF 1 LEMON

JUICE OF 1 ORANGE

1. Preheat oven to 350°F.

2. Grease and line 3 small loaf pans (about 7 x 3 inches) with baking parchment. Set aside.

3. In an electric mixer, cream butter and sugar until light. Add eggs, one at a time, beating well after adding each one. Add marsala. Mix until well blended.

4. In a small bowl, mix flour with baking soda. Add flour mixture to the egg mixture alternately with the sour cream. Begin and end with the flour mixture. Mix just until blended. Stir in orange and lemon rinds, cherries, apricots, and nuts.

5. Spoon batter evenly into prepared pans. Bake for 60 to 70 minutes, or until done. Remove cakes from the oven and place on wire cooling rack.

6. In a small bowl, mix marsala with lemon and orange juice. Pour evenly over hot

(Continued)

cakes. Continue to cool on wire cooling racks. Dust with confectioners' sugar and serve. Store unused cakes in foil or plastic wrap at room temperature for 1 week. For longer storage, freeze.

YIELD: THREE 7 X 3-INCH LOAVES, ABOUT 12 SLICES

ESPRESSO CHEESECAKE

This creamy cheesecake has the subtle flavor of coffee. Serve it with the espresso topping

or with fresh fruit. People often ask me how to prevent cheesecakes from cracking.

There are many causes for the cracking, which usually occurs during the cooling process.

Try to cool the cake gradually by leaving it in the warm oven after baking.

If it still cracks, just use a generous amount of topping.

CRUST:

1 CUP GRAHAM CRACKER CRUMBS	½ CUP SUGAR
4 TABLESPOONS COCOA	¼ POUND BUTTER, MELTED

FILLING:

2 POUNDS CREAM CHEESE, SOFTENED	4 EGGS, SLIGHTLY BEATEN
1 CUP SUGAR	1 CUP SOUR CREAM
4 TEASPOONS INSTANT ESPRESSO POWDER	

1. Preheat oven to 350°F.

2. Grease and line the sides of a 9 x 3-inch springform pan with baking parchment.

3. In a small bowl, combine graham cracker crumbs, cocoa, and sugar. Mix until blended. Add melted butter and mix with your fingers.

4. Press crust into the bottom of the pan. Bake for 5 minutes, or until set. Remove from the oven. Set aside to cool on a wire cooling rack.

5. In an electric mixer on medium-high speed, beat cream cheese until light and fluffy, about 15 minutes. Gradually add sugar and instant espresso. Mix until smooth and well blended. Add eggs gradually, beating well until blended. Stir in sour cream on low speed and mix just until blended.

6. Pour batter into prepared crust. Bake for 1 hour and 20 to 25 minutes, until center is just about set. Turn off oven. Let cake cool in oven for 15 to 20 minutes.

(Continued)

7. Remove cake from the oven and continue to cool on wire cooling rack. When completely cool, cover top of cake with plastic wrap or foil and refrigerate overnight.

8. To remove cake from pan, use a sharp straight knife. Run the edge of the knife along the outside of the cake. Pop open spring on springform pan.

9. Frost with coffee topping (see following recipe) and refrigerate until serving. Serve chilled.

YIELD: ONE 9-INCH CAKE, ABOUT 20 SERVINGS

COFFEE TOPPING

16 OUNCES CREAM CHEESE, SOFTENED	1 TABLESPOON COFFEE LIQUEUR
2 TEASPOONS INSTANT ESPRESSO	½ CUP CONFECTIONERS' SUGAR

In an electric mixer on high speed, beat the cream cheese until fluffy, 4 to 5 minutes. Add instant espresso, coffee liqueur, and confectioners' sugar. Mix until well blended. Using a metal spatula, spread topping on top of cheesecake in a swirling pattern.

AUNT GIULIA'S ORANGE CAKE
TORTE D'ARANCIA

*This is another of my aunt Giulia's specialties. It's a delicious pound cake, perfect
served plain or with a dollop of ice cream or whipped cream. Not only was Aunt Giulia
a great baker, but her basement served as our family party headquarters. It was fully
equipped with a kitchen, player piano, and Ping-Pong table that doubled as our
buffet table. The perfect place for birthday parties, showers, and family reunions.
A lot of memories—and great cakes—were made there.*

4 EGGS, SEPARATED	2½ CUPS CAKE FLOUR
½ POUND BUTTER, SOFTENED	PINCH OF SALT
2 CUPS SUGAR	2 TEASPOONS BAKING POWDER
GRATED RIND FROM 1 ORANGE	1 CUP ORANGE JUICE

1. Preheat oven to 350°F.

2. Grease and flour or line a 9 x 3-inch springform pan with baking parchment. Set aside.

3. In an electric mixer, with wire whisk attachment, beat egg whites until stiff. Set aside.

4. With electric mixer, cream butter until fluffy. Add sugar and orange rind. Add egg yolks, one at a time, beating well after adding each one.

5. In a separate bowl, combine flour, salt, and baking powder. Add the flour mixture to the butter mixture alternately with the orange juice, beginning and ending with the flour mixture.

6. Carefully fold egg whites into the flour mixture. Place batter into prepared pan.

7. Bake for 1 hour and 35 to 40 minutes, or until done.

8. Remove pan from the oven. Place cake on cooling rack and cool for 15 to 20 minutes. Carefully remove cake from the pan. Remove and discard parchment. Use a

(Continued)

long serrated knife to level off the top of cake and remove crust that may form during baking. Turn cake upside down. The flat bottom of the cake will become your level top. Continue to cool on wire cooling rack. Serve at room temperature. Dust top with confectioners' sugar.

YIELD: ONE 9-INCH CAKE, ABOUT 20 SLICES

ITALIAN CHEESECAKE

This ricotta cheesecake can be served plain, topped with fresh fruit or a rich chocolate sauce. I've given this traditional recipe a nutty graham cracker crust that's one of my favorites. It's easy to make and complements the creamy cake perfectly.

NUT CRUST:

1 CUP GRAHAM CRACKER CRUMBS	½ CUP WALNUTS, FINELY CHOPPED
½ CUP SUGAR	¼ POUND BUTTER, MELTED

FILLING:

4 CUPS RICOTTA	¼ CUP FLOUR
½ CUP SUGAR	4 TABLESPOONS AMARETTO
4 EGGS	¼ CUP HEAVY CREAM

1. Preheat oven to 325°F.

2. Grease and line the sides of a 9 x 3-inch springform pan with baking parchment.

3. In a small bowl, combine graham cracker crumbs, sugar, and nuts. Stir until blended. Add melted butter and mix with your fingers. Press crust mixture into the bottom of the prepared pan. Bake for 5 to 8 minutes, or until set. Remove from the oven and set aside to cool on a wire cooling rack.

4. In an electric mixer on medium speed, blend ricotta and sugar. Add eggs and beat until well blended. Add flour, amaretto, and heavy cream. Mix just until blended. Pour batter into prepared crust.

5. Bake for 1 hour and 20 to 25 minutes, until center is just set. Turn off oven. Let cake cool in oven for 15 to 20 minutes. Remove cake from the oven. Continue to cool cake on wire cooling rack. Wrap cake in plastic or foil. Refrigerate overnight.

6. To remove cake from the pan, use a straight knife. Run the edge of the knife

(Continued)

around the outside of the cake. Pop open the spring on the springform pan to release cake. Dust with confectioners' sugar or top with fresh fruit. Refrigerate until
serving. Serve chilled.

YIELD: ONE 9-INCH CHEESECAKE, ABOUT 20 SERVINGS

TUSCAN HARVEST CAKE
TORTE DI TOSCANO

This crumb cake is perfect for breakfast or to take along on a picnic. When grinding almonds in a food processor, add a teaspoon or two of sugar. This will help absorb the oils that are released when chopping nuts. These oils can make the nuts too moist for most recipes.

2 CUPS DICED APPLES (ABOUT 2 APPLES)

2 CUPS SUGAR

GRATED RIND OF 1 LEMON

JUICE OF 1 LEMON

1 TEASPOON CINNAMON

½ POUND BUTTER, SOFTENED

2 EGGS

1 TEASPOON VANILLA

1½ CUPS FLOUR

1 CUP GROUND ALMONDS

1. Preheat oven to 375°F.

2. Grease and flour or line a 9-inch round cake pan with baking parchment. Set aside.

3. In a medium bowl, combine apples, 1 cup of sugar, lemon rind and juice, and cinnamon. With a wooden spoon, mix until well blended. Set aside.

4. In an electric mixer, cream butter and remaining 1 cup of sugar until light. Add eggs and vanilla. Mix until well blended. On low speed, gradually add flour and chopped almonds. Mix just until blended.

5. Spread dough into prepared pan. Spread apple mixture evenly over the top of the dough.

6. Bake for 40 to 45 minutes, or until done in the center.

7. Remove pan from the oven. Place on wire cooling rack. Cool. Cut into wedges and serve warm or completely cool.

YIELD: ONE 9-INCH CAKE, ABOUT 12 SERVINGS

ENGLISH TRIFLE WITH STRAWBERRIES AND MARSALA
ZUPPA INGLESE CON FRAGOLE E MARSALA

A traditional zuppa inglese is an English Trifle with sponge cake, custard, and whipped cream. My updated variation adds fresh strawberries and a hint of marsala wine— delizioso! You'll need a trifle bowl, which looks like a large square brandy snifter, to assemble this dessert. Make your own variations using a different type of wine, liqueur, or fresh fruit.

1 RECIPE SPONGE CAKE (SEE PAGE 46)

½ CUP MARSALA WINE

1 RECIPE VANILLA PASTRY CREAM (SEE PAGE 95)

16 OUNCES STRAWBERRIES, CLEANED, HULLED, AND SLICED

¾ CUP HEAVY CREAM

2 TABLESPOONS SUGAR

1. Cut sponge cake horizontally into thirds. Place the bottom layer, cut side up, in the bottom of the trifle bowl. Using a pastry brush, brush all the layers of sponge evenly with the marsala.

2. Spread half of the pastry cream over the bottom layer of sponge cake. Arrange half the strawberries around the bowl and covering the custard. Place the middle layer of sponge on top of the strawberries. Spread remaining half of pastry cream and strawberries on the middle sponge cake. Top with final layer. Lightly press all the cake down in the bowl.

3. In an electric mixer on high speed, beat heavy cream until stiff. Add sugar and beat until well blended. Spoon dollops or pipe dollops from a pastry bag on top of the trifle. Dust the entire top with confectioners' sugar. Place whole strawberries in the center of the dollop. Refrigerate until serving. Serve chilled.

YIELD: ABOUT 25 SERVINGS

NEAPOLITAN CAKE

This cake is based on the Neapolitan pastry that layers sponge cake with phyllo pastry, fresh fruit, and whipped cream. The result is a light cake with a crunchy surprise layer of baked phyllo.

6 SHEETS OF COMMERCIAL PHYLLO DOUGH, THAWED

2 TABLESPOONS BUTTER, SOFTENED

½ RECIPE SPONGE CAKE

½ RECIPE WHIPPED CREAM FROSTING (SEE PAGE 54)

3 CUPS SLICED STRAWBERRIES AND WHOLE RASPBERRIES

1. Preheat oven to 375°F.

2. Brush each sheet of phyllo with soft butter and layer all 6 layers.

3. Using a sharp straight knife, cut a 9-inch circle from the dough. Place on parchment-lined cookie sheet. Bake for 10 to 15 minutes, or until golden. Cool on parchment.

4. Carefully slice the sponge cake horizontally in half. Place the bottom layer, cut side up, on a serving plate or doily-covered cake circle. Spread a thin layer of whipped cream frosting over the cake. Spread half the berry mixture over the cream. Place phyllo circle on top of the berries. Spread a thin layer of whipped cream on the phyllo circle. Top with layer of sponge cake. Spread layer of cream, and remaining berries, on top.

5. Dust with confectioners' sugar. Refrigerate until serving. Serve chilled.

YIELD: ONE 3-LAYER 10-INCH CAKE, ABOUT 25 SERVINGS

TO MAKE HALF THE SPONGE CAKE

4 EGG WHITES	4 EGG YOLKS
2 TABLESPOONS PLUS ½ CUP SUGAR	½ TEASPOON VANILLA EXTRACT
¼ TEASPOON CREAM OF TARTAR	¾ CUP CAKE FLOUR
¼ TEASPOON SALT	2 TABLESPOONS COLD WATER

1. Preheat oven to 325°F.

2. In an electric mixer with wire whisk attachment, beat egg whites, 2 tablespoons of sugar, cream of tartar, and salt. Start on medium speed, then use high speed until very stiff peaks form, 3 to 4 minutes. Set aside.

3. In a separate bowl, with an electric mixer on medium speed, beat the egg yolks, ½ cup sugar, and vanilla. Beat until light in color, 2 to 3 minutes.

4. Alternate adding flour and water to egg yolk mixture. Begin and end with the flour. Mix just until well blended.

5. Using a rubber spatula, fold egg yolk mixture into beaten whites. When blended, spoon batter into a 10-inch ungreased tube pan with removable bottom.

6. Bake for 30 minutes, or until top is golden brown. Remove pan from the oven. Invert cake and cool in pan for about 1 hour.

7. When cool, carefully remove the cake from the pan. Use a sharp straight knife to loosen the outside of the cake from the pan. Remove inside of pan. Run knife along the bottom and around inside of center column to remove.

THOUSAND-LAYER APRICOT CAKE
MILLEFOGLIE

This cake is really more like a giant pastry. It is simple to make,
impressive to serve, and light to eat. Millefoglie literally means many leaves,
referring to the many layers of the pastry.

1 BOX FROZEN PUFF PASTRY

1 RECIPE APRICOT CREAM (SEE FOL-
LOWING RECIPE)

1. Preheat oven to 400°F.

2. Thaw 2 sheets of puff pastry according to the directions on the box. On a lightly floured surface, roll puff pastry as thin as possible into a rectangle about 9 x 7 inches. Using a sharp straight knife, cut sheet in half so that each piece measures about 4½ x 7 inches. Prick each sheet with a fork several times. Place sheets on a parchment-lined cookie sheet, spacing each sheet about 1 inch apart.

3. Repeat rolling and cutting the second sheet, same as the first. Bake for 15 to 18 minutes, or until well browned.

4. Remove pan from the oven. Cool dough on parchment on wire cooling rack. Wrap in plastic and store at room temperature overnight, if desired, or assemble when cool.

5. Place a piece of baked puff pastry, top side up, on a serving plate or doily-covered cake circle. Using a metal spatula, spread one third of the apricot cream evenly on pastry. Place another sheet on top of apricot cream. Repeat layering another one third of apricot cream and another layer of pastry until plain pastry is at the top.

6. Dust top with confectioners' sugar. Refrigerate until serving. Serve chilled.

YIELD: ONE 4 x 7-INCH CAKE, ABOUT 8 SLICES

APRICOT CREAM

This cream can be used as a filling for the Millefoglie, a sponge cake, or simply spooned into a cup and enjoyed on its own.

1½ CUPS HEAVY CREAM

½ CUP SUGAR

½ CUP APRICOT PIE FILLING OR PRE-SERVES

In an electric mixer with wire whisk attachment, beat heavy cream until thick. Add sugar and beat on high speed until stiff. Add apricot pie filling. Mix until well blended. Use immediately.

AMARETTO CHIFFON CAKE

*This light, flavorful cake has a rich almond taste. The key to this cake is to beat
your egg whites until very stiff, which will produce the most volume and
a light and fluffy cake. Serve with a dusting of confectioners' sugar, a dollop of
whipped cream, and fresh fruit.*

6 EGGS, SEPARATED	2¼ CUPS FLOUR
½ TEASPOON CREAM OF TARTAR	3 TEASPOONS BAKING POWDER
1¼ CUPS SUGAR	¾ CUP AMARETTO
½ CUP VEGETABLE OIL	

1. Preheat oven to 325°F.

2. In an electric mixer with wire whisk attachment, beat egg whites, cream of tartar, and ½ cup of sugar. Beat on high until stiff peaks form. Set aside.

3. In an electric mixer on medium speed, beat egg yolks. Gradually add remaining sugar and oil. Beat until light in color.

4. In a small bowl, combine flour and baking powder. Add the flour mixture alternately with the amaretto to the egg yolk mixture. Begin and end with the flour mixture.

5. Using a rubber spatula, carefully fold egg whites into flour mixture. Pour batter into an ungreased 10-inch tube pan with a removable bottom.

6. Bake for 50 to 55 minutes. Remove cake from the oven. Invert cake to cool. Cool completely. Use a sharp knife to loosen cake from around the sides and bottom of the pan. Dust with confectioners' sugar and serve.

YIELD: ONE 10-INCH CAKE, ABOUT 20 SERVINGS

MANDARIN ORANGE
MERINGUE CAKE

These striking cakes are all over the pastry shops of Italy. The light sponge and chocolate pastry cream is hidden by a covering of meringues and mandarin oranges. Fill and frost the cake first and then arrange baked meringues and mandarin oranges into whipped cream, covering the entire outer surface.

½ RECIPE SPONGE CAKE (SEE PAGE 46)

1 RECIPE CHOCOLATE PASTRY CREAM
(SEE FOLLOWING RECIPE)

1 CUP HEAVY CREAM

¼ CUP SUGAR

1 RECIPE COCOA ALMOND MERINGUES
(SEE PAGE 68)

1 CUP MANDARIN ORANGES

1. Carefully cut sponge cake horizontally into thirds. Place the bottom layer, cut side up, on a serving dish or doily-covered cake circle. Spread half the chocolate pastry cream over the cake. Place the middle layer of sponge on top of the pastry cream. Spread remaining pastry cream over middle layer, and place remaining layer on top. Refrigerate cake while making the whipped cream frosting.

2. In an electric mixer on high speed, beat heavy cream until peaks begin to form. Add sugar and beat until stiff.

3. Using a metal spatula, frost the top and sides of the cake with whipped cream. Don't worry if you have crumbs in your frosting because you're going to cover the cake completely with the meringues.

4. While the frosting is fresh, place meringues and mandarin oranges all over the top and sides of the cake. Place flat side of meringue onto surface of the cake. Refrigerate overnight. Serve chilled.

YIELD: ONE 3-LAYER CAKE, ABOUT 20 SERVINGS

CHOCOLATE PASTRY CREAM

Use this cream to fill cake layers, cream puffs, or cannoli.

3 EGG YOLKS	2 TEASPOONS CORNSTARCH
½ CUP SUGAR	1 TABLESPOON FLOUR
1½ CUPS MILK	¼ CUP COCOA
1 TEASPOON VANILLA	

1. In a medium mixing bowl or the top of a double boiler, whisk egg yolks and sugar until light. Add milk, vanilla, cornstarch, flour, and cocoa. Whisk over boiling water until thickened, 15 to 20 minutes.

2. Cool to room temperature. Cover with plastic wrap and refrigerate until using.

PIES AND TARTS

Italian pies are usually baked in a deep pie dish, with a top crust or without. Tarts are made in shallow-sided pans, usually with removable bottoms to lift the tart out of the pan. They both use similar dough for crusts.

Tips on Making Crust

Most of the pies and tarts in this chapter use a tender dough, or *pasta frolla.* There are many variations of this dough. The master recipe I've included is a rich buttery version.

There are two easy methods to make pie crust dough. You can use either a food processor or a pastry blender to blend cold butter into the flour, or you can use two knives to cut the butter in. This mixture should resemble coarse crumbs. Then add your wet ingredients and knead until blended. Remember to begin with cold butter and cold water. This will give you the flakiest and most flavorful crusts.

For easiest rolling, refrigerate the dough before rolling. To roll, use a rolling pin on a lightly floured surface. You may need to lightly dust the rolling pin as well. (Be sure not to overflour the surface or the rolling pin, which will toughen the dough.) Keep moving the dough as you roll it out to be sure it's not sticking. Roll evenly from the inside out. Do not turn the dough over while rolling. Keep rolling the same side. The crust should be rolled about 1 inch larger than the pan it will fit. This will give you ample room for the sides.

To Make Lattice Top

Roll out dough as thin as the bottom crust, about ⅛ inch thick. Use a fluted pastry cutter to cut strips about ½ inch wide. Carefully lay strips horizontally over the top of the pie, spacing about ½ inch apart. Repeat laying strips ½ inch apart vertically to form lattice. Pinch ends of strips to bottom crust to adhere.

Prebaking a Bottom Crust

For some tart recipes you must bake the bottom crust empty, then cool and fill with filling. Because the tart is empty, there is nothing to hold the crust securely in place. You can use specially made pie weights, available in most kitchen shops, or the old-fashioned way of using dried beans as weights.

Fill the tart pan with bottom crust. Place a small piece of foil on the bottom. Place pie weights or beans on top of the foil. Bake as recipe directs. When cool, remove weights or beans.

You can also partially bake the bottom crust for some of these tarts, to avoid soggy bottoms.

TENDER PIE DOUGH

PASTA FROLLA

Pasta frolla means "tender dough" and is the basis for many of the sweet pies and tarts in this chapter. It is very versatile, buttery, and easy to work with. It freezes easily, so if you need to make just half the recipe, such as for a lemon or fig tart, just wrap the un-used dough in plastic wrap and freeze. You can also use any extra dough to make pasta frolla cookies. This will give you two different desserts with only one dough to mix.

2 CUPS FLOUR	1½ STICKS BUTTER, CHILLED
⅔ CUP SUGAR	1 EGG
PINCH OF SALT	2 TABLESPOONS COLD WATER

1. Combine flour, sugar, and salt in a food processor. Pulse in butter until well blended into dry ingredients.

2. Add egg and water and pulse until blended.

3. Turn out dough onto a lightly floured surface and knead until well blended.

4. Separate dough in half. Wrap each in plastic and refrigerate from 2 to 3 hours or overnight.

YIELD: TWO 9-INCH TART OR PIE CRUSTS

PIE CRUST, OR PASTA FROLLA, COOKIES

These cookies started out as a great way to use any extra pie dough, but they've become popular in their own right, and now I sometimes make pasta frolla just to make them. The dough is rolled out, spread with a very thin layer of jelly, rolled like a jelly roll, and cut into slices.

PASTA FROLLA (SEE PRECEDING RECIPE)	JELLY, ANY FLAVOR

1. Preheat oven to 375°F.

2. Roll out dough on a lightly floured surface into a rectangular shape, about ⅛ inch thick. Using a metal spatula, spread a very thin layer of jelly over the dough. Carefully roll the dough, jelly roll fashion, beginning at the long portion. Roll into cylinder.

3. Place cylinders on parchment-lined cookie sheet. Cover with plastic wrap. Refrigerate 2 to 3 hours or overnight.

4. Cut into ½-inch slices. Place slices cut side up on a parchment-lined cookie sheet.

5. Bake for 20 to 25 minutes, or until lightly browned.

6. Remove cookie sheet from the oven. Use a metal spatula to remove cookies from the cookie sheet and place onto a wire cooling rack. Cool completely.

YIELD: WILL VARY ACCORDING TO HOW MUCH DOUGH YOU ARE USING

LEMON TART

CROSTATA DI LIMONE

A perfect after-dinner treat for any meal, this tart has the fresh taste of lemons that are so popular throughout southern Italy. Because lemons are available in North America year-round, this tart makes both a perfect refreshing summer dessert and a great winter treat.

½ RECIPE PASTA FROLLA (SEE PAGE 78)   5 TABLESPOONS BUTTER, MELTED

¾ CUP SUGAR   JUICE AND RIND OF 2 LEMONS (⅓ CUP)

2 EGGS

1. Make pasta frolla. Chill for 2 to 3 hours or overnight.

2. Preheat oven to 350°F.

3. Roll out dough on a lightly floured surface until ⅛ inch thick. Carefully line the bottom of a 9-inch tart pan with removable bottom with dough. Roll your rolling pin over top of pan to cut dough. Partially cook crust with pie weights 15 minutes. Remove from oven. Cool completely.

4. In an electric mixer, beat sugar and eggs. Add cooled butter and lemon rind and juice. Pour lemon mixture into prepared crust.

5. Bake for 30 minutes, or until filling is set and crust is golden brown.

6. Remove from the oven. Place tart on wire cooling rack. Cool completely. Refrigerate overnight.

7. Carefully remove tart from pan. Refrigerate until serving. Serve chilled. Dust with confectioners' sugar and serve with fresh fruit.

YIELD: ONE 9-INCH TART, ABOUT 8 SERVINGS

FRESH FIG TART
CROSTATA DI FICO

This fresh fig tart is one of my mom's favorite desserts. It reminds me of late summer when figs are in season and plentiful in Italy. It's a perfect dessert to enjoy with coffee at an outdoor café, or on your own porch. I am happily continuing my family's summer ritual of having espresso al fresco every night, weather permitting, and this tart makes it perfect.

½ RECIPE PASTA FROLLA (SEE PAGE 78)

2 EGG YOLKS

½ CUP SUGAR

1 CUP MILK

3 TABLESPOONS FLOUR

3 TABLESPOONS RUM

6 FRESH FIGS, BLACK OR GREEN, CUT INTO THIN SLICES

½ CUP HAZELNUTS, CHOPPED

1. Preheat oven to 350°F.

2. Roll out chilled dough on a lightly floured surface until ⅛ inch thick. Carefully place crust in bottom of 9-inch tart pan with removable bottom. Add pie weights or beans and bake crust for 15 to 20 minutes. Remove crust from the oven. Cool on wire cooling rack.

3. In an electric mixer or with a wire whisk in medium bowl, beat egg yolks and sugar until light. Add milk, flour, and rum. Mix until well blended and smooth. Pour filling into cooled crust.

4. Arrange sliced figs around filling. Sprinkle figs with chopped hazelnuts.

5. Bake for 30 to 35 minutes, or until center is set. Remove from the oven. Cool tart on wire cooling rack. Refrigerate until serving. Serve chilled.

YIELD: ONE 9-INCH TART, ABOUT 8 SERVINGS

FRUIT TART

CROSTATA DI FRUTTA

This versatile tart has a rich pastry cream topped with any type of fresh fruit. I like to arrange the fruit on top in casual clusters rather than the classic concentric circle or structured arrangement. The crumbs that are sprinkled on the base of this tart are a great way to use less-than-fresh amaretti cookies. Another example of Italian recycling!

½ RECIPE PASTA FROLLA (SEE PAGE 78)

½ RECIPE PASTRY CREAM (SEE FOL-LOWING RECIPE)

½ CUP CRUSHED AMARETTI COOKIES (ABOUT 4 COOKIES CHOPPED IN FOOD PROCESSOR)

ABOUT 4 CUPS MIXED FRUIT (SLICED STRAWBERRIES, KIWI, BLUEBERRIES, GRAPES)

1. Preheat oven to 350°F.

2. Roll out pasta frolla on a lightly floured surface until ⅛ inch thick. Place in bottom of 9-inch tart pan. Press into pan. Roll your rolling pin over the top of the pan to cut dough. Save any dough scraps. You can store in freezer and later make cookies (see page 79).

3. Sprinkle chopped amaretti cookies over crust.

4. Bake for 20 to 25 minutes, or until crust is lightly browned. Remove from the oven and cool on wire cooling rack.

5. Carefully remove cooled tart shell from the pan. Place on serving dish. Spread cooled pastry cream into baked tart shell. Arrange fruit slices on pastry cream. Sprinkle with 1 tablespoon additional sugar. Cover with plastic wrap and refrigerate until serving. Serve chilled.

YIELD: ONE 9-INCH TART, ABOUT 6 SERVINGS

PASTRY CREAM

This basic custard is so flexible it is an ideal filling for tarts, cakes, and cream puffs.

2 TEASPOONS CORNSTARCH

½ CUP SUGAR

3 EGG YOLKS

1½ CUPS MILK

½ TEASPOON VANILLA

1. In a mixing bowl over water or double boiler over medium heat, whisk cornstarch, sugar, egg yolks, and milk. Whisk constantly over boiling water until thick, about 20 minutes.

2. Remove from the heat. Stir in vanilla. Let cool before filling tart. Can be prepared 1 day ahead. Just cover and refrigerate.

CHRISTMAS TART
CROSTATA DI NATALE

A vivid red cranberry tart studded with walnuts and finished with a lattice top is a fancy and delicious addition to your holiday dessert table. To make the lattice, use a fluted pastry cutter for a pretty edge. I still have my aunt Giulia's cutter that her brother handcrafted for her in our local factory. It's a large fluted wheel that has had a lot of experience cutting pastry.

1 RECIPE PASTA FROLLA (SEE PAGE 78)	JUICE AND RIND OF 1 LEMON
I CUP SUGAR	1 CUP LARGE WALNUT PIECES
1 TABLESPOON CORNSTARCH	4 CUPS CRANBERRIES
¼ CUP WATER	4 TABLESPOONS BUTTER
½ CUP CORN SYRUP	

1. In a medium saucepan, combine sugar, cornstarch, water, corn syrup, and juice and rind of lemon. Heat over medium heat until boiling. Add walnuts and cranberries. Cook until cranberries pop, about 4 minutes.

2. Remove from the heat. Stir in butter. Let cool.

3. Preheat oven to 350°F.

4. Roll out chilled pasta frolla on a lightly floured surface until about ⅛ inch thick. Line the bottom of a 9-inch tart pan with half of the dough. Pour cooled cranberry filling into crust.

5. Use a fluted pastry cutter to cut ½-inch strips of remaining dough. Arrange strips in lattice fashion on top of the filling. Pinch edges to seal top lattice crust to bottom crust.

6. Bake for 35 to 40 minutes, or until crust is golden brown.

(Continued)

7. Remove tart from the oven. Let cool on wire cooling rack. When completely cool, remove tart from pan.

8. Serve plain or with ice cream or whipped cream.

YIELD: ONE 9-INCH TART, ABOUT 12 SERVINGS

PEAR AND PINE NUT TART

This pear and pine nut combination is a simple rustic treat. Because we had a pear tree in our backyard we always had a bumper crop, and my mom was always looking for desserts to use pears. My brother and I would pick the pears, divide them into portions in brown bags, and use our wagon to distribute to family and neighbors.

½ RECIPE PASTA FROLLA (SEE PAGE 78)

½ CUP PINE NUTS

3 EGGS

1 CUP SUGAR

1 TABLESPOON CORNSTARCH

1 CUP SOUR CREAM

GRATED RIND OF 1 LEMON

½ CUP HEAVY CREAM

4 RIPE PEARS, PEELED, CORED, AND CUBED

1. Preheat oven to 400°F.

2. Grease the bottom and line the sides of a 9 x 3-inch springform pan with baking parchment.

3. Using your fingers, press pasta frolla evenly into the bottom of prepared pan. Sprinkle with ¼ cup of pine nuts. Bake for 15 to 20 minutes, or until lightly browned. Remove from oven and place on wire cooling rack. Let cool.

4. Reduce oven temperature to 375°F.

5. In a large mixing bowl, whisk eggs, sugar, and cornstarch. Add sour cream, lemon juice and rind, and heavy cream. Mix until well blended and smooth. Add pears and stir.

6. Pour batter into cooled crust. Sprinkle top with remaining ¼ cup of pine nuts.

7. Bake for 1 hour and 35 to 40 minutes, or until center is set. Remove pie from the oven and place on wire cooling rack. Cool completely in pan. Remove from pan. Discard parchment. Wrap pie in foil or plastic wrap and refrigerate overnight. Dust with confectioners' sugar and serve chilled.

YIELD: ONE 9-INCH TART, ABOUT 20 SERVINGS

ANTIQUE PIE

PIZZA ANTICO

This crusty "pie" is studded with raisins and nuts. It looks like a large wheel of pastry, impressive and unique, tied with a festive bow. It's the perfect holiday gift—it'll stay fresh for weeks in a cookie tin and actually tastes better with age. Because there are so many inner layers of dough in this pie, it needs to bake for a long time.

CRUST:

2½ TO 3 CUPS FLOUR	6 TABLESPOONS BUTTER, SOFTENED
½ CUP SUGAR	1 EGG
2 TEASPOONS CINNAMON	½ CUP WATER

FILLING:

3 CUPS FINELY CHOPPED WALNUTS	GRATED RIND OF 1 ORANGE
2 CUPS RAISINS	4 TABLESPOONS RUM
2 TEASPOONS CINNAMON	¼ POUND BUTTER
½ TEASPOON NUTMEG	½ CUP HONEY

1. In a food processor, pulse flour, sugar, and cinnamon until uniform. Add butter and process until mixture resembles coarse crumbs. Add egg and water and process.

2. Turn out dough onto a lightly floured surface. Knead until smooth and firm. Wrap dough in plastic wrap and refrigerate overnight.

3. Combine walnuts, raisins, cinnamon, nutmeg, orange rind, and rum in a medium   mixing bowl. Stir until well mixed with a wooden spoon.

4. In a small saucepan, stir butter and honey until mixture boils. Remove from the heat. Pour hot honey mixture over nut mixture. Stir to coat evenly. Set aside. Cool completely.

5. Preheat oven to 350°F.

(Continued)

6. Remove dough from the refrigerator. Separate dough into thirds. On a lightly floured surface, roll each third as thin as possible into strips measuring 5 inches wide by 20 to 25 inches long. Trim the edge of each strip with a fluted pastry wheel.

7. Place one third of the filling onto each strip. Fold over each strip to create strips 2½ inches wide by 20 inches long.

8. Starting with one end, roll the filled strips jelly roll fashion into a big "wheel." Add the other two strips to produce one big wheel.

9. Place base of wheel on a parchment-lined cookie sheet.

10. Use cook's twine to tie around middle of torte to be sure it keeps its shape during baking. Tie gently. Brush entire surface with a beaten egg and sprinkle with additional sugar.

11. Bake for 2 hours. Remove pan from the oven. Place torte on wire cooling rack and cool completely. When cool, remove and discard twine. If desired, use a fancy ribbon to replace twine for presentation. Serve when completely cool. Use a sharp serrated knife to cut into slices.

YIELD: ONE 7½-INCH ROUND TORTE, 25 TO 30 SLICES

GRANDMOTHER'S PIE

TORTA DELLA NONNA

I learned to make this classic dessert at "La Tavola con lo Chef" (at the table with the chef), a beautiful cooking school in Rome. It was amazing to observe master baker Naz-zareno share his experience and love of pastry with a class of aspiring pastry chefs. Watching his techniques and learning about authentic Italian ingredients was a high-light of my last visit to Rome. His version of pasta frolla uses soft butter in place of chilled and confectioners' sugar instead of granulated.

ITALIAN PASTA FROLLA:

6 TABLESPOONS BUTTER, SOFTENED	PINCH OF SALT
½ CUP CONFECTIONERS' SUGAR	ABOUT ¾ CUP FLOUR
1 EGG YOLK	

ITALIAN PASTRY CREAM:

2 CUPS MILK	⅓ CUP FLOUR
1 CUP SUGAR	1 TEASPOON VANILLA
3 EGG YOLKS	½ CUP PINE NUTS

1. With an electric mixer, cream butter and confectioners' sugar until well blended. Add egg yolk. Mix well. Add salt and flour. Turn out dough onto a lightly floured surface and knead until well blended. Dough should be soft but not sticky. Wrap in plastic wrap. Refrigerate 2 to 3 hours or overnight. You can also freeze for later use.

2. In a medium saucepan over medium heat, bring the milk and ½ cup of sugar to a boil. Remove from the heat. In a separate bowl, beat egg yolks and remaining ½ cup sugar with a wire whisk. Add flour and whisk until smooth.

3. Add egg yolk mixture to milk mixture. Return to medium heat, whisking constantly until thickened, about 2 minutes. Remove from heat. Stir in vanilla. Pour into a bowl, cover top with plastic wrap, and refrigerate, up to one day.

4. Preheat oven to 350°F.

(Continued)

5. Roll out dough on a lightly floured surface until ⅛ inch thick. Line a 9-inch tart pan with removable bottom with the dough.

6. Pour cooled pastry cream into the crust. Sprinkle top with pine nuts.

7. Bake for 30 to 35 minutes, or until lightly browned.

8. Remove from the oven and place on a wire cooling rack. Cool completely. Serve at room temperature. Store unused tart in the refrigerator.

YIELD: ONE 9-INCH TART, ABOUT 8 SERVINGS

SWEET RICOTTA PIE

PIZZA DOLCE

Mom's sweet ricotta pie has always been my favorite way to celebrate Easter.
The smell of this pie cooking is one of my favorite sensory memories.
I had the pleasure of learning to make homemade ricotta cheese with Gemma,
our neighbor who made cheese for a living in Italy. Ricotta was actually the by-product
after we made a batch of delicious soft basket cheese. It didn't yield that much, just a
few tasty tablespoons. We would need to make a huge batch of basket cheese to yield a
significant amount of ricotta, but it was fascinating to see how it's produced.

CRUST:

2 EGGS	1 ½ TO 1 ¾ CUPS FLOUR
⅓ CUP SUGAR	PINCH OF SALT
½ CUP MELTED SHORTENING, COOLED	1 TEASPOON BAKING POWDER

FILLING:

6 EGGS	GRATED RIND FROM 1 LEMON
½ CUP SUGAR	3 CUPS RICOTTA
JUICE OF 1 LEMON	

1. For the crust, beat eggs and sugar in an electric mixer until light. Add shortening and mix well. On low speed, gradually add 1¼ cups flour, salt, and baking powder. Turn out dough onto a lightly floured surface. Knead in remaining ¼ to ½ cup flour to make a soft nonsticky dough.

2. Divide dough in half. Using a rolling pin, roll crust on a lightly floured surface to ⅛-inch thickness. Place in an ungreased 9-inch deep-dish pie plate.

3. Roll out remaining dough to the same thickness. Using a fluted-edge pastry cutter, cut dough into strips about ½ inch wide. Set aside and cover with plastic.

4. Preheat oven to 350°F.

(Continued)

5. For the filling, beat eggs in an electric mixer on medium speed. Add sugar, lemon juice, and rind. Beat until well blended. Add ricotta. Blend until smooth.

6. Pour filling into pan lined with bottom crust. Carefully arrange strips of dough to form lattice across the top.

7. Bake for 55 to 60 minutes, or until center is just set. Turn oven off. Leave pie in the oven for 15 minutes.

8. Remove pie from the oven. Cool on wire cooling rack. Refrigerate until serving. Serve chilled.

YIELD: ONE 9-INCH PIE, ABOUT 20 SERVINGS

◆ **AL DENTE** ◆

THIS TERM REFERS TO COOKING PASTA AND RICE. MOST ITALIANS PRE-
FER THEIR PASTA AND RICE FIRMER AND SLIGHTLY MORE UNDERCOOKED
THAN DO MOST AMERICANS. FOR OUR RICE PIE YOU'LL WANT TO COOK THE
RICE A LITTLE FIRM, A BIT HARDER THAN YOU WOULD IF YOU WERE EATING
IT RIGHT AWAY. THE RICE WILL CONTINUE TO COOK IN THE PIE.

EASTER RICE PIE

This crustless Easter pie was my grandmother's specialty. She never really liked pie crusts so she adapted her family recipe to suit her own tastes. The result is a delicious baked rice custard topped with a sprinkle of cinnamon. Be sure to leave the rice a bit undercooked when you make it. It will continue to cook in the pie. You can easily double this recipe and make an 11 x 9-inch pan rice pie if you have a large gathering for Easter. We always do.

2 CUPS WATER	2 TEASPOONS VANILLA
½ CUP RICE	2 CUPS RICOTTA
4 EGGS	1 CUP MILK
¾ CUP SUGAR	2 TEASPOONS CINNAMON

1. In a medium saucepan, bring water to a boil over medium heat. Add rice. Reduce heat to low and cook until al dente, about 20 minutes.

2. Remove from the heat. Drain rice and cool.

3. Preheat oven to 400°F.

4. In an electric mixer on medium speed, beat eggs. Add sugar and vanilla. Add ricotta and beat until smooth.

5. Stir in milk and cooled rice. Pour into ungreased 9-inch round cake pan. Sprinkle cinnamon on top of rice mixture. Carefully place in oven. Bake for 50 to 55 minutes, or until center is just about set.

6. Remove pie from the oven. Cool on wire cooling rack. Refrigerate until serving. Serve chilled.

YIELD: ONE 9-INCH PIE, ABOUT 12 SERVINGS

AUNT ERNESTINE'S CREAM PIE

This unique pie is a specialty of my grandmother's family, the Palmieris. It has an unusual combination of pastry cream, cherry filling, and apricots that sounds odd but tastes delicious when chilled and served. You can make several of the components ahead of time. Just store the pasta frolla, pastry cream, and sour cherry filling in the refrigerator before assembling the pie.

1 RECIPE PASTA FROLLA (SEE PAGE 78)

1 RECIPE SOUR CHERRY FILLING (SEE FOLLOWING RECIPE)

1 RECIPE VANILLA PASTRY CREAM (SEE FOLLOWING RECIPE)

16 OUNCES APRICOT HALVES, PEELED

1. Make pasta frolla according to directions. Divide dough in half. Wrap each half in plastic wrap and refrigerate for 3 hours or overnight.

2. Preheat oven to 375°F.

3. Roll out half the pasta frolla on a lightly floured surface until ⅛ inch thick. Line a greased 9-inch deep-dish pie plate with crust. Press into plate. Let excess hang over.

4. Spread cherry filling on the bottom of the crust. Spread vanilla cream filling over cherries. Place peeled apricots evenly on pastry cream.

5. Roll out remaining half of pasta frolla until ⅛ inch thick. Cover apricots to form a top crust. Use fingers to pinch edges together to seal crusts together. Be sure to tuck edges in so that they do not hang over the rim.

6. Bake for 55 to 60 minutes, until center is golden brown. Remove pie from the oven. Cool on wire cooling rack. When cool, cover with plastic wrap or foil and refrigerate overnight. Serve chilled.

YIELD: ONE 9-INCH PIE, ABOUT 15 SERVINGS

SOUR CHERRY FILLING

1 POUND (16 OUNCES) SOUR PITTED
CHERRIES, PACKED IN WATER, DRAINED

¾ CUP SUGAR

In a small saucepan over low heat, combine cherries and sugar. Simmer, stirring occasionally, until thick and maroon colored, about 50 minutes. Remove from heat. Cool. Set aside.

VANILLA PASTRY CREAM

¼ CUP FLOUR

1 TABLESPOON CORNSTARCH

1 CUP SUGAR

3 CUPS MILK

6 EGG YOLKS, SLIGHTLY BEATEN

1 TEASPOON VANILLA

1. In a mixing bowl over water or double boiler over medium heat, blend together all pastry cream ingredients, except vanilla. Whisk constantly over boiling water until thick, 20 to 25 minutes.

2. Remove from the heat. Stir in vanilla. Set aside to cool.

PASTRY

◆ ◆ ◆

Italian pastry is well known as being some of the world's best. Many of these techniques have been handed down through generations of bakers. In this section I've chosen to include some of the easiest recipes to make at home. They include fried pastries, baked puffs, and miniature pies and cakes that are served as individual desserts.

There are many ways to serve these desserts. Here are a few suggestions:

Place a few tablespoons of fruit or chocolate sauce on the serving dish.

Place a slice of cake or pastry in the center and sprinkle outer edge of plate with a dusting of confectioners' sugar or edible flowers.

Drizzle chocolate sauce or fruit sauce with a fork with light swinging motion over pastry.

Serve with a simple dollop of whipped cream, a chocolate chunk, or assorted fresh fruits arranged on top or to the side.

Use sweet herbs like mint or lavender to garnish.

Use candied citrus peels.

MOCHA CREAM PUFFS

BIGNE

These puffs are international favorites that I've filled with a tasty coffee and chocolate cream filling. Try them simply dusted with confectioners' sugar or drizzled with a chocolate fudge sauce. For freshness, try to fill them as close to serving time as possible. Use this recipe to create small or large cream puffs or éclairs. Be sure to have your eggs at room temperature before adding to the hot dough.

CREAM PUFFS:

7 TABLESPOONS BUTTER	1 CUP FLOUR
1 CUP WATER	4 EGGS, AT ROOM TEMPERATURE
PINCH OF SALT	

MOCHA CREAM:

2 CUPS HEAVY CREAM	1 TEASPOON INSTANT ESPRESSO COFFEE
5 TABLESPOONS COCOA	½ CUP SUGAR

1. Preheat oven to 450°F.

2. In a medium saucepan over medium-high heat, combine butter, water, and salt. Bring to a boil. Add flour quickly, all at once, and stir with a wooden spoon until mixture comes away from the sides of the pan.

3. Remove pan from the heat. In an electric mixer, add eggs, one at a time, mixing well after adding each one. Mix well for a smooth sticky dough. Spoon a heaping tablespoon of hot dough onto a parchment-lined cookie sheet, spacing each about 1 inch apart.

4. Bake for 15 minutes. Reduce heat to 350°F. Continue baking for 30 to 35 minutes, or until golden brown. Remove puffs from the oven. Cool on wire cooling racks.

5. Combine heavy cream, cocoa, espresso, and sugar. With an electric mixer with wire whisk attachment, whip on high speed until soft peaks form, about 2 min-

(Continued)

utes. Scrape down the sides and bottom of mixing bowl using a rubber spatula. Continue whipping on high speed until stiff. Use immediately.

6. Slice the tops of cream puffs off with a serrated knife. Set aside. Using a pastry bag or tablespoon, fill the puffs with cream. Place tops on puffs. Dust with confectioners' sugar and serve. Store in refrigerator. Serve chilled.

YIELD: ABOUT 16 LARGE PUFFS

◆ TRAVELING PASTRY CHEFS ◆

MANY ITALIAN PASTRY CHEFS TRAVELED WITH CATHERINE DE MÉDICI WHEN SHE WENT TO LIVE IN FRANCE. IT WAS THESE CHEFS WHO SHOWED THE FRENCH CHEFS SOME OF THEIR BASIC TECHNIQUES FOR PASTRY MAKING, WHICH THEY THEN ADAPTED TO MAKE SOME OF THEIR LEGENDARY SWEETS.

TRADITIONAL CANNOLI

These crispy shells, filled with sweetened ricotta, originated in Sicily but are found almost everywhere. The secret to making cannoli is to roll the dough very thin and fry the shells in very hot oil. Fill the shells just before serving. If you do it too far in advance, the shell will get soggy. You can find many variations of cannoli, some with a chocolate ricotta, ice cream, or pastry cream filling.

SHELLS:

1¾ CUPS FLOUR	¾ CUP MARSALA
1 TABLESPOON SUGAR	OIL FOR FRYING
PINCH OF SALT	1 CUP MINI CHOCOLATE CHIPS
2 TABLESPOONS BUTTER, MELTED	GRATED RIND OF 1 LEMON

RICOTTA FILLING:

5 CUPS RICOTTA	GRATED RIND OF 1 ORANGE
1½ CUPS CONFECTIONERS' SUGAR	

1. In a medium mixing bowl, combine flour, sugar, and salt. Add melted butter and marsala. Turn out dough onto a lightly floured surface. Knead until well mixed.

2. Wrap dough in plastic wrap and refrigerate for 2 to 3 hours.

3. Roll out dough until very thin. Using a cookie cutter or rim of a glass, cut dough into 4-inch rounds. After cutting, roll each piece again until very thin. Roll each round tightly around cannoli tube. Seal with egg white.

4. Fry in hot oil, turning with a slotted spoon. Fry until golden brown. Remove from oil and drain on absorbent paper. Cool and gently twist tube to remove shell from form.

5. Cool completely before filling.

6. In a medium mixing bowl, stir all filling ingredients with a wooden spoon to mix together. Refrigerate until using. Store unused filling in an airtight container in refrigerator.

(Continued)

7. Fill a pastry bag fitted with a plain or open star tip with ricotta filling. Grab the shell and press tip of pastry bag toward middle of the shell. Press bag to release filling into one side of the shell. Repeat with other side.

8. Continue to fill the shells as needed. Dust with confectioners' sugar and serve. Store filled cannolis wrapped in plastic wrap or foil in refrigerator. Store unfilled shells in an airtight container at room temperature for 2 to 3 days.

YIELD: ABOUT 16 CANNOLI

◆ ITALIAN DESSERTS ◆

ITALY IS A WORLD-CLASS SWEET MAKER. IN PART THIS IS BECAUSE OF ITS DIVERSITY. THE NORTHERN PART OF ITALY DRAWS FROM AUSTRIAN AND GERMAN STRUDEL MAKING AND TRADITIONAL FRENCH TART MAKING. SOUTHERN PORTIONS OF ITALY WERE INFLUENCED BY AFRICAN AND MIDDLE EASTERN CULTURES. IT IS THIS BLENDING OF CULTURES—COMBINED WITH CENTURIES OF ITS OWN TRADITION—THAT MAKES ITALY SUCH A RICH, UNIQUE CULTURE (WITH RICH, UNIQUE DESSERTS).

RUM SPONGE CAKES

These light little sponge cakes are generously soaked in a sweet rum syrup, similar to the traditional "rum baba." They make a precious dessert for a small dinner party. You can serve one per person or one per couple. You'll need to have four mini tube pans to bake these cakes. They measure about 4 inches in diameter and are usually sold in a set of four.

MINI SPONGE CAKES:

4 EGG WHITES	4 EGG YOLKS
½ CUP PLUS 2 TABLESPOONS SUGAR	½ TEASPOON VANILLA EXTRACT
¼ TEASPOON CREAM OF TARTAR	¾ CUP CAKE FLOUR
¼ TEASPOON SALT	2 TABLESPOONS COLD WATER

RUM SYRUP:

1 CUP WATER	1 CUP SUGAR
½ CUP LIGHT OR DARK RUM	2 CUPS ASSORTED BERRIES

1. Preheat oven to 325°F.

2. In an electric mixer with wire whisk attachment, beat egg whites, 2 tablespoons of sugar, cream of tartar, and salt. Start on medium speed, then use high speed until very stiff peaks form, 3 to 4 minutes. Set aside.

3. In a separate bowl, with an electric mixer on medium speed, beat the egg yolks, ½ cup sugar, and vanilla. Beat until light in color, 2 to 3 minutes.

4. Alternate adding flour and water to egg yolk mixture. Begin and end with flour. Mix just until blended.

5. Using a rubber spatula, fold egg yolk mixture into beaten whites. When blended, spoon batter evenly into four 4-inch ungreased mini tube pans.

6. Bake for 20 to 25 minutes, or until lightly browned. Remove pan from the oven.

(Continued)

7. Cool cakes in pan on wire cooling rack.

8. When completely cool, carefully remove cakes from the pan. Use a sharp straight knife to loosen the outside and inner tube of the cake from the pan.

9. Prepare rum syrup or store cakes in plastic wrap overnight at room temperature. Cakes can also be frozen for later use.

10. In a small saucepan, bring water to a boil. Add sugar. Boil on medium-high heat until sugar is dissolved and mixture becomes syrupy, 12 to 15 minutes. Remove from the heat. Stir in rum. Use immediately.

11. Pour a quarter of the rum syrup into a medium baking dish. Place sponge cakes, bottom side down, in syrup.

12. Evenly pour the remaining rum syrup over the cakes. Cover cakes with plastic wrap and refrigerate. Let soak for 2 to 3 hours or overnight.

13. Spoon ½ cup fresh fruit over each cake and serve.

YIELD: 4 MINI SPONGE CAKES, ABOUT 4 SERVINGS

LITTLE MOUTHFULS

BOCCONCINI

These little pies are filled with a sweetened ricotta, cinnamon, and chopped walnuts. This is my comare (godmother) Gloria's recipe, a specialty of her family from the town of Bari. If you don't have a 4½-inch cookie cutter, use the rim of a glass. Even though it's not Italian, I use a margarita glass—it's the perfect size.

CRUST:

2 CUPS FLOUR	¼ POUND BUTTER
½ CUP SUGAR	3 EGG YOLKS
GRATED RIND OF 1 LEMON	½ CUP MILK
½ TEASPOON BAKING POWDER	

FILLING:

3 CUPS RICOTTA	½ CUP SUGAR
2 EGGS	

TOPPING:

4 TABLESPOONS SUGAR	4 TABLESPOONS FINELY CHOPPED WALNUTS
1 TEASPOON CINNAMON	

1. Combine flour, sugar, lemon rind, and baking powder in a food processor. Pulse until blended. Add butter and process until mixture resembles coarse crumbs. Add egg yolks and milk and process to form a dough.

2. Turn out dough onto a lightly floured surface. Knead until well mixed. Dough should be soft but not sticky. Wrap in plastic wrap and refrigerate for 2 hours or overnight.

3. In a medium mixing bowl, combine ricotta, eggs, and sugar. Stir with a rubber spatula until well blended. Refrigerate until using.

4. Preheat oven to 375°F.

(Continued)

5. Grease and flour a standard muffin pan or spray with a nonstick spray. Set aside.

6. On a lightly floured surface, roll out dough until ⅛ inch thick. Cut dough into 4½-inch circles. Press dough circle into prepared muffin pan. Line the pan and form a lip or small pie crust around the edge of each. Repeat until all dough is used.

7. Spoon filling into crusts, until just about full.

8. In a small bowl, combine sugar, cinnamon, and walnuts. Sprinkle filling with cinnamon sugar and walnut mixture.

9. Bake for 25 to 30 minutes, or until middle is set. These will puff up in the center during baking but will fall when cooled.

10. Remove pan from the oven. Cool bocconcini in pan on wire rack. When cool, use a fork to remove from pans. Refrigerate until serving. Serve chilled.

YIELD: 12 BOCCONCINI

BUTTERFLIES

FARFALLE

These little sweet, fried pastries stay crispy for days. They are rolled and then cut to form a bow or butterfly shape. The thinner you roll the dough, the crisper and lighter the butterflies will be.

3 EGG YOLKS	2 TEASPOONS VANILLA EXTRACT
½ CUP SUGAR	2 CUPS FLOUR
½ CUP MILK	OIL FOR FRYING

1. In a medium mixing bowl, whisk egg yolks with a wire whisk. Add sugar and mix until light. Add milk and vanilla. With a wooden spoon, mix in 1½ cups flour.

2. Turn out dough onto a floured surface. Knead in remaining ½ cup flour to make a stiff nonsticky dough.

3. Divide dough in half. Roll one half out with a rolling pin on a lightly floured surface. Roll as thin as possible. Using a fluted pastry cutter, cut dough into strips that measure about 3 x 2 inches. Pinch the dough in the center to form a bow tie. Roll all of the dough, saving all the scraps to reroll at the end.

4. In a medium saucepan, heat about 1 inch of vegetable oil. Fry the butterflies, without crowding the pan, until golden brown. Turn using a slotted spoon or tongs. Remove from the oil and drain on absorbent paper.

5. Cool and dust with confectioners' sugar. Store unused butterflies in an airtight container at room temperature.

YIELD: ABOUT 25 BUTTERFLIES

LEMON RICOTTA FRITTERS

SFINGI DI RICOTTA

These fresh little puffs are like a delicious doughnut. They taste best when freshly fried and slightly warm. Serve with a dusting of confectioners' sugar and a drizzle of fruit sauce for a simple, elegant dessert.

2 EGGS, BEATEN	¾ CUP FLOUR
2 TABLESPOONS SUGAR	1 TEASPOON BAKING POWDER
1 CUP RICOTTA	PINCH OF SALT
2 TABLESPOONS LEMON JUICE	OIL FOR FRYING
LEMON RIND	

1. In an electric mixer, beat eggs. Add sugar and ricotta. Mix until well blended. Add lemon juice and rind. Blend in flour, baking powder, and salt. Transfer mixture to a medium bowl. Cover and refrigerate for 1 hour.

2. Heat about 1 inch of vegetable oil over medium heat in a medium saucepan. Using a teaspoon, drop dough into hot oil. Fry until golden brown, turning with a fork. Use a slotted spoon to remove fritters from the hot oil. Drain on absorbent paper. Dust with confectioners' sugar. Serve immediately.

YIELD: 20 FRITTERS

PASTICIOTTE

These popular little pies are filled with vanilla pastry cream. You can find many variations in Italian pastry shops. Some have chocolate filling or ricotta filling. My dad and I agree that this vanilla-filled version is our favorite. Dad loves them with a cup of espresso with a splash of Sambuca.

To make the crust, use either a pastry blender or food processor.

CRUST:

2½ CUPS FLOUR	¼ CUP WATER
¾ CUP SUGAR	1 EGG
½ TEASPOON BAKING POWDER	2 TABLESPOONS HONEY
¾ CUP SHORTENING	

FILLING:

2½ CUPS MILK	¼ CUP FLOUR
¾ CUP SUGAR	2 TABLESPOONS CORNSTARCH
2 EGG YOLKS	1 TEASPOON VANILLA

1. Preheat oven to 350°F.

2. In a medium mixing bowl, combine flour, sugar, and baking powder. Using a pastry blender, blend in shortening until the mixture resembles coarse crumbs. Add water, egg, and honey. Stir with a wooden spoon. Turn out dough onto a lightly floured surface and knead until well blended. Divide dough in half and wrap dough in plastic wrap and set aside.

3. Make filling. In a double boiler or pan over simmering water, combine milk, sugar, egg yolks, flour, and cornstarch. Whisk over heat until thickened, about 10 to 12 minutes. Remove from the heat. Stir in vanilla. Set aside.

4. Using a rolling pin, roll out one half of the dough on a lightly floured surface. Roll until about ⅛ inch thick. Cut dough into 4-inch rounds using a cookie cutter or rim of a glass.

(Continued)

5. Press a round of dough into a greased muffin pan.

6. Using a tablespoon, fill each dough with about 2 tablespoons of filling. Roll out another set of 4-inch dough rounds. Use these circles to top the filling. Pinch outer edge of the crusts together. Repeat until all circles are filled.

7. Bake for 25 minutes, or until golden brown. Remove from the oven. Cool slightly in pan on wire cooling rack. When cool to touch, carefully remove each pasticiotte from the pan and continue to cool on wire rack. Serve at room temperature or refrigerate and serve chilled. Dust with confectioners' sugar.

YIELD: 12 PASTICIOTTE

◆ BAKERIES IN ITALY ◆

THERE ARE MANY TYPES OF SHOPS IN ITALY THAT CAN BE CLASSIFIED AS WHAT WE CALL BAKERIES. SOME SHOPS SELL BREAD, ROLLS, SWEET BAKED GOODS, AND DELI ITEMS. THESE ARE USUALLY TAKE-OUT SHOPS. OTHERS ARE HIGH-QUALITY PASTRY SHOPS KNOWN AS *PASTICCERIA*. THESE SHOPS HAVE A DIVERSE SELECTION OF PASTRIES AND CAKES, AND SOMETIMES GELATO. YOU CAN USUALLY EAT IN OR TAKE OUT. WHEN YOU TAKE OUT, YOU PICK WHAT YOU'D LIKE AND THEY WRAP IT BEAUTIFULLY. YOU MUST PAY A CASHIER AND THEN GO BACK AND PICK UP YOUR PACKAGE.

THERE ARE ALSO BARS THAT SERVE PASTRY, COFFEE, AND ALCOHOLIC BEVERAGES. AND *TAVOLA CALDA*, WHICH MEANS "HOT TABLE." THESE ARE QUICK-BITE PLACES THAT SERVE SANDWICHES, PIZZA, FOCCACIA, SWEET BAKED ITEMS, COFFEE, AND ALCOHOLIC BEVERAGES. YOU CAN EITHER SIT AT A TABLE FOR AN ADDITIONAL CHARGE, OR STAND UP AND EAT. OBVIOUSLY, SWEETS ARE VERY IMPORTANT—YOU CAN FIND THEM JUST ABOUT EVERYWHERE IN ITALY.

FIG AND MASCARPONE RAVIOLI

These triangle-shaped ravioli are fried and dusted with confectioners' sugar. To elimi-nate the need to make a crust, you can use wonton wrappers (you can use wonton wrap-pers for traditional ravioli as well). These treats are easy to make—in fact, you can fill them about 8 hours before you fry them.

8 OUNCES MASCARPONE CHEESE

¼ CUP CONFECTIONERS' SUGAR

1 TEASPOON AMARETTO

1 CUP DRIED FIGS, COARSELY CHOPPED

20 3-INCH-SQUARE WONTON WRAP-PERS

1 EGG FOR SEALING

OIL FOR FRYING

1. In an electric mixer, cream the mascarpone and confectioners' sugar until well blended. Stir in amaretto and chopped figs. Set aside.

2. Place all the wonton wrappers on a work surface. Brush the edges of each square with beaten egg. Place 1 generous tablespoon of filling in the center of each square. Fold wrapper over to form triangle. Press edges together until sealed. Re-peat filling and sealing all the wrappers. Cover and refrigerate 2 to 4 hours.

3. Fry ravioli, a few at a time, in hot oil. Turn with a slotted spoon. Fry until golden brown. Remove from the oil with a slotted spoon and drain on absorbent paper. Dust with confectioners' sugar or serve with dessert sauce. Serve warm or cooled.

YIELD: 20 RAVIOLI

SWEET BREADS

Many people, myself included, are intimidated by the thought of baking bread that includes yeast. However, with today's easily available active dry yeast, breads can be almost foolproof. I hope you'll try some of these sweet breads—there's nothing quite like the sweet yeasty smell of Easter bread baking, and its perfect taste served warm from the oven with a chunk of butter. It reminds me so much of my childhood and the pending season of spring that always comes after the Easter celebration.

Here are a few tips and general guidelines for baking the sweet breads in this section.

Activating Dry Yeast

It is important that you use lukewarm water, as directed in the recipes, to activate yeast. Water that is too hot will kill the yeast. Water that is too cold will not activate it.

Rising in a Warm Place

Every home bread baker I know has their own personal place for rising bread. My friend Betsy uses a really sunny window in her upstairs bedroom. For me, it's the top of my gas stove at home. If the oven is heated to 375°F the right amount of heat will be vented out onto the top of the stove. I usually place my bread dough here, in a mixing bowl covered with plastic wrap and a dish towel, right between the burners to catch the escaping hot air. A warmed oven, not too hot, 70 to 80°F, is ideal as well.

Doubled in Bulk

This is a widely used term to describe how much the dough has risen. Usually, every time you let the dough rise you're looking for it to be double the size of when you began. Many of the rising times in these recipes are approximate, depending on how warm your warming spot is. You can't be in a hurry to bake bread. You must be sure you've allowed proper time for rising.

Kneading or Punching Down the Dough

Kneading and punching down the dough are important steps to mix and work the dough to its proper consistency.

Storage

Home-baked breads can become stale easily. Be sure to wrap cooled, unused bread in a plastic bag. Store at room temperature for a few days or freeze for later use. Bread that is a couple of days old makes great toast for your breakfast or bread pudding. Do not store bread in the refrigerator. This will make it get stale quicker.

ANISE BREAD

PANE D'ANISE

This dense ring-shaped loaf is a nice breakfast or snack bread. For the strongest anise flavor, use an anise oil or extract. If you like a softer flavor, substitute 2 tablespoons anisette or Sambuca in place of the extract.

1 PACKAGE ACTIVE DRY YEAST

½ CUP LUKEWARM WATER

¼ POUND BUTTER, SOFTENED

1 CUP SUGAR

2 EGGS, PLUS 1 ADDITIONAL EGG FOR EGG WASH

2 TEASPOONS ANISE EXTRACT (OR 2 TABLESPOONS ANISETTE)

3 CUPS FLOUR

PINCH OF SALT

1. In a small bowl, mix yeast with lukewarm water. Set aside.

2. In an electric mixer on medium speed, cream butter and ½ cup sugar until light. Add eggs and anise extract. Mix well. Add 1½ cups flour, salt, and yeast mixture. Mix just until blended. Cover bowl with plastic wrap and a towel and let rise until doubled in bulk, 45 minutes to 1 hour.

3. Stir in remaining ½ cup sugar and 1½ cups flour. Turn out dough onto a lightly floured surface and knead until dough is soft and smooth. If dough is sticky, knead in a bit more flour. Form dough into a ball. Place in a greased mixing bowl. Cover with plastic wrap and a towel. Let rise until doubled in bulk, 45 minutes to 1 hour.

4. Roll and shape dough into a cylinder about 30 inches long. Form into a ring shape and place on a parchment-lined cookie sheet. Be sure to pinch ends together to form a uniformly wide ring. Cover with plastic wrap and a towel and allow to rise in a warm spot for another 35 to 40 minutes.

5. Preheat oven to 325°F.

6. In a small bowl, beat egg with a fork. With a pastry brush, brush top of loaf with beaten egg. Bake for 25 to 30 minutes, or until top is lightly brown. Remove from the oven. Cool on wire cooling rack. Serve warm or cooled. Store unused bread in plastic bag at room temperature for a few days or freeze for later use.

YIELD: ONE 10-INCH RING-SHAPED LOAF, ABOUT 25 SLICES

EASTER BREAD
PANE DI PASQUA

This is my godmother Gloria's new and improved Easter bread. She originally had to let this dough rise overnight, which to me seems like a long time. By changing her original recipe to a sponge method, I've cut down the length of time the bread will take to rise. It's still the same delicious bread, served either plain or toasted.

2 PACKAGES ACTIVE DRY YEAST	GRATED RIND OF 1 LEMON
¼ CUP LUKEWARM WATER	½ CUP SHORTENING, MELTED
6 EGGS	4 TO 4½ CUPS FLOUR
1 CUP SUGAR	

1. Dissolve yeast in lukewarm water. Set aside.

2. In an electric mixer, beat eggs. Add ½ cup of sugar and lemon rind. Add melted cooled shortening. Mix well. With a wooden spoon, stir in 2 cups flour and yeast mixture. Mix until well blended. Cover top of bowl with plastic wrap and a towel. Let mixture rise in a warm spot, free from drafts until doubled and bubbly, 30 to 45 minutes.

3. Remove dough from warming spot. Stir in the remaining ½ cup sugar and 2 cups of flour. Turn out dough onto a lightly floured surface and knead in enough flour for a soft dough, about ½ cup. The dough should not be too sticky.

4. Grease a large mixing bowl. Place dough in the greased bowl. Cover top with plastic wrap and a towel and return to warm spot until doubled in bulk, 45 to 60 minutes.

5. Grease a 10-inch tube pan with removable bottom with butter. Turn out dough on a lightly floured surface. Knead. Roll dough into a long cylinder and place in prepared pan. Cover pan with plastic wrap and a towel and allow to rise again in a warm spot. Let rise until doubled, about 30 minutes. Remove and discard plastic wrap.

6. Preheat oven to 300°F.

7. Bake bread for 30 to 35 minutes, or until golden brown and firm.

(Continued)

8. Remove pan from the oven. Cool pan slightly on wire rack. Carefully remove bread from the pan and continue to cool on wire cooling rack.

9. Serve warm or cool. Serve plain or frost top with lemon confectioners' icing. Store cool unused bread in a plastic bag at room temperature.

YIELD: ONE 10-INCH TUBE PAN, 25 TO 30 SLICES

BRAIDED EASTER BREAD
WITH EGGS
PANE DI PASQUA CON UOVO

This recipe makes a beautiful braided ring-shaped loaf. It can be a festive Easter centerpiece; just place in a basket surrounded by shredded paper grass and jelly beans. The eggs become hard-boiled as you bake the bread, making it the perfect Easter breakfast—eggs and bread.

1 PACKAGE ACTIVE DRY YEAST	JUICE AND GRATED RIND OF 1 LEMON
½ CUP LUKEWARM WATER	¼ TEASPOON SALT
2 TO 2½ CUPS FLOUR	1 EGG
¾ STICK BUTTER, SOFTENED	4 WHOLE UNCOOKED EGGS, PLAIN OR
½ CUP SUGAR	COLORED FOR EASTER

1. In a small bowl, dissolve yeast in ¼ cup of lukewarm water. Set aside.

2. In a medium mixing bowl, add remaining water and 1 cup flour. Using an electric mixer, mix in yeast until well blended and smooth. Cover bowl with plastic wrap and a towel and place in a warm place to rise, 1 to 2 hours. This mixture should double in bulk.

3. In an electric mixer, cream butter. Gradually add sugar and beat until light. Add lemon juice and rind and salt. Add egg.

4. Add raised yeast mixture and mix well.

5. With a wooden spoon, stir in about 1 to 1½ cups of flour. Turn dough out onto a floured surface and knead to form a soft non-sticky dough. Shape into a ball. Place dough in a greased bowl. Cover with plastic wrap and a towel and let rise in a warm place until doubled in bulk, about 2 hours.

6. Punch down the dough with your fist. Divide the dough into 2 equal pieces. Roll each piece of dough into a long cylinder about 1½ inches thick.

(Continued)

7. Loosely twist two pieces of dough together to form a loose braid. Form the braid into a ring shape and place on a parchment-lined cookie sheet. Place uncooked eggs into spaces in braid. Cover with plastic wrap and a towel and let rise until doubled in a warm spot, about 40 minutes. Remove plastic wrap and towel.

8. Preheat oven to 375°F.

9. Bake for 25 to 30 minutes, or until golden brown.

10. Remove from the oven. Cool bread in a pan on wire rack. Serve warm or cold. When cool, if desired, frost top of loaf with confectioners' frosting.

YIELD: ONE BRAIDED LOAF, ABOUT 20 SLICES

CHRISTMAS FRUIT BREAD
PANETTONE

This is a traditional Italian sweet bread that is ideal for breakfast, either plain or toasted. This version with chopped dates and lemon and orange rind has a fresh contemporary flavor. When my mom bakes bread she uses an old fur-collared winter coat to help keep the dough warm while it rises.

2 PACKAGES ACTIVE DRY YEAST	GRATED RIND OF 1 ORANGE
1 CUP LUKEWARM WATER	5 TO 5½ CUPS FLOUR, APPROXIMATELY
¼ POUND BUTTER, MELTED AND COOLED	½ CUP CHOPPED DATES
4 EGGS	1 CUP GOLDEN RAISINS
2 TEASPOONS SALT	1 TABLESPOON BUTTER, MELTED
½ CUP SUGAR	CONFECTIONERS' ICING, IF DESIRED
GRATED RIND OF 1 LEMON	

1. Grease and line a 10 x 3-inch cake pan with baking parchment. Let the paper measure 3 inches above the side of pan, forming a collar. Set aside.

2. In a small bowl, sprinkle yeast over lukewarm water. Set aside.

3. In an electric mixer, beat butter, eggs, salt, sugar, lemon rind, and orange rind. Using a wooden spoon, add yeast mixture and 4 cups of flour. Turn out dough onto a lightly floured surface. Knead dough until not sticky, adding remaining 1 to 1½ cups flour.

4. Knead in dates and raisins. Place dough in a large greased bowl. Cover with plastic wrap and towels and set in a warm place. Let dough rise until doubled in bulk, 1½ to 2 hours.

5. Remove dough from bowl and knead on a lightly floured surface. Form dough into a ball. Place dough into prepared pan.

6. Using a sharp serrated knife, cut a cross in the top of the dough. Brush the top of the dough with melted butter.

(Continued)

7. Cover with plastic wrap and a towel and set dough to rise in a warm spot until doubled again, 30 to 45 minutes.

8. Preheat oven to 425°F.

9. Remove plastic wrap and bake bread until top browns, about 10 minutes. Reduce oven temperature to 325°F. Bake for 35 to 40 minutes, or until golden brown and firm.

10. Remove from oven and cool on wire rack for 10 to 15 minutes. Carefully remove panettone from the pan and continue to cool on wire rack. Remove and discard parchment. Frost with confectioners' icing or serve plain. Store unused bread in plastic at room temperature or freeze.

YIELD: ONE 10-INCH LOAF, ABOUT 25 SLICES

FROZEN DESSERTS

♦ ♦ ♦

Frozen desserts and gelato (Italian ice cream) are hugely popular throughout Italy. There are so many flavors to choose from in Italian gelaterias—everything from lemon, pineapple, watermelon, and kiwi to coffee, pistachio, zabaglione, and cassata. Gelati are commonly served in cups or cones or in a small dish accompanied by a biscotti or two. (If you've made the biscotti yourself, so much the better!)

Many of the frozen desserts included in this section can be made ahead, put in the freezer, and taken out little by little to enjoy. They make perfect endings for company, either planned or unexpected.

Many of the molded frozen desserts, such as Zuccotto and Semi-Freddo, require you to grease and line the bowl or mold with plastic wrap. This will allow for easy unmolding of these desserts. To unmold, set frozen dessert in a large pan of hot water for a few minutes. Turn dessert upside down onto a serving plate or doily-covered cake circle to release.

Ice Cream Makers

For some of these recipes you'll need an ice cream maker. I have an inexpensive one that has a frozen insert that is stored in the freezer. To use it I simply add chilled ice cream ingredients and turn the handle twice every 5 minutes for about 20 minutes. It's really simple. This type of maker will work fine. For the fancier electric makers, follow the manufacturer's instructions.

APRICOT ALMOND SEMI-FREDDO

This half or partly frozen loaf-shaped dessert is very flavorful and rich in texture. Be sure to use a high-quality sipping liqueur in this recipe for the fullest flavor. Try it served plain or drizzled with a rich chocolate sauce.

½ CUP DRIED APRICOTS, CHOPPED	¼ CUP AMARETTO
4 EGG YOLKS	2½ CUPS HEAVY CREAM
6 TABLESPOONS SUGAR	½ CUP SLICED ALMONDS, TOASTED

1. Place dried apricots in a small saucepan. Cover with water and boil over high heat until tender, about 15 minutes. Remove from heat. Drain and cool. Purée in food processor. Set aside.

2. Line a large loaf pan (8 x 4 inches) with plastic wrap. Let the wrap hang over the sides about 3 inches. Place in freezer to chill.

3. In a double boiler, over simmering water, whisk egg yolks, sugar, and amaretto until thick and foamy, 5 to 6 minutes. Remove from the heat.

4. In an electric mixer with wire whisk, whip heavy cream until stiff, 2 to 3 minutes.

5. Fold in egg yolk mixture, apricots, and almonds.

6. Pour into prepared pan. Cover bottom of pan with excess plastic wrap. Freeze overnight.

7. Slice into pieces and serve frozen. Store unused semi-freddo wrapped in plastic in freezer.

YIELD: ONE LOAF, ABOUT 12 SLICES

PISTACHIO DOME

ZUCCOTTO

This dome-shaped ice cream cake is impressive and easy to assemble. You can use your mixer bowl for a mold, to give the cake a nice height. Or you can use a mold that is about 7 inches wide by 9 inches tall.

1 RECIPE POUND CAKE (SEE PAGE 44)   **GARNISH: COCOA FOR DUSTING**

1 QUART PISTACHIO ICE CREAM

1 RECIPE CHOCOLATE WHIPPED CREAM
(SEE FOLLOWING RECIPE)

1. Grease and line mixer bowl or mold with plastic wrap. Let plastic wrap hang 4 to 5 inches out of the bowl. Set aside.

2. Cut pound cake into ½-inch slices. Then cut each slice in half diagonally to form triangles. Line the inside of the mold with triangle slices with points toward the top of the mold. Fit the slices snug so that the mold is completely lined. Use small pieces of cake to fill in gaps where necessary.

3. Scoop pistachio ice cream into the mold, pressing it against the walls of the mold but leaving a well in the center.

4. Spoon chocolate whipped cream into the center of the mold. Press down firmly with the back of a spoon to avoid any air pockets. Cover with any remaining slices of cake. (Be sure this is level before freezing. When you invert the mold, it will become the bottom of the zuccotto.) Cover with excess plastic wrap.

5. Freeze overnight. To unmold, place mold in a bowl of hot water for a few minutes. Invert onto a serving plate or doily-covered cake circle. Dust with cocoa before serving. Let zuccotto stay at room temperature to soften slightly, 15 to 20 minutes, before slicing with a sharp straight knife. Serve frozen. Store unused zuccotto wrapped in plastic in the freezer.

YIELD: ONE ZUCCOTTO, ABOUT 20 SERVINGS

CHOCOLATE WHIPPED CREAM

2 CUPS HEAVY CREAM

½ CUP COCOA

½ CUP SUGAR

In an electric mixer with wire whisk attachment, beat all ingredients until stiff. Set aside.

VANILLA TORTONI

These ice cream cupcakes are great fun for children to make and eat. Make a batch together and take out a few at a time for dessert. Before freezing, decorate tops with colorful sprinkles or nonpareils.

1 CUP HEAVY CREAM	½ CUP WALNUTS, CHOPPED
3 EGGS	½ CUP MARASCHINO CHERRIES, CHOPPED
⅔ CUP SUGAR	
2 TEASPOONS VANILLA	¼ CUP GRAHAM CRACKER CRUMBS

1. In an electric mixer with a wire whisk attachment, beat heavy cream until stiff. Set aside.

2. In another bowl, beat eggs and sugar until light. Add vanilla. Fold in whipped heavy cream, nuts, and cherries.

3. Place 12 paper dessert cups on a cookie sheet. Pour cream mixture evenly into paper cups. Sprinkle the tops with graham cracker crumbs. Place cookie sheet in the freezer. Freeze overnight. Serve frozen. Wrap unused tortoni in foil or plastic wrap and store in the freezer for up to 1 month.

YIELD: 12 CUPCAKE-SIZE TORTONI

COFFEE ICE WITH CREAM
GRANITA DI CAFFE

A popular summer treat in Italy, granita is a frozen shaved ice that comes in many flavors. This coffee and cream version is my favorite.

1 CUP WATER

½ CUP SUGAR

1 CUP DOUBLE-STRENGTH BREWED ESPRESSO

½ CUP HEAVY CREAM

1. In a small saucepan over medium-high heat, combine water and sugar. Stir until boiling. Let boil for about 1 minute, or until sugar dissolves. Remove from the heat. Stir in espresso.

2. Pour mixture into a medium stainless steel bowl. Place bowl in the freezer for about 3 hours.

3. Remove coffee mixture from the freezer. Use a fork to shave flakes of ice off the coffee mixture. Spoon flaked mixture into individual serving cups or place flakes in another bowl. Freeze until ready to serve.

4. Just before serving, whip cream until stiff. Spoon cream over the top of shaved granita and serve.

YIELD: EIGHT ½-CUP SERVINGS

GRAPEFRUIT SORBET
SORBETO DI POMPELMO

This flexible recipe can be made in other flavors. Simply substitute any type of fruit juice for the grapefruit juice. This sorbet is perfect when it is soft and freshly made, or firmer after it is stored in the freezer.

3 CUPS GRAPEFRUIT JUICE **2 TABLESPOONS CORN SYRUP**
1 CUP SUGAR

1. In a medium saucepan, combine 1 cup grapefruit juice, sugar, and corn syrup over medium heat. Heat, stirring occasionally, until sugar dissolves. Remove from the heat.

2. Stir in remaining 2 cups of grapefruit juice. Pour into a bowl and refrigerate for 3 to 4 hours or overnight.

3. Pour juice mixture into an ice cream maker. Process according to instructions. When frozen, serve soft or store in the freezer in an airtight container until firmer. Serve frozen.

YIELD: EIGHT ½-CUP SERVINGS

SPICED GELATO

This gelato uses some of the most popular baking spices—cinnamon, nutmeg, and cloves. It is an ultra-rich ice cream that you'll need an ice cream maker to prepare.

2 EGGS	1 CUP MILK
4 EGG YOLKS	1 TEASPOON CINNAMON
1 CUP SUGAR	½ TEASPOON NUTMEG
2 CUPS HEAVY CREAM	½ TEASPOON CLOVES

1. In a medium mixing bowl, whisk eggs and egg yolks until thick. Add sugar. Beat until light. Add heavy cream, milk, cinnamon, nutmeg, and cloves. Cover with plastic wrap and refrigerate for 2 to 3 hours.

2. Transfer the mixture to an ice cream maker. Follow the manufacturer's instructions for freezing. Place ice cream in an airtight container and freeze until serving. Store in freezer. Serve frozen.

YIELD: ABOUT 1 QUART, 8 SERVINGS

FRUIT DESSERTS

Fruit and cheese make a great, simple, rustic Italian dessert. I love its simplicity. The recipes in this section offer a variety of fruit prepared in several easy ways, each one not too sweet. Many of these desserts can be made ahead of dinner or can be cooking while you're making dinner. Most are perfect on their own with coffee or a sweet dessert wine.

If you'd like to try a fruit and cheese plate for dessert, try one of these cheeses.

BEL PAESE: A soft mild cheese, perfect with a slice of sweet fruit or sweet bread.

GORGONZOLA: A pungent cheese veined with blue is perfect with fresh figs or apples.

PROVOLONE: A sharp firm cheese great paired with pears or peaches.

RICOTTA: Just a few tablespoons of creamy ricotta and a ripe banana are a simple, satisfying way to end a meal.

BAKED PEARS

PERE AL FORNO

Butter, sugar, and a splash of orange liqueur enhance the flavor of ripened pears for this easy dessert. I like to make this for company if I'm serving pasta for dinner—I use the top of the stove for the pasta and the oven for dessert.

3 RIPE PEARS, HALVED, PEELED, AND CORED

1 TABLESPOON BUTTER

4 TABLESPOONS SUGAR

½ CUP HEAVY CREAM

¼ CUP GRAND MARNIER OR OTHER ORANGE LIQUEUR

1. Preheat oven to 400°F.

2. Place pears, cut side up, in a buttered baking dish. To make the pears lie flat in the baking dish, slice a small part off the rounded side. Dot each half with butter. Sprinkle with sugar. Pour heavy cream and orange liqueur over pears.

3. Bake for 30 to 35 minutes, or until tender.

4. Remove from the oven. Serve warm with excess sauce poured over pears.

YIELD: 6 PEAR HALVES, ABOUT 4 SERVINGS

GROWING UP WE ALWAYS HAD PLENTY OF FRUIT IN THE HOUSE. EVERY OTHER MORNING, NICK, OUR PRODUCE MAN, WOULD COME TO SEE MY MOM, AUNTS, AND GRANDMOTHER, WHO ALL LIVED IN THE NEIGHBORHOOD. HE WOULD SIT AND HAVE COFFEE WITH US AND READ THROUGH THE LIST OF WHAT FRUITS AND VEGETABLES HE HAD AVAILABLE THAT DAY ON THE TRUCK. IT WASN'T UNTIL YEARS LATER THAT I REALIZED NOT EVERYONE BOUGHT THEIR PRODUCE THAT WAY.

POACHED PEACHES

This simple dessert is a classic finale to an Italian meal. By absorbing the wine, the peaches take on a delicate sweetness. I enjoy these served warm plain or over ice cream.

2 CUPS WATER

1 CUP SUGAR

3 PEACHES, HALVED, PITTED, AND PEELED

½ CUP MARSALA WINE, OR ANY SWEET WHITE WINE

1. In a medium saucepan, bring 2 cups water to a boil over medium heat. Add sugar. Boil until sugar is dissolved, about 3 minutes. Add peaches. Cover and simmer over low heat until peaches are tender, 10 to 15 minutes.

2. Remove from the heat. Stir in wine. Let sit for 15 to 20 minutes. Serve warm or cool.

YIELD: 6 PEACH HALVES, ABOUT 4 SERVINGS

FRUIT FRITTERS

SFINGI DI FRUTTA

Any firm fruit can be dipped in this batter and fried, but apples are my personal favorite. You can use any variety of apple. For flavor and texture, I prefer McIntosh.

3 EGGS	2 CUPS FLOUR
¼ CUP SUGAR	OIL FOR FRYING
1 CUP MILK	3 MEDIUM APPLES, PEELED, CORED,
½ TEASPOON BAKING POWDER	AND SLICED INTO WEDGES

1. In a medium mixing bowl with wire whisk, beat eggs. Add sugar and milk and mix well. Add baking powder and flour and beat with whisk to make a smooth batter.

2. Heat 1 inch of vegetable oil in a medium saucepan over medium heat. When oil is ready, dip slices of apples into batter, using your fingers, a fork, or tongs. Coat the slice thoroughly and let excess batter fall back into the rest of the batter. Release into oil. Fry the apple slices, a few at a time, without crowding the pan. Turn with two forks or a slotted spoon. Fry until golden brown.

3. Remove from oil and drain on absorbent paper.

4. Sprinkle with cinnamon and sugar or confectioners' sugar, if desired. Serve warm.

YIELD: ABOUT 16 SLICES

MACERATED FRUIT

MACEDONIE

This mixed fruit cup is popular all over Italy. You can use any combination of available fruit and you can substitute a liqueur in place of the wine to suit your taste.

GRATED RIND OF 1 LEMON	½ CANTALOUPE, DICED
GRATED RIND OF 1 ORANGE	1 CUP RED GRAPES (1 SMALL BUNCH)
JUICE OF 1 ORANGE	¼ CUP SUGAR
JUICE OF 1 LEMON	½ CUP WHITE WINE
2 MEDIUM APPLES, PEELED, CORED, AND DICED	1 PINT STRAWBERRIES (1½ CUPS, SLICED)

1. In a large mixing bowl, combine lemon and orange rind and juice, apples, cantaloupe, and grapes. Sprinkle with sugar. Pour over white wine. Stir with a wooden spoon to mix. Cover and refrigerate for 4 to 6 hours before serving. Stir every half hour.

2. Add strawberries right before serving. Spoon into bowls for serving.

YIELD: 6 ½-CUP SERVINGS

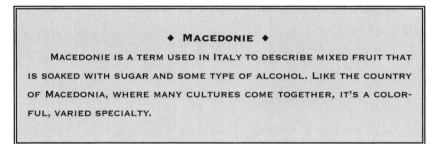

♦ MACEDONIE ♦

MACEDONIE IS A TERM USED IN ITALY TO DESCRIBE MIXED FRUIT THAT IS SOAKED WITH SUGAR AND SOME TYPE OF ALCOHOL. LIKE THE COUNTRY OF MACEDONIA, WHERE MANY CULTURES COME TOGETHER, IT'S A COLORFUL, VARIED SPECIALTY.

OTHER FAVORITES

◆ ◆ ◆

This section includes desserts that are hard to classify. They are casual desserts, such as tiramisù and panna cotta, that are "spooned" out for servings. I've also included pignoli brittle and candied citrus rinds. These are technically candies but are delicious sweets to prepare for yourself or to give as gifts. I've added the popular cordial *limoncello* to round out the book—just as many Italians celebrate the end of a wonderful meal.

CLASSIC TIRAMISÙ

This popular Italian dessert is espresso-soaked savoiardi (ladyfingers) layered with a mascarpone cheese filling and topped with cocoa. It's assembled like a trifle and very easy to make. After assembling, let the tiramisù set in the refrigerator overnight. It really tastes better when the flavors have a chance to ripen.

¾ CUP HEAVY CREAM

8 OUNCES MASCARPONE CHEESE

½ CUP SUGAR

1 TABLESPOON COFFEE LIQUEUR

16 SAVOIARDI (LADYFINGERS) (SEE PAGE 37)

1½ CUPS STRONGLY BREWED ESPRESSO

2 TABLESPOONS COCOA

1. In an electric mixer on high speed, beat the cream until thickened. Add mascarpone cheese, sugar, and coffee liqueur. Beat until stiff. Set aside.

2. Line the bottom of an 8-inch square baking dish with a single layer of savoiardi. They can overlap slightly. Place the bottom of the cookie facing up. This is the spongier side that will absorb the espresso. Pour half the espresso over the savoiardi to soak them.

3. Spread half the mascarpone mixture over the soaked savoiardi. Place another single layer of savoiardi on top of mascarpone mixture. Gently press down with your fingers. Soak with remaining espresso. Spread remaining mascarpone mixture on top. Sprinkle with cocoa. Cover with plastic wrap and refrigerate. Serve chilled

YIELD: ABOUT 8 SERVINGS

VARIATION: CHOCOLATE BERRY TIRAMISÙ

Follow recipe for tiramisù. Add ¾ cup cocoa to the mascarpone mixture. Spread ½ cup fresh raspberries over the first layer of mascarpone filling and ½ cup sliced strawberries on next layer of mascarpone.

CINNAMON RICE WITH MILK

This is my grandmother's loose rice pudding that she always made to celebrate the Assumption of Mary, August 15. This recipe works best with traditional long-grain rice, not the converted or minute rice varieties.

3 CUPS WATER	2 CUPS MILK
1 CUP LONG GRAIN RICE	1 TEASPOON CINNAMON
2 TABLESPOONS SUGAR	

1. In a medium saucepan, bring water to a boil over medium-high heat. Add rice. Cook uncovered, stirring occasionally, until al dente, about 20 minutes. Remove from the heat. Drain.

2. Sprinkle rice with sugar and mix with a wooden spoon to blend. Let cool slightly.

3. Add milk and transfer mixture to a medium serving bowl. Sprinkle with cinnamon. Do not mix in. Serve warm or refrigerate and serve chilled.

YIELD: EIGHT ½-CUP SERVINGS

◆ RICE ◆

RICE IS USED IN MANY WAYS IN ITALIAN COOKING—IN RICE PIES AND PUDDINGS AND OTHER SAVORY DISHES. MANY BELIEVE THIS IS BECAUSE RICE IS A SYMBOL OF ABUNDANCE AND FERTILITY. IT IS SAID THIS IS WHY WE THROW RICE AT WEDDINGS.

COOKED CREAM

PANNA COTTA

This baked cream is the perfect pudding-like dessert. It's just the right thing when you want a little something sweet. Serve it plain, sprinkled with cinnamon, or garnished with fresh fruit.

1 CUP MILK

3 TEASPOONS UNFLAVORED GELATIN

3 CUPS HEAVY CREAM

½ CUP SUGAR

2 TABLESPOONS AMARETTO

1. Spray a 9-inch deep-dish Pyrex pie plate or individual ramekins with a nonstick cooking spray. Set aside.

2. Place ½ cup milk in a small bowl. Sprinkle gelatin over milk. Let stand for 10 minutes to soften.

3. In a medium saucepan, combine remaining milk, cream, and sugar. Over medium heat, heat until boiling. Remove from the heat. Add gelatin mixture. Whisk until dissolved. Stir in amaretto.

4. Cool to room temperature, stirring occasionally.

5. Pour into prepared pan or ramekins. Cover with plastic wrap. Refrigerate for 5 hours or overnight.

6. Loosen edges with knife and turn upside down to remove from pan or ramekins.

7. Top with fresh berries or cinnamon and serve.

YIELD: ONE 9-INCH PANNA COTTA, ABOUT 8 SERVINGS

CANDIED CITRUS PEEL

These addictive little treats can be made from any citrus rind—oranges, lemons, or limes. They're like really fresh gumdrops that you can eat by themselves or use as a garnish for a special dessert, like a cassata. Huge piles of them sparkle in the sunny windows of Sicilian pastry shops.

4 ORANGES	2 CUPS SUGAR
3 CUPS WATER	ADDITIONAL SUGAR TO COAT RIND

1. Using a small sharp paring knife, remove rind from the orange. Score the orange rind into fourths and use your fingers to peel off rind. Cut rind, with pith, into slices.

2. Place pieces in a medium saucepan. Cover with 3 cups of water.

3. Boil on high heat for about 15 minutes. Add sugar and boil until thick, syrupy, and reduced, about 20 minutes. Remove from the heat. Drain pieces in strainer and quickly roll them in sugar. Use two forks to toss and coat. Store in an airtight container at room temperature.

YIELD: 1¼ POUNDS

PIGNOLI NUT BRITTLE

Like a tasty Italian peanut brittle, this is great for munching and lasts for weeks. It's delicious served alone as a candy or broken into pieces and sprinkled over your favorite ice cream. This recipe uses pine nuts but you can substitute any of your favorite nuts.

½ CUP PINE NUTS

½ CUP SUGAR

3 TABLESPOONS WATER

1. Preheat oven to 400°F.

2. Spread pine nuts in a thin layer on a parchment-lined cookie sheet. Toast in the oven for 8 to 10 minutes, or until golden brown. Remove from the oven. Set aside to cool.

3. Line another cookie sheet with parchment. Set aside.

4. In a small saucepan over low heat, combine sugar and water. Do not stir. When golden brown, remove from heat. Stir in nuts. Immediately spread nut mixture in a thin layer on lined cookie sheet. Cool. When cool, break into pieces. Store in an airtight container at room temperature.

YIELD: ½ POUND, ABOUT 6 SERVINGS

ROASTED CHESTNUTS

CASTAGNE

Roasted chestnuts are a real winter treat in Italy. You can pick up a handful from a street vendor for a between-meal snack. Our family usually serves them on Sundays and holidays—after dinner, but before dessert.

1 POUND CHESTNUTS (ABOUT 25)

1. Preheat oven to 400°F.

2. Slit chestnuts. Using a small sharp paring knife, cut a small "x" into the chestnut, going through the outer shell and inner skin. Place on a cookie sheet.

3. Bake for 30 to 35 minutes. Cooking time will vary according to the size of chestnuts and personal preference of softness. I like mine al dente. The best way to check doneness is to take a chestnut out of the oven and try it.

4. Remove chestnuts from the oven. Serve hot. Use a pot holder or cloth napkin to break open chestnuts.

YIELD: ABOUT 25 CHESTNUTS

HOMEMADE LIMONCELLO

*Limoncello is a delicious and potent digestive cordial that is very popular in Italy.
We always keep a bottle and a few cordial glasses in the freezer because it's best served
ice-cold in a chilled glass. This cordial originated in Capri and we had some
difficulty trying to find it in the United States. Luckily, our friend Luciano,
who lives in Rome, shared his recipe.*

750 MILLILITERS GRAIN ALCOHOL   750 MILLILITERS WATER

RIND OF 8 LEMONS   1 POUND SUGAR

1. Combine grain alcohol with grated rind in a large glass sealable container. Store in a cool, dry, dark place for 1 week.

2. Heat water and sugar in a medium saucepan over medium heat. Heat until sugar dissolves and is just about boiling. Remove from the heat.

3. Pour into alcohol mixture. Return mixture to a dark cool place for an additional week.

4. Strain mixture through a fine mesh strainer.

5. Pour into two 750 ml bottles. Cap tightly and store in the freezer. Serve in chilled cordial glasses.

YIELD: TWO 750 ML BOTTLES

◆ CORDIALS ◆

Sweet liqueurs often accompany desserts in Italy. Sweet wines such as Marsala are delicious chilled and sipped. Grappa is a popular liqueur that is made from the skins and seeds of the grapes after the wine is made. Anisette and Sambuca get their anise flavor from the fennel plant, or *finocchio*. Amaretto is a blend of secret herbs and apricot kernels. Strega and Galiano are two popular drinks that are very potent and a striking bright yellow. Many popular Italian cordials are made from age-old secret recipes that include a multitude of herbs and spices.

DESSERT SAUCES

ORANGE SAUCE

This orange sauce enhances an orange dessert or accents a chocolate, mocha, or cheese dessert.

1 CUP ORANGE JUICE

1 TABLESPOON CORNSTARCH

1 CUP CONFECTIONERS' SUGAR

Heat all ingredients in a small saucepan. Whisk until boiling. Boil for 2 minutes, then remove from heat. Let cool. Store in an airtight container in the refrigerator.

RASPBERRY OR STRAWBERRY SAUCE

This versatile berry sauce is great poured over cakes or ice cream.

2 CUPS RASPBERRIES OR STRAWBER-RIES, FRESH OR FROZEN (IF USING FROZEN, LET THEM THAW SLIGHTLY)

1 CUP CONFECTIONERS' SUGAR

In a food processor, pulse berries and sugar until smooth. Store refrigerated in an airtight container.

CHOCOLATE SAUCE

This rich chocolate sauce should be a part of every baker's repertoire.

¼ POUND BUTTER

¾ CUP SUGAR

¾ CUP HEAVY CREAM

½ CUP COCOA POWDER

In a small saucepan, combine butter, sugar, cream, and cocoa. Bring to a boil, stirring constantly until butter melts. Stir until completely blended. Let cool and thicken before use. Store refrigerated in an airtight container. To reheat and thin, heat over simmering water in a double boiler.

YIELD: ABOUT 2 CUPS

INDEX

Page references are preceded by

IT for *Sweet Maria's Italian Cookie Tray*
CJ for *Sweet Maria's Italian Cookie Jar*

CK for *Sweet Maria's Cake Kitchen*
ID for *Sweet Maria's Italian Desserts*